CHINA

The Hardening State

CHINA
The Hardening State

JAYADEVA RANADE

KW Publishers Pvt Ltd
New Delhi

ISBN 978-81-986658-4-3 Hardback

Published in India by Kalpana Shukla

KW Publishers Pvt Ltd
4676/21, First Floor, Ansari Road
Daryaganj, New Delhi 110 002
Phone : +91 11 43528107
Production : kw@kwpub.in
Marketing : sanjeev@kwpub.in
Website : www.kwpub.in

Printed and bound in India
Quiinkit Infotech Pvt. Ltd., Gurugram

To
My Family

Contents

Preface

China's rise and willingness to flex its military, economic and diplomatic strength have made it an inescapable factor in global politics. China's behaviour has also become more assertive and, with its neighbours, more aggressive. India, Japan, the Philippines and Vietnam have all in varying degrees felt Chinese military pressure. Xi Jinping, China's leader since 2012, has publicly announced China's ambition to complete "the rejuvenation of the great Chinese nation" – implying the recovery of all Chinese territories lost through the imposition of unequal treaties by foreign powers – and become "a major world power with pioneering global influence by 2049"! The last challenges the United States' premier position in the world! China has since then pursued more definitive policies towards achieving this.

Taking over as Chairman of more than eighteen of the powerful Central Small Leading Groups that lay down policy for the Chinese Communist Party (CCP) and Chinese government, Xi Jinping has ensured he is able to harness all the resources of the state for achieving national ambitions. By declaring in 2019 that: "Party, government, military, civilian, and academic; east, west, south, north, and center, the Party leads everything", Xi Jinping has once again brought politics to the centre of life in China. China's internal political developments have, therefore, assumed increased importance during Xi Jinping's terms in office. He has demonstrated his control over the CCP by continuing as the CCP General Secretary, Chairman of the Central Military Commission and President of China for a third consecutive term – unprecedented since the CCP informally adopted the convention of the CCP General Secretary not continuing longer than two consecutive terms. Similarly, at the last Party Congress he dispensed with convention and demoted, or dismissed, senior Party Central Committee or Politburo members. The vigorous and relentless CCP-led anti-corruption campaign encompassing the People's Liberation Army (PLA), CCP and the Government, pursued for the first time without interruption for twelve years, has added to Xi Jinping's authority and power. At the same time, the stringent security measures and anti-corruption campaign have simultaneously contributed to the growth and spread of dissatisfaction in the CCP, PLA and the country.

The briefs selected for this book cover the period June 2021 till October 2024. Given China's emphasis on modernisation of the PLA and aggressive foreign policy, the PLA has been discussed in some detail. In addition, China's difficult economic situation, China's relations with other countries and China's attitude and policy towards India have been discussed. The Tibet issue and the XIVth Dalai Lama's reincarnation, which have the potential to seriously escalate tensions between India and China, are also discussed.

The briefs include a fair amount of detail so that it interests serious China analysts as well as the general reader. Footnotes and references have been deliberately omitted to avoid distracting the reader. However, where pertinent the reference has been cited in the text.

I hope the book is successful in providing some clarity and useful insights to the reader especially at this time when economic and military tensions between China and the US and West are rising and no substantive change in China's aggressive posture towards India is discernible.

New Delhi
April 2025

Jayadeva Ranade

1. Xi Jinping and The Portends for His Third Term

The recent rumour that Xi Jinping had been placed under house arrest, confirmed that Xi Jinping is now China's central figure nearly as much as Mao and Deng Xiaoping once were!

Xi's retaining his positions at the helm of affairs after China's 20th Party Congress this October seems a foregone conclusion. He will then become the first Chinese leader since Mao and Deng to lead the country into a second decade. His acolytes had said, soon after he began his first term in November 2012, that 'China under Xi Jinping has embarked on a third new 30- year era like those of Mao and Deng Xiaoping before him'!

Xi Jinping is ambitious, bold and confident in the exercise of power, qualities he would have imbibed as one born into the privileged elite of the Chinese Communist Party (CCP). As the son of Qi Xin and General Xi Zhongxun, one of Mao's trusted lieutenants at the height of his power when Xi was born in 1953, Xi Jinping studied in the special school for children of the CCP elite. He and his co-students, and peers in his social circles, were instilled with the idea that they had a historical destiny to fulfil and carry the torch for restoring China to its 'old' glory. Schools across China teach students that "recovery" of the territories depicted as Chinese territories in a 1840-1919 map is a sacred duty. This mindset has been inculcated not only in Xi Jinping, but other 'princelings' and 'Red Descendants', or children of CCP cadres.

Xi also saw the dark side of the CCP's power politics. His father was 'purged' from the CCP and sent to Henan province in 1963 when he was 10 years old, and in May 1966, the Cultural Revolution cut short his secondary education. 'Red Guards' ransacked the Xi family home and Xi's elder sister, Xi Heping, committed suicide from the pressure. His mother was humiliated and forced to publicly denounce his father when he was paraded before crowds as an enemy of the revolution. The year following his father's arrest in 1968, Xi was sent to work in Liangjiahe Village, Shaanxi.

Despite the misfortunes and suffering that he and his family witnessed in his early years, Xi did not go abroad or opt to join State-owned Enterprises (SoEs) like the children of other senior CCP cadres. Instead, he took the risky decision of joining the CCP at a time he had no 'protector' or patron till Deng Xiaoping returned to power in 1979. The experience undoubtedly toughened him mentally and reinforced his ideological commitment. Subsequently, however, his family connections did facilitate his rise in the CCP as evident from the letter written in the 1980s by his mother Qi Xin, to the Party Secretary of Hebei urging him to promote her son to the provincial party standing committee. The Party Secretary declined and also, against convention, made public the request but was over-ruled!

Within days of taking charge in November 2012, and without a trace of self-doubt because of his pedigree, Xi took the bold step of simultaneously 'rectifying' the Party, Army and government bureaucracy and placing academia – primary schools to universities – into an ideological strait-jacket. He commenced a thorough 'rectification' of the Party, unleashed a relentless anti-corruption campaign intended to also weed out opposition, and undertook the reorganisation and restructuring of the People's Liberation Army (PLA). The last had been pending since the time of his predecessor Hu Jintao, because he hadn't been able to muster adequate support. His fervent commitment to the CCP ideology and sense of destiny were evident. It is very unusual for any leader to simultaneously shake all pillars of a state as Xi did. Inside two years over 40,000 officers of the PLA including 150 above the rank of Major General, and 175 cadres equivalent to and above central Vice Ministers, were dismissed and jailed on various charges of corruption. The cornerstone of Xi's consecutive political re-education campaigns in the Party and PLA has been to ensure the pre-eminence of Party ideology, placement of personnel loyal to him and ensure that the PLA is "absolutely obedient" to the CCP and him. In the process he has made China an even more totalitarian state.

Xi's appointment to China's three top posts at the 18th Party Congress in October 2012 clearly showed that he had the backing and support of the Party, which had mandated him to ensure the spread and supremacy of Party ideology and the Party's pre-eminent position. The Party apparatchiks, current and retired Party members and their families, all of whom are favoured with numerous perquisites and privileges constitute a dependable loyal base for the CCP. They have a personal stake in continuance of the CCP's leadership. They will support Xi and he will depend on them, but if they apprehend that the Party or its leadership is threatened, they could well oust him from the leadership to save the Party. At the same time, Xi's approval by the upcoming 20th Party Congress for a third term will mean that the CCP has endorsed his domestic and foreign policies.

As Xi commences his third five year term in October 2022, he will also have to make good on some of the promises and ambitions he has declared. He is almost certain to incrementally expand the scope of the stringent domestic security laws and continue with the unrelenting anti-corruption campaign. He has already, in fact, linked national development with national security through the Global Development Initiative (GDI)[7] and Global Security Initiative[8] (GSI). But the slowing economy which some months ago necessitated reducing the wages of government employees by 30 percent, burgeoning unemployment, rising living costs, zero-Covid policy and the surge in anti-China sentiment globally, all of which have already made people openly resentful, are likely to follow him through his third tenure.

Resentment continues to simmer among large sections of the populace, especially among China's powerful class of "princelings", intellectuals and students and the private business entrepreneurial class which accounts for 80 percent of the country's employment. These have the potential to severely impact Xi's efforts. If unchecked, they could derail national ambitions and even threaten to erode the CCP's legitimacy which, in turn, would pile inner-Party pressure on Xi to moderate his policies or step down.

As Xi pushes ahead with his foreign policy agenda, he will confront major obstacles in the Indo-Pacific region with opposition from countries like India, Japan, Vietnam and Australia who will not readily acquiesce to China becoming the regional overlord. Tension between the US and China over Taiwan, in the South China Sea and the war in Ukraine is already high. CCP members are apprehensive that any escalation of tension could see the imposition of US sanctions against China, which will seriously affect China's economy and, more importantly, personally impact the approximately 40 million senior CCP cadres and their families.

Impacting the world are Xi's calls for "rejuvenation of the great Chinese nation" and to make "China a major power with pioneering global influence" along with creating a "community of common destiny". These are incorporated in the Constitution. Referred to as the 'Two Centenary' goals, the first entails redrawing China's borders as it "recovers" territories that it claims were taken by the imposition of "unequal treaties by hostile foreign powers". This directly affects China's neighbours. For India it means China will persist with its claims over Ladakh and Arunachal Pradesh and other pockets of territories on the stretch of the border between them. Border tensions and clashes between both the armed forces are a distinct possibility in the years ahead. There will be similar situations with Japan, Vietnam and Taiwan. The second affirms Xi's goal of fashioning a new global world order and surpassing the United States. In addition to generating wider international opposition, this has the real potential for a clash between the two in the near term. If Xi succeeds he will have positioned China as the pre-eminent world power.

It will not be easy for Xi to achieve these objectives, certainly within the time frame he has set. Barring issues of health, however, Xi's qualities of character, personality and mental make-up suggest he will make a determined bid. Having secured the Party's endorsement for his policies, Xi will not easily backtrack on any of the policies – whether economic, security or China's aggressive external posture. Disregarding the slowing economy and fears of China's business entrepreneurs, Xi has continued to tighten regulations on China's Fintech and Real Estate sectors, and called for "common prosperity". He has portrayed discontent, protests etc. as threatening social order and stability and indicative of US efforts to topple the CCP through "colour revolutions"[9]. There will be no easing in the aggressiveness of his foreign policy as that would weaken the self-perception of China as a 'strong' nation. With Xi at the helm, the next five-odd years will be fraught and tense and the outcome will be crucial for the region and the world!

This was first published by the Centre for China Analysis and Strategy (CCAS) and Vivekananda International Foundation (VIF) in October 6, 2022.

2. Troubled Times Ahead for China and Xi Jinping

China is headed for a difficult period. A variety of factors have converged to make this a potentially volatile time. With barely six months to go for the crucial 20th Party Congress, it will be a period of particularly heightened concern for Chinese President Xi Jinping. This is especially as he has been in charge of the economic and foreign policy portfolios, over both of which major problems loom. Chinese academics and strategists have for some years blamed Xi for China's deteriorating relations with the US. Following the Xi-Putin Summit on February 4 in Beijing, he is in addition personally associated with China's support to Russia and Putin, imposing further strain on Sino-US relations. The latter has raised the uncomfortable prospect for Chinese Communist Party (CCP) members and China of being targeted with sanctions by the US and the West.

China's economic situation has been going downhill since 2018 and the trend has accelerated with the onset of the Covid pandemic. The cost of living is increasing, graduate unemployment is above 14 percent and rising, joblessness has spread from the rural countryside, where tens of millions are unemployed, to urban areas, and private businesses and small and medium entrepreneurs(who in 2019 provided an estimated 80 – 90 percent of non-government jobs) — are facing strict new regulatory controls at the same time as they face liquidity problems. Xi's crackdown first on the tech sector and now on the property sector (which accounts for some 29 percent of China's economy) has added to the volatility in the country's economic system.

The growing unemployment and the government's inability to create adequate jobs prompted Chinese Premier Li Keqiang, while on a visit to Chongqing in August 2020, to urge citizens to set up stalls and sell dumplings. This triggered a strong pushback from China's official media suggesting that differences in approach exist in the CCP's echelons. The slowing economy and drop in living standards threatens to erode the legitimacy of the CCP.

There are other indicators of the severity of economic problems that China faces. The budgets of most Ministries which were slashed in 2020 have not yet been fully restored, bonuses paid to employees this year, including those in the more prosperous eastern seaboard provinces, have been recovered, and salaries of employees in almost all provinces have been reduced. This has naturally added to the widespread dissatisfaction. Though the State Council's National Development and Reform Commission (NDRC) this April, sought to play down the impact of the pandemic on consumption, it conceded that "some factors that have exceeded expectations are weighing on consumption", but claimed the impact is phased and consumption will gradually recover once the pandemic is kept under effective control. The claim has been belied by the series of high-level meetings focussing on the economy and on stability.

Nevertheless, the matter is receiving the serious attention of the Politburo and the Leading Group on Economic Affairs headed by Xi and one of his closest sides, Vice Premier Liu He. China's important Central Finance and Economics Committee, an apex body on economic policy chaired by Xi, met for the first time this year on April 26. The meeting emphasised the necessity to coordinate the "two major issues of development and safety, firmly establish bottom-line thinking, effectively strengthen the ability to predict and early warning of major risks, and have practical and effective response plans and specific actionable measures". It urged all regions and departments to accurately understand the spirit of the Central Finance and Economic Commission's decision-making, take responsibility and act actively, guide market expectations, and stabilize market confidence."

Within days, on April 29, 2022, Xi chaired a meeting of the Politburo to "analyse and study the current economic situation and economic work". Liu Yuanchun, Vice President of Renmin University addressed those present on "Regulating and guiding the healthy development of capital in China according to Law". The meeting's assessment of the economy was stark. *Xinhua* (April 29) reported that the meeting observed "that the new crown pneumonia epidemic and the Ukraine crisis have led to increased risks and challenges, the complexity, severity and uncertainty of China's economic development environment have increased, and stable growth, employment, and prices are facing new challenges". The nine-paragraph *Xinhua* report said the meeting stressed that "leading cadres at all levels must have a sense of responsibility" be active and "always take responsibility for their actions, seek truth and be pragmatic, and prevent all kinds of "black swan" and "grey rhino"incidents from happening". Party committees and governments at all levels were directed to "lead the cadres and the masses" and make concerted efforts "to welcome the victory of the 20th Party Congress with practical actions". Giving teeth to this, the meeting warned that more corruption cases are coming. The importance of the meeting was underscored by its extensive coverage in the *People's Daily* and leading official provincial newspapers.

Though since the advent of Xi, the State Council and Premier Li Keqiang have generally been relegated to the background in economic policy-making, the severity of the economic problems has prompted them to become more active. Chinese Premier Li Keqiang presided over a meeting of the Executive State Council on May 5. The difficulties caused by the series of lockdowns affecting numerous cities and regions because of the zero-Covid policy were addressed. The meeting discussed further relief measures for small, medium and micro enterprises and individual industrial and commercial households in order to ensure stable employment of market players. It also determined measures to promote the stability and quality of foreign trade to help stabilize the economy and the industrial supply chain. It noted that "the difficulties of relevant market entities have increased significantly" and unveiled a series of decisions such as tax rebates, tax reductions and fee reductions, logistics guarantees, and promotion of resumption of work and production for enterprises.

All localities were instructed to arrange special funds for the relief of small, medium and micro enterprises and individual industrial and commercial households, and provide subsidies for rent, guarantee fees, loan interest and other subsidies for those with operational difficulties. In order to help foreign trade enterprises cope with difficulties, the meeting decided that the focus should firstly be on securing orders and stabilizing the import and export of key industries and labour-intensive industries secondly on sea and airports and making good use of air cargo capacity etc. It also asked that the RMB exchange rate be kept basically stable.

On May 7, Premier Li Keqiang followed this up with a National Video and Telephone Conference on Employment Stabilization in Beijing. Li Keqiang "pointed out that stable employment is related to the livelihood of the majority of families and is the key support for the economic operation in a reasonable range. The current employment situation is complex and severe". He warned of a "complicated and grave" employment situation as China imposes lockdowns. Politburo member and Vice Premier Hu Chunhua also attended the meeting.

Yet again on May 25 Premier Li Keqiang chaired a 'National Video Conference on Stabilizing Economic Situation' where he addressed more than 100,000 central, provincial, municipal, and county government officials. He emphasised that China is "facing difficulties worse than 2020". He stressed the need to "solidly promote implementation of economic stabilization policies and ensure economic stability within a reasonable range". He said they should ensure "reasonable economic growth" and decline of unemployment rate in Q2, 2022. The meeting came two days after the State Council rolled out a 33-point program to stabilize the Chinese economy, which is buckling under the weight of repeated COVID-19 lockdowns.

The Covid pandemic and particularly the zero-Covid policy and harsh isolation procedures have contributed substantially to the growing discontent. More than 340 million people in regions, including Beijing, that contribute almost 40 percent of China's GDP have been affected by Covid-related lockdowns. The full or partial closure of ports and offices has severely dislocated logistics and affected the supply of food and essential supplies resulting in deprivation or hunger for those in isolation. Shanghai is a vivid example. There is nervousness among Beijing residents too. Despite strict censorship, China's social media is awash with complaints by citizens about the harsh, insensitive measures and financial hardships the zero-Covid policy has caused.

Even Hu Xijin, former Editor-in-Chief of Global Times and a supporter of Xi Jinping, was reported by Reuters (May 5) to have posted on May 4: "Shanghai has fallen," and "Beijing has to either find less costly ways of tackling its outbreak" or "to tell the whole Chinese society the truth" that disruptive consequences cannot be avoided. "The former requires wisdom, the latter courage." The post was swiftly removed and Hu Xijin did not respond to a Reuters request for a comment sent to his Weibo account.

Nevertheless, the Politburo Standing Committee meeting chaired by Chinese President Xi Jinping on May 5, reasserted that the "dynamic zero-Covid" policy will continue. "Persistence is victory" the meeting declared! It asserted: "practice has proven that our prevention and control policy is determined by the nature and purpose of the Party, our prevention and control policies can stand the test of history, and our prevention and control measures are scientific and effective. We have won the battle to defend Wuhan, and we will certainly be able to win the battle to defend Shanghai". It made no mention of balancing Covid prevention and the economy.

Hinting that discontent is high in Party ranks, the meeting issued a sharp warning: "We should have a profound, complete and comprehensive understanding of the epidemic prevention and control policies set by the Party Central Committee, resolutely overcome the problems of inadequate understanding, inadequate preparation and inadequate work, resolutely overcome the ideas of contempt, indifference and self-righteousness, always keep a clear head, unswervingly adhere to the general policy of dynamic zero-Covid, and resolutely oppose all distortions, doubts and denials. We will resolutely struggle against all words and deeds that distort, doubt and deny our epidemic prevention policies".

The other major issue causing anxiety is the protracted conflict in Ukraine which shows no signs of ending despite the lapse of nearly 100 days. This delay is making China's position increasingly difficult. Xi's unwillingness to modulate his support has raised serious concerns within the CCP that sanctions against China are imminent. At least 300 million CCP members will be adversely impacted in case sanctions are imposed. Seventy percent of CCP cadres at the level of Department head or above, across China have children studying in the US and other countries in the West Chinese citizens too have become used to the presence of leading multinational consumer and other outlets and if they withdraw, China will be hit by the economic fallout and, psychologically too, the citizens will begin to question their country's economic might. This will get accentuated as, in the wake of the Covid pandemic, lessons learnt and the surge globally in anti-China sentiment, the US and West begin to restrict access to their markets.

Despite the personal risk, Chinese citizens including academics and CCP cadres have criticised China's support for Putin and Russia's invasion of Ukraine. Indicating that such criticism is widespread and causing Xi a lot of anxiety, are the spate of "political education" campaigns across China and the numerous articles in Party publications like Qiu Shi (Seeking Truth), *People's Daily* and *Guangming Daily* on 'historical nihilism', the contributions to China at this difficult time of the CCP with Xi at the "core of the leadership", "common prosperity' etc. Security and surveillance controls have been elevated and China's official media, which severely criticises the US almost every day, refers frequently to the threat from "colour revolutions". This last was asserted also in the Xi-Putin Joint Statement of February 4. The majority of posts on China's social media, though, continue to support the government, Putin and Russia and demonise the US and West.

Two recent developments suggest this anxiety bordering on apparent paranoia is affecting the Party leadership. One is the directive to all *danwei*, or work units, to return their computers and peripherals by May 1 and replace them with domestic ones to obviate the possibility of foreign hacking or cyber snooping. The second is the subtle, but unmistakable, warning to Chinese citizens in the *People's Daily* of May 3. It publicised that a Chinese citizen had been charged on suspicion of "inciting secession and subversion of state power"! It accused him of being "brainwashed" by foreign anti-China hostile forces online, acting as a domestic agent of foreign hostile forces and being "incited to split the country" etc. Stating that his activities had caused "serious harm to China's national security and social stability", the *People's Daily* declared,"Anyone who attempts to harm the interests of national development, endanger national security, or betray the motherland and nation will be severely punished by the law".

Additionally, at least three major articles strongly endorsing Xi's policy on Putin and Russia and listing the benefits of the conflict to China, were published recently. One was by the Head of the Sichuan Branch of *People's Daily*, the other by a senior researcher of the PLA-affiliated Kunlun Institute and third by well-known Chinese International Relations academic Yan

Xuetong. This has been accompanied by a noticeable effort by most provincial Chiefs to endorse and praise Xi's policies.

Obviously with an eye to career advancement at the 20th Party Congress, there has been a noticeable spurt in political activity in provinces like Chongqing where Politburo member and Party Secretary Chen Min'er eyes a position in the Politburo Standing Committee (PBSC), Tianjin where Party Secretary Li Hongzhong is expecting elevation to the PBSC, and Hunan where the incumbent Party Secretary Zhang Qingwei has been in the Central Committee for four terms and would expect to be promoted to the Politburo. Other provinces like Beijing, Guangxi, Guizhou, Jiangsu and Jiangxi have also been quick to emphasise 'loyalty' and 'political reliability' and support Xi's policies and programmes.

However, the article by Lin Zhibo, head of the Sichuan Branch of *People's Daily*, contained an interesting sentence which could have alluded to Xi. Enumerating Russia's failures in the war in Ukraine, it said: "the information he (Putin) can receive is inevitably one-sided. This kind of information cocoon room is unfavourable for strategic decision-making, and even dangerous".

Dissatisfaction with Xi, noticed since 2017, increased appreciably in 2019-2020. Successful billionaire entrepreneurs signed a letter addressed to Xi asking him to step down and the 'princelings', who normally keep a low profile, posted a letter on social media calling on Xi to quit and suggesting a couple of Politburo Standing Committee members as replacements. This has not dissipated and the rising discontent amid rumours of factional infighting in the CCP just prior to the 20th Party Congress, will cause Xi a lot of anxiety.

If he is unable to control the situation or if conditions worsen and he feels boxed in (by the Indo-Pacific strategy, Quad and AUKUS), Xi could well opt to bolster his domestic image as a 'strong' leader and order a military operation against one of Taiwan's outlying islands, or the South China Sea or India. In the first two cases Xi runs the risk of US intervention. With India there is no such risk, but China has lost the element of surprise and will, this time, face a strong military riposte. The remaining months are ones of high risk for all China's neighbours.

This was first published by the Centre for China Analysis and Strategy (CCAS) and Vivekananda International Foundation (VIF) in May 16, 2022.

3. Xi Jinping Begins Appointing Loyalists to Key Posts

The political situation in China is becoming volatile as the 20th Party Congress draws near and rumours of imminent purges circulating in Beijing gain momentum. The absence of a 'Revolutionary' veteran founding leader with unchallenged authority to decide on leadership appointments has added to the uncertainty. Surviving leaders are those like Song Ping who is over 103 years old now and frail. The failed bids for power in 2012 by the now incarcerated former Politburo (PB) member and 'princeling' Bo Xilai and incarcerated Politburo Standing Committee (PBSC) member and Security Czar Zhou Yongkang continue to haunt the Chinese Communist Party (CCP).

Preparations have also begun for the important annual confidential conclave of senior and veteran CCP leaders scheduled to be held at the Beidaihe seaside resort in August where major decisions are usually taken. The platform has traditionally been used by senior veteran communist leaders to voice their views — which carry considerable weight — and approve through consensus the promotions of cadres to the PBSC, PB and Party Secretaries of provinces. But cadres of pre-eminent stature, like former CCP CC General Secretary Jiang Zemin or PBSC member Zeng Qinghong, are very few in number, are 'tainted', and individually limited in their potential to pose an effective challenge to Chinese President Xi Jinping at the Beidaihe conclave. Unless there are a sizeable number of cadres in the Party Central Committee (CC), or Delegates to the Congress, who are agitated enough to criticise Xi Jinping, many veteran leaders are unlikely to throw their weight behind them and oppose Xi.

Xi is simultaneously securing his next term, and possibly beyond, at the upcoming 20th Party Congress. His acolytes have been saying since 2013 that 'under Xi Jinping, China has embarked on a new thirty-year era like those of Mao and Deng before him! The official Chinese media has stepped up its almost daily promotion of Xi, his thoughts and his leadership. Many provincial Party leaders, those in central leadership positions and others within the CCP appear to have assessed that Xi will secure a third term and have expressed overt support for Xi and lined up behind him. Reflecting confidence that he will secure the third term, unprecedented since Deng Xiaoping, Xi has commenced promoting and positioning his loyalists in key positions. He has also cautioned prospective opponents that the anticorruption campaign will continue and prominent 'tigers'[3] might fall.

At the meeting of the Politburo's Group Study Session in Beijing on June 17, Xi warned that corruption in the country remains severe and complicated even though progress has been made in the battle against graft. He said its "stubbornness and danger" cannot be underestimated. Indicating that senior cadres are now in the crosshairs of the anti-corruption campaign, Xi Jinping vowed "zero tolerance" on corruption and asked senior government officials to keep themselves, their family and relatives in check and ensure a moderate and clean relationship between the government and business community.

Soon after, on June 20, the Shanghai-based 'Paper' publicised that the CCP CC General Office had issued "Regulations on the Management of Leading Cadres' Spouses, Children and Their Spouses to Run Business and Run Enterprises". Stating that "You can't have both fish and bear's paw. When you are an official, don't make a fortune. If you are rich, don't become an official. This is a car that runs on two roads", the regulations quoted Xi as saying that "the requirements for leading cadres are to be stricter". It clarified that "Centrally-managed cadres, cadres at the bureau level and equivalent positions in the provinces, autonomous regions, municipalities and central units are all included in the scope of the specification, leaving no blank spots". The *Discipline Inspection and Supervision News*, a newspaper of the CCP's powerful anti-corruption watchdog, the Central Discipline Inspection Commission (CDIC), reiterated the warning. In a commentary on managing the children and families published on June 21, it said "Leading cadres must study the spirit of the "Regulations" in depth, take the lead in strictly implementing the rules and regulations, accept the supervision of the party and the people, take the lead in improving family style and family style".

Wu Guoguang, Canada-based Chinese Political Science Professor and former editor of *People's Daily* and member of the Central Policy Group on Political Reform during the term of Premier Zhao Ziyang who resigned in protest against the Tiananmen events, said "Since Xi came to power, he has continued to carry out high-level political purges in the party through anti-corruption. It should come as no surprise that he did so at such a crucial stage of preparation for such a reorganization of power." He predicted that around July or August, Xi Jinping may purge high-level political figures in order to further deter the elites in the party, and warn the various forces that may challenge him to dare not act lightly.

The Politburo meeting of June 17 and the other regulations and newspaper articles together sparked speculation inside China that Xi intends to neutralise opposition from Jiang Zemin and Zeng Qinghong and that among those who could be targeted in a new anti-corruption campaign are Jiang Zemin's two sons, Jiang Mianheng and Jiang Miankang. Taiwan's media quoted Zhang Yushao, a researcher at the Cross-Strait Policy Association, as saying the Jiang Zemin family used to have a close relationship with Chinese tycoon Jack Ma. Jiang Mianheng, Jiang Zemin's eldest son is known to have an influential shareholding ratio in many listed companies. Zeng Wei, the son of former Vice Chairman and Jiang Zemin's right hand, Zeng Qinghong, is engaged in the oil trade and is rumoured to be involved with Shanghai Volkswagen, Beijing Hyundai, and Shanghai Eastern Airlines. The Shanghai Municipality responded that after it started conducting inspections in 2014-15, requiring leading cadres to declare businesses of spouses and children, 2133 leading cadres of Shanghai Municipality had made 'special declarations' on their spouses and children running businesses. Speculation has been reinforced by the report that Xiao Jianhua, who was taken away from the Four Seasons Hotel in Hong Kong in January 2017, would be tried in Shanghai before the end of the month.

The speculation links Xiao Jianhua's case with the larger enquiries into Jiang Zemin's family and claims that after his arrest Xiao Jianhua has probably "cooperated" in the investigations with the authorities. These reports add that in view of his relationship with Jiang Zemin, Zeng Qinghong, and other powerful families, the authorities would have obtained relevant evidence of the power and money transactions that have been discussed. Xi and his loyalists will use this evidence to neutralise Jiang Zemin, Zeng Qinghong and others likely to oppose him, which includes incarcerated former PB member Bo Xilai's supporters.

Discontent is, however, simmering below the surface. Many 'princelings', businessmen and entrepreneurs, Party cadres, intellectuals, students and others are dissatisfied with the slowing economy which has seen unemployment and the cost of living soar. Writing in the Ziyou Yazhou *diantai*[1] on May 24, a retired NDRC official and CCP cadre who writes under the pseudonym Liang Jing, forecast that US President Biden would see the fall of Putin and Xi Jinping, probably in 2022. He said that unlike Russia under Putin, China has seen no gains during Xi's terms and the elite is very unhappy.

More recently on June 18, Radio France International published a Chinese-language article that was originally published by the CDIC's "China Disciplinary Inspection and Supervision Magazine" on June 1. Titled "Abandoning Exquisite Egoism", the article criticised "Prime Minister Li" and generated a lot of speculation. Once it went viral the article was deleted, leaving only screenshots and snippets of quotes. WeChat accounts and WeChat groups that disseminated the article were censored. The article, which cites two negative examples, one is the prime minister of the Qin Dynasty, Li Si, and the other is the prime minister of the Tang Dynasty, Li Linfu, said: "Exquisite egoism refers to making good use of superbly realistic acting skills and high-sounding reasons to carefully embellish and subtly cover up the nature of selfishness and greed." Speculation was rife in China that Chinese Premier Li Keqiang was the article's target. It is strange that the CDIC issued such an article at this sensitive period and it points to ongoing inner-Party factional struggles.

Signalling his confidence, Xi has begun appointing loyalists to important senior CCP posts without waiting for either the Beidaihe conclave or the 20th Party Congress. He has also sidelined some who were expected to be elevated like former Xinjiang Party Secretary Chen Quanguo and International Liaison Department Chief Song Tao. Both have been appointed to bodies under the National People's Congress (NPC) and Chinese People's Political Consultative Conference (CPPCC). Chen Quanguo has been appointed Deputy Head of the Central Rural Work Leading Group.

The 35th meeting of the 13th NPC Standing Committee on June 24, presided over by NPC Chairman and PBSC member Li Zhanshu, approved new appointments among which were Pan Yue as Secretary of the Party Leadership Group of the State Ethnic Affairs Commission, while he continues as Deputy Minister of the United Front Work Department. Pan Yue relinquished the post of Director of the Overseas Chinese Affairs Office. Wang Xiaohong was promoted and appointed Minister of Public Security. The appointment of 64-year-old loyalist and former Executive Vice Minister of Public Security Wang Xiaohong as Minister of Public Security at this juncture is particularly important. He is the first professional police officer to lead the Ministry in 24 years.

Wang Xiaohong is likely to be 'cleared' for promotion as State Councillor, or even the PB, at the Party Congress in October-November and formally appointed at the "two sessions" (*lianghui*) meetings in March 2023. Other important appointments made by Xi are those of Liu Jianchao as head of the important CCP CC International Department (formerly the International Liaison Department), replacing Song Tao, on June 6. The following day the appointments of other Xi loyalists to Ministerial-level posts were also announced. These include: Cui Maohu as Director of the State Administration for Religious Affairs (SARA); Fu Hua as President of Xinhua News Agency; and Lv Yansong as Editor-in-Chief of Xinhua News Agency.

Fu Hua, is a long-time media veteran who served four years (2010-2014) as Deputy Propaganda Chief for the city of Beijing, and nearly two years (2018-2020) as the top propaganda official in Guangdong province. He has risen rapidly through the ranks and is regarded as a thoroughly loyal Party apparatchik. Fu Hua has given priority to Xi Jinping's notion of "telling China's story well" and the need to find new ways for the CCP to control public opinion domestically and globally. For example, shortly after joining *Beijing Daily*, Fu Hua referred to Xi's first major speech on propaganda and ideology on August 19, 2014, where he stressed the need for propaganda officials to "be bolder in raising the banner and showing their swords".

Before being promoted as Director of the State Administration for Religious Affairs (SARA), 1965-born Cui Maohu was Deputy Director of UFWD, in which capacity he has worked closely with Xi. Another Xi loyalist to be elevated is Xie Chuntao who, in a rare internal promotion was appointed Executive Vice President of the Central Party School.

Born in 1963, Xie Chuntao used to be the President and Editor-in-Chief of the CCP CC Party School and in May 2018, served as the Vice President (Dean) of the Central Party School (National School of Administration). Soon after his appointment, on June 30 Xie Chuntao published an article in the *People's Daily* where he declared "In the face of economic and trade frictions provoked by the United States, General Secretary Xi Jinping personally led the response, effectively safeguarding China's sovereignty, dignity. The core interests show the leadership level and the art of struggle of a leader of a big party and a big country strategizing and directing. In the people's war, the overall war and the blocking war in the prevention and control of the new crown pneumonia epidemic, General Secretary Xi Jinping took the overall situation and made decisive decisions, which provided the most fundamental guarantee for major strategic achievements in epidemic prevention and control. In the face of external forces interfering in Hong Kong affairs and rampant "anti-China chaos in Hong Kong" activities, the CPC Central Committee with Comrade Xi Jinping at its core maintained its determination and adopted a series of measures to address both the symptoms and the root causes, so as to push the situation in Hong Kong to achieve a major transition from chaos to governance".

The Ministry of Foreign Affairs (MoFA) has two potential vacancies to be filled at the Party Congress, namely those of Politburo member Yang Jiechi in case that position is to be retained and that of 69-year old Wang Yi as Foreign Minister. A surprise was the sideways movement and 'demotion' of Vice Foreign Minister and Russia expert Le Yucheng, widely regarded as Wang Yi's successor. It is probable that he was side-lined because of a factional struggle. Reports have long suggested that there are differences between Yang Jiechi and Wang Yi. Vice Foreign Minister Ma Chaoxu, and the current Director of the Taiwan Affairs Office Liu Jieyi are possible successors to Wang Yi. There are rumours too that Wang Yi's term could be extended by a year or two, but his elevation to the Politburo is doubtful. There is speculation, however, that Xi has someone else in mind for the job of Foreign Minister.

Senior CCP cadres have been competing for some months now to demonstrate their loyalty to Xi in the run up to the 20th Party Congress, further confirming that personal loyalty to Xi Jinping has become an important criterion for promotion in the CCP. Till June 29 a total of 11 Party Secretaries were noticed praising Xi Jinping and extolling his leadership qualities in their reports to the respective Provincial People's Congresses. Some of them are vying for a seat in the CCP CC Political Bureau.

The Party Secretaries include: Lou Yangsheng, Party Secretary of Henan, who wrote (June 22) in the *Learning Times* that cadres should "hold high the ideological banner and keep in mind the leader's entrustment", regard Xi Jinping's political theory as a "lifelong career", and call for "item-by-item" implementation of Xi Jinping's decree; Li Hongzhong, Party Secretary of the Tianjin Municipal Party Committee, who was the first to shout the slogan of "Xi's core", also mentioned "two safeguards" in his report to the Tianjin Party Congress (June 17), while calling on officials to strengthen "Xi's "core status", political identity, ideological identity, and emotional identity," and "unswervingly" follow Xi; Jiangxi Provincial Party Secretary Yi Lianhong in his speech (June 13) called Xi "the leader at the helm", and urged cadres to "keep in mind the entrustment and keeping up with the leader's pace"; Shandong Party Secretary Li Ganjie published (May 30) an article on the front page of the *Study Times* calling Xi Jinping "the man at the helm" and describing Xi's instructions as a "compass", "golden key" and "fulcrum". In addition, provinces and Municipalities have held several seminars to study the red pocket book and some have organised special exhibitions.

There are others too, like Zhejiang Party Secretary Yuan Jiajun whose report to the 15th Party Congress of Zhejiang on June 20 included 19 references in praise of Xi Jinping. He additionally ensured that eye-catching banners of "Practicing the 'Eight-Eight Strategy' faithfully, resolutely achieving the 'Two Maintenance', and striving to promote socialism with Chinese characteristics for common prosperity and provincial modernization in high-quality development" were placed on the balcony on the second floor of the venue! Fifty nine-year-old Yuan Jiajun is an aerospace engineer best known for his role as chief of the Shenzhou program and is a Full Member of the 19th CC who would be hoping for elevation to the PB. 1960-born

Jing Junhai, Jilin Party Secretary, in his report to the Jilin Party Congress on June 20, declared "The people of Jilin are infinitely grateful, highly trusted, and sincerely support General Secretary Xi Jinping" and "sincerely appreciate General Secretary Xi Jinping's care and concern". In his report to the Hubei Province Congress on June 18, Hubei Party Secretary Wang Menghui mentioned Xi Jinping 10 times. Attributing Hubei's successes to Xi Jinping, he ended with the exhortation "Let us unite more closely around the CPC Central Committee with Comrade Xi Jinping at the core, hold high the great banner of Xi Jinping Thought on Socialism with Chinese Characteristics for a New Era ... and make new and greater contributions to ... realizing the Chinese dream of the great rejuvenation of the Chinese nation!" Ningxia Party Secretary Liang Yanshun referred to Xi Jinping 39 times in his report to Ningxia's 13th Party Congress on June 10! Xinjiang Uyghur Autonomous Region Party Secretary Ma Xingrui too praised Xi in his report to the Eighth Congress of the Xinjiang Production and Construction Corps.

This was first published by the Centre for China Analysis and Strategy (CCAS) and Vivekananda International Foundation (VIF) in July 27, 2022.

4. Xi Jinping Appears Set for The Next Term at China's Helm

After a fortnight's absence from public events, Chinese President Xi Jinping and Chinese Premier Li Keqiang appeared in the Liaoning and Guangdong provinces respectively. Their absence since July 31 and appearance subsequently on August 16 confirmed that the secretive conclave of senior veteran cadres at the Beidaihe seaside resort had concluded after a fortnight. Additionally, none of the Politburo Standing Committee (PBSC) members were noticed either during this period. The extended duration of the Beidaihe conclave, which normally lasts 8- 10 days, has sparked some speculation in China. So also has the fact that instead of the other PBSC members appearing earlier;(National People's Congress (NPC) Chairman and PBSC member Li Zhanshu was the first to appear after the previous two conclaves at Beidaihe)– it was Xi Jinping and Li Keqiang who were seen.

What transpired at the Beidiahe conclave is not yet known and rumours will probably begin to circulate in a couple of weeks. However, the visits and speeches by Xi Jinping and Li Keqiang do suggest that the economy would have been discussed at length at Beidaihe and will be a priority for China's leadership. Reports that Xi Jinping may possibly physically attend the Shanghai Cooperation Organisation (SCO) Summit in Uzbekistan and Indonesian President Joko Widodo's disclosure that Xi Jinping plans to attend the G-20 Summit in Bali this November, also suggest that Xi Jinping is confident that he will continue to be at China's helm after the 20th Party Congress.

Xi has been preparing for another term as China's leader and reports circulating in China claim that he may even be designated Chairman at the upcoming 20th Party Congress! This would place him on par with Mao Zedong. More importantly, it would make him the pre-eminent member of the PBSC and imply that decisions in the PBSC or Politburo (PB) will no longer be by consensus. Another term for Xi Jinping also means that the CCP has decided to set aside the informal convention laid down by Deng Xiaoping of no more than two 5-year terms for any leader in order to prevent undue concentration of power in a single leader. Chinese Premier Li Keqiang has already announced that he would be stepping down as Premier on completion of his second term in March 2023.

What is interesting is that Xi Jinping, during his inspection of Jinjiang City, Shenyang and other places in Liaoning province on August 16 and 17, where he was accompanied by Liaoning Party Secretary Zhang Guoqing and Liaoning Governor Li Lecheng, emphasised water conservation, food production, common prosperity as well as the economy. He gave "important" instructions on flood control and improving disaster management capabilities. He also spoke of the need to cultivate young 'Red' cadres[4].

During his visit to Guangdong and the Shenzhen Special Economic Zone, Li Keqiang stressed on economic reforms. He emphasized that under the guidance of 'Xi Jinping Thought on Socialism with Chinese Characteristics for a New Era', the decisions of the Party Central Committee and the State Council must be fully implemented along with the new development concept. He called for efficient coordination of epidemic prevention and control and economic and social development, and economic stability. He also, pointedly, visited Lianhuashan Park to pay homage to the bronze statue of Deng Xiaoping. Careful to acknowledge Xi Jinping's contributions, Li Keqiang said 'It is hoped that under the strong leadership of the CCP Central Committee with Comrade Xi Jinping as the core, we will forge ahead, reform and innovate, and push development to a new level!'

Underscoring the leadership's focus on the economy, Li Keqiang presided over a symposium on August 16, with the principals of the provincial government in Shenzhen. Four Party Secretaries and Governors including Li Xi, Secretary of the Guangdong Provincial Party Committee, together accounting for more than 40 percent of the national economy, delivered speeches via video. Li Keqiang urged the economically large provinces to take the lead, ensure that market players stabilize the economy, and stabilize the employment of local and migrant workers. He said it is necessary to promote a higher level of opening to the outside world, stabilize foreign trade and foreign investment, and achieve mutual benefit and win-win results. A stable economy, he asserted, is also a stable source of money.

China's deteriorating economy is a serious concern and Li Keqiang's successor will have a difficult task. Amid rumours that Chinese Vice Premier Hu Chunhua will be promoted to the PBSC and appointed the next Premier, he attended a national teleconference, on stabilizing foreign trade and foreign investment and expanding consumption, in Beijing on August 17. On August 19, Hu Chunhua attended the National Employment Work Teleconference and the plenary meeting of the State Council's Employment Work Leading Group in Beijing. He emphasized that "we should make greater efforts to further stabilize the employment situation and make positive contributions to the overall economic and social development."

Hu Chunhua has the necessary qualifications for elevation to the PBSC and appointment as Premier. A young, low-key cadre on the fast-track, he has served as Party Secretary of Guangdong and the Inner Mongolia Autonomous Region and has served two terms in the Tibet Autonomous Region. He is a Vice Premier and has also been entrusted with implementation of Xi Jinping's flagship poverty alleviation programme. However, Hu Chunhua has risen through the ranks of the Communist Youth League (CYL) and is considered close to Hu Jintao.

There are at least three other candidates in the central organisations with experience of economic work who would be contenders for the job of Premier. Liu He, who is one of Xi Jinping's closest friends and has studied Economics in the US, is Xi Jinping's foremost adviser on economic matters. But he is 71 years old. He Lifeng heads the powerful National Development and Reform Commission (NDRC) under the State Council and is a Politburo (PB) member. He is 67 years old and eligible for elevation to the PBSC. Both accompany Xi Jinping on his tours within China and appear in the official photographs.

Finally, there is Han Zheng who is already in the PBSC and a Senior Vice Premier and at 68 years is just eligible to continue. Han Zheng was close to former Chinese President Jiang Zemin and, while he has switched allegiance to Xi Jinping, is still not regarded as entirely in Xi Jinping's camp. There was also some apparent unhappiness at the delay in his handling of the 'democracy' protests in Hongkong. If Han Zheng is retained in the PBSC or appointed Premier, it would mean that Xi Jinping has not been able to pack the PBSC with his loyalists.

There are others in the provinces who are also aspiring for elevation to the PBSC and could be considered eligible for the job of Premier. Front runners among them would be Li Jiang (63 years), Party Secretary of Shanghai; Chen Min'er (62 years), Party Secretary of Chongqing and long considered a rising star; Li Xi (66 years), Party Secretary of Guangdong; and Li Hongzhong (66 years) Party Secretary of Tianjin. Li Jiang and Chen Min'er are closely associated with Xi Jinping. Li Hongzhong has been vocal in his support for Xi Jinping and was the first cadre to refer to him as 'lingxui'. All of them have experience of managing provinces that are economic powerhouses.

Whoever takes over as Premier will have to contend with major economic difficulties in the years ahead. The rising graduate unemployment – already 19.9 percent by June this year, officially acknowledged ten percent rise in the costs of production, closure of businesses, imposition of strict regulatory controls on China's tech and fintech industries that has reduced their profitability, massive rural and urban unemployment, closure of businesses, anticipated food shortages etc., all threaten the legitimacy of the Chinese Communist Party (CCP). In addition, the deteriorating international environment and mounting anti-China sentiment globally could also shrink China's export markets abroad especially in the US and Europe. Xi Jinping and China's new Premier will have a difficult task ahead of them after the 20th Party Congress.

This was first published by the Centre for China Analysis and Strategy (CCAS) and Vivekananda International Foundation (VIF) in August 29, 2022.

5. Xi Jinping is Taking Steps to Avoid Any Surprise by the Opposition

It would be unwise today to discount reports of opposition to Chinese President Xi Jinping. This especially since opposition to him burst into the open first in 2017-2018 when Xi Jinping abolished term limits for the top Party posts at the 18th Party Congress. Dissatisfaction with the Chinese Communist Party (CCP) and Xi Jinping personally, surfaced again in 2020, when the authorities mishandled the outbreak of the Covid pandemic. The period leading to the 20th Party Congress, crucial for Xi Jinping if he wants to continue to lead China, is sensitive.

Chinese history is full of accounts of plots and attempted, or successful, coups against the Emperor. The more contemporary history of the Chinese Communist Party (CCP) has been no different. Despite Mao Zedong's preeminent stature in China and the CCP, he often suspected he was the target of plotters. Those suspected of plotting against him, including close comrades, were ruthlessly eviscerated. Deng Xiaoping faced opposition from his colleagues on issues of policy, but his proteges had to contend with sustained efforts to oust them. Efforts to create factions and make a bid for power continue, especially with the revolutionary veterans having faded from the scene. In fact, at the time of Xi Jinping's predecessor Hu Jintao, another 'princeling' Bo Xilai, successfully cultivated factions in the Party, military and security apparatus in his failed bid for Xi Jinping's position. He is now under house arrest!

Born in 1953, Xi Jinping is a 'princeling', or son of a senior Party leader with revolutionary credentials, who spent many years growing up in the confines of the leadership compound in Zhongnanhai in Beijing. He went to the 'August 1' special school for children of senior Party leaders. This enabled him to closely watch the inner workings of the CCP, including how deadly it can be as during the Cultural Revolution which he barely survived. Unlike many of his school comrades, Xi Jinping chose to join the CCP. He became a party apparatchik and rose through its ranks without the 'protection', or helpful influence, of his father who had been purged by Mao. Things changed after Deng Xiaoping captured power in 1979 and rehabilitated Xi Jinping's father, Xi Zhongxun, as Vice Premier.

The extent and stridency of criticism in 2012 and 2020 by Chinese intellectuals, professors, students, journalists, the public and even members of the CCP, of the Party and Xi Jinping personally, would have caught him unawares. Many of the criticisms were posted on social media and the offending posts were not taken down immediately by censors of the China Cyber Administration, suggesting that elements sympathetic to the critics were present in the security apparatus. The steps being taken by Xi Jinping to strengthen his grip on the levers of power confirm that opposition continues to simmer.

With his experience and insights into the inner workings of the CCP, Chinese President Xi Jinping has been taking measures to prevent being surprised in the run up to the Party Congress next year. In the midstream of criticism and in the wake of China's 'princelings' posting an 'open' letter on social media calling for an "emergency enlarged meeting of the Politburo to discuss Xi Jinping's removal" — which remained posted on social media for weeks — Xi Jinping set up the 'Safe China Constructing Coordinating Small Group' in April 2020. This new security body comprised Xi Jinping loyalists and Guo Shengkun, Politburo member and Chairman of the powerful Political and Legal Affairs Commission (PLAC), was appointed its head. This high-powered group reports directly and only to Xi Jinping. Its tasking is interesting: to "prevent and crackdown on activities that endanger the political security of the country". Later, the 26th 'collective study session' of the Politburo chaired by Chinese President Xi Jinping on December 11, 2020, decided on ten measures to tighten security. Among these, prioritising political security was identified as a top-level concern. References to "political security" and "political stability" in China's official media have visibly increased thereafter.

Around this time Wang Xiaohong, Executive Director of the Ministry of Public Security (MPS) and Director of the Secret Service Bureau charged with protecting the senior retired veteran cadres and Politburo members, suggested to Xi Jinping that "We must increase the monitoring of the 'top leaders' decision-making power, staff appointment power, and financial approval power, to let the 'top leaders' get used to working and living under monitoring". The implications are obvious.

The following month the Party's leading theoretical fortnightly journal *Qiu Shi* began calling for "protecting" Xi Jinping as the "core" of the Party. The People's Liberation Army (PLA) had already started exhorting cadres to "protect" Xi Jinping as the "core" of the Party from 2019.

Obviously keeping in mind the pivotal role of the public security apparatus, Xi Jinping loyalist Chen Yixin announced a three-month (July-October) pilot programme to prepare for a penetrating "rectification" of China's security apparatus in July 2020. Chen Yixin was handpicked by Xi Jinping as Secretary General of the PLAC. Indicating that the campaign would be far reaching and thorough, Chen Yixin called the pilot programme the beginning of "a self-restoration with the blade inward and bone scraping to cure the poison"![10]

On June 10, 2021, Chen Yixin announced that in the initial phase 75,084 security personnel had been disciplined, 1760 were placed in 'liuzhi' (detention), and 1012 sent for prosecution. As indicated by Guo Shengkun while addressing a meeting of the Political and Legal Education and Rectification Leading Group on June 16, the campaign is far from over. 10. Xi Jinping has been attentive to other aspects too. In October 2020 he strengthened his grip on the Party apparatus and assumed the authority to not only convene meetings of the Politburo (PB) and Politburo Standing Committee (PBSC) but also to explicitly set the agenda for the meetings. This precautionary move allows him to exclude topics that could question his decisions or undermine or embarrass him.

With an eye on the elections to the subordinate bodies that elect delegates to the Party Congress, certain changes were mandated by the CCP Central Committee (CC)'s 'Opinions on Selection of First Secretaries and Task Forces in Key Villages' on May 12, 2021. The main emphasis is "on building a team of leaders and cadres that are politically sound and capable of leading modernization." In this context, the CCP CC's instructions call for emphasising both, ability and political integrity, but with greater emphasis on the latter. It stated "It is necessary to thoroughly investigate political loyalty, political determination, political responsibility, political ability, political self-discipline, political judgment, political understanding, political execution, etc. Those who fail to observe political discipline and political rules and have problems such as "seven haves" shall not be selected as candidates."

Xi Jinping has also sought to ensure that the wealthy Chinese private entrepreneurs and businessmen who have been critical of his policies and called for reforms do not impede his efforts. While billionaire founder of Alibaba, Jack Ma has been brought down, Liu Changle of Phoenix Television has been compelled to sell his shares in Phoenix TV and its holding company. Wang Ting, billionaire founder of Meituan is also being investigated by China's financial regulators. Xi Jinping has additionally got Chinese Mainland businesses supportive of him to buy out or get controlling shares in the Hongkong media which is critical of his policies.

In addition, in late April 2021 China's Ministry of State Security issued a notice warning against attempts by the US and West to instigate a 'colour revolution' in China. A subsequent Global Times editorial singled out the US. Such calls for vigilance against efforts by Americans and westerners will fan xenophobia.

Whether opposition to Xi Jinping gets any traction will depend largely on whether it receives the support of the influential retired veteran leaders. What is important is whether the number of CCP cadres, particularly in the CCP CC, will reach a critical mass. These will mainly comprise Party cadres and members who feel strongly about the Cultural Revolution and are unhappy with present policies. Meanwhile, though Xi Jinping presently controls all the levers of power and is taking measures to neutralize any opposition, there have been subtle hints of opposition in recent months. The extent of pressure that the deteriorating Sino-US relations exert on the CCP's leadership in the coming months would be potentially important.

This was first published by the Centre for China Analysis and Strategy (CCAS) and Vivekananda International Foundation (VIF) in June 21, 2021.

6. Purges in Security Apparatus Indicate Xi Jinping Faces Resistance

The months till the 20th Party Congress, scheduled for late next year, are fraught with risk for China and its neighbours. It is a particularly crucial year for Chinese President Xi Jinping, who is trying to secure a third term, unprecedented since Mao Zedong, at the 20th Party Congress. At the same time there are signs of enhanced political activity, albeit subterranean, which suggest that Xi Jinping's opponents are also active, thereby raising the stakes.

A fairly clear indication is the attention being paid by China's leadership to the powerful security apparatus, known among Party cadres as "the knife handle" (*daobazi*, 刀把子). After Politburo Standing Committee member and Security Czar Zhou Yongkang's ouster and imprisonment immediately prior to the 18th Party Congress in November 2012, Xi Jinping downgraded the position of Chairman of the Political and Legal Affairs Commission (PLAC), which oversees the entire security apparatus, to that of a Politburo member reporting directly to him thereby taking direct charge of the security establishment. By 2013-14 he had replaced much of the senior leadership of the central security establishment with his loyalists. He appears, however, not to have looked at the senior to middle rungs of the security establishment and there are indications that sections within the establishment are not entirely loyal to him. Examples are the numerous instances between 2017-18 and again between 2020 and early 2021 when posts critical, or opposing, Xi Jinping and the CCP were permitted to stay for long periods on Chinese social media websites before being deleted. There have also been reports at regular intervals of dismissals of senior security personnel. Xi Jinping has now begun addressing this since late last year.

After the 26th 'collective study session' of the Politburo chaired by Chinese President Xi Jinping on December 11, 2020, ten measures were identified as necessary to tighten security. Among these, political security was prioritised as a top-level concern and references to "political security" and "political stability" in China's official media increased visibly thereafter. This session was held amidst growing concern that the increasing tensions with the United States could spark more political turmoil inside China. The following month the Party's leading theoretical fortnightly journal *Qiu Shi* began calling for "protecting" Xi Jinping as the "core" of the Party. The People's Liberation Army (PLA) had already started exhorting cadres to "protect" Xi Jinping as the "core" of the Party from 2019.

Earlier, in July 2020, Xi Jinping loyalist Chen Yixin had announced a three-month (July-October) pilot programme for the entire security apparatus to prepare for the beginning of "a self-restoration with the blade inward and bone scraping to cure the poison"! Chen Yixin was handpicked by Xi Jinping as Secretary General of the powerful PLAC.

On June 10, 2021, Chen Yixin announced that in the initial phase itself 75,084 security personnel had been disciplined, 1760 were placed in 'liuzhi' (detention), and 1012 sent for prosecution. As indicated by Guo Shengkun while addressing a meeting of the Political and Legal Education and Rectification Leading Group on June 16, the campaign is far from over.

The CCP's powerful anti-corruption watchdog body, the Central Discipline Inspection Commission (CDIC), recently indicated that the rectification is not yet over. A notification on its official website on August 7, 2021, stated that over 90 "leading cadres" of the Political and Legal system at the department level or above were investigated and dealt with in the first half of the year.

State Councillor, Secretary of the Party Committee of the Ministry of Public Security and Minister of Public Security Zhao Kezhi subsequently confirmed on October 16, that the rectification drive is continuing. He disclosed that the bureau and eight bureau-level units under the Ministry have "promoted investigations and corrections" on the work of "eliminating the effects of poisoning". The term "poisoning" is a reference to the existence of ideas contrary to those of the CCP or opposing factions or groups. A month ago the campaign was expanded to include all of China's 1,355 counties. There is no doubt that more personnel will be weeded out.

While senior cadres who have been in the system for many years could have been expected to forge loyalties to previous General Secretaries of the CCP, the charges leading to the dismissal of Fu Zhenghua and Sun Lijun were surprising. Both were promoted by Xi Jinping. Though Fu Zhenghua never served under Xi Jinping, both were considered by Beijing-based Chinese observers to be among hissupporters. Punitive action was taken against them within days of each other. Sun Lijun was dismissed as Vice Minister of Public Security on September 29, and on October 2, the CDIC's State Supervision Commission announced that 66-year-old Fu Zhenghua, former Justice Minister and at the time Deputy Director of the Social and Legal Affairs Committee of the CPPCC National Committee, had been placed under disciplinary review and supervision and was under investigation on suspicion of "serious violations of discipline and law". Fu Zhenghua and Sun Lijun had worked together in the Ministry of Public Security from 2013-2018. Their dismissal appears to have had repercussions in the public security apparatus with top leaders holding a series of meetings warning cadres to oppose factions and stressing the need for loyalty.

Fu Zhenghua's case is particularly interesting. It could have far reaching implications and signal the start of more senior security cadres, affiliated to Jiang Zemin or other opposing factions, being weeded out or pulled out of retirement and punished. Fu Zhenghua is the highest-ranking security official, after Politburo Standing Committee member and Security Czar Zhou Yongkang, to have been dismissed from the CCP and be put on trial. His last assignment before retirement was as Minister of Justice. Born in Hebei province, Fu Zhenghua rose through the ranks of the public security hierarchy of Beijing Municipality and in 2010, was promoted to the Beijing Municipal Public Security Bureau and appointed Secretary of the Party Committee. The same year he was made a member of the Standing Committee of the Beijing Municipal Party Committee and Deputy Secretary of the Municipal Committee of Political and Legal Affairs. From January 2015 to February 2018, Fu Zhenghua served as Deputy Minister and Deputy Secretary of the Ministry of Public Security, and was concurrently a member of the Central Political and Legal Committee and Director of the Central "610" Office[11]. He served as Deputy Secretary of the Party Leadership Group of the Ministry of Justice and Minister of Justice from March 2018 to April 2020. From May 2020 till his dismissal, he was Deputy Director of the Social and Legal Committee of the CPPCC National Committee. A report says that Fu Zhenghua was brought in to the Beijing Public Security Bureau by Liu Qi, a former secretary of the Beijing Municipal Party Committee and member of Jiang Zemin's faction.

According to *Epoch Times* (October 2), five years ago Wuhan billionaire businessman Xu Chongyang had accused Fu Zhenghua of 'mobilising 4000 political and legal personnel against Xi Jinping'. During the Chinese New Year in 2019, Xu Chongyang again accused Fu Zhenghua, in an 18,000-character complaint. He alleged that Fu Zhenghua has close ties to the sacked security 'tigers' Zhou Yongkang and Meng Jianzhu and also that he has close ties to Guo Shengkun, currently Politburo member and Secretary of the CCP CC's Central Political and Legal Commission!

The case of Sun Lijun, who till his dismissal and expulsion from the Party was a security cadre on the fast-track, is of particular interest. He was formally arrested on November 4. Sun Lijun was the deputy head of a high-level team sent by Beijing to Wuhan, Hubei province in February 2020 to help contain the Covid-19 outbreak. The charges levelled against him were more serious than the usual instances of corruption and having mistresses and clearly suggested that Sun Lijun was actively working against Xi Jinping.

On September 30, China's official media reported that 52-year-old Sun Lijun, a former Chinese Vice Minister of the Public Security Bureau, has been sacked and expelled from the CCP and will face trial for "serious violation of discipline rules and law". The charges against Sun Lijun publicised by *Xinhua* were very serious and unusual. Xinhua quoted the CDIC as saying that "[Sun] has never had any real faith or ideals ... He harboured hugely inflated political ambitions, and was of extremely bad political quality. To achieve his political objectives ... [he] resorted to whatever means ... forming gangs and factions, seizing control of key [security] departments, seriously undermining the unity of the party, and causing extreme danger to the political security [of the party]." It added that Sun Lijun "had secretly possessed a large amount of confidential materials, and engaged in superstitious activities for a long time" [For a long period of time, Sun] lived a decadent life, accepting huge amounts of bribes and expensive gifts ... [He] is a man with no morals, trading power for money and sex." More seriously the report disclosed that Sun Lijun had been under investigation for 17 months from April last year, had resisted the investigation and "did not explain [his] problems truthfully" to the investigators. The CDIC said Sun Lijun's "case has been transferred to prosecutors who will arrange for a trial in accordance with the law." Interestingly, Sun Lijun was secretary to Meng Jianzhu, a former Politburo member and Minister of Public Security (2012-2017) with strong patron-client ties to former CCP General Secretary Jiang Zemin. He is also reported to be a close ally of Politburo Standing Committee member and Vice Premier Han Zheng, who heads the central leading group on Hong Kong and Macau affairs.

The charges levelled against Sun Lijun also reveal that while he was actively working against Xi Jinping, there are other factions or groups in the security apparatus which are also opposed to Xi Jinping. These could include pro-Bo Xilai groups. The series of meetings being held in the security apparatus following the dismissals of Fu Zhenghua and Sun Lijun appear to confirm this and suggest that news of involvement of other senior security cadres may soon follow. Of special interest is the meeting convened by Guo Shengkun, Politburo member and Secretary of the CCP CC's Central Political and Legal Committee. Of particular importance is the language he used. Xinhua (October 8) reported that Guo Shengkun chaired the second 'national political and legal team education and rectification work promotion meeting' on October 8 where he emphasised that he "firmly supported the Party Central Committee's decision to thoroughly implement the Party Central Committee's deployment and increase efforts to promote the education and rectification of political and legal teams". Guo Shengkun also expressed "firm support" for the Party Central Committee's decision to deal with Sun Lijun's serious violations of discipline and law and the decision to conduct disciplinary review and supervision and investigation of Fu Zhenghua's suspected serious violations of discipline and law. He added "We must resolutely and thoroughly eliminate the poisonous influence, insist on real hard work, and resolutely clean up in place". State Councilor and Minister of Public Security Zhao Kezhi, the Chief Justice and President of the Supreme People's Court of China Zhou

Qiang and Procurator-General, Supreme People's Procuratorate Zhang Jun were present at the meeting.

Later, on October 19, the *Legal Daily* reported that an enlarged meeting of the Party Committee of the Ministry of Public Security was held on October 16 to convey the "spirit" of the Ministry of Public Security's third work report. State Councilor, Secretary of the Party Committee of the Ministry of Public Security and Minister of Public Security Zhao Kezhi presided over this meeting. The *Legal Daily* disclosed that "the bureau and 8 bureau-level units under the Ministry" were carrying out "investigation, correction, rectification" and "the work of eliminating the effects of poisoning". Zhao Kezhi stressed the need to "thoroughly study and implement the important instructions of General Secretary Xi Jinping and the spirit of the CPC Central Committee decisions" and to enhance and continue "to deepen political understanding" and "eliminate the pernicious influence of Sun Lijun" and "gangs". It said "the education and rectification of the second batch of political and legal teams across the country entered the stage of investigation, correction and reform".

Underscoring the importance of the case, the *Legal Daily* report included at least five references to "Sun Lijun's political gangs" and their serious violation of law, elimination of "the pernicious influence of political gangs as a top priority" and the serious violation of law by the Sun Lijun political gangs. The meeting asserted: "We must focus on political loyalty, persist in learning and education throughout, thoroughly study and implement the spirit of the important precepts of General Secretary Xi Jinping's important speech, and earnestly build the foundation of faith, supplement the spirit of the spirit, and stabilize the ideological rudder, from the ideological, political, and organizational In the above and work style, thoroughly eliminate the poisonous influence of Sun Lijun's political gang, and strive to build a loyal and vigilant soul". It insisted "We must continue to deepen the rectification of stubborn diseases". Wang Xiaohong, Deputy Secretary of the Party Committee and Executive Vice Minister of the Ministry of Public Security and a close associate and loyalist of Xi Jinping attended the meeting along with members of the Party Committee of the Ministry of Public Security. The main "responsible" officials of various bureau-level units under the Ministry, "relevant responsible" officials of the

CDIC and Supervision Group and the State Immigration Administration attended the meeting as non-voting delegates.

The charges levelled against Sun Lijun and the inordinately long time of 17 months taken to carry out the investigations make clear that a number of elements opposed to Xi Jinping are present in China's security apparatus. Sun Lijun's expulsion from the Party and arrest and the repeated references to "political gangs" appear to confirm that the authorities have identified other "disloyal" elements and placed them under investigation. Xi Jinping loyalists are now carrying out a thorough rectification of the public security apparatus. More persons with suspect loyalties will be weeded out or punished. The involvement of Xi Jinping loyalists in the rectification campaign is indicated by the presence of Zhao Kezhi and Wang Xiaohong, both Xi Jinping loyalists, in the meetings. There are also other signs suggesting a heating of political activity and of Xi Jinping retaliating against opponents.

This was first published by the Centre for China Analysis and Strategy (CCAS) and Vivekananda International Foundation (VIF) in November 7, 2021.

7. Xi Jinping's New Security Satraps

China's powerful security apparatus has become even more important for Xi Jinping as he makes a bid for a third term at China's helm at the upcoming 20th Party Congress in 2022. The unease and dissatisfaction simmering just below the surface make it imperative that the security apparatus is unquestioningly loyal to Xi.

The appointment on November 19 of Wang Xiaohong, a long-time associate of Chinese President Xi Jinping, as Secretary of the Ministry of Public Security's Party Committee makes it certain that he will replace Zhao Kezhi as Minister in the Ministry of Public Security (MPS), at least in the short term. Zhao Kezhi is 68 years old and due to retire. The appointment is out of the ordinary as it is normally the Minister who is concurrently Secretary of the Party Committee of the Ministry. News of the appointment comes within days of the conclusion of the Chinese Communist Party (CCP) Central Committee (CC)'s Sixth Plenum (November 8-11), suggesting that the Plenum considered personnel appointments, which will finally be announced after the 20th Party Congress late next year. Wang Xiaohong's appointment also coincides with the intensive purge, or cleansing, of China's security apparatus — called by Party cadres as "the knife handle" — which now appears to be in its final stages.

The choice of Wang Xiaohong to head the sensitive Ministry of Public Security (MPS) is undoubtedly deliberate. The months leading up to the 20th Party Congress scheduled for late next year are crucial for Xi Jinping who is making a bid for a third term. After Mao Zedong, Chinese leaders have not continued in office for more than two terms. If appointed Minister MPS, 64-year-old Wang Xiaohong, who is a member of the 19th CCP CC, can be expected to be promoted to State Councillor or Politburo member and will probably hold this powerful post till almost the 21st Party Congress in 2027. It is equally likely that Xi promotes him after the 20th Party Congress to the Politburo to head the all-powerful Central Political and Legal Committee.

There are, additionally, signs of enhanced political activity, albeit subterranean, which suggest that Xi's opponents are active thus raising the stakes. Clear pointers were the charges levelled against former Vice Minister of Public Security Sun Lijun which included "forming gangs" and even "causing extreme danger to the political security [of the party]" – code for Xi! The uncertainty implies that Xi will not give even a hint of weakness by relaxing policies. This includes his aggressive foreign policy which will continue to pose a risk for China's neighbours.

Wang Xiaohong convened a meeting of the Ministry of Public Security's Party Committee on November 21, within days of being appointed its Secretary, where, according to HongKong's Sing Tao Daily, he emphasized that "purging out Sun Lijun and other people's poisonous influence should be placed in a more prominent position, and resolutely eliminate political hidden dangers." The implication is that more dismissals can be expected.

Sing Tao Daily also reported on November 23, that Wang Xiaohong is placing his former loyal subordinates at leadership-level in the MPS to replace those dismissed. Identified among them are the former Vice Governor and Director of Public Security of Henan, Xu Ganlu who has very recently been inducted as Vice Minister in the MPS. Wang Xiaohong's subordinate in the Fujian Public Security, Lin Rui, is another who has been appointed MPS Vice Minister. The Vice Minister and Director of the First Bureau (China Domestic Political Security Bureau) Chen Siyuan is a former subordinate of Wang Xiaohong in the Beijing Public Security Bureau. Another subordinate of Wang Xiaohong's in the Henan Public Security, Feng Yan, has been appointed Director of the Political Department. With these appointments and those yet to come, Wang Xiaohong is clearly ensuring that the MPS stays loyal to him and Xi.

Wang Xiaohong has a long and close association with Xi and is counted among his closest friends. He began his career in Fujian, where he remained until August 2013. Wang Xiaohong was Xi Jinping's subordinate during the latter's entire term in Fujian. In December 2013, Wang Xiaohong was appointed Deputy Governor of Henan province in charge of the provincial public security department. Wang Xiaohong served 34 years (1993-2013) in Fujian and held positions such as Director of the Minhou County Public Security Bureau and Director of the Fuzhou Public Security Bureau. He later became police chief of Xiamen, before moving to Henan province.

Wang Xiaohong was promoted to the post of Director of Public Security of Beijing in March 2015. That he was trusted by Xi is evident from not only his appointment as Police Chief of Beijing (2015-2020) – a job entrusted only to a person of the CCP CC General Secretary's confidence – but that he was concurrently Deputy Mayor of Beijing, Party Secretary of the Beijing Municipal Public Security Bureau, and the Director of the Public Security Bureau. He was appointed Vice Minister of Public Security in May 2016. A source has reportedly disclosed: "I have heard Wang served as a ban lang (the best man or head groomsman) at Xi Jinping's private wedding with Peng Liyuan, attended by only close relatives. They are so close to each other."

The most important post in China's security apparatus is that of the Secretary of the Central Political and Legal Committee who is a member of the CCP Politburo. The Central Political and Legal Committee supervises and is directly responsible for the MPS, Ministry of State Security (MoSS) and Procuratorate. The Minister of Public Security often takes over as Secretary of the Political and Legal Committee, but this year the incumbent MPS Minister Zhao Kezhi and Secretary of the Central Political and Legal Committee Guo Shengkun are likely to retire at the same time. This could provide an opportunity for Wang Xiaohong to be promoted to the Politburo and appointed Secretary of the Central Political and Legal Committee. Xi loyalist, Chen Yixin, already Secretary General of the Central Political and Legal Committee, could be another contender.

Born in 1959 in Zhejiang Province, Chen Yixin is a 'Cultural Revolution Rusticated Youth'. He joined the CCP in 1982. Having spent his entire career in Zhejiang Province, Chen Yixin was Secretary of the Wenzhou City Party Committee from 2013-2015 when he is reputed to have played a central role in helping it recover from its worst debt crisis in decades. Xi Jinping brought Chen Yixin, already regarded a rapidly rising cadre of the loosely labelled 'Zhejiang faction', to Beijing as Deputy Director of the CCP CC's Central Leading Small Group (LSG) for Comprehensively Deepening Reform in the

General Office. The CLSG was created by Xi Jinping and is chaired by him. In 2018, Chen Yixin was appointed to the powerful post of Secretary General of the Central Political and Legal Committee. In April 2020, Chen Yixin initiated a thorough 'rectification' of the entire security apparatus, comprising the MPS, MoSS, Central Political and Legal Committee, Supervisory Commission, Procuratorate etc, which he described as "a self-restoration with the blade inward and bone scraping to cure the poison".

Chen Yixin is an Alternate Member of the 19th CCP CC and a year younger than Wang Xiaohong. In case Xi promotes Wang Xiaohong to the Politburo and the powerful job of Secretary of the Central Political and Legal Committee, he could appoint Chen Yixin as Minister MPS and promote him as State Councillor. With age on his side, Chen Yixin could then wait till 2027 for elevation to the Politburo, unless Xi decides to use his talents in the economic sphere.

Yet another candidate for elevation to the Politburo and choice for the powerful post of Secretary of the Central Political and Legal Committee is Chen Wenqing, a member of the 19th CCP CC. Born in 1960, Chen Wenqing is younger than Wang Xiaohong or Chen Yixin. Chen Wenqing is a professional security cadre and well acquainted with the central security apparatus after Xi named him Deputy Director of the Central State Security Office, part of the new Central State Security Commission (CSSC) set up by Xi to tighten party oversight of the security apparatus, in May 2018. If appointed Secretary of the Central Political and Legal Committee, Chen Wenqing will bring to his job the experience of ordinary police work as well as that of the more sophisticated domestic security and foreign intelligence. In view of China's current hostile external environment, Chen Wenqing's experience may be considered useful.

Chen Wenqing is also a 'Red Descendent'.His father was in the Sichuan Province Public Security.After graduation, he entered the Ministry of Public Security in 1984. In 1988, he was decorated for bravery for his role in the capture of two armed criminals. Chen Wenqing moved to the MoSS in 1994 and became Deputy Director at the Sichuan provincial State Security Department. He was appointed Director of the State Security Department in Sichuan in 1998 and held this position until 2002, when he was appointed

Chief Prosecutor at the Sichuan provincial People's Procuratorate. In 2006, Chen Wenqing moved to Fujian, where he served until 2012 as Deputy Party Secretary and concurrently head of the provincial Commission for Discipline Inspection. Following the 18th Party Congress at which Xi came to power, Chen Wenqing was brought to Beijing to become one of the Deputy Secretaries of the Central Discipline Inspection Commission (CDIC). He was appointed Party Secretary of the MoSS in October 2016 and MoSS Minister in November.

This was first published by the Centre for China Analysis and Strategy (CCAS) and Vivekananda International Foundation (VIF) in December 20, 2021.

8. Chinese President Jiang Zemin's Demise Reveals Extent of Discontent in China

Recent events have confirmed the considerable subterranean discontent in China. The death of former Chinese President Jiang Zemin, who was handpicked by the late Chinese leader Deng Xiaoping to steer the Chinese Communist Party (CCP) and the country in the immediate aftermath of the Tiananmen massacre in 1989, has occurred at a critical time for Chinese President Xi Jinping. It complicates an already difficult situation when numerous cities across the country have witnessed protests against the stringent restrictions to implement the zero-Covid policy and the economic situation is worsening.

Clear confirmation that China's authorities were apprehensive that Jiang Zemin's funeral could trigger another nationwide wave of protests was the decision announced on December 1, that 'No funeral service will be held' for Jiang Zemin. The authorities would have had in mind the rash of protests in the wake of former Chinese Communist Party (CCP) Central Committee (CC) General Secretary Hu Yaobang's funeral in 1989 which culminated in the use of military force against students and workers at Tiananmen. This is a break with past practice. Instead, the 206-member 'Jiang Zemin Funeral Committee' ruled (December 1) that there will be a big ceremony to honour him at the Great Hall of the People, in Beijing.

Interestingly, the funeral committee included the name of former General Secretary Hu Jintao along with those of all former and current Politburo members. Hu Jintao, it may be recalled, was 'removed' from the meeting of the 20th Party Congress on its final day on October 23. Hu Jintao was also reported by the state-owned CCTV as visiting the PLA hospital to pay his respects to Jiang Zemin and later shown standing next to Chinese President Xi Jinping at the Great Hall of the People. This confirms that Hu Jintao was 'removed' from the venue of the 20th Party Congress on October 23, due to ill health. Interesting also is that the funeral committee included Xi Jinping's wife, Peng Liyuan.

As previously anticipated, Xi Jinping will face a range of problems through his third term with his zero-Covid policy and its after-effects tenaciously dogging him. Provoked by the disastrous fire accident in Urumqi where nearly 10 people died, protests against the zero-Covid policy erupted across China within days. One of the main centres of protest was Foxconn's giant iPhone plant in Zhengzhou, which began on November 23, when workers angry over unpaid wages and Covid-19 lockdowns clashed with hazmat-clad riot police. The violence followed disturbances last month that resulted in thousands of workers fleeing the facility after a Covid outbreak and a failed attempt at keeping workers isolated from the outside world. The immediate provocation was the failure of plant administrators to deliver adequate food and water to the 200,000 Foxconn workers. Matters were aggravated when the company also failed to fulfil the promises of higher wages made to workers. Apple was prompted to announce that customers will face delays for iPhone 14 deliveries as Apple was committed to "ensuring the health and safety of every worker."

China's official media blanked out news of the protests, but social media has been peppered with reports from citizens, of protests in different places and the movement of PLA troops, tanks and trucks. The Hongkong-based *Intium* has reported that 79 tertiary educational institutions, including Beijing's prestigious Tsinghua University, have participated in the protests. Protests have occurred in Tsinghua University, Beijing, Wuhan, Urumqi, Korla, Chengdu, Nanjing, Zhengzhou, Chongqing, Guangzhou and Shanghai with crowds shouting "Down with Xi Jinping", "Get off CCP", and having stand-offs with police as late as on December 7 at Beijing's Haidian University District. Public Security personnel began arresting protesters on November 27 night. PLA tanks, heavy vehicles and ambulances were seen being deployed on November 29, outside Tsinghua University and Zhengzhou. China's official media, including the China Daily and Global Times, had blanked out reports of the protests till November 28.

Though apparently against the Covid restrictions, the protests in at least ten cities across the country have quickly been joined by students, citizens and workers and surfaced earlier than anticipated, suggesting that leadership elements opposed to Xi Jinping could be stirring things. The protests continued till December 8, including in educational institutions like the Nanjing University. While indications are that the protests may die down soon, the authorities have already hinted at the involvement of "hostile foreign elements" trying to instigate a "colour revolution" and begun trying to identify the protesters. Many have been brought in for questioning by public security officials, but efforts to question the majority of protesters is expected to continue.

Meanwhile Jiang Zemin's supporters, upset as their futures become more uncertain with their 'leaders' death, will add to the pools of discontent. Their apprehensions will have been heightened with the CCP's anti-corruption outfit, the Central Discipline Inspection Commission (CDIC), beginning to list disloyalty to Xi Jinping as one of the charges. On October 30, the CDIC disclosed that Li Xiaobao, former Secretary of the Party Group and Director of the Jiangxi Provincial Department of Culture and Tourism, was being re-investigated because, it said, "Li Xiaobao lost his ideals and beliefs, betrayed the "two safeguards" etc. This is probably the first political verdict to mention the "two safeguards" after they were included in the Party Charter at the just concluded 20th Party Congress. The slogan of "Two Safeguards", first coined in 2018, is to "resolutely safeguard General Secretary Xi Jinping's core position of the Party Central Committee and the core position of the whole party" and to "resolutely safeguard the authority and centralized and unified leadership of the Party Central Committee".

An additional worry for Jiang Zemin's supporters would be the reports circulating in Beijing since around a fortnight that Xi Jinping has drawn up plans to purge Jiang Zemin's faction. The reports state that more than 15,000 CCP officials and 3000 entrepreneurs will be purged or punished and their assets confiscated.

China's economy has also been slowing down. The cost of living has been rising, urban and rural unemployment is burgeoning, and graduate unemployment has touched 20 percent. The people are feeling the pain more directly too with those who find employment getting half the salaries than before Covid, salaries of central and provincial government employees slashed by 30 percent and bonuses already paid being recovered. The Institute of International Finance in early November estimated that foreign investors pulled out US$ 8.8 billion from China's financial market in October. Of that US$ 7.6 billion was from the stock market and US$ 1.2 billion was from the bond market. It added that since Russia's invasion of Ukraine in February, about US$ 105 billion has been pulled out from China's bond portfolio.

Despite this Xi Jinping showed no inclination towards taking economic initiatives and assisting China's private entrepreneurs who provide 80 percent of the jobs and 90 percent of the revenues. On the contrary, the Work Report approved by the 20th Party Congress spoke of 'common prosperity'[12]. It was only on December 6 that a meeting of the Politburo was convened to discuss the economic situation in 2023.

The protests have, quite unusually, persisted for nearly twenty days. Realising that they have the potential to gain momentum, the official *Xinhua* news agency reported that the CCP's apex security outfit, the Central Political and Legal Affairs Commission (CPLAC), met and decided to "resolutely crack down on infiltration and sabotage activities by [foreign] hostile forces..., resolutely crack down on illegal and criminal acts that disrupt social order, and effectively maintain overall social stability." Soon, thereafter, the Cyberspace Administration of China issued instructions making the act of "liking" something on the web a criminal offense. China's leadership has simultaneously set up "small leadership groups" to investigate the reasons and identify protesters.

Action against those who took part will certainly follow soon. The CCP believes, as the Tiananmen events have shown, that any demonstration of opposition must be crushed so that it doesn't resurface for the next "25 years"! Xi Jinping and the leadership will not brook a challenge and certainly not if they suspect, as is very possible, that Xi Jinping's opponents within the CCP have already begun mobilising to coerce him to step down.

This was first published by the Centre for China Analysis and Strategy (CCAS) and Vivekananda International Foundation (VIF) in December 9, 2022.

9. Xi Jinping Preparing to Initiate Another 'Party Rectification'

Since Chinese President Xi Jinping withdrew the stringent zero-Covid restrictions overnight and eased the campaign against China's tech platforms, there has been considerable speculation in the international media to suggest that Xi Jinping had been weakened by the popular protests. A few observers suggested that some members of the Politburo or its Standing Committee had together urged Xi Jinping to amend the policies. There are, however, no indications that point to a weakening of Xi Jinping's power or authority.

On the contrary, since the 20th Party Congress (October 6-22, 2022) there have been clear indications that the Chinese Communist Party (CCP) is gearing up to begin another round of its 'rectification' campaign. It is clear that this time the rectification campaign will especially evaluate the loyalty of the cadres to Xi Jinping and investigate senior cadres. Party Cadres who have retired will also be investigated where necessary.

In an announcement seemingly timed to emphasise that there will be a focus on senior cadres, the CCP's anti-corruption watchdog Central Discipline Inspection Commission (CDIC) disclosed that 61-year-old Li Chunsheng, former Guangdong Deputy Governor and Public Security Chief for eight years until he stepped down in 2021 and currently Deputy Director of the provincial legislature's standing committee, had been placed under investigation. The announcement also conveyed the importance of loyalty to Xi Jinping as Li Chunsheng happened to have worked with Sun Lijun when the latter took charge of the Public Security Ministry's Hong Kong, Macau and Taiwan Affairs Office, in which the Guangdong's police department plays a key role.

A series of articles and statements by senior CCP officials have set the tone for the campaign. The first indications were in the speeches by Chen

Wenqing, Politburo member and Secretary General of the CCP CC's powerful Central Political and Legal Affairs Commission, during his inspection visit to Shaanxi province on November 16-18, 2022. The *People's Daily* (November 19) observed that while speaking to cadres of the procuratorates, public security, national security, and judicial administrative agencies, he emphasised that they should "always maintain a firm and correct political direction on the political and legal front, defend the "two establishments" with practical actions, and achieve the "two safeguards." The phrase "Two Safeguards" was, incidentally, incorporated in the CCP Constitution in October 2022.

This was reinforced by Chen Xi, former Politburo member and the outgoing head of the CCP Central Committee (CC) Central Organization Department, in a major article published by the *People's Daily* on November 23. The article on "building a team of high-quality cadres worthy of the important task of national rejuvenation" insisted the organizational line must be to ensure a high degree of awareness of the political line and that strengthening and improving the work of cadres in the new era "is related to the prosperity and long-term stability of the party and the country". Importantly, he emphasised the necessity of "vigorously selecting cadres who firmly support the "two establishments"[13], resolutely achieve the "two safeguards", and maintain a high degree of consistency with the Party Central Committee with Comrade Xi Jinping at the core in terms of ideology, politics and actions, and resolutely put those political "two maintenances" in line". The phrase "Two Safeguards" was incidentally incorporated in the CCP Constitution in October 2022.

The following day the *People's Daily* (November 24) published animportant article by Guo Shengkun, outgoing Secretary of the Central Political and Legal Affairs Commission. Underscoring "the absolute leadership of the party", he stressed the need to "deeply understand the decisive significance of the "two establishments", and strengthen the "four consciousnesses".He added that, "The new strategic environment, the risks and challenges that need to be dealt with, the contradictions and problems that need to be resolved are more complicated than before, and the promotion of the modernization of the national security system and capabilities is of greater and far-reaching significance". He reiterated that "various "black swan" and "grey rhinoceros" incidents may occur at any time and that China faces increasing risks.

An important article authored by the Central and State Organ Working Committee Theoretical Learning Center Group and published in the *People's Daily* on December 26, outlined the scope of the rectification campaign. It declared that "consolidating the longterm ruling position of the party and ensuring that the party will always be the strong leadership core of the cause of socialism with Chinese characteristics", thus clarifying that loyalty to Xi Jinping will be the key criteria in the evaluation of cadres. Setting out the scope of the rectification campaign, it said "The central and state organs are the closest to the Party Central Committee and serve the Party Central Committee most directly. They are the first phalanx for practicing the "two safeguards" and the "first mile" for implementing the decisions and deployments of the Party Central Committee. To deepen comprehensive and strict party governance and carry out self-revolution, we must start with the central government and state organs, and start with the party building of the organs". The article warned party members and cadres "to deeply understand the decisive significance of the "two establishments" and strengthen the "four Consciousness", strengthen the "four self-confidences", achieve "two safeguards" ... and provide a strong guarantee for the implementation of various work responsibilities assigned by the Party Central Committee to the central and state organs".

Days later the *Guangming Daily* (December 28) asserted "There is no unity without struggle, and no struggle without unity". It stressed that "Unity and struggle are the source of stability for Marxist party organizations. Organizational unity is the foundation of political party unity". It urged the people to "Adhere to and strengthen the party's overall leadership and forge a firm "backbone" and added that it is necessary to "adhere to and strengthen the overall leadership of the party, resolutely safeguard the authority of the Party Central Committee and the centralized and unified leadership, and implement the party's leadership in all aspects of the party and the country's business, so that the party will always be the best when storms strike". It emphasised "the decisive significance of the "two establishments", strengthen the "four consciousnesses", strengthen the "four self-confidence", and achieve the "two safeguards", so as to ensure that the whole party and the whole country have a strong political cohesion and develop self-confidence".

The clearest warning that a rectification campaign was to get underway in the CCP was, however, the Politburo's "democratic life" meeting held on December 26-27, 2022, and chaired by Xi Jinping. Its agenda reported by the *People's Daily* (December 28) was unambiguous. *Xinhua* stated it was "to fully implement Xi Jinping's new era of socialism with Chinese characteristics, deeply understand the decisive significance of "two establishments", and strengthen the "two establishments". It said the "Four Consciousnesses", firm "Four Confidences", and "Two Maintenances", unite and lead party members and cadres to implement the major decisions and deployments made by the 20th National Congress of the Party ... take the lead in achieving the "two safeguards" ... sum up achievements, investigate and address deficiencies, conduct party analysis, and carry out criticism and self-criticism". *Xinhua* added that in their speeches the Politburo members focused on the need to "have a deeper understanding of the decisive significance of the "two establishments", and to further enhance the ideological, political and action consciousness of "two maintenances"; and "to have a deeper understanding of the role of leading cadres in comprehensively and strictly governing the party. They must be stricter than self-revolution, and consciously set an example for the entire party in abiding by rules and disciplines". Calling for "comprehensively and strictly governing the party", it said "the meeting emphasized that this year is an extremely important year in the history of the party and the country".

In its reporting, the state-owned CGTN asserted that the previous year had seen "the decisive significance of establishing Comrade Xi Jinping's core position on the Party Central Committee and in the Party as a whole" and quoted Xi Jinping as saying that the "unity, readiness to meet challenges and cohesion of the CPC central leadership" had been beneficial. Xi Jinping told the Politburo's "democratic life" meeting that "upholding the centralized, unified leadership of the Party Central Committee is one of the founding principles of the ruling party" and "called on members of the Political Bureau to maintain a high degree of unity with the Central Committee, follow the course and the will of the Party, and maintain loyalty to the Party at all times and under all circumstances". Xi Jinping said, "For a party and a country as big as ours, if the Central Committee can't exercise strong, centralized and unified leadership, party members will act in their own separate ways and nothing can be accomplished." Citing political ability as "the most important competence for members of the Political Bureau to perform their duties", Xi Jinping underscored that Politburo members should set an example in abiding by the code of honest conduct and taking the lead in fulfilling the political responsibility for the governance of the Party. He said they should be strict with their family members, relatives and those around them, and never allow them to seek illegitimate interests by taking advantage of their power and influence.

The warnings got sharply accentuated this month when the *People's Daily* (January 6) used language for Xi Jinping's opponents last used in the years between2017-2019 which stressed the need to heighten political supervision to improve cohesion in the CCP. The *People's Daily* article emphasised that cadres must "deeply understand the decisive significance of Two Establishments, resolutely achieve the Two Safeguards and ensure that the whole Party moves forward in unison." It highlighted Xi Jinping's position as the core of the CCP. The article cited cases investigated by the CDIC's National Supervision Commission to enforce political discipline and rules, "purify the political ecology within the Party", and fight "against people and things that threaten the authority and centralised and unified leadership of the CPC Central Committee". While doing so it revealed that "many leading cadres have been investigated and dealt with for violating discipline and law." In a thinly veiled suggestion that loyalty to Xi Jinping will be the focus, the article quoted an unidentified discipline official as saying that the aim is to "resolutely eliminate the 'two-faced people' who betray the Party". It similarly referred to the task to "eradicate political gangs that form cliques and serve private interests, eliminate serious hidden political dangers in the Party, safeguard political security, and ensure the political position and political interests of the whole Party."

This was followed by another toughly worded article (January 19) by Fu Mingxian, Member of the Standing Committee of the Zhejiang Provincial Party Committee, Secretary of the Provincial Commission for Discipline Inspection and Director of the Supervisory Commission, which was posted on the official website of China's Central Discipline Inspection Commission (CDIC). It bluntly declared that "the political supervision system must more consciously assume the major political responsibility for the "Two Safeguards" and described the "Two safeguards" as the highest political principle of the party and the fundamental task of strengthening political supervision in the new era". Injecting a sense of urgency, it called for the "accurate identification and timely investigation of "seven existing" problems", prompt elimination of "political "double-faced people" and "double-faced factions"," and resolutely preventing all kinds of "low-level reds" and "high-level blacks" that undermine the unity and unity of the party". In a warning to senior echelon cadres, it called for "strengthening the joint supervision of the "top leaders" and the leadership team" and said "the reason why leading cadres, especially the "top leaders" are difficult to supervise, is closely related to the lack of supervision and coordination".

While Xi Jinping has been able to place loyalists in crucial senior positions at the 20th Party Congress held last October, it is apparent that he is now focussing on the senior and middle echelons of the CCP. Many of them are supporters of the former CCP General Secretary Jiang Zemin, or younger cadres who are nominees of Xi Jinping's loyalists. Separately there are indications that the security apparatus is also likely to be subjected to a rectification. The Party rectification campaign will have also been prompted by the slowing economy which has resulted in burgeoning unemployment, closure of thousands of businesses, reducing of incomes of central and provincial government employees and withdrawing of bonuses. Another factor would be the residual resentment at the stringent zero-Covid rules and the adverse growing international environment which Xi Jinping has been candidly referring to in his speeches.

This was first published by the Centre for China Analysis and Strategy (CCAS) and Vivekananda International Foundation (VIF) in January 26, 2023.

10. Xi Jinping's Leadership Appears to be Facing Opposition

From the time Xi Jinping made his ambition for a third term clear, and for months before the 20th Party Congress (October 6-12, 2022), China's official media has been publishing a series of articles highlighting the importance of safeguarding Xi Jinping's position as the 'core of the Chinese Communist Party Central Committee'. They have emphasised that Xi Jinping and the Chinese Communist Party (CCP) Central Committee (CC)'s leadership were essential if China was to achieve its modernisation and reunification with Taiwan.

Though the CCP CC made clear that Xi Jinping had personally vetted candidates for the new CC, there were indications soon after the 20th Party Congress that the CCP will be subjected to another 'rectification' campaign. A similar campaign is underway in the People's Liberation Army (PLA). "Political security", a euphemism for protecting Xi Jinping's position as the 'core of the Chinese Communist Party Central Committee', 'absolute' obedience to the CCP CC, and unity, are among their main themes. The 'rectification' campaign this time will also specifically evaluate the loyalty of cadres to Xi Jinping. Retired cadres will be investigated as will senior cadres where necessary. The focus will be on the middle and junior level cadres.

The start of a rectification campaign so soon after the Party Congress and with emphasis on loyalty to Xi Jinping suggests dissatisfaction within the CCP. Much of the dissatisfaction would be because of the slowdown in the economy, unemployment, closure of businesses, and reductions in salaries etc. Some would be because of Xi Jinping having secured a third term. A large number of senior and retired cadres have earlier publicly expressed unhappiness at this break with convention. Other factors include the dashed aspirations of hundreds of cadres who have been denied promotions in favour of those affiliated with Xi Jinping or his loyalists. Yet other reasons would include broader issues like Xi Jinping's support for Putin's war against Ukraine, which prompted senior cadres to write, advising against such support. The deteriorating Sino-US relations is a particularly major worry for CCP cadres especially because of the ever-present threat of US sanctions which, if imposed, will directly impact millions of Chinese. In the last couple of months a few of the more reputed Chinese scholars in China's prestigious think-tanks and universities have advised restraint in responding to 'America's provocations' and suggested that efforts be made to improve ties.

A bluntly worded article in the CCP's official newspaper *People's Daily* on January 6, 2023, contained numerous references to political issues and dangers. These suggest that the rectification is to safeguard Xi Jinping's position and expel those influenced by western liberal ideas. The article declared that the aim is to "resolutely eliminate the 'two-faced people' who betray the Party, resolutely investigate and deal with violations of laws and regulations that are intertwined with political and economic issues, eradicate political gangs that form cliques and serve private interests, eliminate serious hidden political dangers in the Party, safeguard political security, and ensure the political position and political interests of the whole Party." The implication clearly is that rival factions and disloyal cadres exist.

Within days of its publication, while speaking at the second plenary session of the CCP's powerful anti-corruption watchdog body, the Central Discipline Inspection Commission (CDIC) on January 9, Xi Jinping issued a sharp warning that the CDIC would enforce "a high degree of awareness of compliance and discipline" and asked every member of the Communist Party, especially leading cadres, to abide by Party discipline and "get into the habit of working and living in a supervised and restrained environment". The current Minister of Public Security and close associate of Xii Jinping Wang Xiaohong had in 2021 suggested to Xi Jinping that particularly all Politburo and Central Committee members should be monitored. Xi Jinping added "It is necessary to combine the theme education that will be carried out in the whole party, focus on pure thinking and pure organization as prominent issues, effectively strengthen political education and party spirit education, strictly enforce the law and discipline, resolutely eliminate black sheep, and build a loyal, clean and responsible iron army with iron discipline". He called for a severe crackdown on those so-called "political liars" who have "backgrounds".

The seriousness of the problem was further highlighted on January 19, 2023, when the CDIC's official website posted an article by Fu Mingxian, Member of the Standing Committee of the Zhejiang Provincial Party Committee, Secretary of the Provincial Commission for Discipline Inspection and Director of the Supervisory Commission. It was titled 'Carry out the spirit of the second plenary session of the 20th Central Commission for Discipline Inspection - Promote the improvement of the party's self-revolutionary institutional normative'. Stressing that "the political supervision system must more consciously assume the major political responsibility for the "two safeguards", it described the "Two safeguards" as the highest political principle of the party and the fundamental task of strengthening political supervision in the new era". It called for the "accurate identification and timely investigation of "seven existing" problems, promptly eliminating political "double-faced people" and "double-faced factions"," and resolutely preventing all kinds of "low-level reds" and "high-level blacks" that undermine the unity of the party. The article particularly emphasised that senior cadres would be closely monitored and said "strengthening the joint supervision of the "top leaders" and the leadership team is the top priority. From a practical point of view, the reason why leading cadres, especially the "top leaders" are difficult to supervise, is closely related to the lack of supervision and coordination. It is necessary to conscientiously implement the "Opinions of the Central Committee of the Communist Party of China on Strengthening the Supervision of "Top Leaders" and Leading Groups" and supervise superiors, peers, and subordinates."

Meanwhile reports indicate the existence of factions which are not all affiliated to Xi Jinping or his loyalists. Some are affiliated to former veteran cadres while others are associated with some of Xi Jinping's loyalists. With the passage of time and the growing gap in age and seniority, Xi Jinping will become more dependent on his loyalists to select cadres for senior positions. New factions will undoubtedly emerge and not all will support Xi Jinping.

On October 30, the CDIC disclosed that Li Xiaobao, former Secretary of the Party Group and Director of the Jiangxi Provincial Department of Culture and Tourism, had again been placed under investigation. In probably the first political verdict to mention the "two safeguards" after they were included in the Party Charter at the recently concluded 20th Party Congress, it said "Li Xiaobao lost his ideals and beliefs, betrayed the "two safeguards" etc. The slogan of 'Two Safeguards', first coined in 2018, is to "resolutely safeguard General Secretary Xi Jinping's core position of the Party Central Committee and the core position of the whole party" and to "resolutely safeguard the authority and centralized and unified leadership of the Party Central Committee".

More recently on January 6, 2023, the Chinese financial publication Caixin disclosed that Xu Ming, former Deputy Head of the State Administration of Grain, had pleaded guilty on January 4 at the Xiamen Intermediate People's Court to taking more than 52.4 million yuan ($7.6 million) in bribes. He was accused of taking advantage of his positions between 1995 and 2021 at the Ministry of Commerce and earlier the State Economic and Trade Commission. The report implied that by charging Xu Ming who had previously worked under Bo Xilai, the former Politburo member who was sentenced to life in prison in October 2013, Xi Jinping was still actively uncovering members of opposing factions.

The CDIC also announced that 61-year-old Li Chunsheng, former Guangdong Deputy Governor and Public Security Chief for eight years until he stepped down in 2021 and currently Deputy Director of the Guangdong People's Congress Standing Committee, had been placed under investigation. This announcement carried an implicit message of the importance of loyalty to Xi Jinping. Li Chunsheng had worked with Sun Lijun when the latter took charge of the Public Security Ministry's Hong Kong, Macau and Taiwan Affairs Office, in which the Guangdong's police department plays a key role. Sun Lijun was a former Deputy Minister of Public Security who had been awarded a suspended death sentence and jailed for life for "seriously damaging the unity of the party" and leading a "political clique". China's Public Security Ministry, where Sun was a deputy minister until 2020, held a meeting to denounce him and vowed to eradicate the "venomous" influence of his "political clique".

Another faction with the potential to cause Xi Jinping trouble is that of the former Chinese President Jiang Zemin who died last October. They constitute a powerful Shanghai faction, but with their leader's death its members are leaderless and their futures have become more uncertain. They will add to the pool of discontented elements. Reports that Xi Jinping has prepared plans to purge members of Jiang Zemin's faction and that more than 15,000 CCP officials and 3000 entrepreneurs affiliated to Jiang Zemin are slated to be purged and have their assets confiscated, will have unnerved them further.

By appointing loyalists to all top posts in China's security establishment Xi Jinping will be able to detect discontent, but it is unlikely that he will be able to get all factions to fall in line. Resolving the economic problems will be important for Xi Jinping to stabilise the political situation. Till then Xi Jinping is likely to impose increasingly stringent measures to ensure discipline in the Party and the general populace.

This was first published by the Centre for China Analysis and Strategy (CCAS) and Vivekananda International Foundation (VIF) in February 16, 2023.

11. Xi Jinping Tightens His Grip on the Security Apparatus

Moving rapidly after the 20th Party Congress (October 6-12, 2022) approved his policies and endorsed him for a third term, Chinese President Xi Jinping has over the past year and a half further tightened his grip on the Party, the People's Liberation Army (PLA) and especially the security apparatus. Since last year Xi Jinping has increased the country's priority for security, as seen at the Politburo study session on January 31 when security was placed on equal footing with development. He has enhanced attention to strengthening his grip on the Ministry of State Security (MoSS) and Ministry of Public Security (MPS), referred to by Chinese Communist Party (CCP) members as the "knife handle".

Xi Jinping removed or neutralised people and appointed loyalists to head security organisations including the Party's security-related United Front Work Department (UFWD) and International Department, earlier known as the International Liaison Department. Indicating the importance Xi Jinping attaches to national security and the united front strategy, the heads of both these organisations are now members of the Politburo. China's new Foreign Minister Qin Gang too, is a Xi Jinping loyalist and has an intelligence background in the CCP having served many years in the International Liaison Department (ILD), which could mean greater synergy in the functioning of these departments.

With Politburo member Guo Shengkun's retirement at the 20th Party Congress, Xi Jinping now has loyalists in all key security-related positions. Though Guo Shengkun was elevated to the Politburo at the start of Xi Jinping's second term as General Secretary of the CCP Central Committee (CC) in 2017, he has long been assessed as affiliated with former Chinese President Jiang Zemin.

The new heads of the Ministry of Public Security (MPS) and Ministry of State Security (MoSS) are persons who have worked for many years with Xi Jinping. Wang Xiaohong, formerly Executive Vice Minister of Public Security who was Xi Jinping's head of security in Fujian and followed him to Beijing, is a very close associate. Chen Wenqing, a professional public security official and the former Minister of State Security has been elevated to the Politburo and becomes the first professional security official in over a decade to become a member of the Politburo. Chen Yixin, then Deputy Secretary of the Central Political and Legal Affairs Commission (CPLAC) is the current Minister of State Security and Secretary General of the Central Political and Legal Affairs Commission. Chen Yixin is a close ally of Xi Jinping and worked with him in Zhejiang and was brought to Beijing when Xi Jinping moved there.

The current tense social and adverse international environments require that the security establishment is not compromised. The rash of protests between October-December and the protests by pensioners in three major cities earlier this month will have been unsettling. Indications are that appointing loyalists to head these key ministries and departments, is preparatory to launching a 'rectification' campaign, or purge, that will mainly target its middle and lower levels and make the security outfits fully loyal to him. That the security apparatus will undergo another rectification drive, or a purge, was mentioned during the Party Congress. The rash of protests across China in the past few months seem to have spurred Xi Jinping to eliminate elements who are lax or not fully committed to his ideology.

The security apparatus was last investigated in 2012-13 immediately after Bo Xilai, then a Politburo member and son of one of China's "Eight Immortals" failed in his bid to oust Xi Jinping and become CCP CC General Secretary. In 2013, Xi Jinping established a National Security Commission and passed a number of laws reinforcing national security. It was, however, only in 2021 that the security apparatus was subjected to intense scrutiny and 'rectification'. The rectification campaign was spearheaded by Chen Yixin, then Deputy Secretary of the Central Political and Legal Affairs Commission (CPLAC). Interestingly, the call for the rectification campaign to control the "knife" was given by Chen Yixin and not Guo Shengkun who, as a Politburo member, was senior to him!

In the past two years high-profile senior Party members of the 'Sun Lijun Political Group' opposing Xi Jinping were successively expelled and awarded severe sentences by the Party authorities. Efforts to unearth them still continue and one prominent case was publicised last October. An overseas Chinese commentator observed that the group was backed by former CPLC Secretary Meng Jianzhu, former Politburo Standing Committee member Zeng Qinghong, and former Party Chief Jiang Zemin. He assessed that once Xi Jinping returned from Yan'an after the 20th Party Congress, a major rectification, and possibly showdown, is inevitable. Chen Yixin has since been promoted and appointed Minister of State Security and Secretary General of the Central Political and Legal Affairs Commission.

Since Xi Jinping focussed on the security apparatus its budget and personnel have steadily increased and the CCP's vision of security now includes 16 areas. Unsurprisingly, national security had its own section in the Work Report approved at the 20th Party Congress. It declared that: "We must take the people's security as our ultimate goal, political security as our fundamental task, economic security as our foundation, military, technological, cultural, and social security as important pillars, and international security as a support". The 'Decision of the Central Committee of the Communist Party of China on Conscientiously Studying, Propagating and Implementing the Spirit of the Twentieth National Congress of the Communist Party of China', published by the *People's Daily* on October 31, 2022, clarified that while food, energy, resources, cyber, financial and other forms of security are important, considerable importance is to be given to the need to 'improve the level of public security governance, improve the social governance system, and resolutely safeguard national security and social stability.' Developing the 'Fengqiao model' and improving 'grid-based management, meticulous services, and IT support' are euphemisms for tightening control and surveillance over society.

The top echelons of the security hierarchy have moved rapidly under its new leadership. On November 28, 2022, two days after the outbreak of nationwide protests against the zeroCovid policy (also called the 'White Paper Revolution'), the Chinese Communist Party's (CCP's) apex security body, the Political and Legal Affairs Committee (PLAC), held a plenary session emphasizing the need to "resolutely crack down on the infiltration and sabotage activities of hostile forces, and resolutely crack down on illegal and criminal acts that disrupt the social order."

Chen Wenqing, the new head of the PLAC, presided over the meeting. Wang Xiaohong, the Minister of Public Security, Zhou Qiang, the President of the Supreme People's Court, and Zhang Jun, the President of the Supreme People's Procuratorate — all Xi Jinping loyalists — also attended. The meeting was the CCP's response to the protests. It called for strengthening the "combat spirit" and accelerating the construction of a higher level of "a safe China under the rule of law." it stressed the need to promptly channel and resolve conflicts and disputes and to help solve the practical difficulties of the people. It asked cadres to "resolutely combat the infiltration and sabotage activities of hostile forces, to resolutely combat illegal and criminal acts that disrupt the social order, and effectively to maintain the general stability of society."

Outgoing Politburo member Guo Shengkun published a lengthy and important article in the *People's Daily* (November 24, 2022) where he disclosed that Xi Jinping is actively involved with the security apparatus. It credited him with promoting the modernization of the national security system and its capabilities, and "pointing out the direction for us to do a good job in maintaining national security and social stability". Guo Shengkun stressed the "two establishments" and "two safeguards" and the absolute and "strong leadership of the Party Central Committee with Comrade Xi Jinping at the core". He said "modernization of the national security system and capabilities is an inevitable requirement for preventing and defusing risks and challenges" and added that "National security is the foundation of national rejuvenation, and social stability is the prerequisite for national prosperity". He reiterated: "Various "black swan" and "grey rhinoceros" incidents may occur at any time. The risk tests we face are becoming more and more complicated. Get ready for a big test with rough seas and even rough seas." He stressed "we must closely focus on upholding the Party's absolute leadership over national security work, upholding the Party Central Committee's centralized and unified leadership over national security work, unswervingly follow the path of national security with Chinese characteristics, and improve institutional mechanisms and institutional systems". Guo Shengkun also, importantly, emphasised the need to "Strengthen the party building on the national security front, adhere to the party's political construction as the guide, and forge a loyal, pure and reliable national security cadre team". The same day the *Guangming Daily* published an article captioned 'Promoting the Transformation of Public Security Governance Model', which similarly detailed the areas of focus of the public security apparatus.

Later, the National Conference of Directors of Public Security Bureaus met in Beijing on January 8, 2023. The meeting, inter alia, emphasized the importance of deeply comprehending "the decisive significance of the "two establishments", strengthen the "four consciousnesses", strengthen the "four self-confidence", and achieve the "two safeguards", and stated that "the Party Central Committee with Comrade Xi Jinping as the core attaches great importance to public security work, leading the public security work in the new era to achieve historic achievements and undergo historic changes". It instructed public security organs and cadres across the country to be loyal to the party, "faithfully fulfil their missions and tasks" in the new era, and ensure long-term social stability. The meeting emphasized "that the next five years will be a critical period for the start of building a modern socialist country in an all-round way".

Three days later on January 11, the *People's Daily* (January 11) published an article by Chen Yixin, Minister of State Security and the Secretary General of the Central Political and Legal Affairs Commission, captioned 'Improve the social governance system (conscientiously study, publicize and implement the spirit of the 20th National Congress of the Communist Party of China)'. It said "Improving the social governance system is a major task proposed by the Party Central Committee with Comrade Xi Jinping as the core, from the strategic height of promoting the modernization of the national security system and capabilities, and resolutely maintaining national security and social stability." It said "The Party Central Committee has strengthened its leadership over social governance, established a Safe China Construction Coordination Group, and promoted the establishment of a strong and powerful organizational leadership system, a systematic and complete institutional system, and an integrated and coordinated working mechanism." It added "The establishment and improvement of the legal system and enforcement mechanism for the

Hong Kong Special Administrative Region to safeguard national security has achieved a major turning point in the situation in Hong Kong from chaos to order. Preventing and cracking down on infiltration, sabotage, subversion, and separatist activities by hostile forces has resolutely safeguarded the security of state power, system, and ideology."

The article focussed on social stability and activities of "hostile foreign forces". It revealed: "Adhering to and developing the "Fengqiao Experience" in the new era, and strengthening the construction of grassroots organizations, the country's towns (streets) have basically been equipped with political and legal committee members, and more than 583,000 comprehensive management centers at all levels have been established, with a total of 4.5 million grid members. "The article explained: "Political security is the foundation of national rejuvenation. It is necessary to effectively prevent the infiltration, sabotage, subversion, and separatist activities of foreign hostile forces, and to promptly detect and quickly deal with the illegal activities and movements of hostile forces and related organizations. It is necessary to effectively remove the soil that affects political security in the country, promote the "de-radicalization" work to achieve remarkable results, and maintain "zero occurrence" of serious violent and terrorist activities in the country; Social stability is the prerequisite for a strong country. It is necessary to prevent and control stability-related "variables" and effectively prevent social risks from turning into political risks, regional risks from turning into global risks, and overseas risks from turning into domestic risks; and that people's safety is a very important livelihood".

To achieve a continuous decline in criminal cases, the eight types of serious violent cases have decreased year by year, and the high incidence of new cybercrime has been effectively curbed. It called for improving the party committee leadership system and said "Adhere to the party's overall leadership, implement the system of requesting instructions, reporting, decision-making, and execution, strengthen the organization and command system, and improve mechanisms such as overall planning and implementation. Fulfil the duties of the Political and Legal Committee of the Party Committee to take the lead in coordination, organization and promotion, and supervision and implementation, and mobilize the enthusiasm of various departments and units to participate in social governance. Give full play to the role of grassroots party organizations as a battle fortress, and build a new work pattern of regional overall planning, block coordination, and joint construction and sharing."

National security received increased prominence with Xi Jinping's ascendance to office in 2012. It received a boost in 2021 with the "new development phase" — two of its three main points related to security and stability – and is among the main themes in official propaganda. The widespread domestic dissatisfaction and the CCP leadership's fears that "hostile foreign powers" could instigate a "colour revolution" will ensure that emphasis on security will continue through Xi Jinping's third term. It will be further enhanced with data controls and the application of technology.

This was first published by the Centre for China Analysis and Strategy (CCAS) and Vivekananda International Foundation (VIF) in February 20, 2023.

12. China's Big Two Sessions' Confirm Xi Jinping as China's Pre-Eminent Unrivalled Leader

The plenary sessions of the 14th National People's Congress (NPC), China's version of a parliament, and the 14th Chinese People's Political Consultative Conference (CPPCC),— China's top political advisory body—that concluded on March 13, were, as anticipated, a success for Xi Jinping. Having again been elected as General Secretary of the Chinese Communist Party (CCP) Central Committee (CC) at the 20th Party Congress last October, 2952 Deputies to the NPC unanimously re-elected Xi Jinping for a third term as President of China. In his first speech after the NPC session, Xi Jinping exulted that he was honoured to be elected to "the lofty office of President". He also claimed to have lifted the people out of poverty and wiped out the centuries of humiliation they had suffered!

Xi Jinping is the first leader of the People's Republic of China (PRC) to hold the position of Head of State for such a long period. Even Mao Zedong was Chairman for only one year. His named successor Liu Shaoqi was Chairman for a year and a half and Xi Jinping's two immediate predecessors Hu Jintao and Jiang Zemin were President for two terms each. With this Xi Jinping has established himself as the unrivalled pre-eminent leader of the PRC. By also endorsing Xi Jinping's nominees as State Councillors, members of the Central Military Commission and in all top appointments, the NPC plenum solidified Xi Jinping's authority over the Party and Government apparatus. Today, Xi Jinping has his loyalists in all key positions. To reinforce that message China's official media, including the Global Times, acclaimed (March 12): "Xi Jinping's unanimous election as Chairman of the Central Military Commission has greatly inspired and motivated the whole Party, the whole army and the whole nation to embark on a new journey".

While Xi Jinping was unanimously elected, the second-ranked in the CCP CC hierarchy and candidate for Premier, Li Qiang, received three votes against and eight abstentions. The NPC session also endorsed the two PLA Generals, Zhang Youxia and He Weidong, as Vice Chairmen of the PRC Central Military Commission (CMC). General He Weidong's 'helicopter' promotion to the CCP CC Politburo and as Vice Chairman of the CMC is important as he has experience of postings in the Western Theatre Command facing India and the Eastern Theatre Command opposite Taiwan – both important military theatres for China. He Weidong is credited also with having planned and overseen the major air and sea military operations against Taiwan within days of US Congress House Leader Nancy Pelosi's visit to Taipei.

The NPC approved the following loyalists nominated by Xi Jinping as new members of the PRC State Council: Premier Li Qiang; Executive Vice Premier Ding Xuexiang (long time, trusted Secretary to Xi Jinping); Vice Premiers He Lifeng (former Head of NDRC), Zhang Guoqing (former Party Secretary of Liaoning), and Li Guozhong (former Party Secretary of Shaanxi). It also approved his nominees for the position of State Councillors: General Li Shangfu (as Defence Minister), Wang Xiaohong (Minister for Public Security), Wu Zhenglong (as Secretary General of the State Council), Shen Yiqin (the only female and former Party Secretary of Guizhou), and Qin Gang (Foreign Minister). Indicative of the importance being accorded to reviving the economy and in a bid to reassure markets and investors as the country focuses on fighting economic headwinds, the NPC approved retention of China's Central bank Governor 65-year old Yi Gang and Finance Minister 66-year old Liu Kun.

Among the key appointments are those of former Shanghai Party Secretary and long-time Xi Jinping associate Li Qiang as Premier. Though there were three "nos" and eight abstentations in his election, this could have been because he complied with Politburo member Sun Chunlan's instructions and implemented the centre's 'zero-Covid' policy and locked-down Shanghai for three months. However, having been Governor and Party Secretary of Zhejiang, Jiangsu and Shanghai – three of China's wealthiest provinces – Li Qiang is well qualified for the position which requires him to revive the country's economy.

Zhao Leji, also a close friend and protégé of Xi Jinping, was appointed NPC Chairman replacing Li Zhanshu, one of Xi Jinping's closest friends. Two other key appointments which showed that national security remains a high priority for the Chinese leadership, are the elevation of the Minister of Public Security Wang Xiaohong as a member of the powerful CCP CC Secretariat and promotion and appointment of General Liu Zhenli as Head of the PLA Joint Staff Department, in addition to raising the national defence budget by 7.2 percent. For the past two years the quantum of increase was under 6.5 percent.

Of particular interest was the appointment of former Politburo Standing Committee member Han Zheng as PRC Vice President in place of Wang Qishan who retired. Han Zheng has not been regarded as particularly close to Xi Jinping despite his efforts, and his elevation may indicate an element of compromise. It may have been a move intended to keep the discontented Jiang Zemin faction from creating complications in the months ahead. There have been reports that Xi Jinping has prepared plans to purge members of Jiang Zemin's faction and that more than 15,000 CCP officials and 3000 entrepreneurs affiliated to Jiang Zemin are slated to be purged and have their assets confiscated. In any event the post of PRC Vice President is not powerful. Chinese observers have suggested that Li Qiang's appointment could also help assuage this group.

The NPC also authorised a major restructuring of Party and government departments. Their apparent emphasis was on enhancing the Party's control and making it more powerful. The restructuring confirmed the Chinese leadership's three top priorities for the next five years, namely national security, economic development (or high-quality development), and self- sufficiency in agriculture. The budgets for security, national defence, science and technology and agriculture all registered increases.

The NPC approved the plan for reform and restructuring of Government Departments submitted to it by China's State Council on March 7. The plan proposed that:

1. A new National Financial Regulatory Authority will be set up, which will absorb the China Banking and Insurance Regulatory Commission (CBIRC). It will take over some of the functions of the People's Bank of China and the China Securities Regulatory Commission;

2. The China Securities Regulatory Commission will become a government agency directly under the State Council;
3. The regional branches and business management departments of the People's Bank of China, as well as the business management departments directly under the headquarters and the central branches in provincial capitals will be revoked. Instead, the central bank will establish provincial-level branches in 31 provinces, autonomous regions, and municipalities, in addition to branches in cities specially designated in the state plan, including Shenzhen, Dalian, Ningbo, Qingdao, and Xiamen. The People's Bank of China Beijing Branch will retain the brand of the People's Bank of China Business Management Department, while the People's Bank of China Shanghai Branch will share an office with the People's Bank of China, Shanghai Headquarters;
4. The Ministry of Science and Technology will be restructured. It will absorb the China Rural Technology Development Centre, China Biotechnology Development Centre, the Administrative Centre for China's Agenda 21 and the Hi-Tech Research and Development Centre;
5. A National Data Bureau Authority will be set up. It will take over certain functions of the Office of the Central Cyberspace Affairs Commission and the NDRC;
6. The Ministry of Agriculture and Rural Affairs will add the brand of the National Rural Revitalization Administration;
7. The National Public Complaints and Proposals Administration will be an institution directly under the State Council; and
8. the number of Central Government Department Employees will be reduced by 5 percent in a shakeup.

There were reports just prior to the NPC that the Ministry of State Security and Ministry of Public Security would be merged and removed from the purview of the State Council and placed under one newly established Central Internal Affairs Commission (CIAC), or *neiwehui*. That has not yet been announced. However, reports filtering out of Beijing suggest that there are differences between two of Xi Jinping's closest proteges, Ding Xuexiang and Wang Xiaohong, on who will head the newly established Central Internal

Affairs Commission, or *'neiwehui'*. There are also differences on whether it will have the legendary anti-espionage and other State Security functions.

On March 16, Xinhua published the detailed "Party and State Institutional Reform Plan" jointly issued by the CCP CC and the State Council. It specified that Reform tasks at the central level should be completed by the end of 2023, and reform tasks at the local level should be completed by the end of 2024. Apart from previously announced government reforms, the reform of Party organs include: (i) Creation of a Central Finance Committee; (ii) Creation of a Central Finance Work Committee; (iii) Creation of a Central Science and Technology Commission; (iv)Creation of a Central Social Work Department; and (v) Creation of the Central Office of Hong Kong and Macao, among others. Among these the Central Social Work Department appears akin to the former Central Social Affairs Department and appears to be an entirely new system reaching down into the grassroots, outside of the existing bureaucracies, including the Ministries of Public Security and State Security.

The restructuring of the Ministry of Science and Technology (MOST) and creation of a new Central Science and Technology Commission reinforces the Chinese leadership's unwavering focus on science and technology. China retains its ambition of becoming one of the most advanced technology powers in the world despite increasingly restrictive US sanctions.

The outgoing Chinese Premier Li Keqiang's Government Work Report that he presented to the NPC on March 4 is important. The Report, which was approved by Xi Jinping, outlined the plans for the coming period and indicates the Chinese Communist Party (CCP)'s priorities. The 29 page report, which included 14 mentions of Xi Jinping, expectedly credited his leadership as having surmounted the difficulties of the past few years, difficulties which include, economic difficulties, adverse international environment and the Covid pandemic!

In his hour-long speech, Li Keqiang lauded Xi Jinping as "the core of the party leadership" seven times, stressing that "We owe our achievements ... to the strong leadership of the party central committee with comrade Xi Jinping at its core and the sound guidance of Xi Jinping Thought." However, in what many analysts interpret as a note of caution, Li Keqiang conveyed a cryptic message for his staff: "While people work, heaven watches. Heaven has eyes."

The Report kept the spotlight on security and development and its emphasis on the "unpredictable" and "grim" difficulties that lie ahead for China is significant. Echoing Xi Jinping's warnings of the past some months, it too warned of the probability of "black swan" and "grey rhinoceros" events. Li Keqiang anticipated difficult times ahead and asked China to gear up for "rough seas and even rougher seas". Another indicator of the economic difficulties was the announcement that the number of central government employees would be reduced by five percent. In his first press conference after the NPC on March 13, new Chinese Premier Li Qiang too was cautious on the economy and, played down the five percent GDP growth target, saying achieving it would be difficult as the base was high.

The key economic targets announced by Premier Li Keqiang in his report are: i) GDP - around 5 percent; ii) CPI - around 3 percent; iii) deficit-to-GDP - 3 percent; iv) Special Purpose Bonds - 3.8T Yuan; v) Defence - 1.55T Yuan (US$ 225 Billion), up 7.2 percent from 2022.

The highlights of Chinese Premier Li Keqiang's 29 page Work Report are:

- While recognizing our achievements, we are keenly aware that China is still a large, developing country. It remains in the primary stage of socialism with prominent imbalances and inadequacies in its development. Today, many difficulties and challenges still confront us.
- Uncertainties in the external environment are on the rise. Global inflation remains high, global economic and trade growth is losing steam, and external attempts to suppress and contain China are escalating.
- At home, the foundation for stable growth needs to be consolidated, insufficient demand remains a pronounced problem, and the expectations of private investors and businesses are unstable. MSMEs and self-employed individuals face multiple difficulties in business and production operations. The task of maintaining employment stability is challenging, and the budgetary imbalances of some local governments are substantial. There are many risks and hidden dangers in the real estate market. The operating risks of some small and medium financial institutions have been exposed.
- There are still many institutional barriers hindering development. Our capacity for scientific and technological innovation needs to be further

improved. We still have a long way to go in protecting the environment. There are still major weak links in urban and rural infrastructure for disaster prevention and mitigation and other purposes. Weak links also persist in areas important to the people's lives.

- Pointless formalities and bureaucratism remain acute issues. Some local governments have used one-size-fits-all approaches or taken excessive measures when implementing policies. Some officials fail to fulfil their duties, act arbitrarily, or have a narrow focus in work. Some are detached from reality, go against the public will, or disregard the legitimate rights and interests of the people. Corruption remains a common problem in some fields, sectors, and localities. Regarding government work, the people have expressed some views and suggestions which deserve our full attention.

Sharing his recommendations for the direction of government work of 2023, Premier Li Keqiang said that 2023 is the first year for fully implementing the guiding principles from the Party's 20th National Congress. He said for the government to deliver, it is important, under the strong leadership of the Party Central Committee with Comrade Xi Jinping at its core, to do the following:

- follow the guidance of Xi Jinping Thought on Socialism with Chinese Characteristics for a New Era;
- implement the guiding principles from the Party's 20th National Congress;
- act on the guidelines of the Central Economic Work Conference;
- make solid progress in advancing Chinese modernization;
- act on the general principle of pursuing progress while ensuring stability;
- fully and faithfully apply the new development philosophy on all fronts and move faster to create a new pattern of development;
- promote high-quality development;
- respond to Covid-19 and pursue economic and social development in a more coordinated way;
- better ensure development and security;
- deepen reform and opening up in all respects; - boost market confidence;
- pursue the strategy of expanding domestic demand and deepen supply-side structural reform;

- give priority to ensuring stable growth, employment, and prices;
- effectively prevent and defuse major risks;
- effectively pursue higher-quality growth and appropriately increase economic output;
- keep working to improve people's lives and maintain overall social stability.

He further listed the main projected targets for development this year and stressed prioritizing economic stability and pursuing progress while ensuring stability. He listed the following targets:

- GDP growth of around five percent;
- around 12 million new urban jobs;
- surveyed urban unemployment rate of around 5.5 percent;
- CPI increase of around three percent;
- growth in personal income that is generally in step with economic growth;
- steady increases in both the volume and quality of imports and exports;
- grain output of over 650 million metric tons;
- steady improvements in the quality of the eco-environment.
- This year, it is essential to prioritize economic stability and pursue progress while ensuring stability.
- A deficit-to-GDP ratio of three percent has been projected for this year. We should improve preferential tax and fee policies, and extend and further refine policies on tax and fee cuts, tax rebates, and tax deferrals as the situation requires. We should see that at the primary level, basic living needs are met, salary payments are ensured, and normal government functioning is maintained.
- The RMB exchange rate should be kept generally stable at an adaptive, balanced level.
- In adopting industrial policies, we should give consideration to both, development and security imperatives.
- Scientific and technological policies should aim at building up our country's strength and self-reliance in science and technology. The new system for mobilizing resources nationwide should be improved, we should better leverage the role of the government in pooling resources

to make key technological breakthroughs, and enterprises should be the principal actors in innovation.

- We should take concrete measures to fully implement the employment-first policy and place a higher priority on promoting the employment of young people, particularly college graduates.

Li Keqiang additionally listed eight key priorities of the government work for 2023.

In his first speech after the 14th NPC Plenum, Chinese President Xi Jinping addressed the First Session of the Fourteenth National People's Congress on March 13. Declaring that he had been elected for the third time to "the lofty office of President", he asserted that he "will faithfully perform the duties entrusted by the Constitution". At the outset Xi Jinping recalled that China, after "more than 5,000 years of civilization, has created countless brilliance and experienced many hardships in history. After modern times, China had gradually become a semi-colonial and semi-feudal society, suffering from bullying by foreign powers, fragmentation, frequent wars, and misery. After the founding of the Communist Party of China, it closely united and led the people of all ethnic groups in the country. After a century of struggle, the national humiliation was wiped out, and the Chinese people became the masters of their own destiny. The Chinese nation ushered in a great leap from standing up, getting rich, and becoming strong. The great revival has entered an irreversible historical process".

Asserting that "The baton of building a strong country and national rejuvenation has historically fallen on our generation", Xi Jinping emphasised implementing "the strategy of rejuvenating the country through science and education, the strategy of strengthening the country with talents, and the strategy of innovation-driven development, focus on improving the ability of self-reliance and self-improvement in science and technology, promote industrial transformation and upgrading, and promote the coordinated development of urban and rural areas" so as to "continuously strengthen China's economic strength, scientific and technological strength, and comprehensive national strength". In an implicit reference to common prosperity, a term that generates considerable unease among China's private businessmen and entrepreneurs, he said the achievements of modernization should benefit all the people more and more equitably.

Calling for better coordination of development and security, Xi Jinping said "Security is the foundation of development, and stability is the prerequisite for prosperity. It is necessary to implement the overall national security concept, improve the national security system, enhance the ability to maintain national security, improve the level of public security governance, improve the social governance system, and guarantee the new development pattern with the new security pattern. It is necessary to comprehensively promote the modernization of national defence and the army, and build the people's army into a steel Great Wall that effectively safeguards national sovereignty, security, and development interests". Xi Jinping also dwelt on "the great cause of the reunification of the motherland" and, stating that "Building a strong country cannot be separated from the long-term prosperity and stability of Hong Kong and Macau", declared that "Realizing the complete reunification of the motherland is the common aspiration of all Chinese people, and it is the essence of national rejuvenation. We must implement the Party's overall strategy for resolving the Taiwan issue in the new era, adhere to the one-China principle and the "1992 Consensus,"[17] actively promote the peaceful development of cross-strait relations, resolutely oppose interference by external forces and separatist activities for "Taiwan independence," and unswervingly advance the process of reunification of the motherland".

Xi Jinping said, "China's development benefits the world, and China's development cannot be separated from the world." He stressed the need to, "Promote the implementation of global development initiatives and global security initiatives, add more stability and positive energy to world peace and development, and create a favourable international environment" for China's development. In conclusion, declaring that "The great rejuvenation of the Chinese nation has entered an irreversible historical process", Xi Jinping stressed that to build a strong country, "we must adhere to the leadership of the Communist Party of China and the centralized and unified leadership of the Party Central Committee" ... "unswervingly oppose corruption, always maintain the unity and unity of the party, and ensure that the party will never deteriorate, change colour, or change".

Chinese Foreign Minister Qin Gang, whose proximity to Chinese President Xi Jinping was evident in his appointment and now elevation at this NPC to State Councillor, held a press conference on the side-lines of the NPC plenum on March 7. In fairly tough language aimed at the US, he said that 'containing and suppressing China won't make the US great, and it will not stop the rejuvenation of China'. He said 'the United States' China policy has entirely deviated from the rational and sound track'. Qin Gang said "The US claims that it seeks to out-compete China but does not seek conflict. Yet in reality, its so-called 'competition' means to contain and suppress China in all respects, and get the two countries locked in a zero-sum game." Comparing China and the US to two athletes competing in an Olympic race, Qin Gang said if one of the athletes, instead of focusing on giving one's best, always tries to trip or even injure the other,that is not fair competition but malicious confrontation and a foul. Qin Gang said the US rhetoric of "establishing guardrails" and "not seeking conflict" simply means China should not respond in words or action when slandered or attacked; "That is just impossible." "If the US does not hit the brake but continues to speed down the wrong path, no amount of guardrails can prevent derailing and there will surely be conflict and confrontation." Qin Gang added that China is firmly opposed to such competition, which is a reckless gamble with the stakes being the fundamental interests of the two peoples and even the future of humanity. "If the US has the ambition to make itself great again, it should also have a broad mind for the development of other countries."

The 'Big Two' sessions, while confirming Xi Jinping's authority over the Party and Government apparatus and re-election as PRC President, also affirmed China's objectives for his third term. These are: consolidation and strengthening of the CCP, economic reforms and high-quality development, strengthening national security, and ensuring China's self-sufficiency in agriculture. Emphasis was also given to national rejuvenation and reunification.

This was first published by the Centre for China Analysis and Strategy (CCAS) and Vivekananda International Foundation (VIF) in March 19, 2023.

13. Xi Jinping's Latest Campaign: 'Theme Education'

Within months of securing a third term at the 20th Party Congress last October and successfully packing the Politburo Standing Committee (PBSC) with loyalists, Chinese Communist Party (CCP) Central Committee (CC) General Secretary Xi Jinping launched a new political education campaign – his sixth — on April 3, 2023. It is the largest, most vigorous and intense ideological campaign since Xi Jinping took office in October 2012 and has penetrated the CCP, People's Liberation Army (PLA) and Government. This new "themed education" programme aims at embedding 'Xi Jinping Thought' into the minds of CCP members and cadres all the way from the central cadres in Beijing down to the country's more than 2,800 county-level areas. It is a long-term move intended to ready successive generations of communists to lead China.

The campaign was unveiled at a meeting of the CCP CC Politburo in Beijing on March 30. Presided over by Xi Jinping the Politburo decided that starting from April this year, the whole party from top down will be divided into two batches to carry out "education on the theme of learning and implementing Xi Jinping's new era of socialism with Chinese characteristics". Xi Jinping delivered an "important" speech at the meeting which reviewed the "Regulations on Leading Cadres Reporting Personal Matters". In his speech, Xi Jinping pointed out "that focusing on leading cadres above the county level, the whole party will carry out in-depth study and implementation of Xi Jinping's new era of socialism with Chinese characteristics theme education, and use the party's innovative theory to unify thinking, unify will, act in a unified manner, carry forward the great spirit of party building, keep in mind the "three musts", and promote the united struggle of the whole party to comprehensively build a socialist modern country and comprehensively promote the great rejuvenation of the Chinese nation". It emphasised that in-depth study and implementation of the theme education of Xi Jinping's new era of socialism with Chinese characteristics in the whole party "is a major effort made by the Party Central Committee to fully implement the spirit of the 20th National Congress of the Party and mobilise all comrades in the party to unite and struggle to complete the central task of the party".

Describing it as "a major deployment of the new great project of further advancing the party building in the new era", it said the purpose "is to use Xi Jinping's new era of socialism with Chinese characteristics to condense the heart and soul, and promote the whole party to more consciously and deeply understand the decisive significance of the "two establishments", strengthen the "four consciousnesses"[19], strengthen the "four self-confidences", achieve "two safeguards", and maintain a high degree of consistency with the Party Central Committee in terms of ideology, politics and actions". It added that one objective is to promote the "self-revolution" of the party. The meeting instructed party committees (party groups) at all levels to attach great importance to the campaign and carefully strengthen the mastery and application of the party's innovative theories, do a good job in the transformation of investigation and research results and solve the urgent problems and worries of the masses. Cautioning Party members against duplicity in work it said combining 'theme education' with promotion of the centre's work is to prevent "two skins".

The meeting recalled that since the 18th Party Congress, 'the Party Central Committee with Comrade Xi Jinping at its core' has incorporated the strict implementation of the reporting system for leading cadres on personal matters for strictly governing the party, strictly enforcing the party's discipline rules and strictly managing and supervising cadres. Emphasising the importance of the system, it stressed that leading cadres must "deeply understand the decisive significance of the "two establishments", strengthen the "four consciousnesses", strengthen the "four self-confidence", and achieve the "two safeguards". It mandated Party committees (party groups) at all levels to conscientiously and strictly implement the measures and govern the party. In addition to China's official media, the state-owned China Central Television (CCTV) also publicised the Politburo meeting on March 31.

The Politburo meeting's decision, on the new intra-Party thematic education campaign, heralded the start of a rigorous and thorough political education campaign aimed primarily at the senior cadres. It follows other recent articles warning against "double-faced" cadres, "political liars" and Xi Jinping's speech (*Qiu Shi*; April 30) that cadres with "mediocre abilities" still remain in the Party as do "prominent problems such as impure thinking, impure organization, and impure style of work within the party". To monitor the campaign's progress, the CCP leadership dispatched 58 "guidance" teams across China. This is the sixth education campaign since 2012. The earlier ones were in 2013 (Mass line educational practice activities); 2015 ('Three strict and three honest'[20]); 2016 ('Two learning and one doing'); 2019 ('Do not forget the original intention, keep in mind the mission'); and 2021 (Party history study and education).

Coinciding with the start of the Theme Education campaign, CCTV (April 3) telecast a report that the first and second volumes of "Selected Readings of Xi Jinping's Works" edited by the CCP Central Committee have been published by the People's Publishing House and will be distributed nationwide on April 3. The publication of the first and second volumes of "Selected Readings of Xi Jinping's Works" has been categorised as "a major event in the political life of the party and the country, with great and far-reaching significance". The report also unambiguously elevated Xi Jinping's status describing "Comrade Xi Jinping as the main representative of the Chinese Communists" since the 18th Party Congress. Crediting major issues of the times with creating 'Xi Jinping Thought on Socialism with Chinese Characteristics for a New Era', CCTV further announced: "As the core of the Party Central Committee and the core of the whole party, General Secretary Xi Jinping is the main founder of Xi Jinping Thought on Socialism with Chinese Characteristics for a New Era". This assertion by the CCP CC is important. It could possibly be the prelude to formally designating it "Xi Jinping Thought" and placing Xi Jinping at par with Mao!

From the next day China's major newspapers began publishing articles explaining and eulogising 'theme education'. Senior Party cadres, commentators and academics have been writing articles in China's official media almost daily explaining, or expounding, on different facets of the campaign. Senior Party cadres of central organisations and Central Ministries and departments promptly organised 'study' meetings and publicised these. Provincial Party Committees followed and organised special meetings presided over by the Party Secretaries. So did universities and educational institutions. 'Theme education' soon became a nationwide campaign. *Qiu Shi* (April 30) said that the central government had dispatched a steering group to supervise and guide the development of theme education and that provincial, autonomous, and municipal party committees and party groups (party committees) of the competent departments had dispatched roving steering groups to strengthen the supervision and guidance of their regions, departments and units. City and county levels were directed to emulate this.

On April 6, 2023, CCTV telecast that the CCP CC had issued a notice on printing and distributing the "Outline for Studying Xi Jinping's Thought on Socialism with Chinese Characteristics for a New Era (2023 Edition)" as an important auxiliary reading on 'theme education' for the majority of party members, cadres, and the masses. The Notice emphasised that party committees at all levels should make careful arrangements and organize all party members to carefully read the original works. The *People's Daily* (April 23) disclosed that an official website was set up to help the study of 'theme education' together with an official account for the campaign on the social media platform WeChat.

To dispel any doubt about the importance of the first and second volumes of "Selected Readings of Xi Jinping's Works", Politburo Standing Committee (PBSC) member, member of the CCP CC Secretariat and Director of the CCP CC General Office Cai Qi addressed a symposium on their publication in Beijing on May 22, 2023. Cai Qi, incidentally, also supervises Propaganda work. According to *People's Daily* (May 23), Cai Qi stressed the importance of the two books and said they "are an authoritative resource for the whole Party and the entire nation to thoroughly study and implement Xi Jinping Thought on Socialism with Chinese Characteristics for a New Era." He called for genuine efforts to translate the study into concrete actions to build China into a modern socialist country and advance the rejuvenation of the Chinese nation on all fronts.

The Party's leading theoretical fortnightly '*Qiu Shi*' (Seeking Truth) published (April 30) a Commentary captioned 'Tightly anchor the target tasks of theme education', which listed the five goals of 'theme education'. It listed these as: (i) build a solid foundation by concentrating on the soul, tempering character and strengthening loyalty; (ii) promoting development through hard work; (iii) practicing the purpose to benefit the people; (iv) establishing a new style of honesty; and (v) public service. It added that achievements in these areas will test the effectiveness of thematic education. Separately, Shuang Chuanxue, Secretary of the Party Committee and President of the Xinhua Daily, published an article on understanding 'theme education' in the *Guangming Daily* (April 7). He said 'theme education' is an "opportunity to strengthen the party's innovative theoretical arm and continuously improve the level of Marxism in the whole party".

China's Supreme People's Court commenced study of 'theme education' on April 12. At its first mobilisation meeting Zhang Jun, Secretary of the Party Leadership Group and President of the Supreme People's Court, emphasised the seriousness of the new campaign when he said, "There will be no gusts of wind, no "two skins", and no formalities". Xu Yousheng, leader of the 22nd Central Steering Group, attended the meeting and said 'theme education' is important for strengthening party building in the new era.

On April 17, the Public Security Department of the Tibet Autonomous Region (TAR) held a work conference on studying theme education. Zhang Hongbo, TAR Vice Chairman, Secretary of the Party Committee of the Public Security Department, and Director of the Department, attended the meeting and delivered a speech. He emphasised the maintenance of stability as the top priority along with "severely cracking down on hostile forces and the Dalai clique's separatist and sabotage activities" and fully safeguarding the country's political security and overall social stability in Tibet.

By April 20, the *People's Daily* published a special report declaring that central and state agencies, departments and units are all carrying out in-depth study and implementation of the theme education of Xi Jinping's new era of socialism with Chinese characteristics. It listed numerous Party Committees of Ministries as having initiated the study. It mentioned the Party Committee of the Ministry of Public Security, which said it regarded high-standard and high-quality thematic education as a major political task. It said the Ministry had also quickly established a leading group and office for thematic education.

Highlighting the progress of the theme education campaign, CCTV (April 22) said a number of 'study' sessions, meetings, training courses and 'theme party days' had been held in central organisations and Ministries. It mentioned the Ministry of Culture and Tourism, the China Federation of Literary and Art Circles, the China Writers Association, the Ministry of Foreign Affairs, the Central Taiwan Affairs Office, the General Administration of Sports, the State Administration of Radio, Film and Television and other units as having "organised party members and cadres to unremittingly use Xi Jinping's new era of socialism with Chinese characteristics to build their souls". The *Guangming Daily* (April 30) disclosed that the Ministry of Civil Affairs had begun studying the 'theme education of studying and implementing Xi Jinping's new era of socialism with Chinese characteristics'. It said the Ministry of Civil Affairs had also established a leading group and office for themed education of the Ministry of Civil Affairs, which would be led by the Secretary of the Party Group of the Ministry and Minister Tang Dengjie along with members of the Party Group and Deputy Minister of the Ministry Tang Chengpei.

In a telecast on "the theme education of Xi Jinping's socialist ideology with Chinese characteristics in the new era" on May 2, CCTV disclosed that 31 central management colleges and universities, including Sun Yat-sen University, Sichuan University, Central South University and other central management colleges had carried out in-depth study and implementation of the theme education.

The Party Committee of China's Ministry of Foreign Affairs (MoFA), according to *People's Daily* (May 23), held a meeting 'immediately to study and understand the spirit of General Secretary Xi Jinping's important speech' and set up a 'reading class for the party committee of the ministry, arranged 14 half-days to concentrate on reading, and sent five roving steering groups to supervise and guide the development of themed education in 36 affiliated units within the Ministry and 265 party committees of embassies and consulates stationed abroad'. The Office of the Central Foreign Affairs Commission held five rounds of reading classes for all staff in addition to organising a series of special counselling report meetings and other activities. It said the CCP CC International Liaison Department, had organized reading classes for the leading group of the Ministry and 'three batches of cadres at the bureau level carried out a sevenday reading class, focusing on 28 specific research topics' and 42 special seminars were held. It also reported the activities of the China International Development Cooperation Agency, the Chinese People's Association for Friendship with Foreign Countries and the Chinese People's Institute of Foreign Affairs.

CCTV (June 5) reported that the National Development and Reform Commission (NDRC) has "solidly studied" the theme education. It held 'Party group reading classes and theoretical study centre group studies, conducted in-depth examination of deficiencies, and made solid progress in rectification'. Members of the NDRC Party group had led teams for 28 investigations, and relevant departments and bureaus conducted more than 180 investigations. They went to 19 cities in 9 provinces, held 23 symposiums, and visited 40 companies.

CCTV (June 8) publicised that by early summer, the party committees and organs of units above the military level had carried out in-depth study and implementation of Xi Jinping's education on the theme of socialism with Chinese characteristics in the new era. All departments and units had implemented the decisions of the Party Central Committee, the Central Military Commission, and Chairman Xi Jinping. It added that, "The army carries out theme education and ... ultimately it must fall on being able to fight and win battles. From government agencies to troops, from training grounds to mission frontlines, from the western border to the southeast coast, party committees at all levels focus on realizing the goal of the army's centennial struggle as scheduled, and learn from the party's innovative theory the spirit of fighting hard and forging ahead." It emphasised that theme education would "radiate into a powerful driving force for preparing for wars and overcoming difficulties" and promote the high-quality development of the military.

The 'theme education' campaign is the most comprehensive and far-reaching political education campaign initiated by Xi Jinping since he came to power. It further consolidates Xi Jinping's authority. The campaign, which penetrates all levels of the Party apparatus down to the county, is being closely monitored. Apart from raising the ideological level of Party members and cadres, one of its main objectives would be to instil 'Xi Jinping's socialist ideology with Chinese characteristics in the new era' throughout the CCP's rank and file and especially in academia. The campaign will almost certainly identify and eliminate Party cadres of doubtful loyalty to Xi Jinping. At least one CCP cadre has already been accused of "betrayal" of the "Two Establishments". This campaign also credits Xi Jinping as "the main founder of Xi Jinping Thought on Socialism with Chinese Characteristics for a New Era". The next step could well be to elevate it to "Xi Jinping Thought" and Xi Jinping to the level of Mao Zedong.

This was first published by the Centre for China Analysis and Strategy (CCAS) and Vivekananda International Foundation (VIF) in June 12, 2023.

14. Former Chinese Foreign Minister Qin Gang's Absence Points to Discord in Senior Echelons of the CCP

The decision taken by members of China's National People's Congress Standing Committee (NPCSC) at an emergency meeting on July 25 to replace Qin Gang as Foreign Minister with his predecessor Wang Yi was very unusual. The NPCSC did not, however, divest him of his rank as State Councilor though it is empowered to do so. The NPCSC resolution also pointedly stated that Xi Jinping had signed-off on the decision to replace him as Foreign Minister. The NPCSC decision was, incidentally, taken when Wang Yi was attending a BRICS conference in South Africa. Regardless of whether it is finally revealed that Qin Gang is seriously unwell or resurfaces, the recent developments point to the political situation in China not being all that stable as some analysts maintain.

Pools of potential opposition to Chinese President Xi Jinping have existed in Chinese society at least since around 2017, when he made known his intention to break with convention and continue in power beyond the two terms for China's top three posts. Dissatisfaction against Xi Jinping has simmered since then among senior and veteran cadres, Chinese entrepreneurs and businessmen, and unemployed graduates or those who haven't got jobs commensurate with their qualifications. The low growth rates and China's slowing economy have contributed to this. The excessively stringent quarantine restrictions imposed during Covid fuelled popular anger and added to the economic slowdown. Though the NPCSC resolution did acknowledge Xi Jinping's authority by saying he had approved their decision, there have been other indicators that resentment against Xi Jinping is building.

The latest episode of Qin Gang's unexplained absence since June 25 and his "removal" from the post of Foreign Minister is one instance of probable inner-Party opposition to Xi Jinping. There is as yet no official report on Qin Gang's whereabouts or the reasons for his absence. While he has been replaced as Foreign Minister, Qin Gang continues to retain his rank of State Councilor, which places him above a Minister but below a Vice Premier. His retaining the rank suggests that Xi Jinping has not yet decided to abandon Qin Gang. In case Qin Gang is not under investigation, he could either return to his former position or be appointed elsewhere. The appointment of Wang Yi as Foreign Minister appears to be temporary; the last time a Politburo member was Foreign Minister was in the late 1980s when Qiao Shi was Foreign Minister. More importantly, if Qin Gang is indeed placed under investigation in the next few weeks, it would undermine Xi Jinping's position since he had promoted Qin Gang twice in the last two years, bypassing other senior candidates, to two prominent positions, namely China's Ambassador to the US and as Foreign Minister. Xi Jinping had also approved his selection as a member of the Central Committee (CC) of the Chinese Communist Party (CCP) at the 20th Party Congress in October 2022 when he was not even an Alternate Member of the CCP CC.

Within the CCP an affair by itself is not cause enough to punish a cadre. The case of retired Vice Premier Zhang Gaoli, who was accused by Chinese national Tennis player Peng Shuai of sexual assault in November 2021, was definitively suppressed with Peng Shuai subsequently retracting her allegation. They had been having an affair for many years. There are reports of many senior CCP cadres who have been divorced and have numerous liasons! Speculation about Qin Gang's affair with Phoenix TV anchor Fu Xiaotian and her having been recruited by British Intelligence also appear unfounded. However, the email allegedly originated by her while on her way back to China did suggest she was under some coercion by China's Ministry of Public Security, also called the "knife handle", but doubts persist as to whether it is linked to Qin Gang.

Qin Gang himself has a strong Intelligence background. He served many years in the Chinese Communist Party (CCP)'s International Liaison Department (ILD) before being brought by Xi Jinping to the Ministry of

Foreign Affairs (MoFA) in 2008. In 1988, Qin Gang did not graduate from China's training academy for diplomats, namely the China Foreign Affairs University. He graduated instead from Beijing's University of International Relations, wellknown for its affiliation with the CCP's Intelligence services. A report by the Australia Strategic Policy Institute (ASPI) cautions that UIR "is designated very high risk for its affiliation with the Ministry of State Security (MoSS), China's foreign intelligence agency." As was to be expected, upon his graduation, Qin Gang was assigned to the MoSS-run "Beijing Diplomatic Services Bureau" (北京外交人員服務局), from where he was deputed to work in the Beijing bureau of United Press International.

At the same time, competent reliable analysts say there are indications to suggest that former Politburo Standing Committee (PBSC) member Zeng Qinghong is orchestrating opposition to Xi Jinping. The appearance of reports of Qin Gang's affair with the Phoenix TV anchor Fu Xiaotian bear the fingerprints of Zeng Qinghong. An affair is not enough to discredit a CCP official. However, involvement with a foreign Intelligence organisation is a different matter and viewed very seriously. This especially after Chongqing Public Security Chief Wang Lijun sought asylum in 2012 in the US Consulate General in Chengdu in a bid to avoid capture by China's Ministry of Public Security (MPS) or Ministry of State Security (MoSS). But Zeng Qinghong's style has been to put out such rumours to discredit cadres. He is also known to be vindictive. In China's political circles the saying is that no one wants to get on Zeng Qinghong's wrong side! Former CCP General Secretary Jiang Zemin and his aide Zeng Qinghong are known to have regretted agreeing to Xi Jinping's appointment as Party Secretary of Shanghai and been opposed to him.

In addition, the MoFA is an intrigue-ridden bureaucracy. China's Foreign Service officials are reported to be very competitive, the number of posts at higher levels are few, and iswell known for its officials stabbing each other in the back. Qin Gang's rapid rise will have antagonised not only people in MoFA but also China's former Foreign Minister Wang Yi. Wang Yi would have resented that while he had to wait almost double the time as Qin Gang to be appointed Foreign Minister, Qin Gang was appointed Foreign Minister and State Councilor. Further, with Qin Gang's appointment Wang Yi's authority within the MoFA will have got diluted as Qin Gang had a direct link to Xi Jjinping.

But one thing is certain, namely that Xi Jinping will not go down without a fight. The fact that it took nearly 30 days,from June 25th to remove Qin Gang from his position as Foreign Minister suggests that it was preceded by protracted and tough negotiations. This despite the position of Foreign Minister being one that is constantly in the public eye. Furthermore, in addition to Xi Jinping being credited with promoting Qin Gang as Ambassador to China and soon thereafter as Foreign Minister, Qin Gang was approved by Xi Jinping as CCP CC Member. The *People's Daily* and *Xinhua* had, at the time of the 20th Party Congress, specifically said that all candidates for elevation as CC or Alternate CC members had been vetted by a special group in the CCP CC's Organisation Department and been personally confirmed by Xi Jinping. For Qin Gang to now have been removed from his position certainly dents and undermines Xi Jinping's authority. Interesting in this context is that while MoFAs official website promptly erased all references to Qin Gang as far back as March 2023 by June 26, raising the prospect of his being placed under investigation, all references to him were restored last weekend on the official website. Further, his actions and remarks as State Councilor remain on China's official websites. Other moves are visible in the economics sphere where some concessions are being given to the tech sector and China's private entrepreneurs.

At the same time, Xi Jinping has begun shoring up his position. A significant move was the promotion and appointment of Wang Zhizhong as a new Deputy Minister of Public Security (MPS). He is a veteran of the MPS Special Duty Bureau (SDB), which oversaw Xi Jinping's security when he was Vice President from 2008-13, and is likely to continue to oversee the SDB. Wang Zhizhong worked under Minister Wang Xiaohong from 2019-21 and the current CDIC Chief Li Xi in Guangdong from 2021-22. Xi Jinping will use him and the Minister of Public Security Wang Xiaohong to closely monitor senior CCP cadres, weed out those whose loyalty is suspect and keep them in line.

This was first published by the Centre for China Analysis and Strategy (CCAS) and Vivekananda International Foundation (VIF) in July 31, 2023.

15. Unusual Developments in China

The interest of governments and observers of China have been heightened with some unusual developments taking place in China, particularly since the past few months. These have included the "removal" of high Chinese Communist Party (CCP) officials, purges of high officials of the People's Liberation Army (PLA) and changes in Chinese President Xi Jinping's work pattern. Countries are also concerned at the implications of China's deteriorating economic situation.

The sudden disappearance from public view of Qin Gang, who occupied the high-profile post of China's Foreign Minister, sparked numerous rumours including that he was under investigation. Two months later, this July, the Standing Committee of the National People's Congress (NPC) (China's version of a parliament) formally announced his "removal" as Foreign Minister. Curiously, and though the NPC SC is empowered to divest him of the higher post of State Councilor, he has been allowed to retain that.

Soon thereafter, Chinese Defence Minister Li Shangfu, who was also appointed a State Councilor, disappeared from public view from August 29. His whereabouts are still not known, though rumours abound that he too is under investigation. Giving credence to these rumours, neither he nor Qin Gang were present at the Politburo 'study session' presided over by Chinese President Xi Jinping on September 27. The other three State Councilors were all present. Furthermore, Li Shangfu and his predecessor General Wei Fenghe, also rumoured to be under investigation, did not attend the 74th anniversary celebrations of the People's Republic of China at the Great Hall of the People in Beijing attended by former and serving PLA officers. In case they are being investigated then an announcement could be expected around October this year.

That both Qin Gang and Li Shangfu 'disappeared' almost at the same time is intriguing. Both are very close associates of Xi Jinping who has been instrumental in their rise.

Qin Gang is a protégé of Chinese President Xi Jinping. Xi Jinping brought him in to China's Ministry of Foreign Affairs (MoFA) and then sent him as Ambassador to Washington ignoring other senior contenders for this prestigious appointment. Well before completion of his term, Qin Gang was recalled to Beijing and at the 20th Party Congress in October 2022, he was appointed Foreign Minister and State Councilor. He was also appointed a full member of the CCP Central Committee (CC) though he was not even an alternate member of the CC earlier.

Li Shangfu, who is a "military princeling" has close second generation family ties with Xi Jinping. Xi Jinping and Li Shangfu's fathers served together in the Army and Li Shangfu's father was brought into the mainstream by Xi Jinping's father, Xi Zhongxun. Xi Jinping brought Li Shangfu into the CCP CC at the 19th Party Congress and retained him in the CC at the 20th Party Congress. He also promoted him as a member of the Central Military Commission (CMC) and appointed him Defence Minister and State Councilor in October 2022.

In case the two are confirmed to be under investigation it would convey a number of messages. Chinese cadres could interpret it as either a push back by some group or coalition of cadres against Xi Jinping's accumulation of power or, more likely, as Xi Jinping being unable, or unwilling, to protect his protégés. Rumours have also been circulating since late last week that Chinese Premier Li Qiang, another close associate of Xi Jinping, could be in trouble because he has a foreign "son-in-law". Chinese social media said that the son-in-law, a British national named Forbes, and Li Qiang's daughter had started an architecture company when she was 23 years old and got a major contract in the first year. It published photographs of his daughter and son-in-law's house in the UK. These developments are likely to dent Xi Jinping's image.

The sudden removal of General Li Yuchao as PLA Rocket Force (PLARF) Commander and Xu Zhongbo as PLARF Political Commissar, both Generals promoted by Xi Jinping, confirms that corruption is widespread in the PLA. More importantly it indicates that despite the successive year-long political education campaigns in the PLA and bringing the PLA within the purview of the CCP's anti-corruption outfit, namely the Central Discipline Inspection Commission, Xi Jinping has not been able to eradicate corruption in the PLA. The appointments of PLA Navy (PLAN) General Wang Houbin as Commander of the PLARF and PLA Air Force (PLAAF) General Xu Xisheng as Political Commissar, additionally suggests an effort to break up existing groups of associates and friends. It indicates that instead of informing the authorities about cases of corruption, PLA officers band together and 'protect' each other. PLA Rocket Force officers normally earn their promotions and stay within the Rocket Force.

The PLARF was recently allocated a large budget for expansion and enlarging its inventory of missiles. Reports reinforced by satellite photos in late 2021 showed that China is building nearly 170 new silos for intercontinental ballistic missiles in a desert near the northwestern cities of Yumen, Hami and Ordos. There are reports that the PLARF has added 15 Brigades to its strength. PLARF officers would have had access to a lot of money. A notice issued by the military's anti-corruption organisation, the PLA Discipline Inspection Commission, in late July 2023, said it will be investigating irregularities in the tender bidding process for the period between 2017 and 2022. This implies that in addition to the PLARF Commander and Political Commissar, former senior PLARF officers including Generals Li Shangfu and Wei Fenghe would be involved as well. Li Shangfu was the PLARF Commander during that period. Citing two unnamed sources, Reuters recently reported that eight senior officials from the Chinese military's procurement unit are also under investigation.

This was strongly brought out in an important sternly-worded article published by the CCP's People's Daily on September 22. Titled 'Purify the social circle, life circle, and friend circle', the article was written by Chen Qinghua of the Reform and Establishment Office of the Central Military Commission. This *People's Daily* article is significant in the backdrop of the purges and "removals" of PLA Officers in recent months and points to the effort to break up existing groups of associates and friends.

It recalled that,"When talking about the need for leading cadres to strengthen self-discipline, President Xi once quoted the story in 'Journey to the West' vividly: 'Sun Wukong put Tang Monk there and drew a circle with a golden hoop, and the monsters could not get in.Draw a circle for yourself". It said this should be "a strong inspiration for leading cadres to purify their social circle, life circle and friend circle" adding that this is "The most effective way to stay away from dangers and temptations is to conduct "physical isolation". It asked cadres "Never overestimate your determination or superstition about your abilities. Don't participate in activities that you can avoid, and don't go to dinner appointments that you can avoid. ...Party members and cadres do not live in a vacuum. Necessary interpersonal interactions are inevitable, but interactions must be principled and rule-based". It warned that "Especially for leading cadres, once the power in their hands is targeted by people with ulterior motives, problems such as abuse of power for personal gain and power-for-money transactions will easily occur" and drew their attention to the "Code of Conduct for Social Interactions of Military Leading Cadres" issued recently by the Political Work Department of the Central Military Commission and the Commission for Discipline Inspection. The Code emphasises "that military leading cadres should strengthen their party spirit, strengthen self-discipline, constantly purify their social circles, living circles, and friend circles, and consciously achieve social interaction, have principles, boundaries, and rules". It said "This requires leading cadres at all levels to firmly guard the relationship between people, consciously maintain pure, healthy and civilized interactions, and build fresh and clean interpersonal relationships".

Addressing leading cadres it said "Judging from the corruption cases investigated and dealt with in recent years, many "hunting" behaviors are cloaked in the guise of human relations, and under the banner of fellow villagers, classmates, comrades, etc., like "boiling a frog in warm water", unknowingly turning the "circle of friends" into a "circle of friends" "Encirclement" made the "small circle" weave into a "big trap", and "careless making of friends" was an important reason for individual leaders to surrender. As the saying goes, "The success or failure of a life depends on the virtuousness of your friends." The article added that "There is politics in communication, discipline in communication, principles in communication, and image in communication. Because of their special status, soldiers should interact more with positive people, whether internally or externally, in order to establish a good image as a soldier. Only by making friends with people who are dedicated to fighting can they better focus on their main responsibilities. Leading cadres at all levels should always tighten the strings of discipline and rules, work in a down-to-earth manner, interact with each other in a clear and refreshing manner, mind their own mouths and not eat what they shouldn't eat; mind their hands and take things they shouldn't. Don't take it; take care of your legs and don't go where you shouldn't go. We should resolutely abandon the utilitarian exchanges of "friendship based on profit", the pragmatic exchanges of "friendship based on power", and the vulgar exchanges of "friendship based on wealth", and beware of "talking" by relatives and friends, and "walking around" by classmates. "Move around" and "liaise" with neighbors near and far, and truly be politically savvy, contact wise, economically clean and decent people in life."

A couple of other features of Chinese President Xi Jinping's third term at the helm, are his absences from some international events. Xi Jinping skipped attending the ASEAN Summit held in Indonesia and a week later the G-20 Summit in New Delhi though it could have been advantageous to China. He would have met leaders of advanced countries at a time when China is facing economic pressures including that of de-risking, from countries and runs the risk of coming under increasing economic and political pressure. He also avoided attending the UNGA session, where he sent Vice President Han Zheng. Earlier, Xi Jinping used to attend all these meetings. There is speculation whether he will attend the APEC Summit in the US where he would have the opportunity to personally meet US President Biden.

Finally, unlike in the past decade during Chinese President Xi Jinping's previous terms, there is an apparent imbalance in the portfolios of the Politburo Standing Committee members. While in the past all, except to a degree Chinese Premier Li Keqiang, had a similar profile with Xi Jinping surpassing all others including his predecessors, this term is different. Number five ranked Politburo Standing Committee member 1955 born Cai Qi holds more important portfolios than his other colleagues except for Chinese Premier Li Qiang. As in charge of the CCP Central Secretariat and Director of the CCP CC General Office, Cai Qi is effectively Xi Jinping's chief of staff. He accompanies Xi Jinping on all his travels and oversees security and other arrangements. He is also in charge of ideology and propaganda. Unlike his predecessors in this job, Cai Qi is also a Deputy Director of the CCP CC National Security Commission and a Deputy Director of the Central Comprehensively Deepening Reforms Commission, both chaired by Xi Jinping.

Chinese Premier Li Qiang another confidante of Xi Jinping was promoted as Premier at the 20th Party Congress. He is charge of the economy and State Council, which gives him authority over personnel appointments. Li Qiang has, however, not been able to make much headway in tackling the economy because of Xi Jinping's stress on security.

Both Cai Qi and Li Qiang are in important positions and have been able to place some of their proteges in the central apparatus. They need to be discreet and subtle, however, because if they are perceived to be strengthening their positions their downfall could be sudden. At the same time, while the appointment of Cai Qi and Li Qiang in these important positions demonstrates Xi Jinping's confidence in them it also sows the seeds of potential future factional infighting.

This was first published by the Centre for China Analysis and Strategy (CCAS) and Vivekananda International Foundation (VIF) in October 2, 2023.

16. Chinese President Xi Jinping Beset by Growing Popular Discontent

Faced with increasing popular discontent, Chinese President Xi Jinping and the Chinese leadership have, since the 19th Party Congress in 2017, been focussed on trying to assert the Chinese Communist Party's (CCP) pre-eminence in all sectors and ensure social stability. The legitimacy of the CCP and its continuance as the sole ruling party of China are the top priorities. There are various indicators that confirm that popular discontent in China, including within the CCP, is rising. This has the potential to adversely impact the CCP's leading role and Chinese President Xi Jinping's position. China's security apparatus has consequently been appreciably increased as reflected in the expanded budgets and leadership appointments of the Ministry of Public Security (MPS) and Ministry of State Security (MoSS).

Reflecting the leadership's sensitivity to the rising discontent was the decision of the Chinese authorities in recent months to prohibit official Chinese organisations from reporting the number of protests and strikes taking place. These showed that the number of protests and strikes by workers due to poor working conditions or non-payment of dues were rising across China. Nikkei Asia (November 21) disclosed that "around 50 to 70 demonstrations are now occurring monthly, though August saw about 100 worker-led protests, three times as many as the same month a year earlier. Since June 2022, demonstrations have occurred in 276 cities nationwide". It said Freedom House's China Dissent Monitor project tallied 1,777 demonstrations linked to the property sector between June 2022 and October 2023.

Human Rights in China (HRIC) reported that on December 27 and 28, 2023, thousands had gathered in Henan to protest the death and possible gruesome murder of a 14-year-old student, as well as the government's apparent complicity in helping the school cover it up. The demonstrations drew crowds of over ten thousand, becoming the largest Chinese protest of 2023. The authorities quickly cracked down, with police and blockades shutting down the whole city. Separately, in Sichuan, doctors perched on windowsills to protest unpaid wages, amid a series of protests over wage arrears. The Hongkong-based China Labour Bureau reported in January this year,that in the last six months there were 1104 strikes in China and 976 calls for help by workers striking for wage arrears etc. with the latest incident occurring in Guangdong Province. On January 4, 2024, Radio Free Asia reported that amidst the waves of layoffs across China, Beijing bus companies are hiring security guards so that each bus has at least two to "prevent emergencies".

China's economic situation is more stressed than it has been for decades. The magnitude of the problem can be gauged from the government's efforts to curb spending. Cuts in wages of government employees are quietly being effected across China. The National Financial Work Conference held in Beijing on December 21-22, 2023, emphasized the need to vigorously promote financial management reform next year. It stressed the importance of practicing frugality to instil the concept of tightening belts and establishing a system of living within tight financial constraints. Reports from China's provinces on December 28, 2023, revealed that the policy of reducing salaries of civil servants is spreading to the more prosperous areas and regions including Beijing, Hubei, the Yangtze River Delta, and the Pearl River Delta.

A civil servant in a Beijing municipal agency said that although the basic salary has not changed this year, various subsidies and bonuses have been reduced by tens of thousands of yuan. He said a Salary Reduction Office had been established to eliminate the "unreasonable" benefits provided earlier. An article on the official WeChat account of Hubei Province disclosed that the wave of salary reductions began quietly in 2023 before the year's end. It mentions a town-level civil servant in Xiantao, Hubei, who joined in 2018, experiencing a reduction of about 280 yuan in monthly salary that month and a halving of the year-end performance bonus of over 10,000 yuan, resulting in an overall salary reduction of around 15 percent.

The annual income in Shenzhen has dropped from over 360,000 yuan to just over 250,000 yuan, and in Zhuhai, it has decreased from 280,000 to about 200,000 yuan. After the reduction, the annual income for provincial government employees in Guangdong is over 220,000 yuan, in Foshan and Dongguan it's 200,000 yuan, and in Zhongshan it ranges from 150,000 to 200,000 yuan, with Huizhou and Jiangmen at 140,000 yuan. Reports also suggest that civil servants in various regions are undergoing structural adjustments in their salary, which is a "disguised" pay cut. A netizen on Xiaohongshu, a social media and e-commerce platform with over 300 million registered users, claimed that Shandong Province has issued a document eliminating the basic performance bonuses but leaving room for discretionary distribution. A notice on "strengthening budget management and adhering to the concept of living within tight financial constraints" issued by the Xiamen Municipal Government in Fujian Province has circulated widely online. It strictly prohibits the unauthorized construction of buildings and facilities and forbids projects solely for political achievements or image building. Meanwhile, China's state-backed Zhengzhou Public Transport Group is seeking opinions internally on its plan to encourage employees to start their own businesses.

Radio Free Asia (RFA) reported on November 16 that the authorities have reduced wages for public security and national security personnel by about 20 percent. It quoted a wellknown dissident in Beijing who did not want to be named for security reasons as saying, "The National Security Bureau told me that they have reduced wages by about 20 percent. Now they are more polite than before". A human rights activist in Chengdu who did not want to be named for fear of retaliation told RFA, "The national security guards in Chengdu have all had their salaries reduced, with each person receiving a reduction of one to two thousand yuan. No wonder they are now more polite than before. In fact, they have also begun to get dissatisfied with the government, after all, the wage cut affects their interests." Separately, Radio France International (RFI) reports that there are numerous posts by citizens on Sina complaining about delayed payment of wages and non-payment of wages for up to eight months. When wage cuts were announced by the National People's Congress (NPC) across the board for all government ministries and departments from 2020 till 2022, the Ministries of Public Security and State Security were exempt as was National Defence. That they also now face wage cuts indicates the Chinese government's severe financial constraints.

The authorities apparently hope to offset any consequent laxity in discipline and enforcement of the security personnel with the introduction of a whistle-blowers programme to help maintain social stability. For example, on October 25, Beijing's Tongzhou District issued confidential documents to various industries and offered rewards to encourage people to provide "hints of instability". The documents explain that intelligence clues combined with the results of actual application have different levels of rewards for the whistle-blowers. From first-class clues to fourth-class clues and other clues, rewards range from 10,000 yuan to 500 yuan. The final reward amount will be determined based on the actual effect. If multiple people report the same clue, only the first citizen to report will be rewarded. Posts on social media by citizens critical of the programme say that the "Big Whistle blowing Campaign" is the fifth largest intelligence organization in China after the "Chaoyang Masses", "Xicheng Aunt", "Haidian Netizens" and the "Fengtai Persuasion Team". Some netizens feared that this campaign to involve citizens in maintenance of stability will lead to the recurrence of the mutual revelations of the Cultural Revolution, and the emergence of a large number of so-called "secret agents" and will help the CCP divert social conflicts and consolidate its power.

There are a number of other indications that China's economy is slowing. For example, graduate unemployment has been officially declared to be 21.8 percent which, in a one-child society further accentuates dissatisfaction. After releasing such data twice in six months, with both data sets reflecting steadily growing figures, the National Statistics Bureau (NSB) was stopped from issuing this data. Similarly, the NSB has ceased releasing data on joblessness. The number of marriages have declined as girls say that with housing shortages and jobs paying less, they would rather live at home and share their salaries with their parents. This has raised fears of a declining population which would lower national productivity and CCP cadres have been directed to talk to youth and persuade them to marry. There is also a rising trend of young graduates applying for government jobs in contrast to looking for employment in the private sector. The lack of appropriate jobs has had a deleterious effect on Chinese youth and led to the social phenomenon called 'tangping', or losing hope and 'lying flat'. Party cadres are trying to dissuade the youth from adopting such an attitude as it could adversely affect China's productivity and economy. China's social media shows another similar attitude impacting the youth who, instead of striving harder, are hosting "quitting" parties and leaving their jobs.

There is, additionally, a high outflow of funds from China indicating that Chinese businessmen are uncertain about the country's economy and its policies. China's State Administration of Foreign Exchange (SAFE) recently revealed that there had been an outflow of US$ 53.9 billion in September 2023. This is the largest amount since January 2016, when China logged a net outflow of nearly US$55.8 billion. Al Jazeera (May 2) quoted the rights group 'Safeguard Defenders' as reporting that China has stepped up use of 'exit bans' against government critics with more than 15 laws and legal instruments in place. It noted that mentions of 'exit ban' on the Supreme People's Court database rose from less than 5,000 in 2016 to 39,000 in 2020. It added that only administrative, criminal, and civil case-related exit bans appear on the court's 'China Judgments Online database' so the figure is probably an underestimation, noting that it can also take up to two years for data to be uploaded.

In just the past few weeks China's NSB was instructed not to release official data on joblessness in China and the rise in graduate unemployment. The implication clearly is that release of such information confirms the economic downslide and raises questions on the leadership of the Chinese Communist Party (CCP). Meanwhile, Xi Jinping has consistently laid stress on stability over development. This appeared to change last month, however, when the once-in-five-year Central Economic Work Conference mentioned progress and stability and placed progress ahead of stability. The CCP's mouthpiece *People's Daily* also published an editorial stressing that reforms were necessary for the rejuvenation of China. However, stability continues to receive greater prominence.

The growing dissatisfaction, which appears to exist within the CCP too, has moved Xi Jinping to increase the number and enlarge the scope of the security-related organisations and appoint 'loyalists' to head them. It is telling that China's apex security body, the National Security Commission, which is chaired by Chinese President Xi Jinping, has Premier Li Qiang and

Politburo Standing Committee member and Director of the important CCP CC General Office, Cai Qi — both long time confidants and loyalists of Xi Jinping – as its two Vice Chairmen. An expanded national anti-espionage law is also to soon be made applicable in all provinces and Autonomous Regions in China.

At the Central level, in 2023 just prior to the 20th Party Congress, Xi Jinping curtailed the authority of the five other Politburo Standing Committee (PBSC) members to appoint and pay staff members and authorised the Ministry of Public Security (MPS) to monitor members of the CCP CC Politburo. Unless the economy begins to grow and people's lives improve, Xi Jinping will continue to face increasing popular discontent.

This was first published by the Centre for China Analysis and Strategy (CCAS) and Vivekananda International Foundation (VIF) in January 18, 2024.

17. Xi Jinping Reinforces Security Apparatus Amidst Growing Popular Discontent'

The slowing economy and increasing joblessness have contributed to the growing popular discontent in China. This has affected China's entrepreneurs and there are indications that discontent has spread also to the 'princelings' and cadres in the Chinese Communist Party (CCP). The uncovering recently of corruption in the senior echelons of the People's Liberation Army (PLA) and punishments to those found guilty will add to the number of discontented elements. While Chinese President Xi Jinping and the CCP leadership have been increasingly emphasising security and stability, Xi Jinping has simultaneously been strengthening China's security apparatus.

The threats perceived by China's leaders were highlighted in a statement by China's Ministry of State Security (MoSS) on its WeChat account on August 15, 2023, which declared that "Political security directly relates to the stability of political power and the survival of the system, and is the most essential need and the foundation for a country's survival and development. National security is impossible without political security". It stressed that "the core of political security lies in the security of the political power and system, which is to uphold the leadership and ruling status of the Communist Party of China (CPC) and safeguard the socialist system with Chinese characteristics". The MoSS also pointed out that safeguarding political security will be the primary task, while coordinating efforts to strengthen security in all other areas such as military and territorial security, as well as nontraditional. One concern, it identified the centrally administered organisations, were the persistent efforts by various hostile forces to instigate 'colour revolutions' across China posing a real danger and long-term harm to China's political security.

To contain and curb the spread of dissatisfaction, Xi Jinping has enlarged the security apparatus and expanded its scope as well as placed 'loyalists' to head the security-related organisations. It is telling that China's apex security body, the National Security Commission, which is chaired by Chinese President Xi Jinping, has Premier Li Qiang and Politburo Standing Committee member and Director of the important CCP CC General Office, Cai Qi — both long time confidants and loyalists of Xi Jinping – as its two Vice Chairmen. Chairing the first meeting of the Central National Security Commission (CNSC) on May 30, 2023, Chinese President Xi Jinping called for accelerated efforts to modernise the country's national security system and capacity. The meeting was attended by PBSC members Li Qiang, Zhao Leji and Cai Qi, who are deputy heads of the CNSC. By August, the centrally administered Chongqing Municipality announced an expanded national anti-espionage law and the MoSS welcomed the move and indicated that the law will soon be made applicable in all provinces and Autonomous Regions in China. It also urged people to be on the lookout for spies and report them.

At the Central level, in 2023 just prior to the 20th Party Congress, Xi Jinping curtailed the authority of the five other Politburo Standing Committee (PBSC) members to appoint and pay staff members and authorised the Ministry of Public Security (MPS) to monitor members of the CCP CC Politburo. The MPS and MoSS have both reportedly increased their nationwide personnel strength three-fold. Xi Jinping has also encouraged them to harness technology to reinforce efficacy. For instance the Director of Public Security of Sichuan Province announced in April 2023 that the province became the first to build a new generation of public security information network and build a police cloud computing platform that integrates the whole police. The MPS also has a technology centre, where "the latest scientific, technical and technological developments" aligned with police missions are developed. Chinese President Xi Jinping has additionally added at least two organisations to the national security apparatus, namely the 'Safe China Construction Coordinating Small Group' and the CCP's Social Work Department.

The security-related organisations under the CCP and State Council are all (except the CNSC) under the CCP CC's Political and Legal Affairs Commission (PLAC). They are the:

1. National Security Commission (CNSC), which was initially proposed in 1997, but finally established in 2013;

2. PLAC with subordinate offices across the country down to the county level;
3. State Supervision Commission (with subordinate offices across the country down to the county level);
4. The 'Safe China Construction Coordinating Small Group', established in April 2020 and chaired by Xi Jinping. Its wide ambit includes preventing "activities that endanger the political security of the country".
5. Ministry of Public Security (MPS) with a network of subordinate offices across the country down to the village level and which is augmented by inputs from informers and the ubiquitous 'neighbourhood committees';
6. Ministry of State Security (MoSS) which is authorised to conduct espionage operations abroad in addition to counter-espionage operations domestically and, of late, investigate financial matters. Over the past two years it has become more active and adopted a higher public profile;
7. United Front Work Department (UFWD) — after Xi Jinping took over as Chairman of the United Front Central Small Leading Group in 2016, he doubled its budget and personnel strength. The UFWD's scope of duties was expanded to include surveillance of Chinese dissidents abroad, Chinese students studying abroad, and recruiting and winning over influential people and opinion-makers abroad in addition to members of ethnic Chinese minorities like Tibetans, Uyghurs and Mongols. It is now reported to function more closely with China's Ministry of Foreign Affairs (MoFA).
8. International Liaison Department (ILD).
9. CCP's Social Work Department, which was re-established in 2023. This office was set up by Mao Zedong as an Intelligence and Counter-Intelligence unit within the CCP. Its charter is not entirely public except to deepen the Party's reach in society. Its head is 60-year-old Wu Hansheng, who has spent most of his career in the Central and State Organs Working Committee (CSOWC) and its predecessor organizations. He is a close associate and one time chief of staff of Politburo Standing Committee member Li Xi,

Announcing the enlarged scope of the security apparatus last year while on an inspection of Jiangxi province, Politburo member and Secretary of the Political and Legal Affairs Commission Chen Wenqing said political-legal organs should "address risks in public finance", strengthen "internet governance", and contribute to "new development pattern", among other things.

An expansion of the domestic security apparatus was visible since the end of 2023 when Municipalities began setting up Armed Police Departments. Apart from being a clear indication of the widespread and spreading discontent in China, these departments will augment the police and security apparatus. On September 28, 2023, the Shanghai Municipal Investment Corporation established a People's Armed Forces Department responsible for "security and emergency management". Subsequently at least 12 other municipal investment bureaus in China have followed Shanghai's example and done the same, including in the Wuhan and Huizhou Municipalities. Many of these investment bureaus are already heavily in debt and facing default. All the Armed Police Departments are nominally charged with maintaining social stability and order. Radio Free Asia reported (October 3) that the new people's armed forces departments are being rapidly established not only in municipal investment bureaus, but also in at least 23 of China's state-owned enterprises.

These efforts are being augmented by engaging the public in security work. In a WeChat article published on August 1, the MoSS said that security agencies would "need the broad participation of the people and their joint prevention" to tackle the current "grim and complex" state of anti-espionage efforts. Consequent to the reduction last year in wages of security personnel by up to 20 percent, the authorities, in an apparent bid to offset any consequent laxity in discipline and effectiveness of the security personnel, introduced a "whistle-blowers" programme to help maintain social stability. On October 25, the authorities of Beijing's Tongzhou District issued confidential documents to various industries and offered rewards to encourage people to provide "hints of instability". The documents explain that intelligence clues combined with the results of actual application have different levels of rewards for the whistle-blowers. From first-class clues to fourth-class clues and other clues, rewards range from 10,000 yuan to 500 yuan. The final reward amount will be determined based on the actual effect. If multiple people report the same clue, only the first citizen to report will be rewarded. Posts on social media by citizens critical of the programme say that the "Big Whistle blowing Campaign" is the fifth largest intelligence organization in China after the "Chaoyang Masses", "Xicheng Aunt", "Haidian Netizens" and the "Fengtai Persuasion Team". Some netizens feared that this campaign to involve citizens in maintenance of stability will lead to the recurrence of the mutual revelations of the Cultural Revolution, and the emergence of a large number of so-called "secret agents" and will help the CCP divert social conflicts and consolidate its power.

The MoSS has also enlarged the scope of its activities. Since last year it began publicising its success in uncovering espionage cases involving an MI6 officer inside China, neutralising an espionage effort near a critical Chinese Navy base, and arresting a software engineer working for foreign intelligence. An article in the South China Morning Post (December 24) disclosed that China is building up private security to protect overseas interests in hostile, unstable regions. It said conflicts have necessitated that Beijing make new contingency plans to safeguard Chinese interests abroad. At a seminar in early December, jointly held by the China-Africa Business Council and the MoSS-affiliated China Institutes of Contemporary International Relations, participants pushed for Chinese firms to become more internationalised, more localised with regional staff and political support, and more commercialised. The seminar saw the presence of some large domestic security companies, including Huayuan Security Guard; Dewe Security, a subsidiary of Hong Kong-listed Frontier Services Group; Huaxin Zhongan Group; Shanghai-listed Anbang Save-Guard Group; representatives from the China Security Association; and others. Officials from China's foreign ministry attended the conference and the MoSS said it would ensure the security of China's overseas mining projects, personnel and assets, adding it is ready "to ensure the safety of Chinese companies 'going global', and safeguard the security of key mineral-resource supply chains." Many of the private security companies have recruited ex-PLA or police personnel.

These efforts to strengthen the security apparatus, and especially the use of technologies like facial recognition, amid growing popular discontent have been criticised by some Chinese. Many have resented the use of technologies like facial recognition. At a two day Global Public Security Cooperation Forum in Lianyungang, Jiangsu province on September 21, Xu Jin, a researcher with the Chinese Academy of Social Sciences, said Beijing should be cautious about going too far on security, do more research and be more flexible in its approach. He said, "While pursuing security goals, it needs to take into account the needs of different stakeholders, especially by giving adequate attention to vulnerable groups." He said there was a dilemma for policymakers trying to find the right balance on public security, adding that excessive measures could result in "wasted resources, panic among the public and inappropriate policies".

This was first published by the Centre for China Analysis and Strategy (CCAS) and Vivekananda International Foundation (VIF) in January 19, 2024.

18. Chinese President Xi Jinping Bolsters Position at National People's Congress

The plenary sessions of the Chinese People's Political Consultative Conference (CPPCC), the top political advisory body, and the National People's Congress (NPC), China's version of a parliament, both important events in China's political calendar opened in Beijing's Great Hall of the People on March 4 and March 5 respectively amid high security. The observations by the NPC deputies and CPPCC delegates give some insight into the mood and thinking of the Chinese authorities. This NPC session (March 4-11) signalled that Xi Jinping had still further consolidated his stature as China's preeminent leader and more firmly stamped the Chinese Communist Party (CCP)'s imprimatur on the state. Equally importantly, it reaffirmed China's global leadership ambitions.

The authority of the CCP was explicitly stated at the ceremonial closing on March 11, when the National People's Congress (NPC), voted 2883 to 8, with 9 abstentions, to revise the State Council Organic Law and increase the number of Articles from 11 to 20. This was the first revision since its enactment in December 1982 and it made explicit the CCP's primacy over the State Council and government. The changes bring the Vice Premiers and the Governor of the People's Bank of China (PBoC) within the State Council's top leadership group. The new Article 18 confirms the primacy of the CCP when it stipulates "The constituent members of the State Council shall resolutely uphold the Party Central Committee's authority and its centralized and unified leadership...". Article 19 mandates that the State Council and CCP shall "closely cooperate with one another to ensure that the Party Central Committee's and the State Council's work plans are implemented in all aspects".

Despite the high security across Beijing and its adjoining provinces including the troubled Autonomous Regions of Tibet, Xinjiang and Inner Mongolia, early in the morning on March 10, an incident occurred in Beijing. A black sedan was observed stopped just outside Xinhuamen, the entrance to Zhongnanhai – the gated, walled residential compound of China's top leadership — and someone, most likely the driver, was dragged out of the vehicle and carried away spread-eagled from the scene by a squad of policemen. The event was videorecorded by a passer-by.

Of the 2,162 delegates who should have attended the second meeting of the 14th National Committee of the CPPCC only 2,085 actually attended. The NPC session was attended by 2900 Deputies with 56 absent. Some of those absent were individuals who had died or were removed as deputies and delegates on charges of corruption and included those from the People's Liberation Army (PLA).

The 40-page Government Work Report presented by Chinese Premier Li Qiang on the opening day is an important policy document that indicates the government's plans for the year ahead. It is a record of the government's performance, assessment of China's economic situation and outlines the leadership's ambitions. While Government Work Reports since the 18th Party Congress have regularly included laudatory references to Xi Jinping, what was striking in this year's report was that Premier Li Qiang singled out Chinese President Xi Jinping for special praise. Li Qiang asserted that "we owe our achievements in 2023 to General Secretary Xi Jinping, who is at the helm charting the course". He, of course, also included the mandatory acknowledgement of "the strong leadership of the Party Central Committee with Comrade Xi Jinping at its core, and the concerted efforts of the whole Party, the armed forces, and Chinese people of all ethnic groups".

Taking over 50 minutes to read the Report on March 5, Chinese Premier Li Qiang mentioned Xi Jinping 16 times, the most number of times in a Government Work Report since Xi Jinping took office in 2012. This underscored Xi's preeminent status. Among the highlights of the report was that security remained Beijing's top concern and was mentioned 28 times, three times more than in last year's report. Li Qiang asserted "We should adhere to the principles of pursuing progress while ensuring stability, promoting stability through progress, and establishing the new before abolishing the old." "Stability is of overall importance, as it is the basis for everything we do. All localities and government departments should adopt more policies that are conducive to keeping expectations, economic growth, and employment stable". Formulations in all reports and speeches by Chinese leaders mention security and progress but place security ahead of progress.

The work report of the Supreme People's Court (SPC) again highlighted the theme of stability and security. On March 8, the NPC session heard the work report delivered by SPC President Zhang Jun and started deliberations on the work report. In his report Zhang Jun, who mentioned the 'Fengqiao' (Mao-era mechanism to eliminate threats to social stability at the grass-roots level) experience at least twice, said that in 2023, the Supreme People's Court accepted 21,081 cases and closed 17,855 cases, a year-on-year increase of 54.6 percent and 29.5 percent respectively. Courts at all levels across the country accepted 45.574 million cases and closed 45.268 million cases, a year-on-year increase of 15.6 percent and 13.4 percent respectively. While mentioning the composition of the first-instance criminal cases concluded by the People's Court in 2023, he said there were "0.04 percent of the other cases". The latter are defined as "including harming national security, harming defence interests...". Zhang Jun's figures suggest that 70,520 national security and defence related cases were tried in 2023. An analyst pointed out this means just under 1 in 20,000 Chinese are doing something subversive and being brought to court for it!

The National Defence budget was increased by 7.2 percent, or 1.67 trillion yuan (US$ 231.4 billion) making 2024 the ninth straight year to see a single-digit hike in the country's defence budget. The National Defence budget has doubled since 2013 when Xi Jinping took over. This increase, in spite of China's slowing GDP growth rate, confirms that China continues its efforts to build a modern, technologically-advanced world class army and harbour ambitions to 'recover' its so-called 'lost' territories. Noticeable too is the fresh thrust towards advanced technology and emphasis on building the Navy. Delivering an "important" speech to PLA Deputies and Delegates to the NPC and CPPCC plenary sessions on March 7, according to Xinhua, Chinese President Xi Jinping "emphasised that the strategic capabilities in emerging fields are crucial components of the national strategic system and capabilities, which are related to the high-quality development of China's economy and society, national security, and the initiative of military struggle". He stressed the need to "promote the efficient integration and two-way stimulation of new productive forces and new combat forces".

Xi Jinping stressed the need to comprehensively enhance the strategic capabilities in emerging fields and said it is important to "integrate preparation for maritime military warfare, safeguarding of maritime rights and development of the maritime economy". On the side-lines of the NPC session, Yuan Huazhi, Political Commissar of the PLA Navy and NPC Deputy, told the Hong Kong Commercial Daily (March 5) that China will unveil its fourth aircraft carrier soon. He said there is no bottleneck in China's aircraft carrier technologies, and the development is progressing smoothly. The appointment of General Dong Jun, a PLA Navy officer and submariner, as Defence Minister will ensure adequate funds for the Navy.

Xi Jinping also mentioned building a network space defence system and enhancing the ability to safeguard national network security. Alluding to Civil-Military fusion, he called for strengthening the coordinated implementation of major projects in science and technology, promoting independent and original innovation, and fostering a vibrant ecosystem for innovation. Zhang Yuzhuo, Chairman of the State-owned Assets Supervision and Administration Commission (SASAC) of the State Council, disclosed (March 5) that investment by central SOEs in strategic emerging industries increased 32.1 percent year on year in 2023. He said the SASAC's goal envisaged income derived from strategic emerging industries by central SOEs as accounting for 35 percent of their total income by 2025. He said it is important to increase the layout of industries "especially in brain-like intelligence, quantum information and controlled nuclear fusion."

As anticipated, the Government Work Report glossed over China's economic problems. However, projecting a GDP growth rate of five percent, the same as in the previous year, - and estimating the inflation rate at three percent -revealed the country's economic difficulties. Both estimates remain unchanged since last year, indicating the government's reluctance to set a figure it cannot reach, or a realistically low figure which would further undermine confidence. Unlike last year, when Beijing's abrupt exit from Covid Zero saw a sudden burst in economic activities in the first half, this time there is no such advantage favouring China. The government also continues to see inflation at around 3 percent, even as the National Statistics Bureau reports the economy is slipping into deflation. The CCP's failure to hold the Third Plenum, which stipulates the country's economic goals, in October or November suggests differences within the Party.

The main points in Li Qiang's Work Report are:

1. Beijing's economic expectations are mainly in line with last year's, with the GDP growth target still set at 5 percent.
2. Industrial policy is still the No: 1 priority. Although Premier Li Qiang incorporated the 'new quality of productivity' proposed by Xi Jinping last year into this government report, this did not show any changes in China's industrial direction.
3. Expanding domestic demand now seems to be more important than supply-side reform. Li Qiang elevated expanding domestic demand to the third most important issue in the government report and devoted a full chapter to talk about how to stimulate consumption, while supply-side reform was only briefly mentioned twice without detailed explanation. Li Qiang has not mentioned supply-side reform much since becoming Premier last year.
4. Clearly revealing its economic difficulties, Beijing has further tightened constraints on local governments. Not only does the Report suggest that Beijing will tighten controls on wasteful local fiscal spending, but it will also clamp down on local protectionism.
5. Amidst the persistently sluggish real estate market, Premier Li Qiang omitted the phrase "houses are for living, not for speculation" for the first time. The phrase was first articulated by Chinese President Xi Jinping. However, the Minister for Housing and Urban-Rural Development Ni Hong did mention it. He also said (March 9) property developers "that must go bankrupt should go bankrupt" and warned that those who "harm the interests of the masses" will be probed and punished.
6. There has been a definite move to encourage foreign investment. Beijing will fully abolish restrictive measures on foreign investment access in

the manufacturing sector and liberalize market access in services such as telecommunications and medical care.

7. The National Defence budget has increased by 7.2 percent, or 1.67 trillion yuan (US$ 231.4 billion) making 2024 the ninth straight year to see a single-digit hike in the country's defence budget. The National Defence budget has doubled since 2013 when Xi Jinping took over.
8. The Government Work Report mentioned "peaceful development" but not "peaceful reunification," a departure from the standard phraseology. It used the term "China's reunification." This implies greater attention by Beijing to the Taiwan issue and signals it is keeping open the option for the possible use of force.
9. Security is still Beijing's top concern. Last year, it was mentioned 25 times in the government work report, and this year it was mentioned 3 more times i.e. 28 times. The high incidence of "other cases" in the SPC report corroborates the warnings repeatedly issued by Chinese leaders and China's security agencies against "hostile forces" and "colour revolution".
10. In a disappointment to business and especially private entrepreneurs, Beijing did not announce any major economic adjustments or stimulus measures during the "Two-sessions". The establishment of crucial economic directions and personnel changes might be postponed until the Third Plenum.

The main targets for development this year are projected as follows:

1. GDP growth of around 5 percent;
2. over 12 million new urban jobs;
3. urveyed urban unemployment rate of around 5.5 percent (same as last year);
4. CPI increase of around three percent;
5. Deficit Ratio: three percent (same as last year);
6. Government debt ratio — (last year was 50 percent);
7. Special Government Bond Issue — Yuan 3.9 trillion;
8. The government will issue Yuan 1 trillion yuan (US$139 billion) in ultra long-term special bonds in this and coming years to support "major national strategies" and build "security capacity" in key industries;

9. Yuan 10.4 billion (US$1.4 billion) will go to upgrading industries and modernizing manufacturing;
10. growth in personal income in step with economic growth;
11. a basic equilibrium in the balance of payments;
12. grain output of over 650 million metric tons;
13. a drop of around 2.5 percent in energy consumption per unit of GDP; and
14. continued improvements in the environment.

China's Politburo member and Foreign Minister Wang Yi gave a two hour long press conference on March 7, where he spoke on China's role as a peacemaker in the middle-east and Myanmar, its relations with Russia and the US. Regarding Russia he emphasised that "Maintaining and developing China-Russia relations is a strategic choice made by both sides .... and "is also an inevitable requirement in line with the general trend of world development". He used tough language on Taiwan saying "Anyone in Taiwan who wants to pursue "Taiwan independence" will be liquidated by history. Anyone in the international community who condones and supports "Taiwan independence" will surely get burned and suffer the consequences".

After listening to the Premier's report on March 5, senior CCP leaders joined provincial and other delegations in their deliberations. Chinese Premier Li Qiang joined NPC Deputies from Yunnan Province; Politburo Standing Committee (PBSC) member and NPC Chairman Zhao Leji joined his fellow Deputies from Sichuan Province; PBSC member and CPPCC Chairman Wang Huning joined Deputies from Guizhou Province; PBSC member and Vice Premier Ding Xuexiang joined legislators from Liaoning Province; PBSC member and CDIC Secretary Li Xi joined Deputies from Fujian Province; Vice President Han Zheng met deputies from Shandong Province; Politburo (PB) member and Vice Premier Zhang Guoqing attended a review meeting of the TAR delegation presided over by TAR Party Secretary and Leader of the TAR to the NPC, Wang Junzheng; PB member and Foreign Minister Wang Yi participated in the deliberations of the Guangxi delegation; PB member and Director of the CCP CC Propaganda Department Li Shulei met the Jiangxi delegation; PB member and NPC Vice Chairman Li Hongzhong attended the deliberations of the

Gansu province delegation; and PB member and Vice Premier He Lifeng met the Deputies from Inner Mongolia.

The closing meeting of the plenary session of the 14th National People's Congress (NPC) was chaired by CCP CC Politburo Standing Committee (PBSC) member and NPC Chairman Zhao Leji, Executive Chairman of the Presidium of the Conference. Chinese President Xi Jinping, Premier Li Qiang and PBSC members Wang Huning, Cai Qi, Ding Xuexiang, Li Xi, Han Zheng and members of the presidium of the conference took their seats on the rostrum. Li Hongzhong, Wang Dongming, Xiao Jie, Zheng Jianbang, Ding Zhongli, Hao Mingjin, Cai Dafeng, He Wei, Wu Weihua, Tiening, Peng Qinghua, Zhang Qingwei and Lobsang Gyaltsen, were among those present.

Also sitting on the rostrum were: Ma Xingrui, Wang Yi, Yin Li, Shi Taifeng, Liu Guozhong, Li Ganjie, Li Shulei, He Weidong, He Lifeng, Zhang Youxia, Zhang Guoqing, Chen Wenqing, Chen Jining, Chen Min'er, Yuan Jiajun, Huang Kunming, Liu Jinguo, Wang Xiaohong, Wu Zhenglong, Chen Yiqin, Zhang Jun, Ying Yong, Hu Chunhua, Shen Yueyue, Wang Yong, Pabala Glenelg, Ho Hau Wah, Leung Chun-ying, Battelle, Su Hui, Shao Hong, Chen Wu, Mu Hong, Xian Hui, Wang Dongfeng, Jiang Xinzhi, Jiang Zuojun, He Baoxiang, Wang Guangqian, Qin Boyong, Zhu Yongxin, Yang Zhen, and members of the Central Military Commission Liu Zhenli, Miao Hua, Zhang Shengmin, etc.

Responsible persons from relevant departments of the central and state agencies, relevant units of the People's Liberation Army and the Armed Police Force, and various people's organizations attended or observed the conference. Foreign envoys stationed in China attended the conference.

This year, unusually, Chinese President Xi Jinping did not address the closing session of the NPC, something he normally does. For the first time since the practice was instituted in 1993, there was no press conference by the Chinese Premier after the NPC session this year. The announcement said "unless there are special circumstances there will be no press conferences by the Premier for the next few years". This press conference is one of the rare events for the media to interact with the Premier. NPC spokesman Lou Qinjian said (March 5) that China's former Defence Minister Li Shangfu is no longer a NPC representative. The NPC has, however, not yet named a Foreign

Minister to replace former Foreign Minister Qin Gang – who continues to be a member of the 20th CCP CC.

The week-long (March 5-11, 2024) NPC plenary session strengthened and reconfirmed Xi Jinping and the CCP's pre-eminent position. It indicated an emphasis on preserving China's position in the global supply chain and also that Beijing regards manufacturing as important. No measures were announced, however, to stall its slide and give a fillip to China's economy. China's private entrepreneurs will also have been disappointed at the absence of any incentives and the favoured status accorded by the Politburo to State owned Enterprises (SoEs). At its meeting on March 29, the Politburo reiterated that "state-owned enterprises (SoEs) are important material and political foundation of socialism with Chinese characteristics, and they should uphold and strengthen Party leadership, and guard against and defuse risks to safeguard high-quality development". Of importance was the attention given by Xi Jinping to strengthening the armed forces for multi-dimensional warfare (land, air, cyber, space and sea) by using advanced technology and to enhance the PLA Navy's maritime capabilities.

This was first published by the Centre for China Analysis and Strategy (CCAS) and Vivekananda International Foundation (VIF) in March 31, 2024.

19. Signs of Disquiet in Chinese Communist Party as 20th Congress Draws Near

Amid efforts by Chinese President Xi Jinping to marshal resources to imprint his image on people's minds as one among those in the pantheon of China's Greats, there are signs of possible disquiet in the Chinese Communist Party (CCP).

The 20th Congress of the Chinese Communist Party (CCP) scheduled for late next year is crucial for Xi Jinping. Seeing himself as the Child of Red Destiny, Xi Jinping feels he needs to be at the helm to lead China to its rise. To all intents, therefore, he appears to be making a definite bid for securing China's three top and most powerful posts for a third time, unprecedented since 1980!

In addition to the extensive coverage of Xi Jinping's activities in the official media, there have been efforts to project Xi Jinping's personality. On May 7, 2021, for example, a lengthy special Xinhua article captioned: *Studying in progress | "He is really super kind - Xi Jinping in the eyes of college students* listed students in different places praising Xi Jinping's personal qualities over the years at varying stages of Xi Jinping's career. They highlighted his "simplicity, approachability, kindness and caring nature".

Xi Jinping's efforts to reduce opposition has gone down to the provinces. At a seminar in Beijing for the "main leading cadres" at the provincial and ministerial level on January 11, Xi Jinping pointed to the "success" of his signature project for poverty alleviation. He emphasised that great historical achievements have been made in building a moderately prosperous society, and asserted that "Realizing common prosperity is not only an economic issue, but also a major political issue related to the party's ruling foundation". Underscoring the benefits of the CCP's leadership, he told the cadres: "Our country's economic strength, scientific and technological strength, comprehensive national power, and people's living standards have jumped to a new great level, becoming the world's second largest economy, the largest industrial country, the largest trading country of goods, and the country with the largest foreign exchange reserves, a gross domestic product of over 100 trillion yuan, a per capita GDP of over 10,000 US dollars, an urbanization rate of over 60 percent and a middle-income group of over 400 million people."

The Chinese financial magazine Caixin (May 7) reported that five provincial capitals namely Changchun, Nanjing, Nanchang, Shijiazhuang and Lanzhou announced the appointment or departure of top officials during the month. It added that leadership changes in provincial capitals are the most important part of local government personnel reshuffles. A month later there were leadership changes in Shenzhen. These efforts and the CCP's ideological campaigns have been augmented by that against corruption. This year alone, at least 129 senior provincial officials have been placed under investigation by the Party's anti-corruption watchdog the Central Discipline Inspection Commission (CDIC). There are also reports of the dismissal of a couple of members of the CCP Central Committee (CC) and National People's Congress (NPC).

But there is discontent among intellectuals, academics, students, and business entrepreneurs. Many are critical of Xi Jinping and the CCP leadership for the deterioration in relations with the US and what they perceive as China's growing isolation. Such negative sentiments increased in 2020 with the perceived mishandling of the coronavirus pandemic outbreak and criticism spilled over onto China's tightly controlled social media despite the personal risk to the authors of the posts. Many of those who criticised Xi Jinping were later detained, jailed or punished. Aware of the discontent among academics, students and intellectuals, the CCP has imposed progressively stringent controls on them. On April 16, the CCP CC promulgated the revised "Regulations on the Work of Primary Organizations in Ordinary Higher Education Institutions of the Communist Party of China" and issued a notice requesting urgent compliance to all regions and departments. These Regulations highlighted the Party's central role in academia and pointed out that they are guided by 'Xi Jinping Thought on Socialism with Chinese Characteristics for a New Era'.

Over the past couple of years Xi Jinping has launched successive ideological campaigns in the CCP and People's Liberation Army (PLA) to instil greater adherence to more purist Marxism-Leninist-Mao Zedong Thought to counter any "liberal" thinking and disseminate his own thoughts on various subjects. A 'Party History Study and Education' campaign was launched earlier this year to mark the CCP's centenary and is being rigorously implemented. China's official media, including the *People's Daily*, have publicised that as part of this campaign 'study sessions' have been organised in China's provinces, Ministries and departments in the government, in universities, colleges and schools and the PLA.

The *People's Daily* (April 16) reported that a Central Propaganda Group for Party History Study and Education had travelled to various parts of China to spread the education campaign among the masses. It disclosed that the group held sessions in more than 30 localities and 110 government organs and universities, and organised more than 70 interactive exchange activities. It said the group reached out to more than 22 million people through television and online broadcasting. The *People's Daily* said the propaganda group had successfully explained the "glorious course of the Chinese Communist Party's century of struggle," its contributions to the nation and the major theoretical achievements of sinicized Marxism.

The Ministry of Foreign Affairs (MoFA) too recently disclosed that the MoFA's Party school had carried out various activities and a 12-day "special study" of Party history which were attended by more than 400 directly affiliated party organizations and tens of thousands of party members. It said experts from the Central Party History and Literature Research Institute gave lectures to more than 50 department-level leading cadres.

Similarly, the state-owned CCTV reported on May 13 that the powerful Central Political and Legal Commission, which is at the apex of China's security apparatus, was "guiding" party members and cadres to study party history. It quoted the Central Political and Legal Commission as saying "The soul is forged, the sword is inwardly rectified, and the party and the people are trustworthy, reliable, and can be assured of an iron army of politics and law".

Possible signs of disquiet inside the Party, however, seem to be emerging. Chinese leaders have, over the decades, often used the Hongkong media to overcome opposition or float controversial ideas which could face opposition within the Chinese leadership.

A prominent example is Deng Xiaoping's well-known "southern tour" (or nanxun). Deng Xiaoping's 'open door' and reform policies were threatening to stall because of opposition from cadres within the party who blamed the policies for letting in foreign influences and ideas that had led to the Tiananmen events of 1989 and polluted China's atmosphere. To bypass opposition and mobilise popular supports for the policies, Deng Xiaoping undertook an unannounced 'southern tour' and visited Shenzhen, Zhuhai, Guangzhou and Shanghai, from January 18 to February 21, 1992. It was only when the Hongkong media reported his presence in southern China that the Chinese media picked up the reports and provided extensive coverage of his visit.

Another more recent example was when Prof Jin Wei, a senior faculty of the Central Party School gave an interview on June 6, 2013, to the Chinese-language Hongkong-based Asia Weekly captioned 'Reopen talks and resolve Tibetan Issues'. There had been no talks between the Chinese and the Dalai Lama's envoys since 2010. This interview proposed a new initiative, obviously floated by a group of very senior CCP cadres, but which could be controversial. Jin Wei's backers were powerful enough to send her to the UK, US etc to publicise the ideas but, in the end, no contact materialised because those opposed were able to prevail.

Now 80-year-old former Chinese Premier Wen Jiabao has written an article which was serialised (March 25-April 15) by the little-known 'Macau Guide'. In the article, Wen Jiabao recalled the difficult times of poverty of his childhood and his mother's lessons to him, but it were his concluding remarks that attracted public attention. He wrote, "However, only sincere, simple and kind emotions cannot be faked. I sympathize with the poor and the weak, and oppose bullying and oppression. In my mind, China should be a country full of fairness and justice, where there will always be respect for the human heart, humanity, and always have the temperament of youth, freedom and struggle. I have screamed and fought for this. This is the truth that life taught me, and it was also given by my mother"." His remarks resonated with Chinese netizens and went viral on China's social media.

Wen Jiabao had, when he was Premier (2003-2013), also occasionally made carefully crafted yet ambiguous statements hinting at the need for reform, democracy and more openness. His recent remarks could, therefore, have been interpreted as hinting at the need for reform and more openness as well as a critique of Xi Jinping's policies. Implicit endorsement of this was evident in the decision of the authorities to take down the post overnight.

More recently on May 13, the CCP's official authoritative newspaper *People's Daily* published a box item on its front page to remember the dead on the 13th anniversary of the Wenchuan Earthquake which occurred on May 12, 2008, and killed nearly 70,000 people and injured more than 370,000 with 18,000 missing. It is the 10th, 15th or 20th anniversaries that are normally commemorated in China. The appearance of the *People's Daily* box item is, therefore, intriguing. Its appearance would suggest allusion to former Chinese Premier Wen Jiabao whose popularity was boosted when he visited the site of the earthquake within hours of its occurrence. In contrast, Chinese President Xi Jinping failed to visit Wuhan at the height of the Covid-19 pandemic. This had provoked comments on China's social media at the time.

In the run up to the 20th Party Congress, Chinese President Xi Jinping is taking tough measures to thin out, if not suppress, opposition. It will be interesting to observe whether other hints of opposition to Xi Jinping and his bid to continue for a third term emerge. In the interim, Xi Jinping cannot afford to appear weak and this will dictate his policies on domestic and international issues. On territorial issues there will certainly not even be a suggestion of weakness or willingness to yield ground. The situation on the India-China border needs to be viewed in this backdrop.

This was first published by the Centre for China Analysis and Strategy (CCAS) and Vivekananda International Foundation (VIF) in May 17, 2021.

20. 'Xi Jinping and CCP Leadership Wary of Colour Revolution before 20th Party Congress'

Anxiety in the leadership echelons of the Chinese Communist Party (CCP) of the possibility of a "colour revolution" in China has transparently risen in the past month or so. While Chinese cadres, including Xi Jinping, have harboured such apprehensions since the disintegration of the Communist Party of the Soviet Union (CPSU) in 1991, these concerns have increased markedly since the rapid deterioration in relations with the United States. There is growing consensus in China that Beijing and Washington will remain locked in a power competition in the foreseeable future despite the change of leadership in the US. Wang Jisi, President of the Institute of International and Strategic Studies at Peking University and one of China's top experts on America, stated this January, that the rivalry had gone far beyond great-power competition and ideological differences.

A clear illustration of this heightened concern was the appearance of an editorial authored by the Ministry of State Security (MoSS) in the *People's Daily* on April 15. It said "We must be soberly aware that various hostile forces have not stopped...subversion and sabotage of the Party leadership...and are always planning 'colour revolutions' in our country." The editorial asserted that the MoSS is standing firm against: "All kinds of risks and challenges to the Party leadership and the socialist system"; "All kinds of risks and challenges to sovereignty, security, and development interests"; and "All kinds of risks and challenges that endanger China's core interests and major principles". The same day the Global Times published an article warning: "West backed color revolution a 'top threat' to China's national, political security!"

A subsequent editorial in the Global Times (April 19) was more specific. Asserting that the US has supported "colour revolutions" around the world, it described the US as "extremely untrustworthy". The editorial argued "China, as a newly targeted "strategic competitor" of the US, is fortunate that we have witnessed all the colour revolutions in the world in the past 30 years. This is equivalent to having gotten politically vaccinated and received a boost shot to enhance the effectiveness. The Chinese people must protect the fruitful achievements of the People's Republic of China, and remain sober-minded about the US' repeated deceptive clamour that the strategic game between the US and China is a battle between "democracies and autocracies." China must continue to grow its national strength and weaken the ability of the US to pressure it 'from a position of strength' China can only be a friend with whom the US has to coexist because it cannot crush."

In a related move the Chinese Institutes of Contemporary International Relations (CICIR), among China's more influential think-tanks and directly subordinate to the MoSS, on April 14 established the 'Research Center for Overall National Security Concept' in Beijing.

The *People's Daily* editorial was reinforced with the release of new anti-espionage regulations by China's Ministry of State Security (MoSS). These were publicised by the *People's Daily* and Xinhua on April 26, 2021.

The new anti-espionage regulations, which became effective immediately, allow the national security authority to draw up lists of a broad range of entities including companies, organisations and, potentially universities and private businesses, as if they are sensitive government agencies susceptible to foreign infiltration. MoSS officials explained (April 26) that "Overseas espionage and intelligence agencies and hostile forces have intensified their infiltration into China, with more diverse methods and in broader fields, which pose a serious threat to China's national security and interests." Stating that "the core and vital areas still have issues such as which organizations bear the primary responsibilities for anti-espionage security and prevention measures that are not institutionalized", they said the regulations clarify "what, who and how" to guard against foreign espionage. The MoSS will provide companies and organisations susceptible to foreign infiltration with work manuals, guides, and other publicity and education materials. The authorities will also issue written guidance, organize trainings, hold work meetings, and supervise anti-espionage work using different methods.

It should normally have been the task of the Ministry of Public Security (MPS), responsible for domestic security and counter espionage, to issue such regulations. However, a Party inspection group that was sent into the MPS in late 2020 submitted its report on February 3, where it criticised the MPS for "not doing enough to remove the remaining poison" of the ex-Head of the Political and Legal Affairs Commission Zhou Yongkang and Vice Ministers of Public Security Meng Hongwei and Sun Lijun. A campaign was, thereafter, launched to "cleanse" the country's security apparatus. A shake-up of the powerful MPS seems to still be underway as indicated by the removal recently of the heads of three powerful law enforcement bodies in Shenzhen.

The warning sounded by the Ministry of State Security has been buttressed by China's Provincial Party Secretaries. They have also in recent weeks been stressing the need for heightened vigilance.

Fujian Province Party Secretary Yin Li explained that the security agenda includes protecting governance, ideological security, critical infrastructure, strategic resources and technology etc. Ruan Chengfa, Party Secretary of the border province of Yunnan, wrote a lengthy article captioned,"In-depth practice of the overall national security concept - Build a strong security barrier in the southwest of the motherland', which was published by the *People's Daily* on April 22. It praised Xi Jinping for having "creatively put forward the concept of overall national security". The article stressed "We will comprehensively strengthen anti-infiltration, anti-subversion, anti-terrorism, and anti-separatism struggles, strictly prevent and accurately combat infiltration and sabotage activities by foreign hostile forces, and firmly maintain regime security and institutional security." It referred to border security and said China will "Strengthen the protection of overseas interests and take all measures to protect the safety of our enterprises and personnel in neighboring countries". Meanwhile, in the Tibet Autonomous Region (TAR) a vigorous campaign has been underway with leaders from Beijing and TAR exhorting local cadres, especially in border prefectures and counties, that "the efforts should centre on safeguarding the country's unity and strengthening ethnic solidarity, resolutely combating separatism, forestalling and defusing major risks and challenges and continuously consolidate the foundations of long-term peace and stability in Tibet".

Concern about 'colour revolution' seems to have been rekindled in the People's Liberation Army (PLA) too. In a publication of the Chinese Academy of Social Sciences (CASS), two PLA officers from the Political College of the National Defense University and the Joint Logistics Support Force Longyan Comprehensive Warehouse Support Team respectively, admitted there are "new challenges to the party's absolute leadership over the army to take root at the grassroots level". It said "the officers and soldiers of the new era generally lack the training in the severe and complex environment and the baptism of blood and fire on the battlefield" and "often lack understanding and mastery of the party's absolute leadership over the military" and "the extremely deceptive political propaganda of the hostile forces".

Underscoring that it is important "to clear out the fog of thought", it said "President Xi Jinping pointed out that some Western countries are stepping up instigation of 'color revolutions' in our country, stepping up the implementation of online "Cultural Cold War" and "political genetic modification" projects in an attempt to root out our military officers and soldiers and pull the military out of the party banner. The challenges we face in the field of ideology and political security are very serious". In conclusion the article recommended "as young officers and soldiers of the "media generation", they will inevitably be involved in the struggle of public opinion. This urgently requires us to change our minds, carry out online struggles like a war, and continuously strengthen the ability of officers and soldiers to resist the erosion of social corruption and the infiltration and destruction of hostile forces."

Such a candid article on ideological weakness in the PLA has not been noticed for quite some time. Between 2011-2013, numerous intellectuals, university professors and "liberal" Chinese economists were noticed advocating 'new liberalism", calling for political reform and arguing that the PLA should be an army of the State and not subservient to the CCP. The CCP and PLA leadership was troubled by the circulation of this 'hostile' foreign-inspired propaganda. A Liberation Army Daily article on June 17, 2012, raised for the first time the issue of factional "sub-loyalties" in the PLA. Promptly thereafter year-long political education campaigns were launched throughout the PLA consecutively. These continue.

With the PLA moving to become a technology-based armed force, it started focussing on recruiting high school and college graduates since 2001. Data from China's Ministry of Education and *Xinhua News Agency* reveals that by 2019, the total number of high school and college students enlisted in the Army were 1.24 million. The PLA Military Academies also enrol students and in 2018 they enrolled 30,500 students. These college and high school graduates presently comprise the largest single source of recruits. Concern persists in the senior echelons of the PLA that such recruits might have got influenced by "liberal" ideas from their teachers and professors. Consecutive year-long political education campaigns are now being conducted throughout the PLA.

Academics and students were prominent in the criticism of Xi Jinping and his policies when the authorities mishandled the outbreak of the Covid-19 pandemic. In 2020-2021, Chinese businessmen and intellectuals were also complicit. Though Xi Jinping has cracked down on the critics and many have since been detained or severely penalised, resentment continues to linger below the surface.

Accordingly, the Central Discipline Inspection Commission (CDIC) announced (April 28) that in its latest round of "discipline inspections" it will 'inspect' 31 universities and the Ministry of Education. The Paper (April 28) said that while details of the upcoming inspections have not been released, a priority will be to make sure that university faculty and administrators are loyal CCP members or abide by Party discipline.

Warnings of efforts by the US and West to promote colour revolution under the garb of 'universal values' are, therefore, being sounded in universities. An article by two Anhui University Professors published in the China Education Daily (May 13) emphasised the importance of "resisting the negative impact of "universal values" on young students". Describing 'universal value' as the "strategic attempt of ideological struggle", the article explained that the usual tactic is to "slander and vilify other countries at the ideological level under the banner of freedom, democracy, and human rights". It cautioned that following "the disintegration of the Soviet Union, some Western countries intensified their efforts to promote the so-called 'universal values' necessitating "our high vigilance".

A lengthy article in the *Global Times* (May 16) highlighted these anxieties. Titled "US embassy increasingly offensive in pushing 'peaceful evolution' in China by roping in activists with money", the article pointed to a recent initiative of the US Embassy in China to "support non-governmental organizations (NGOs) including think tanks, civil society organizations and individuals ... to carry out activities to spread American values and enhance the understanding of the US among the Chinese people, among other objectives. The maximum amount for each award is $30,000." Li Haidong, Professor at the Institute of International Relations at China Foreign Affairs University, was quoted as warning that this program is being initiated by the US State Department "to propagate and infiltrate all parts of China, including Hong Kong and Macao". He said it provides funding and transfer benefits to "specified individuals" or "organizations" possibly even to instigate a "color revolution". The *Global Times* said "analysts pointed out that in addition to directly propagandizing Western democracy and its rule of law, it often uses the guise of caring for women's, animal and minority rights to export "color revolution"." It quoted other Chinese experts who claimed that US cultural and other programmes were designed to further "peaceful evolution".

The 20th Congress of the Chinese Communist Party (CCP) scheduled to be held towards the end of next year, is crucial for incumbent Chinese President Xi Jinping who appears intent on securing China's three top posts for the third time. The run up to the Congress is a sensitive period and the Chinese leadership will be aware that popular resentment, and the opposition to Xi Jinping that exists inside the CCP, could find public expression. China's leadership would also perceive the recently stepped-up US and Western criticism of human rights violations in Xinjiang and Tibet as attempts to fan the existing restiveness in these border provinces. The CICIR and CASS had warned the Politburo in April 2020 of such a possibility. Xi Jinping has visibly started taking steps to counter any such efforts.

This was first published by the Centre for China Analysis and Strategy (CCAS) and Vivekananda International Foundation (VIF) in May 31, 2021.

21. China's Communist Party Revises its History Yet Again in Time for Use by Xi Jinping

History and the power of the narrative have always been important to authoritarian regimes. Communist regimes have elevated their importance by using them to indoctrinate entire generations with sanitised versions of events authorised by those in power. Under Chinese President Xi Jinping the Chinese Communist Party (CCP) has further refined the impact of the narrative by using propaganda and technology to keep the media and social media in check. Since the last few years, China's security apparatus has also been co-opted to try and prevent western 'liberal thinking' from infiltrating and swaying China's students, academics and intellectuals.

Using the media and school history text books, the CCP has not only been able to airbrush out leaders who crossed the line so that they no longer exist, but blank out entire events from public memory. As part of this effort, 'revised' versions of the Chinese Communist Party (CCP)'s history have been published every ten years. Editions of the Party History were published in 1999, 2001, 2011 and the latest now in 2021. But this is probably the first time in the history of the Chinese Communist Party that the CCP Central Committee (CC) has simultaneously launched a year-long, nationwide 'Party History Study and Education Campaign'. Interestingly, the important 20th Party Congress, crucial for Xi Jinping, is scheduled to be held next year!

The CCP CC's Party History and Literature Research Institute released a new 'Brief History of the Communist Party of China' on April 13, 2021. Its release coincided with the new campaign to study the history of the Party. The study-campaign encompasses the 92-million strong CCP, the People's Liberation Army (PLA) and schools and universities across China. It is listed as a mandated teaching resource in schools. Its importance can be gauged from the reports, articles and commentaries that publicise it daily in the Party's official *People's Daily*, the *PLA Daily*, the State-owned CCTV and other media. The CCP's leading fortnightly theoretical journal Qiu Shi (Seeking Truth) on March 31, reproduced a hitherto unpublished speech on the importance of studying Party History delivered by Xi Jinping on February 20. It specifically listed eight important points identified by CCP CC General Secretary and Chinese President Xi Jinping for study.

The *Brief History of the Communist Party of China*' is the latest updated version of the Party's history. Its release has coincided with the hundredth year of the CCP's founding anniversary. The 'Brief History' and the study campaign have political significance. They promote Xi Jinping's image and elevate him as one of China's three most important communist leaders at par with Mao Zedong and Deng Xiaoping. The Brief History reinforces the narrative pushed since 2013 that China, under Xi Jinping, has embarked on another thirty-year era like those of Mao and Deng before him!

Among the important differences noticed between the latest version of the 'Brief History of the Communist Party of China' and the older version is the apparently reduced emphasis on Mao's era. While there were three or four chapters on Mao Zedong's 30-year era, the new version encapsulates it in only two chapters. Further, the old edition of "The History of the Party" covered the ten-year period of the Cultural Revolution in one lengthy 11,000-word chapter with at least six sections. It discussed the destruction of the "Lin Biao Group", efforts to correct the "ultra-leftist trend" and smashing of the "Gang of Four". The new version has shrunk this to just one page with a superficial description. References to party rectification, the anti-rightist struggle, "Great Leap Forward" etc. are absent.

An initial comparison of the various editions reveals the difference in treatment of the tumultuous Cultural Revolution decade. The titles of the relevant sections in the different Editions make this self-evident:

1991 Edition:

Chapter: The initiation of the Cultural Revolution

1. The full-scale civil strife that "overthrew everything";
2. The destruction of the Lin Biao Group and the frustration of efforts to correct "Left" errors;

3. Opening up a new situation in diplomatic work;
4. The collapse of the Jiang Qing Group

2001 Edition:

Chapter: Ten Years of Civil strife of the Cultural Revolution

1. The launch of the "Cultural Revolution"; and total civil strife
2. The destruction of the Lin Biao Group and the efforts to correct the ultra-leftist trend
3. The struggle against the "Gang of Four"; and the overall rectification in 1975
4. The victory of crushing the Jiang Qing Group

2011 Edition:

Chapter: The 10-year civil strife of the Cultural Revolution

1. The launch of the Cultural Revolution.
2. From the "full seizure of power" to the Party's Ninth Congress and the Third Party.
3. The destruction of the Lin Biao Group and the efforts to correct the ultra-leftism.
4. The new situation in diplomatic work.
5. The overall rectification in 1975.
6. The smashing of the "Gang of Four". The victory of the counter-revolutionary group

2021 Edition:

Chapter: The Exploration and Tortuous Development of Socialist Construction

1. The Eighth National Congress of the Communist Party of China and a good start for China's socialist construction.
2. The arduous exploration of the socialist road.
3. The development of socialist construction amid twists and turns.

In its analysis of the *Brief History of the Communist Party of China*, the Hongkong-based *Apple Daily* (April 13) said this version has put a "more hawkish and nationalistic touch on major events, including foreign sanctions and Hong Kong's handover, compared with an older version". The authors, it added, "have concentrated on how the party stepped up efforts to deal with sanctions imposed on China by Western countries following the bloody Tiananmen Square crackdown in 1989" and noted that the US and Europe imposed an arms embargo on China for its bloody crackdown on pro-democracy protesters in Beijing on June 4, 1989.

The *Apple Daily* observed that while not negating Deng Xiaoping's assessment of Mao Zedong, "The new book has also significantly downsized coverage of the Cultural Revolution, a decade of national turmoil starting 1966, to one page of sketchy descriptions instead of an entire 11,000-word chapter in the old edition". While the older version held Mao Zedong responsible for initiating the Cultural Revolution, which became a "serious disaster" for the Chinese people, the latest edition does not blame Mao. Instead, it credits Mao with "exploring ways in his incessant fight against corruption, special privileges and bureaucratism within the party and government ... Many of his correct ideas for building socialism were not thoroughly implemented, leading to internal turmoil."

Predictably the new version endorses the aggressive foreign policy being pursued by Xi Jinping. *Apple Daily* pointed out that "instead of focusing on former leader Deng Xiaoping's low-profile diplomacy approach, as in the older edition, the latest version recalled Deng's hawkish remarks during a meeting with former US President Richard Nixon in November 1989". At that time Deng Xiaoping told Nixon that the Chinese people would "never beg for the cancellation of the sanctions" even if they dragged on for 100 years.

Owned by Hong Kong media tycoon Jimmy Lai, who has just this fortnight been awarded a one-year prison sentence under the National Security Law for supporting pro-Hong Kong independence demonstrators, the *Apple Daily* naturally has a particular focus on Hong Kong. It observed that unlike the 2011 edition, which said Hong Kong enjoyed a high degree of autonomy and kept its previous social and economic systems unchanged under the "one country, two systems" principle, the new version of Party History describes the handover as a "brilliant and great achievement in the history of the Chinese race," and as an event that placed Hong Kong under "China's national governing machine to share an inseparable path of development".

The latest version of the CCP's history endorses Xi Jinping's policies. This week the *People's Daily* publicised that a leading group under the CCP CC Propaganda Department has been tasked with disseminating the contents of the latest 'Brief History of the Communist Party of China' nationwide. It said the Leading Group has made over 30 reports in various localities, organized more than 70 interactive exchange activities, and delivered more than 110 reports to government organs and universities. It had reached more than 22 million people through television and online broadcasting. This campaign reinforces the other efforts to enhance Xi Jinping's image.

Xi Jinping has also flashed the steel of the security apparatus to mobilise nationalism and buttress the History campaign and rein in dissenters. The National Security Education Campaign appears more robust this year with some Provincial Party Secretaries noticed as writing articles emphasising its importance. A *Global Times* (April 15) article highlighted: 'West-backed colour revolution a 'top threat' to China's national, political security'. Separately, in a rare editorial in the *People's Daily* (April 15), the Ministry of State Security (MoSS) publicised China's security concerns. It warned: "We must be soberly aware that various hostile forces have not stopped...subversion and sabotage of the Party leadership...and are always planning 'colour revolutions' in our country." The MoSS assured it is standing firm against: "All kinds of risks and challenges to the Party leadership and the socialist system"; "All kinds of risks and challenges to sovereignty, security, and development interests"; and "All kinds of risks and challenges that endanger China's core interests and major principles".

These campaigns are especially important this year as Xi Jinping prepares to secure a third term - unprecedented since 1980 - at the next Party Congress in 2022!

This was first published by the Centre for China Analysis and Strategy (CCAS) and Vivekananda International Foundation (VIF) in April 24, 2021.

22. Quick Glimpse into China's Upcoming Annual 'Big Two' Sessions

With just a couple of weeks to go before China's 'Big Two' (the popular name for the plenary sessions of China's version of a parliament), the National People's Congress (NPC) and the top political advisory body, the Chinese People's Political Consultative Conference (CPPCC) – there are no signs of any easing in the Chinese Communist Party (CCP)'s efforts to promote Chinese communist ideology. The deliberations at the NPC and CPPCC sessions will reveal China's priorities for this year and the longer term. The Reports are expected to bear the unmistakable imprimatur of Xi Jinping.

As done last year, the authorities are taking precautions to ensure the health and safety of the well over 5,000 Deputies, delegates and officials who will gather in Beijing for the sessions at a time when the pandemic has not yet abated. The *People's Daily* (February 2) disclosed that the number of journalists permitted to cover the Fourth Session of the Thirteenth National People's Congress (NPC) and the Fourth Session of the Thirteenth CPPCC National Committee, which will open in Beijing on March 5 and March 4, 2021, respectively, will be restricted. It clarified that some Chinese and foreign journalists in Beijing would be invited to cover the conference, but foreign journalists will not be invited on temporary visits to Beijing. Interviews would mainly be conducted through the Internet, video, written, etc. In accordance with past practice, stringent security measures can be anticipated to blanket Beijing.

Preparatory to the annual plenary sessions the CCP has continued the steady build-up of Xi Jinping's personality cult. Media coverage of Xi Jinping has been increasing since he took over the country's three top posts in November 2012 and, according to a very recent analysis it today surpasses even that of Mao Zedong. A recent example is the article in the CCP's official newspaper

People's Daily on February 24. The article was spread over the entire first three pages of the newspaper and lauded Xi Jinping's personal contribution and role in the poverty alleviation campaign that was pronounced to have been successfully completed on schedule in November 2020. The article left no doubt of Xi Jinping's role mentioning him 139 times!

Ideological campaigns to fortify China with communism and reinforce the commitment of Party members have continued to be initiated. In February alone two campaigns were launched. Most recent is the campaign to 'study the development of Party history learning and education'. It was kicked-off with Xi Jinping's "important" speech at the Party History Study and Education Mobilization Conference held in Beijing on February 20, which was telecast by the state-run CCTV the same day. In his speech Chinese President Xi Jinping emphasised that the development of party history learning and education in the whole party is a 'new starting point for the party Central Committee based on the party's century-old history, coordinating the overall strategy of the great rejuvenation of the Chinese nation and major changes in the world unseen in a century, and mobilizing the whole party and the country'. He exhorted "all comrades in the party" to learn history, learn party history etc. *Xinhua* (February 21) explained that "As the Communist Party of China is about to usher in its centennial birthday, the Party Central Committee with Comrade Xi Jinping at its core requires the development of party history learning and education throughout the party, declaring the firm determination of the Communists in the new era to keep their original aspirations in mind and keep their mission in mind." The Xinhua article marks the start of a new education campaign in the CCP to study Party history.

Earlier on February 4, the *People's Daily* front-paged an important over 6000-character editorial signalling the start of a campaign to energise the CCP's 130 million-strong Young Pioneers that was created in 1949. Outlining the start of a serious effort, it said the Young Pioneers is "a school for children to learn socialism and communism with Chinese characteristics, and is a reserve team for building socialism and communism". It stressed that the "Young Pioneers, comprehensively strengthen the building of the party ... and focus on training Communism successor, focusing on inheriting the red gene".

It was interesting that the article, published by the Editorial Department of the *People's Daily*, included references to 'Xi Jinping' and 'Xi Jinping Thought' six times, but mentioned none of China's other leaders like Mao Zedong or Deng Xiaoping!

The centrepiece and focus of the NPC and CPPCC sessions will be the 'Report on the Work of the Government' that will be presented by Chinese Premier Li Keqiang. The report will detail China's achievements over the past year despite the deleterious economic effects of the Covid-19 pandemic. The economy will be a focus of Li Keqiang's Work Report. Some CPPCC Delegates have been quoted by Asia Times as saying that Premier Li Keqiang would set a "soft" GDP growth target, around 4-5 percent, for the year. Other important aspects in the Work Report would include the need to promote agriculture and increase food-grain production, the decline in China's working-age population, and the crucial technology sector, which after former US President Trump targeted China's 'Made in China' programme was set back by at least five years. Professor Wong Kam-fai, a CPPCC Delegate and Deputy Dean of the Chinese University of Hong Kong's Department of Systems Engineering and Engineering Management, was quoted by *Asia Times* as saying China's chip and integrated circuit sector would need eight to 10 years to play catch-up and even pull ahead of Western competitors to eventually tackle the United States' export bans. It said he expressed optimism that China may narrow the gap in chip design and manufacturing in the mid-2030s and create a TSMC-like chipmaker by then.

Agriculture and grain production are sensitive issues for China's leadership. The Chinese leadership's apprehensions of a potential global food grain shortage within the next 10 years were highlighted in April last year by a current member of the CPPCC National Committee and former Vice Minister of the CCP Central Committee (CC)'s International Liaison Department (ILD). As it has done for the past 18 years, the CCP CC issued its Central Document No: 1 on Agriculture the first Document of 2021. The document stressed that efforts will be made to vitalise China's rural sector, modernise agriculture and raise farmer's incomes. Reporting the issue of Document No: 1, the state-owned CGTN explained that rural income growth is expected to outpace urban income growth and that the modernisation of agriculture and rural areas will make significant progress and construction of rural infrastructure facilities will be basically completed by 2025. The Document urged governments at all levels to retain the "red line" of 1.8 billion mu (120 million hectares) of arable land. These will undoubtedly find mention in the Work Report.

The steady decline in China's population despite the full removal of birth restrictions on the population in 2015 are causing concern to China's leadership. There was a 15 percent decline from the 11.8 million babies registered in 2019 combined with the drop in China's marriage rate, which plunged to 6.6 per 1,000 people in 2019, the lowest level in 14 years. China's National Statistics Bureau has estimated that China had 254 million elderly residents aged 60 or above in 2019, or 18 percent of the whole population of 1.4 billion. China's Ministry of Civil Affairs expects that number to rise to 300 million by 2025, prompting concerns that China's state pension scheme could run out of funding by 2035. This is a vital issue of maintaining social stability for the Party. The "Recommendations of the Central Committee of the Communist Party of China on Formulating the Fourteenth Five-Year Plan for National Economic and Social Development and the Long-term Goals for 2035", dwelt on the need to formulate a long-term population development strategy. Recently on February 19, China's National Health Commission suggested to the Heilongjiang, Jilin and Liaoning regional governments that they should submit a pilot program for implementing a comprehensive family planning policy in the region. The suggestion was made in a response to a proposal by some NPC Deputies.

Technology is an important area of endeavour for China's leaders and will feature prominently in Chinese Premier Li Keqiang's Work Report. The state-owned CCTV News highlighted on February 14, that "Technological independence and self-reliance is the strategic support of national development" and that the Central Economic Work Conference at the end of last year had prioritised that strengthening the national strategic scientific and technological capabilities is the first key task of this year. It disclosed that during his inspections on the eve of the Spring Festival over the years, General Secretary Xi Jinping has visited scientific and technological workers many times and that "General Secretary Xi Jinping is very concerned about technological innovation". *Xinhua* separately noted that President Xi Jinping or Premier Li Keqiang may attend the panel discussions of NPC and CPPCC deputies from the nation's research institutes as well as private tech companies to seek policy recommendations.

Li Keqiang's Work Report will state the progress made in this sector. The Beijing-based *Economic Observer* newspaper noted that sectors like chips, jet engines, next-generation telecommunication solutions and vaccines and drugs against infectious diseases, would receive ample funding. Civil-Military Fusion is also playing a role. Huawei, under the auspices of the Ministry of Industry and Information Technology, was reported by *Asia Times* at the end of January 2021, as having initiated the pooling of scientific human resources of Peking University, Tsinghua University, the People's Liberation Army's National University of Defense Technology as well as 90 Chinese chip designers and foundries for the establishment of a national integrated circuit standardization committee. NPC deputies from Shenzhen, who have been lobbying for more state-private sector joint platforms to foster tech breakthroughs, may present proposals at the NPC session. Politburo Standing Committee member and NPC Chairman Li Zhanshu, is reported to have instructed the NPC secretariat to draft legislative proposals based on recommendations from Huawei, its partners and the science ministry.

An interesting focus will be the deliberations of NPC Deputies and CPPCC Delegates in the various panels. The PLA Deputies will hold discussions in separate panels, but they usually share some views with the media. The NPC will, additionally, approve the Long-Term Goals for 2035 thereby implicitly endorsing confidence in Xi Jinping's leadership.

This was first published by the Centre for China Analysis and Strategy (CCAS) and Vivekananda International Foundation (VIF) in February 25, 2021.

23. Highlights of Chinese Premier Li Keqiang's Government Work Report Presented to NPC and CPPCC Deputies on March 5, 2021

Chinese Premier Li Keqiang presented a 36-page Report on the Work of the Government to the NPC session on March 5, 2021. Delegates to the CPPCC, among others, attended the session and will discuss the Report but not vote on it. The Government Work Report, the draft of which had been discussed and approved at the Politburo meeting chaired by Chinese President Xi Jinping, contained 13 references to Xi Jinping.

The Report highlighted that China had "achieved major strategic success in our response to Covid-19 and China was the world's only major economy to achieve growth". Specifically mentioned was that Xi Jinping had taken personal charge of the fight against Covid-19. It highlighted that China had "attained a complete victory in the fight against poverty, and we scored decisive achievements in securing a full victory in building a moderately prosperous society in all respects", adding that the achievements had received the "approval of our people and global recognition" and "will be remembered in history".

It stressed that despite "facing shocks of a severity rarely seen before", China had maintained security and stability. It claimed "a total of 11.86 million urban jobs were added, and the year-end surveyed urban unemployment rate dropped to 5.2 percent". Credit for the achievements last year was given "to the strong leadership of the Party Central Committee with Comrade Xi Jinping at its core, to the sound guidance of Xi Jinping Thought on Socialism with Chinese Characteristics for a New Era, and to the concerted efforts of the Party, the armed forces, and the Chinese people of all ethnic groups".

Highlights of the Report on the Work of the Government for 2021 are:

- Discussing agriculture, the Report stressed that "The total area of China's farmland must stay above the red line of 120 million hectares". It also disclosed that "Agricultural belts for national food security will be developed. Subsidies for grain growers will be maintained, and minimum purchase prices for rice and wheat will be increased as appropriate. Pilot insurance programs covering total production costs and incomes will be expanded. Grain acreage will be kept stable, per unit crop yield will be increased, and the quality of grains will be raised". It added that China "will adopt multiple measures to expand the production of oil-bearing crops, develop livestock, poultry, and aquaculture farming, and promote stable hog production. Prevention and control of animal and plant diseases will be enhanced.
- It disclosed that "The statutory retirement age will be raised in a phased manner".
- Among the 15 major tasks listed for 2021 to be implemented "under the strong leadership of the Party Central Committee with Comrade Xi Jinping at its core", the first was to "follow the guidance of Xi Jinping Thought on Socialism with Chinese 2 Characteristics for a New Era". Among the others are ensuring stability; creating a new pattern of development; applying systems thinking; ensuring better coordination in pursuing development and upholding security; ensuring stability on six key fronts and maintain security in six key areas; keeping major economic indicators within an appropriate range; expanding domestic demand; strengthening science and technology to provide strategic support for development; and maintaining social harmony and stability.
- Among the main projected targets for this year are: GDP growth of over six percent; creation of over 11 million new urban jobs; maintaining CPI increase of around 3 percent; steady increases in the volume and quality of imports and exports; steady growth in personal income; a drop of around three percent in energy consumption per unit of GDP; and grain output of over 650 million metric tons.
- Offering relief to citizens, the Report said "Government subsidies for basic medical insurance for rural and non-working urban residents will

increase by an average of 30 yuan per person, and subsides for basic public health services will increase by 5 yuan per person". It assured that the government "will increase the basic pension for retirees and the subsidies and living allowances for entitled groups, and work toward unified national management of old-age insurance funds" and will also "increase the benefits for service members and their families, ex-service members, and other entitled groups, while also refining work systems and support mechanisms for ex-service members".

- The Report extended the duration of several temporary policies such as VAT relief for small-scale taxpayers. The VAT threshold for small-scale taxpayers will be raised from 100,000 yuan to 150,000 yuan in monthly sales. The income tax of micro and small enterprises and self-employed individuals on annual taxable income below one million yuan will be halved.
- The Report said China "will continue to implement the three-year action plan for SOE reform, and work to strengthen, expand, and increase the returns on state capital and enhance the strength, quality, and size of SOEs". China, it said, "will also push ahead with mixed-ownership reform in SOEs".
- On Science and Technology and Innovation, the Report said the government "will ensure the stable functioning of funding mechanisms for basic research and boost spending in this area by a considerable sum. Central government expenditures on basic research will increase by 10.6 percent. Research institutes will have more say about how funds should be used, and the mechanisms for assessing projects and evaluating personnel will be refined". As part of the effort and to encourage increase in R&D spending, the government "will continue to implement the policy of granting an extra tax deduction of 75 percent on enterprises' R&D costs, and will raise this to 100 percent for manufacturing enterprises".
- China will this year issue 3.65 trillion yuan of local government special purpose bonds and additionally earmark a total of 610 billion yuan for investment in its budget for key projects already under construction.
- The Report said China will pursue the BRI and promote multilateral trade arrangements including with Japan, ROK, and the US.

- The Report also said China continue to "forge a strong sense of community among the Chinese people and encourage all China's ethnic groups to work in concert for common prosperity and development" and that it "will fully implement the Party's basic policy on religious affairs, and work to guide religions in adapting to socialist society".
- There were five brief paragraphs on China's armed forces. Asserting that "Last year, major success was attained in the development of national defense and the armed forces". It said China's "people's forces, with complete competence and fine conduct, safeguarded China's national security and participated in epidemic control. This year, we will thoroughly implement Xi Jinping's thinking on strengthening the armed forces and the military strategy for the new era, ensure the Party's absolute leadership over the people's armed forces, and strictly implement the system of ultimate responsibility resting with the chairman of the Central Military Commission. We will, bearing in mind the goals set for the centenary of the People's Liberation Army, continue to enhance the political loyalty of the armed forces, strengthen them through reform, science and technology and the training of capable personnel, and run them in accordance with the law. We will boost military training and preparedness across the board, make overall plans for responding to security risks in all areas and for all situations, and enhance the military's strategic capacity to protect the sovereignty, security, and development interests of our country. We will improve the layout of defense-related science, technology, and industry, and enhance the defense mobilization system. We in government at all levels should vigorously support the development of national defense and the armed forces, and conduct extensive activities to promote mutual support between the civilians and the military, so as to forge an ever-closer bond between the people and the military in the new era".
- The Report declared that China "will resolutely guard against and deter external forces' interference in the affairs of Hong Kong and Macao" and reiterated its strong commitment to "the one-China principle and the 1992 Consensus, and to promoting the peaceful growth of relations across the Taiwan Strait and China's reunification".

The Report concluded with the call: "Let us rally more closely around the Party Central Committee with Comrade Xi Jinping at its core, hold high the great banner of socialism with Chinese characteristics, follow the guidance of Xi Jinping Thought on Socialism with Chinese Characteristics for a New Era, and push forward in a concerted effort to complete the objectives and tasks for this year and celebrate the centenary of the Communist Party of China with outstanding achievements. Let each and every of us keep making tireless efforts to build China into a great modern socialist country that is prosperous, strong, democratic ... and fulfill the Chinese Dream of national rejuvenation".

(Comment: There were no references in the Report to Pakistan, North Korea or India or any other countries except, in the context of multilateral trade, to Japan, ROK, and the US. Neither did the Report mention, obliquely or otherwise, the military tension with India.)

This was first published by the Centre for China Analysis and Strategy (CCAS) and Vivekananda International Foundation (VIF) in March 5, 2021.

24. Xi Jinping's Centenary Speech Exudes Confidence and Determination

Centenaries are celebrated around the world. These are occasions for special celebration when it is the centenary of the ruling political party, as well as an opportunity for it to share its assessment of the journey thus far and give a broad sense of direction for the future. The Chinese Communist Party (CCP) Central Committee (CC) General Secretary Xi Jinping did just that in his speech. He also mentioned the Belt and Road Initiative and the 'community of shared destiny', both his personal projects, possibly hinting that he will continue in office beyond the Party Congress scheduled for late next year. The CCP's centenary celebrations held in Beijing on July 1, and especially its General Secretary Xi Jinping's speech, will be closely scrutinised for the clues they yield of the path that the CCP's incumbent leadership hopes to tread over the next hundred years.

An indication that the CCP leadership is adequately sensitive to the military's morale to make an on-course correction was the visible departure from the CCP's announcement in late March that there would be no military parade to mark the Party's centenary. Instead, there was a military parade and a flypast led by the People's Liberation Army Air Force (PLAAF)'s latest generation J-20 'stealth' fighter aircraft and latest ZL-10 transport helicopters flying in the formation '100' at Tiananmen Square. A carefully vetted crowd of 70,000 watched the ceremony.

Earlier on June 28, there was a grand musical extravaganza. It was witnessed by the entire Politburo Standing Committee (PBSC). Among the other invitees were: Ding Xuexiang, Wang Chen, Liu He, Xu Qiliang, Sun Chunlan, Yang Jiechi, Yang Xiaodu, Zhang Youxia, Chen Xi, Hu Chunhua, Guo Shengkun, Huang Kunming, Cai Qi, Li Ruihuan, Jia Qinglin, Zhang Dejiang, Yu Zhengsheng, Zeng Qinghong, Wu Guanzheng, Li Changchun,

He Guoqiang, Liu Yunshan, Zhang Gaoli, You Quan, Cao Jianming, Zhang Chunxian, Shen Yueyue, Ji Bingxuan, Chen Zhu, Wang Dongming, Bai Ma Chilin, Ding Zhongli, Hao Mingjin, Cai Dafeng, Wu Weihua, Wei Fenghe, Wang Yong, Wang Yi, Xiao Jie, Zhao Kezhi, Zhou Qiang, Zhang Jun, Zhang Qingli, Liu Qibao, Pabala Grelange, Wan Gang, He Houhua, Lu Zhangong, Ma Biao, Chen Xiaoguang, Liang Zhenying, Xia Baolong, Li Bin, Battelle, Wang Yongqing, He Lifeng, Su Hui, Zheng Jianbang, Gu Shengzu, Liu Xincheng, He Wei, Shao Hong, Gao Yunlong and Wang Lequan, Wang Zhaoguo, Hui Liangyu, Liu Qi, Wu Yi, Cao Gangchuan, Liu Yandong, Li Yuanchao, Ma Kai, Li Jianguo, Fan Changlong, Meng Jianzhu, Guo Jinlong, He Yong, Du Qinglin, Zhao Hongzhu, Gu Xiulian , Raidi, Wuyunqimuge, Chen Zhili, Zhou Tienong, Wang Shengjun, Chen Changzhi, Zhang Ping, Xiangba Puncuo, Chang Wanquan, Jia Chunwang, Wang Zhongyu, Zhang Huaixi, Li Meng, Bai Lichen, Chen Kuiyuan, Abulaiti Abdure Xiti, Li Zhaozhuo, Huang Mengfu, Zhang Meiying, Zhang Rongming, Qian Yunlu, Sun Jiazheng, Li Jinhua, Zheng Wantong, Wang Zhizhen, Han Qide, Luo Fuhe, Li Haifeng, Chen Yuan, Zhou Xiaochuan, Wang Jiarui, Qi Xuchun, Liu Xiaofeng, Wang Qinmin, and Li Zuocheng, Miao Hua, Zhang Shengmin, Chen Bingde, Li Jinai, Qiao Qingchen, Jing Zhiyuan, Zhao Keshi, Wu Shengli, Ma Xiaotian, Chief Executive of Hong Kong Special Administrative Region Carrie Lam, Chief Executive of Macau Special Administrative Region He Yicheng.

The celebrations culminated with the ceremony at Tiananmen Gate on July 1, where honour guards, military musicians, youthful choristers and thousands of flag-waving guests provided pomp and circumstance for the occasion. The proceedings stretched for nearly two hours and began and ended with the chorus singing patriotic songs like "Without the Communist Party, There Would be No New China"! The Party was honoured with a 100-gun salute and 56 artillery guns fired 56 salvoes acknowledging China's 56 officially recognized ethnic minority nationalities. Among the 29 individuals awarded the 'July 1st Medal', however, there was only one Tibetan and one Uyghur.

On the rostrum were the entire Politburo Standing Committee (PBSC) and Xi Jinping's predecessor Hu Jintao. Xi Jinping was observed on state-owned CCTV deferentially walking a step behind the grey-haired Hu Jintao and, as he walked to the lectern to deliver his speech, politely gesturing Hu Jintao to his seat. Many former Politburo Standing Committee members attended the ceremony on the Tiananmen Gate Tower, including 104-year-old Song Ping, as well as Wen Jiabao, Jia Qinglin, Yu Zhengsheng, Wu Bangguo, Li Ruihuan, Zhang Dejiang, Zeng Qinghong, Li Changchun, Liu Yunshan, Li Lanqing, Wu Guanzheng, He Guoqiang and Zhang Gaoli. Interesting was the presence of Bo Xicheng, brother of Bo Xilai, reported by China's social media, as one of the guests invited to attend the July 1st ceremony on the Tiananmen Gate Tower. Hongkong Chief Executive Carrie Lam was also present.

However, 95-year Jiang Zemin, 93-year ex-Premier Zhu Rongji and former Politburo Standing Committee (PBSC) member and Vice Premier Luo Gan who is 88 years of age, were absent, possibly because of their age and reported ill health.

The CCP's International Liaison Department had requested political parties from around the world to send congratulatory letters to the CPP on the occasion. Such requests were made to Indian political parties too, but only the Communist Party of India (CPI) and Communist Party of India (Marxist) (CPI-M) responded positively.

Xi Jinping's nearly hour-long speech was crafted to exude confidence blended with aggression and nationalism. It was calculated as much to concretise the CCP's monopoly on power in China as to rally nationalist sentiment against anti-China foreign forces and mobilise the people for achieving the second centenary goal under the CCP's leadership.

Xi Jinping subtly directed credit towards himself when he declared "we have brought about a historic resolution to the problem of absolute poverty in China, and we are now marching in confident strides toward the second centenary goal of building China into a great modern socialist country in all respects." This was subliminally reinforced early in his speech with the assertion that "Following the Party's 18th National Congress, socialism with Chinese characteristics entered a new era". He elaborated: "In this new era, we have upheld and strengthened the Party's overall leadership, ensured coordinated implementation of the five-sphere integrated plan and the four-pronged comprehensive strategy, upheld and improved the system of socialism with Chinese characteristics, modernized China's system and capacity for governance, remained committed to exercising rule-based governance over the Party, and developed a sound system of intraparty regulations. We have overcome a long list of major risks and challenges, fulfilled the first centenary goal, and set out strategic steps for achieving the second centenary goal." In other words, these achievements followed Xi Jinping coming to power. There was no mention of any other Party Congress.

Xi Jinping paid the ritual obeisance and genuflected before the veteran Chinese communist revolutionaries. He acknowledged "Mao Zedong, Zhou Enlai, Liu Shaoqi, Zhu De, Deng Xiaoping, Chen Yun, and other veteran revolutionaries who contributed greatly to China's revolution, construction, and reform, and to the founding, consolidation, and development of the Communist Party of China". The mention of Chen Yun is interesting. Xi Jinping also said "We owe all that we have achieved over the past hundred years to the concerted efforts of the Chinese Communists, the Chinese people, and the Chinese nation. Chinese Communists, with comrades Mao Zedong, Deng Xiaoping, Jiang Zemin, and Hu Jintao as their chief representatives, have made tremendous and historic contributions to the rejuvenation of the Chinese nation. To them, we express our highest respect". As if to especially emphasise the contribution of the Party and its members, on a few occasions in his speech Xi Jinping placed "Chinese communists" ahead of the "Chinese people".

Intended primarily for the domestic audience, Xi Jinping's speech did nevertheless convey some clear messages for other countries. The tough remarks about not allowing China to be humiliated by foreign powers bore Xi Jinping's imprimatur. Xi Jinping announced that the "new democratic revolution put an end to China's history as a semi-colonial, semi-feudal society, to the state of total disunity that existed in Old China and to all the unequal treaties imposed on our country by foreign powers and all the privileges that imperialist powers enjoyed in China". He declared "the time in which the Chinese nation could be bullied and abused by others was gone forever". These remarks echoed those he made in Mexico in February 2009 as Vice President, when he said: "There are some well-fed foreigners who have nothing better to do than point fingers at our affairs. China does not, first, export revolution; second, export poverty and hunger; third, cause troubles for you"! The remarks will arouse nationalist sentiment among the Chinese people, something the Party feels is necessary as it is convinced that the US and West have stepped-up efforts to instigate a 'colour revolution' and bring about the downfall of the CCP.

He made pointed mention of the Belt and Road initiative (BRI), an essential part of China's second centenary goal and personally backed by him, indicating that China will continue to push it. Similarly, he referred to the concept of 'community of shared destiny for mankind' which is also being advocated by him.

The dominant strain that ran through Xi Jinping's 5515-word (*Xinhua's* English version) speech was that of the Party's indispensability to the people and country. The Party was mentioned 133 times. It was credited with having raised China to its present level: "only socialism could save China, and that only socialism could develop China". This was highlighted while praising the "Chinese communists, Chinese people and the Chinese nation" for their hard work. Equally emphatic was the assertion that China cannot do without the Party's leadership. For good measure and to convey an unmistakable message to those wanting to weaken the Party — by separating the Army from the Party or trying to deprive the Party of its monopoly on power — Xi Jinping declared we "must uphold the firm leadership of the Party. China's success hinges on the Party. Without the Chinese Communist Party there will be no new China and no national rejuvenation".

Xi Jinping stressed the importance of the peoples' support to the Party and said the Party has to "earn and keep the people's support". In this context he assured that "the Party has no special interests of its own – it has never represented any individual interest group, power group, or privileged stratum". In a thinly veiled reference to the anti-China efforts of the US that the CCP leadership is convinced of, Xi Jinping insisted that the Party cannot be dislodged. He said: "Any attempt to divide the Party from the Chinese people or set the people against the Party is bound to fail. The more than 95 million Party members and more than 1.4 billion Chinese people will never allow such a scenario to come to pass". In the weeks leading up to the celebrations the Chinese authorities had warned the people that foreign powers were trying to instigate a "colour revolution".

Alluding to the increasing pressure on China from the US, Xi Jinping declared that China will not be intimated by threats of force. He said "The Chinese people will not allow any external forces to bully, oppress, or enslave us; anyone who deludes themselves into doing so will suffer a crushing and bloody head-on collision with the great wall of steel (PLA) made of the flesh and blood of 1.4 billion Chinese people". China's official news agency Xinhua subsequently released a toned-down version of this phrase as official Chinese interlocuters explained that the language was part of the imagery of Chinese vocabulary. The revised version quoted Xi Jinping as saying "Anyone who would attempt to do so will find themselves on a collision course with a great wall of steel forged by over 1.4 million people".

There were references to Hongkong, Macau and Taiwan. Xi Jinping promised Hongkong and Macau the rule of law, but tempered with the promise of greater autonomy. On Taiwan he specifically mentioned the 1992 consensus and reiterated China and the Party's commitment to the "full reunification" of China. He did not omit to mention the word "peaceful". Suggesting that Beijing will continue its psywar against Taiwan, the CCP-owned Global Times on July 2, cited a Taiwan Public Opinion Foundation (TPOF) poll which shows that among adult Taiwan residents, favourable views of the CPC have increased by four percent and negative views decreased by 16 percent as compared to October 2020.

Xi Jinping's assurance that China will achieve "full reunification", however, is of import for China's neighbours. It is particularly relevant for those with whom it has unresolved, outstanding territorial disputes whether on land or at sea.

But throughout this year-long period there was no mention of the CCP's major policy disasters. These include the Great Leap Forward, and Great Proletarian Cultural Revolution, which together resulted in the deaths of over 60 million people and left millions more disabled or scarred for life. Similarly, Xi Jinping did not at all mention the difficulties that China will confront in the next few years. Issues like the rapidly greying Chinese population and reducing labour force which will impose increasing strain on the national treasury; the slowing economy which is unlikely to pick up if anti-China sentiment in the US and Europe remains high; the closure of over 60 percent of small and medium businesses; concerns about inflation; and likely drop in living standards leading to popular discontent, were ignored. So too was the rising pressure from the US and West and the growing threat of conflict. These have the potential to derail China's "march" to its second centenary goal.

The CCP's hundredth founding anniversary was a major event in its history. The Party has effectively used it to project its contribution to China's 'rise' and future relevance to China and its people. But the repeated references in Xi Jinping's speech to foreign bullying, efforts to separate the Party from the people and his emphasis that the Party needs the people's support, do indicate the fears of the CCP leadership. Xi Jinping has nonetheless deftly highlighted his contributions and demonstrated his unchallenged position. The manner in which Xi Jinping implied that it was his policies and programme that had seen China achieve its first centenary goal and would guide China in "it's March to the second century goals" was particularly notable.

This was first published by the Centre for China Analysis and Strategy (CCAS) and Vivekananda International Foundation (VIF) in July 6, 2021.

25. China's Communist Party Celebrates its Centenary – What Next?

The Chinese Communist Party (CCP)'s centenary celebrations were extensively covered in the Chinese media. Xi Jinping, who holds China's three top positions of CCP General Secretary, Chairman of the Central Military Commission (CMC) and Chinese President, delivered an important speech on the occasion on July 1, 2021. His speech provided a few pointers about future plans including an indication that he intends to remain in power. His speech affirmed that the Party will adhere to the prescription Xi Jinping gave in 2017: "the party, government, military, civilian and academic, east, west, south, north and center, the party leads everything".

The highlights and Xi Jinping's speech

An interesting and possibly little noticed sidelight was the reversal of a decision regarding the People's Liberation Army (PLA)'s participation in the CCP's centenary celebrations. On March 23, 2021, the spokesman of China's Ministry of National Defense stated at a press briefing that there will be no parade by the PLA and it will not have a role in the Party's celebrations. Yet on July 1 there was a fly-past by PLA Air Force (PLAAF) aircraft, a parade and a 100-gun salute for the Party by PLA contingents. The CCP leadership probably decided that PLA participation is essential to demonstrate its "absolute obedience" to the party and to underscore the Party's firm grip on the PLA.

The emphasis of Xi Jinping's 7000-character speech was on the Chinese people, the CCP, ideology and 'rejuvenation'. Its focus was sharp as it was one-third the length of Jiang Zemin's 21,000-character speech delivered at the CCP's 80th anniversary in 2001. Xi Jinping mentioned the CCP 200 times and 'rejuvenation' 26 times. The emphasis on ideology sought to justify the Party's policies and push for ideological education in schools, colleges, and universities as well as enhanced ideological monitoring of the academic fraternity. The assertion that 'only socialism could save China and only socialism could develop China' accorded legitimacy to the Party's policy. It also explains the thrust to establish Party cells in State owned Enterprises (SoEs) and private, including foreign, enterprises. Adding emphasis, he said the Party is indispensable for China's progress. Xi Jinping declared: "China's success hinges on the Party" and "without the Chinese communist party, there will be no new China and no national rejuvenation".

Noteworthy was the apparent, albeit oblique, acknowledgement of the criticisms — many, rather unusually, directed at Xi Jinping personally and the CCP — that had spilled over into China's social media and cyberspace since 2020. These were prompted by various factors, like his ignoring the term limits for appointments of senior cadres, mismanagement of the outbreak of the COVID pandemic in its initial stages etc. In an attempt to deflect the criticism, Xi Jinping said "the Party has to earn and keep the peoples support". In the same context he said "the Party does not represent any individual interest group, power group, or privileged stratum". Coincidentally, around this time the Chinese media publicised the incident of Zhang Tao, Chairman and Communist Party Secretary of China Aerospace Investment Holdings, who severely beat two senior academicians and scientists of the China Aerospace Corporation on June 6 resulting in their hospitalisation. Zhang Tao is a highly connected 'princeling' and was punished only after July 4. Xi Jinping's remarks reinforce his insistence that Party cadres need to live simply and once again get closer to the people.

Pointing to the serious and publicised apprehensions of the CCP leadership that the US and West are trying to destabilise China, Xi Jinping warned foreigners not to interfere in China's internal affairs. Otherwise, he said, they will "smash their heads against the solid steel of the Chinese people". His remark comes in the wake of public warnings by the Chinese media and China's Ministry of State Security (MoSS) of attempts by the US and Western powers to instigate a 'colour revolution' in China.

Significant was Xi Jinping's reference to the Belt and Road Initiative (BRI), China's flagship project personally backed by Xi Jinping. It was the only concrete project of China's "second century" goal that was mentioned in his speech and he stressed that it "will continue to progress". The BRI is intended to project state power and represents Xi Jinping and China's global ambition. Its mention clearly hints that Xi Jinping fully intends to continue pursuing his expansive global agenda to make China a leading world power by 2049. Xi Jinping's mention of the "full reunification" of China, while referring to Taiwan, reinforces this.

China's 'Second Century' Goal

China has now embarked on its 'second century' goal. Crucial, however, will be the next 20 to 30 years — by when Xi Jinping intends to make China a "power with pioneering global influence" and rival or surpass the US – till 2049/2050. Present indications are that China's leadership will find it difficult to achieve this goal. In addition to Xi Jinping continuing in power for at least the next two terms if not longer, there are at least two other issues that China's leaders will have to confront.

Internal Difficulties

The informal annual Autumn conclave of veteran leaders at the seaside resort of Beidaihe, during their discussions this year reportedly agreed that China is facing a 'severe economic crisis'. This confirms reports that China's economy is in dire straits despite the upbeat reporting by China's official media. The second is China getting potentially isolated internationally, especially by the world's major advanced countries. In addition to reacting to China's aggressive polices, an important factor for governments will be the public pressure because of surging global anti-China sentiment due to the Covid pandemic. These are exacerbated by the worsening Sino-US ties. Even as the US and EU begin to recover from the devastating effects of the Covid pandemic, they are very unlikely to open their markets to China to anywhere near the same extent as earlier. This will push China's export-dependent economy into deeper distress.

There are other economic difficulties currently confronting China. Around 300 million workers who left urban centers and went to their villages have, according to official Chinese data, not yet returned to work. This was indirectly confirmed by China's National Bureau of Statistics when it announced in

August 2021 that inequality in urban and rural incomes is already 32 percent and widening. 60 percent of small and medium businesses in China are officially acknowledged to have closed. The weak recovery in services—which absorbs most college graduates—has aggravated the already high youth joblessness with unemployment among the 16 to 24 age group averaging 14 percent since 2019. A drop in living standards is likely and inflation is rising. An important indication of China's economic difficulties is that the budget approved by the National People's Congress (NPC) — China's version of a Parliament — in March 2021 effected a 50 percent reduction for all government ministries and departments and a further five percent in March 2022. The budget of China's public security apparatus, however, increased both years while the budget of the Ministry of Foreign Affairs increased marginally this year.

There are other longer-term issues, like the graying of China's population which has begun to burden revenues, pension and social welfare funds. It has also reduced the labor force and affected productivity.

At the same time, in an apparent bid to regulate the industry and ensure enhanced Party control in a growing adverse international environment, the Chinese authorities began cracking down on big business and FinTech since last year. In a number of instances, they intervened on the eve of the companies being listed on foreign stock exchanges leading to a sharp fall in stock prices and heavy losses by foreign investors. The first to be 'disciplined' was Jack Ma's Alibaba. Others under investigation, or who have been punished, are Wang Xing of Meituan and Liu Changle of Phoenix TV.

An additional political price was recently imposed on China's successful billionaire businessmen entrepreneurs and profitable businesses under the slogan "common prosperity", enunciated by Xi Jinping on August 17. Reflecting apparent fear, many businesses complied promptly. On August 18, Tencent pledged to contribute 50 billion yuan (US$ 7.73 billion) to low-income groups, basic healthcare and education. On August 24, internet commerce firm Pinduoduo and a rival of Alibaba announced a donation of this year's entire first quarter profit totaling US$ $374 million to support agriculture and rural areas. It promised to donate future profits up to a total of 10 billion yuan. Meituan founder Wang Xing donated 10 percent of his stake to his philanthropic foundation in June.

The *Economist* reported that the number of Chinese nationals seeking asylum abroad went up from 15,362 in 2012 to 1,07,864 in 2020. This does not include those leaving China illegally or who have funneled money abroad through illegal channels. These actions have hurt China's investment climate and foreign investors are becoming increasingly averse to investing in China. Chinese businesses have also become cautious about listing on foreign stock exchanges.

China's External Environment

Deteriorating Sino-US relations are a major concern for the Chinese leadership. There is bipartisan consensus in the US Congress that China needs to be contained and, the Biden Administration is continuing with its predecessor's tough policies. The hardened US attitude is visible across a number of areas including Taiwan and Tibet — areas of "core concern" for China — with the passing of the US Policy Act on Tibet. US pressure on China's 'Made in China-2025' hi-tech programme has resulted in it slipping behind its deadline by at least a decade with an adverse fallout likely in other sectors.

There is also the possibility of clashes. China's leadership and analysts are very apprehensive of more US actions aimed at China, especially now that the US has withdrawn from Afghanistan. The US-led exercises in the South China Sea and adjacent waters and of the Quad are being watched very carefully. The arrival of British, French and German warships, evoking memories of China's 'century of humiliation', would be disconcerting for Beijing. Apprehensions have increased with senior US Admirals speaking of the enhanced possibility of clashes between the US and China in the South China Sea.

Taiwan's profile as an area of potential conflict has increased in recent months. Aggressive actions by the PLAAF and PLA Navy have raised temperatures. US weapons sales to Taiwan and elevated prominence given to Taiwan by Trump and the successor Administration have added to the pressure. The international environment has become more adverse with Japan's Defense Minister identifying Taiwan and the waters around it as of "vital importance" to Japan, and observations in Japan's Defense White Paper, and the talks in the last week of August between leaders of the LDP and Taiwan's ruling DPP.

The considerable tension between China and India is unlikely to ease for quite some time and has the potential to suddenly escalate sparking serious clashes. China continues to claim Ladakh and other territories in India's possession with Chinese President Xi Jinping showing no inclination to discuss the issue with India's leaders. Reports of China's continuing military build-up and Chinese President and Chairman of the Central Military Commission Xi Jinping's "special" meeting with PLA officers in Lhasa on July 23, suggest additional preparations. Till the Chinese leadership withdraws the PLA to its positions prior to May 2020, tension will remain. Any further Chinese actions raise the high possibility of armed clashes.

In this backdrop, China needs markets abroad. With US and European markets unlikely to open to China as earlier, the Indian market getting progressively restricted, and global supply chains reorienting to restrict, or eliminate, China's role, Beijing faces serious economic difficulties ahead. If China's economic condition deteriorates, popular discontent and dissatisfaction will grow, and this will adversely impact Xi Jinping's credibility and the CCP's legitimacy. Chinese analysts already privately blame Xi Jinping's aggressive policies for antagonising China's neighbours and the rapid deterioration in relations with the US.

Chinese Leadership

With the 20th Party Congress next year probably approving Xi Jinping continuance for the third term, he is very unlikely to compromise his agenda or make the concessions necessary for repairing ties with the US. The current thinking in the CCP leadership appears to be that the US is now in irreparable terminal decline and this is China's window of opportunity. Recent initiatives for contact taken by the US are being viewed as "weakness" and Chinese Foreign Minister Wang Yi's lecture to the US Special Envoy on Climate John Kerry showed this. This assessment, of course, appreciably raises the risk of clashes. Xi Jinping's ambition to make China the pre-eminent regional power will mean the continued pursuit of aggressive policies to 'recover' territories claimed by China and maintain pressure on India, Taiwan, Japan and others with clashing maritime territorial claims. If China's leadership assesses that the US is too weak, or unwilling, to intervene then Xi Jinping could well gamble on a military effort to 'reunify' Taiwan with the Mainland. Xi Jinping's big ambitions, the changing situation in Afghanistan and temptation to advance the BRI, could also entice Xi Jinping into 'assisting' the Taliban with men and material.

Emerging Internal Political Scenario

It is improbable that domestic discontent will compel Xi Jinping to temper policies or withdraw from his bid to continue in office. Measures taken by him in the past 2-3 years have strengthened his control on the CCP CC, Politburo and Politburo Standing Committee and minimised the possibility of his being surprised by an unanticipated agenda or development. Unless the number of discontented or dissatisfied cadres in the CC reach a critical mass, it is very unlikely that veteran cadres will extend their support to Xi Jinping's ouster. Neither do reports suggest that Xi Jinping was criticised at the recent Beidaihe meeting.

If popular dissatisfaction rises, Xi Jinping will exponentially increase his already heavy reliance on the security apparatus. The latter, including the PLA and People's Armed Police Force (PAPF), would visibly gain in influence. The PLA's obedience and loyalty to the CCP and Xi Jinping is already being continuously reinforced and tested through consecutive ideological campaigns and emphasis on political reliability. During travels outside Beijing, Xi Jinping makes it a point to visit nearby PLA establishments and talk to personnel. Despite earlier denials, the PLA was given a role during the party centenary celebrations. Additional allowances were announced for retired PLA veterans and families of serving personnel just before the Party's centenary. Increased dependence on the security forces could see their inclusion in larger numbers in the CCP Central Committee or Politburo.

A lot depends on the attitude of the US and China's neighbours. It is very unlikely that India, Japan, Vietnam and, probably Indonesia, will easily yield to Chinese dominance. The US and Europe too have finally begun to see that China views dominance of Asia, or the Indo-Pacific, as the stepping stone to becoming the leading world power. The stakes are high for the US with Beijing having openly challenged Washington's status as the sole superpower. Unless the US seeks a compromise with China and yields its position, China's neighbours can anticipate a difficult next 30 years. If, as is likely, US-China relations continue to deteriorate and Washington steadily ratchets pressure then China's rise will get derailed. The next ten years will be crucial in global geopolitics.

This was first published by the Centre for China Analysis and Strategy (CCAS) and Vivekananda International Foundation (VIF) in September 9, 2021.

26. Assessment of China's 20th Party Congress

The 20th Party Congress (October 6-22, 2022) is a watershed event in China's political history and marks a new phase. It exemplified Chinese Communist Party (CCP) Central Committee (CC) General Secretary Xi Jinping's absolute control and firm grip on the CCP. From selection of members of the Politburo and its Standing Committee to finalisation of the Work Report presented to the 20th Party Congress, all carried Xi Jinping's firm imprimatur. Xi Jinping has pushed China into becoming a one-man totalitarian state.

As on previous occasions a tight security blanket comprising an estimated over a million personnel was thrown over Beijing and the restive provinces. Despite the security precautions the atmosphere was marred by a 'worker' who unfurled a banner atop a bridge in Beijing's Haidian university district protesting the government's policies. Bloomberg reported that protests had also been staged in eight cities across China, but there are no corroborative reports.

The meticulously choreographed 20th Party Congress intended to display Xi Jinping's unchecked power was, however, disrupted on the last day by the unprecedented removal in front of the cameras of former Chinese President Hu Jintao. While it appeared that Hu Jintao might have suddenly taken ill and therefore taken away as stated by the state-owned CCTV, reports now suggest that the video showing the incident has been erased from Chinese social media and references to Hu Jintao have been deleted along with his photographs. The episode remains shrouded in mystery.

Each of the six other Politburo Standing Committee (PBSC) members and 23 members of the Politburo (PB) – one less than the previous 25 — is unmistakably a Xi Jinping loyalist. Xi Jinping has personally selected them and not followed any single criteria for selecting cadres. No cadre affiliated or associated with another leader, or group like the Communist Youth League

(CYL), has been inducted. These top-level personnel selections mean that the PBSC will no longer take decisions on the basis of consensus. It will ensure faithful implementation of Xi Jinping's directives. This also leaves open the possibility of 69-year-old Xi Jinping continuing in office for another term or even longer.

It was interesting to see that while retired senior veteran cadres were invited and those who attended were seated on the front row of the rostrum, an explanatory report on the 20th Party Congress released by Xinhua pointedly omitted any mention of Xi Jinping having consulted them on the appointments of PBSC and PB members. This is a departure from past practice.

It is significant that by approving the Work Report the 20th Party Congress has endorsed the policies followed by Xi Jinping thus far, including the concentration of power in his person and building of his personality cult. This means the continuance of the tough policies on ensuring the CCP's pre-eminent position, national and domestic security, 'zero-Covid', economic regulation and reform, and foreign policy.

Aware of the adverse international environment, Xi Jinping avoided abrasive rhetoric in his Work Report, but was defiantly uncompromising in reiterating the goals that he had set out at the two earlier Congresses in 2012 and 2017. He reiterated "we will continue to work hard and build China into a great socialist country that leads the world in terms of composite national strength and international influence by the middle of the next century".

For the region and China's neighbours, like Taiwan and Japan, the 20th Party Congress signals increasing tensions. Tougher language has been used for Taiwan with Xi Jinping hinting that reunification could be achieved during his tenure in office.

India merited special negative attention. Party Congresses do not usually name individual countries, but this time a film clip of the clashes between Indian and Chinese military personnel in Galwan was screened at the meeting for all the Delegates, special invitees and officials numbering nearly 5000 people in the Great Hall of the People. This indicates that China will not change its attitude towards India and is prepared for a long period of strained relations. Reflecting current tensions, the Work Report approved by the 20th

Party Congress also included language not used by the 19th Party Congress in 2017. Discussing military training and deployment it said: "This will enable us to shape our security posture, deter and manage crises and conflicts and win local wars". For India, this means increased pressure on the borders with the high probability of further clashes.

A detailed assessment is appended.

Appendix (October 30, 2022)

ASSESSMENT OF THE 20TH PARTY CONGRESS

Presenting the Work Report titled 'Hold High the Great Banner of Socialism with Chinese Characteristics and Strive in Unity to Build a Modern Socialist Country in all Respects', at the opening session of the 20th Party Congress on October 16, 2022, Chinese Communist Party (CCP) Central Committee (CC) General Secretary Xi Jinping read out excerpts for over one hour 43 minutes instead of the entire report as at the 19th Party Congress.

The once in five-years political event is meticulously choreographed to project the incumbent leader. As on previous occasions a tight security blanket, estimated to comprise over a million personnel, was thrown over Beijing and the restive provinces. Despite the security precautions the atmosphere was marred by a 'worker' who unfurled a banner atop a bridge in Beijing's Haidian university district protesting the government's policies. Bloomberg reported that protests had also been staged in eight cities across China, but there were no reports in the Chinese media.

The meticulously choreographed 20th Party Congress intended to display Xi Jinping's unchecked power was, however, disrupted on the last day by the unprecedented removal in front of the cameras of former Chinese President Hu Jintao. While it appeared that Hu Jintao might have suddenly taken ill and therefore taken away as stated by the state-owned CCTV, reports now suggest that the video showing the incident has been erased from Chinese social media and references to Hu Jintao have been deleted along with his photographs. The episode remains shrouded in mystery.

The 20th Party Congress should have been attended by 2,296 delegates and 83 specially invited delegates, totalling 2,379 people, but 39 people had asked for leave due to work or illness. Resultantly there were 2,340 actual delegates and specially-invited delegates.

It was interesting that while retired senior veteran cadres were invited and those who attended were seated on the front row of the rostrum in the Great Hall of the People, an explanatory report on the 20th Party Congress released this time by Xinhua pointedly omitted any mention of Xi Jinping having consulted them on the appointments of Politburo Standing Committee (PBSC) and Politburo (PB) members.

Among the veteran cadres seated on the front row of the rostrum were former Chinese President Hu Jintao (seated to the left and next to Xi Jinping), Li Ruihuan, Wen Jiabao, Jia Qinglin, Zhang Dejiang, Yu Zhengsheng, Song Ping, Li Lanqing, Zeng Qinghong, Wu Guanzheng, Li Changchun, He Guoqiang, Liu Yunshan, Zhang Gaoli (who was accused in November 2021 by Chinese Tennis star Peng Shuan of sexually molesting her, but later withdrew the charge and acknowledged that they had been having an affair for many years), You Quan and Zhang Qingli (a former Party Secretary of the Tibet Autonomous Region (TAR) who called the XIVth Dalai Lama a "wolf in sheeps clothing and the heart of a beast". He has been dropped from the 20th CCP CC). Former Chinese President Jiang Zemin did not attend.

The list of new members of the PBSC, PB and Central Committee (CC) were disclosed only on the final day of the Congress on October 22. The new PBSC includes: Xi Jinping, Li Qiang, Zhao Leji, Wang Huning, Cai Qi, Ding Xuexiang and Li Xi. Each of the six other Politburo Standing Committee (PBSC) members and 24 members of the Politburo (PB) – one less than previously — is a Xi Jinping loyalist. No cadre affiliated to another leader, including retired veteran cadre, or group like the Communist Youth League (CYL) has been inducted. Equally importantly, they all owe their positions to him – a Xinhua release illustrated Xi Jinping's role at each stage of the selection process — as he has not followed any single criteria for selecting cadres. Xi Jinping has neither observed the convention of age limits for cadres in the PBSC or PB as borne out by the retention of 72-year-old General Zhang Youxia on the Politburo.

Significantly, he has also demoted cadres. The ouster of 59-year-old Hu Chunhua from the Politburo and retention only as a member of the Central

Committee (CC) is a prominent example. So also is the removal from the Politburo of 66-year old Chen Quanguo, former Party Secretary of Xinjiang and earlier Tibet, who is now not even a member of the Central Committee. Chen Quanguo was handpicked by Xi Jinping for appointment as TAR Party Secretary and later promoted to the Politburo and sent to Xinjiang. These are clear signals to senior cadres that they can be removed from their positions! Apparently to drive the point home, an official Xinhua release of October 24 asserted that "Party and national leadership positions are not 'iron chairs'!" These top-level personnel selections also mean that the decisions of the PBSC will no longer be on the basis of consensus. It will ensure faithful implementation of Xi Jinping's directives.

The new 20th CC has 138 new members out of 204 members, or 67.6 percent, suggesting that Xi Jinping has packed it with loyalists. The 19th CC had 85 new members out of 205 full members – or 41.5 percent. The 20th CC has 11 female members, up one compared to the 19th CC, and only 9 from the Ethnic Minorities— a sharp drop from the 15 in the 19th CC. In the new 20th CC among the 43 People's Liberation Army (PLA) members, 13 are PLA Lt. Generals and the remaining 30 are PLA Generals. The service-wise distribution of members is: PLA Air Force (5); PLA Navy (10), People's Armed Police (3), PLA Army (23), and PLA Rocket Force (2). Of the Alternate Members of the CC, 4 have retained their positions, 25 have been elevated as Full Members of the CC and 114 are newly appointed CC Members. There are 22 women and 20 representatives of ethnic minorities.

The 72-page, 33,273 (Chinese)-character Report presented this time to the 20th Party Congress was slightly longer than the Report (31,750 Chinese-characters) that Xi Jinping presented at the 19th Party Congress in 2017. This Work Report has 15 sections compared to the 13 in the Report for the 19th Congress. Three are new, namely: Section 5 titled 'Invigorating China through Science and Education and Developing a Strong Workforce for the Modernization Drive' on Science, education and innovation; Section 7 on legal reform and titled 'Exercising Law-Based Governance on All Fronts and Advancing the Rule of Law in China'; and Section 11 on National Security titled 'Modernizing China's National Security System and Capacity and

Safeguarding National Security and Social Stability'. There was a separate section on National Defence.

Reasserting the CCP's objective, Xi Jinping said "we will continue to work hard and build China into a great socialist country that leads the world in terms of composite national strength and international influence by the middle of the next century". It announced no policy changes. Instead, Xi Jinping appeared to double down on certain issues like arresting the erosion in the Party's image and credibility — unusually blunt references to which he made in the Work Report — and rectifying the Party, persisting with the 'zero-Covid' policy, further strengthening the national security apparatus, science and technology, achieving national rejuvenation and reunification of the country, and modernising and strengthening the army to "win local wars". While Xi Jinping omitted the term "local wars" from the excerpts that he read out, "local wars" is mentioned in the Work Report.

National security, the CCP, political ideology and political reliability, science and technology and innovation were among the predominant themes in the Work Report presented to the 20th Party Congress. In fact, the Work Report listed "upholding the leadership of the Chinese Communist Party and socialism with Chinese characteristics" as the first among the "essential requirements" of modernisation. These illustrate the leadership's priorities and are areas where China is investing huge sums of money and manpower. The importance of Science and Innovation as thrust areas has clearly been elevated in the wake of the restrictions imposed by the US on the sale of hi-tech components, microprocessors etc.

The Work Report acknowledged the major challenges China faces and efforts by unnamed foreign powers to destabilise China and topple the CCP. Unlike at the 19th Party Congress where Xi Jinping spoke of the "window of opportunity", in this report he was more cautious and said "Both China and the world are in the midst of profound and complex changes. China is still in an important period of strategic opportunity for development; the prospects are bright but the challenges are severe. All comrades must aim high and look far, be alert to dangers even in times of calm, have the courage to pursue reform and break new ground, and never become hardened". This was emphasised in the areas of focus identified for the next five years.

Despite the serious problems in the economy, it didn't get priority in the Report. The number of references to the economy dropped from 70 in the Report of 2017 to 60 in this Report. Similarly, economic reforms were mentioned only 48 times in contrast to the 68 times in 2017. The issues of unemployment, slowing economy and economic reforms etc found little space and no new economic initiatives were announced. The solitary mention of the Belt and Road Initiative (BRI) — Chinese investment in which has dropped by nearly 50 percent in the past couple of years — was, however, indicative of the difficult economic conditions. There were also only two brief mentions of "common prosperity". The Report did, though, talk of more equitable distribution of incomes and China's official media discussed it at length during and immediately after the Congress indicating that it will be pursued. It addressed the urban-rural development and income imbalances suggesting acknowledgement of the wide gaps in development and income distribution between urban and rural areas.

At the same time, implying that efforts to enhance Party control will continue, the Report asserted that the Party will build its presence in the economic enterprises including mixed enterprises. The market reacted immediately to the Report. On October 24, the Hongkong China Index, which includes the top 50 Chinese companies, dropped 6 percent on heavy volume. Alibaba, Tencent and Meituan each dropped over 10 percent and overseas investors sold a record US$ 2.5 billion worth Mainland shares via the Shanghai-Hongkong Stock Connect. Wealthy Chinese are reportedly trying to move almost US$40 billion out of China.

Aware of the adverse international environment, Chinese Communist Party (CCP) Central Committee (CC) General Secretary Xi Jinping avoided abrasive rhetoric in his Work Report, but was defiantly uncompromising in reiterating the goals that he had set out at the two intervening Congresses in 2012 and 2017. He exuded confidence in his assertions — directed mainly at the domestic audience — to make China a major world power. Xi Jinping declared that "scientific socialism" and "Chinese wisdom"[30] enabled China to offer a "new choice for humanity"!

The CCP was prominent in the Work Report. It figured the most with 261 mentions as compared to 331 times in the 2017 Report. Cognizant of the challenges confronting China, Xi Jinping doubled down on issues like arresting the erosion in the Party's image and credibility — unusually blunt references to which he made in the Work Report — and 'rectifying' the Party. There was emphasis on ensuring that Party members "follow the Central Committee in terms of political stance, orientation, principles, and path and that the Party's solidarity and unity are maintained". It said the Party will strengthen centralisation and its leadership and "enforce strict political discipline and rules" and make "full use of criticism and self-criticism". He devoted considerable space to the spread of Marxist ideology, the Party and raising the ideological standards of Party members. Keeping them corruption-free was accorded priority. He indicated that the stringent standards set for Party members, and especially high-ranking cadres and leadership teams and their heads, would be scrupulously enforced and stipulated that "political commitment is the primary criterion for selection" of cadres and officials. He made it clear that efforts to promote the CCP and consolidate its premier position will continue.

National security dominated the report with Xi Jinping referring to it 91 times in this Report in contrast to the 42 mentions in 2017. Highlighting its importance, it declared that "National security is the bedrock of national rejuvenation". The Report said steps are being taken to coordinate "external and internal security, homeland and public security, traditional and non-traditional security" and that popular support for national security and social stability will be strengthened. Though not mentioned by name, the implication that the US was the main threat was explicit. Xi Jinping referred to the "external attempts to blackmail, contain, blockade and exert maximum pressure on China" and said "external attempts to suppress and contain China may escalate at any time". He promised to "crack down hard on infiltration, sabotage, subversion and separatist activities by hostile forces". Xi Jinping declared China's "firm determination to never yield to coercive power". The regular references by Chinese officials and in the official Mainland media over the past few years to attempts by "hostile" foreign powers to instigate "colour revolutions" and holding of the annual National Security Week have been pointing to the CCP's and Chinese leadership's concerns about national security.

Official Chinese media reports have independently disclosed that over the past couple of years there has been a three-fold increase in the number of public security personnel with provinces recruiting large numbers. China spent approximately 1.38 trillion yuan on public security in 2018, a threefold increase in the past decade. The public security expenditure includes state security, police, domestic surveillance, armed civil militia, and other measures to deal with public disturbances. Since 2010, it has surpassed the country's military spending. It exceeded military spending by approximately 200 million yuan in 2018. Guangdong, Jiangsu, and Xinjiang were the top three provinces in terms of public security spending.

Two appointments specifically underscore the focus on security. Chen Weiming, the Minister of State Security (MoSS), was elevated to the Politburo. He is likely to be appointed Secretary of the Political and Legal Affairs Commission (PLAC), China's apex security body. The other was the appointment just prior to the 20th Party Congress of Wang Xiaohong as Minister of Public Security. While he continues as a CC member, he has also been appointed member of the five member CCP CC Secretariat, a powerful body that oversees the functioning of the CC and its organisations and reports directly to Xi Jinping. The only other member of the Secretariat who is not in the Politburo is Liu Jinguo, who also has a strong background in Public Security and was till recently in the CCP's top anti-corruption watchdog body, the Central Discipline Inspection Commission (CDIC).

Xi Jinping has also linked security with development. Apprehensions about the US and West's attempts to contain China — as also indication that China is preparing for a long period of strained ties with the US and West — surfaced again later in the report when Xi Jinping announced that "mechanisms for countering foreign sanctions, interference and long-arm jurisdiction will be strengthened". Stating that "strategic opportunities, risks and challenges are concurrent and uncertainties and unforeseen factors are rising", Xi Jinping cautioned cadres that "various "black swan" and "gray rhino" events may occur at any time" and "We must therefore be more mindful of potential dangers, be prepared to deal with worst-case scenarios, and be ready to withstand high winds, choppy waters, and even dangerous storms." But he also sought to dispel speculation that China was closing itself to the world by announcing that China is "committed to its fundamental policy of opening to the outside world" and will "contribute its share to building an open global economy.

As evident from inclusion of the new section titled 'Invigorating China through Science and Education and Developing a Strong Workforce for the Modernization Drive', Science, Technology and Innovation are thrust areas. The Report said "Innovation will remain at the heart of China's modernisation drive" and that education and strength in strategic science and technology will be boosted. Alluding to the restrictions imposed by the US on the sale of hi-tech components, microprocessors etc., it said "to meet China's strategic needs, we will concentrate resources on original and pioneering scientific and technological research to achieve breakthroughs in core technologies in key fields". On October 7, the US announced a ban not only on the sale of chips to China but also the advanced equipment needed to make them and "knowledge" from any US citizens, residents or green card holders, effectively banning them from working for Chinese chipmakers. On the same day it added 30 Chinese companies to a list of "unverified" firms its officials had been unable to inspect.

The Report mentioned no policy changes. In apparent disregard of extant resentment, Xi Jinping has persisted with the zero-Covid policy.

The section elaborating the 'Centenary goal of the People's Liberation Army (PLA) and further modernising National Defence and the Military' is important. It reiterates the goal of accelerating the elevation of the PLA to world-class standards "through mechanisation, informatisation and application of smart technologies" by its centenary in 2027. It promises to "carry out operations" and boost combat preparedness. Of import is disclosure of the decision to establish "a strong system of strategic deterrence, increase the proportion of new-domain forces with new combat capabilities". This confirms reports that China is increasing its nuclear arsenal and also that it intends to enlarge the PLA Strategic Support Force and PLA Rocket Force and enhance their combat capabilities. Hinting that the PLA is being prepared for multiple roles, Xi Jinping said the PLA will be "flexible" in its operations.

Of special significance to the region and its neighbours are Xi Jinping's observations on Taiwan and the military. Language on containing Taiwan's independence was inserted and stronger phrases used to reaffirm "two countries, one system". Striking an uncompromising stance on Taiwan and "realising China's complete reunification", Xi Jinping asserted that "We will implement our Party's overall policy for resolving the Taiwan question in the new era". He added "complete reunification of our country must be realised and it can, without doubt, be realised." This assertion, hinting at efforts to achieve it during Xi Jinping's term in office, was greeted with resounding applause by the Delegates. Earlier, Xi Jinping had said that while China will strive for peaceful reunification "we will never promise to renounce the use of force".

India merited special negative attention. In the backdrop of China's plans for a massive border defence infrastructure build-up in Tibet and enhanced naval capability, the reference to winning local wars is pertinent. It has immediate implications for India. Party Congresses do not usually name individual countries, but this time a film clip of the clashes between Indian and Chinese military personnel in Galwan was screened at the meeting for all the Delegates, special invitees and officials numbering nearly 5,000 in the Great Hall of the People. This indicates that China will not change its attitude towards India and is prepared for a long period of strained relations. Reflecting current tensions, the Work Report approved by the 20th Party Congress also included language not used by the 19th Party Congress in 2017. Discussing military training and deployment it said: "This will enable us to shape our security posture, deter and manage crises and conflicts and win local wars". For India, this means fresh deployments and increased pressure on the borders with the high probability of further clashes.

This was first published by the Centre for China Analysis and Strategy (CCAS) and Vivekananda International Foundation (VIF) in October 30, 2022.

27. Xi Jinping further Strengthens Chinese Communist Party's 'Magic Weapon' – The United Front Work Department

China is making efforts to arrest the slide in US-China relations and lower temperatures after Joe Biden takes over as President on January 20. In addition to Chinese Politburo member and former Foreign Minister Yang Jiechi's plans for visiting Washington this week, a Chinese trade delegation is likely to travel to the US shortly. Confirming that China will use all the levers it possibly can, Chinese President Xi Jinping on January 6 wrote to Howard Schultz, Honorary Chairman of the Board of Directors of Starbucks Corporation of the United States, emphasising that China "will provide a broader space for companies from all over the world, including Starbucks and other American companies, to develop in China". He hoped "that Starbucks will make active efforts to promote Sino-US economic and trade cooperation and the development of bilateral relations". Well informed Chinese academics have separately spoken recently of using their influence with some of the big corporations and prominent figures, including on Wall Street, to influence the new Biden Administration.

Meanwhile, China has further strengthened what it calls its "magic weapon" — the United Front Work Department (UFWD) of the Chinese Communist Party (CCP)'s Central Committee (CC). The UFWD has not only stepped-up influence operations in the past couple of years, but the CCP CC has just this month issued revised rules for the UFWD.

Responsible for intelligence and influence operations, establishing and maintaining contacts with non-Party and foreign entities, and China's ethnic minority nationalities, the United Front functions in China and abroad. It has played a crucial role for the CCP especially during the years it was struggling to capture power and become China's sole ruling party. Many of the CCP's founding and early cadres used a nom-de guerre[31] and worked "underground" for the Party's cause for many years. Many chose to retain these names long after the CCP became China's ruling party and died without disclosing their real names. In some cases the real names were revealed only when their obituaries were published!

After a period of dormancy during the Cultural Revolution and reign of the Gang of Four when China withdrew and became inward looking, Deng Xiaoping revived the United Front. Always a shadowy but important arm of the CCP CC, the UFWD got re-energised in recent years with Xi Jinping's ascent to power. After he took over as head of the central leading small group on united front work and later the new foreign affairs commission in 2017, Xi Jinping doubled the budgets and personnel strength of China's Ministry of Foreign Affairs and the CCP CC's UFWD. A recent report funded by the Netherlands Ministry of Foreign Affairs disclosed that the UFWD presently has more than 600 senior bureaucrats and half a dozen Ministers which makes it equivalent in strength to many Ministries put together. It claimed also that six new bureaus have been added to the UFWD. The six bureaus cover: (i) Xinjiang affairs; (ii) new social strata individuals/urban professionals and elites; (iii) overseas Chinese affairs; (iv) building up and strengthening intelligence and propaganda networks in foreign countries; (v) monitoring and managing religious schools; and (vi) monitoring specific religions within China. The US$ 6.6 billion allocated for an international propaganda offensive is at the disposal of the UFWD as are the Confucius Institutes set up under China's Ministry of Education in 2014.

Earlier this month on January 5, 2021, the CCP CC issued a circular confirming the revised regulations comprising 14 Chapters and 61 Articles approved at a meeting of the Politburo in November 2020. You Quan, head of the UFWD and member of the 19th CCP Central Committee, stated that these prominently reflect the "Party's centralized and unified leadership in united front work". Some of the more important new regulations among the 61 promulgated are listed below.

New chapters include one on "United front work of new social strata" and a chapter on "Overseas United Front Work and Overseas Chinese Affairs

Work". The latter emphasised that "we should devote ourselves to maintaining and promoting China's reunification, realising the great rejuvenation of the Chinese nation, enhancing the friendly cooperation and exchanges between the Chinese people and the people of the world, and promoting the building of a community of human destiny."

The Head of the UFWD in an interview with the *People's Daily* (January 6) explained that the revised regulations had been finalised after getting the views of 20 provinces, autonomous regions and municipalities and "the opinions of the member units of the Central United Front Work Leading Group, relevant departments of the central and state agencies, various provinces, autonomous regions and municipalities, and the United Front Work Department of the Xinjiang Production and Construction Corps" and those "of the head of the Federation of Industry and Commerce and representatives of non-party personages, as well as the heads of the United Front Work Department of some provincial party committees". He described them as of "great significance" and said they "will strengthen the party's centralized and unified leadership over the united front, consolidate and develop the most extensive patriotic united front, and unite efforts to build a modern socialist country and realize the Chinese Dream of the great rejuvenation of the Chinese nation".

Some of the new or more important of the Articles are: Article 3 - stipulates that the patriotic united front should "comprehensively build a modern socialist country and realize the great rejuvenation of the Chinese nation" ... and "achieve the complete reunification of the motherland". It enumerated eight principles of united front work as:

1. Uphold the leadership of the Communist Party of China;
2. Persist in holding high the banner of patriotism and socialism;
3. Persist in focusing on the 'center' and serving the overall situation;
4. Persist in great unity and great union;
5. Persist in correctly handling the relationship of consistency and diversity;
6. Persist in respecting, safeguarding and taking care of the interests of allies;
7. Persevering in making friends from outside the party and making deep friendships; and
8. Adhere to the work pattern of the grand united front.

Among the twelve specific areas of the united front that were identified, of particular interest are:

1. Non-public ownership economy persons;
2. People from new social classes;
3. Those who have gone abroad and returned to study abroad;
4. Overseas Chinese, returned overseas Chinese and their relatives;
5. Other personnel who need contact and unity. It clarified that people outside the party, and representatives of the various groups are the targets.

Article 7 - concretised establishment of the Central United Front Work Leading Group under the "leadership of the Political Bureau of the Central Committee and its Standing Committee".

Article 8 - includes the direction that "the main person in charge of party committees (party groups) at all levels" should be "the first person in charge of the united front work of the local department and unit". It instructed local party committees to set up a united front work leading group, adding that the group leader should generally be at the same level as the party committee secretary.

Article 10 - directed that there should be united front personnel at all administrative levels down to the township and village, universities and State-owned Enterprises (SoEs).

Article 35 - dealt solely with Taiwan and said the united front would "Continuously promote the process of peaceful reunification of the motherland and realize the great rejuvenation of the Chinese nation with one heart".

Article 44 - stipulated the number of positions that must be filled by non-Party persons. It said: "Non-Party representatives shall occupy a large proportion in the CPPCC at all levels, with no less than 60 percent of the members and no less than 65 percent of the standing committee members; and no less than 50 percent of the vice-chairmen of the leading groups of the CPPCC at all levels". Significantly, this does not include ethnic autonomous areas. Similar provision was made for its subordinate bodies at lower administrative divisions and the Supreme People's Procuratorate.

An important backdrop for promulgation of the revised regulations for the United Front is the tension in the Sino-US relationship. While China perceives that with the new Biden Administration it will have a window of opportunity to ease tensions, Beijing is unlikely to offer any substantial compromises. The United Front Work Department can be expected to intensify influence operations to ease tensions with the US. As China steps up its effort for "peaceful reunification of the motherland" and to "realize the great rejuvenation of the Chinese nation", the United Front will have a larger role and will step up its activities and influence operations in other countries of interest to China. India, Taiwan and countries with a large number of Tibetans, Uyghurs and overseas Chinese will be prominent among those that witness elevated United Front activity.

This was first published by the Centre for China Analysis and Strategy (CCAS) and Vivekananda International Foundation (VIF) in January 18, 2021.

28. Xi Jinping's New Slogan of Common Prosperity is Worrying People

'Common Prosperity' has become the new buzzword in the People's Republic of China since August 2021. The term provokes varying emotions ranging from fear and apprehension to a sense that the government is finally addressing the rising Gini coefficient and reining in the private entrepreneurs who have become multi-billionaires. Chinese President Xi Jinping, who mentioned common prosperity in a speech on August 17,2021, definitely had in mind the steadily widening income disparities, the growing urban-rural income divide and the concentration of enormous wealth in the hands of just a small handful of people. While his announcement will have been welcomed by ordinary Chinese people, Chinese Communist Party (CCP) cadres particularly will wait to see the details of the policy and whether it heralds a return to the harsh and devastating Cultural Revolution decade.

The international business magazine Forbes, in September disclosed that mainland China has 626 dollar-billionaires, the second-highest number in the world and that in 2020, the wealthiest one percent of people held 30.6 percent of the country's wealth, an increase of 10 percent from 10 years ago. Official Chinese statistics also reveal that China's Gini coefficient (a measure of inequality that ranges from 0 to 1) has reached 0.47. This inequality is accentuated by the rising cost of living and urban real estate and the 9 am to 9 pm six days a week work culture which has triggered the social phenomenon of tang ping, or "lying flat" among China's graduate youths. These youth say they are giving up on life as there is little point in striving for better opportunities which are out of reach. Communist Party officials, however, are worried about its deleterious effects on society, the country's labour force and manufacturing capacity, and the additional strain it will impose on the already burdened state exchequer.

Though announced by Xi Jinping as part of efforts to strengthen his position before the upcoming 20th Party Congress scheduled for late next year, the "common prosperity" initiative has triggered opposition including from leading Chinese economists. People's University Vice President Liu Yuanchun spoke about the need to stabilize market expectations and warned that the new regulatory measures would lead to volatile market sentiment not conducive to economic development. Zhang Weiying, an Economics Professor at Peking University, said the slogan of "common prosperity" indicates loss of faith in the market and that "introducing more and more market interventions, will only lead China toward common poverty." Li Daokui, a former adviser to the People's Bank of China was quoted by *Nikkei Asia* (September 29) as saying "We must be vigilant against common prosperity becoming a Great Leap Forward or something that blights development."

Meanwhile, the initiative has sparked apparent vigorous debate within the CCP. One example of its fallout is the proposal for a national property tax, under discussion since 2003. Wanting to reduce speculation, lower prices, and make life easier for middle-class families, Xi Jinping backed the proposal with his remark "Housing is for living, not for speculation". Politburo Standing Committee member and Vice Premier Han Zheng was tasked with steering a pilot rollout of the tax. On October 23, China's NPC Standing Committee (NPCSC) adopted a decision authorizing the State Council to carry out property tax pilots in selected, as yet unspecified, regions, for at least five years. Based on negative feedback, Vice Premier Han Zheng scaled back plans for the pilot from 30 to only 10 cities although earlier plans approved by Xi Jinping had called for its introduction in 30 cities.

Meanwhile concerns that 'common prosperity' could be a prelude to return of the days of the Cultural Revolution has aroused apprehension and discussion within the Chinese Communist Party (CCP). "Ultra-Leftists" and others, including supporters of Xi Jinping like Hu Xijin, the nationalist Editor-in-Chief of Global Times, are discussing 'common prosperity'. The crackdown against prominent Chinese billionaire private entrepreneurs has not helped.

Li Guangman, a former Editor-in-Chief of the Central China Electric Power News, which was closed in 2013, posted an article on August 28 on

WeChat where he lauded the announcement of "common prosperity." He said a "profound transformation" was underway in China and that "This transformation will wipe away all the dust." Indicating that the article had official approval, it was promptly picked up by other official newspapers including the CCP's official People's Daily. On October 9, Li Guangman posted another article on his WeChat account where he again asserted that a "profound transformation" is underway, but this time added "It's changing our society, thoughts, concepts and lives and it will not be stopped by the will of some people or groups with vested interests." He railed against private businesses investing in and controlling the media and listed two examples to substantiate how politics, business, culture and the media could be affected. He urged tougher policies against "unregulated" capitalism, "effeminate male pop stars" etc.

Hu Xijin responded to Li Guangman's with a warning against creating "confusion and panic." A number of articles authored by academics justifying "common prosperity" have been published over the past month in the *Guangming Daily*, *People's Daily* and other national newspapers.

On September 19, Cai Fang a former Vice-President and Professor at the Chinese Academy of Social Sciences, explained that the concept of "common prosperity" is not new in Chinese politics and is compatible with the reform policies. It had, he said, appeared when former Chinese leader Deng Xiaoping initiated economic reforms in the late 1970s, and again at the 14th Party Congress in 1992, which declared that the aim was "to build a socialist market economy". The 18th and 19th CCP Central Committees under the leadership of President Xi Jinping included the term in all major Party and Government policy documents. Cai Fang argued there is consensus that the Chinese people had benefitted from the reform and opening, but said that despite growing prosperity income inequality had widened. He pointed out that in 2019, the rural–urban income ratio and Gini coefficient was 2.325 and 0.465, respectively, which was "hardly satisfactory". He said the leadership's reiteration of common prosperity as a principal policy goal, therefore, comes at the right time. He identified three reasons for the goal of common prosperity: 1. it is a logical continuation of the long-term task of eliminating poverty and pushing the low-income to the middle-income group, building a welfare society by 2020 and building a modern socialist country by 2049; 2. it is the key to "growing the pie" and a "skilful response" to alleviating discontent caused by income inequality, social immobility and low-wages of workers, youth and the less-educated groups; and 3. using redistribution tools along with charity and social responsibility will strengthen the level of social welfare and social protection and inequality will be reduced as common prosperity is realised.

At the China International Digital Economy Exposition in Shijiazhuang, Hebei Province on September 6, 2021, Vice Premier Liu He, who is among Xi Jinping's closest confidants and the principal economic adviser, also sought to assure China's private sector. He said, "China's policy of supporting the development of the private economy remains unchanged. There is no change now, and there will be no change in the future."

Xi Jinping personally sought to address and allay these concerns and explain that the intention is not to bring about "common poverty". The CCP's leading theoretical fortnightly Qiu Shi (October 15) published an article by Xi Jinping captioned 'Solidly promoting common prosperity', which contained remarks on common prosperity made by him in speeches in 2021. Xi Jinping stressed that the Party realises that poverty is not socialism and had broken traditional institutional constraints to allow some people and some regions to get rich first. He said since the 18th Party Congress, the Party Central Committee has "put the gradual realization of common prosperity for all people on a more important position" and is promoting coordinated regional development to create "good conditions for promoting common prosperity". Emphasising that there are acute problems of unbalanced and inadequate development with "a large gap between urban and rural regional development and income distribution", Xi Jinping said China "must resolutely prevent polarization, promote common wealth, and achieve social harmony and stability". He declared "Common prosperity is the essential requirement of socialism and an important feature of Chinese-style modernization" and that this is the goal for the middle of this century.

Chinese President Xi Jinping's remarks on "common prosperity", which were intended to consolidate his position in the run up to the upcoming 20th Party Congress late next year, appears to have instead provoked robust inner-Party debate. This has spilled out into China's official media and brought to the surface the discontent among academics, economists and CCP cadres with Xi Jinping and his policies. Apprehension of a swing back to the days of the Cultural Revolution were articulated during the 19th Party Congress in 2017, when Xi Jinping abolished the term limits for the position of President of China and senior cadres especially voiced fears of a return to the one-man rule of Mao. These apprehensions have resurfaced. While Xi Jinping still appears to have a firm grip on the CCP, it is clear that sections of the Party are discontented and this introduces a degree of political uncertainty until the Party Congress late next year.

This was first published by the Centre for China Analysis and Strategy (CCAS) and Vivekananda International Foundation (VIF) in October 27, 2021.

29. 'China's Central Economic Work Conference Flags the Difficulties Ahead'

China's important annual Central Economic Work Conference was held in Beijing from December 8 – 10, 2021. The conference is an important forum where Chinese leaders map out the country's economic priorities for the coming year and when analysts can gauge the state of China's economy.

This Central Economic Work Conference was held in the backdrop of the continuing deterioration in Sino-US relations, global economic and social distress and surge in anti-China sentiment caused by the Covid pandemic, China's plateauing economy, and looming severe socio-economic problems. Difficulties are accentuated by issues like rising prices, growing unemployment, closure of businesses — official Chinese data revealed that 4.37 million micro and small businesses, described as the "backbone" of China's private sector, closed in the first 11 months of 2021 – and banks and bank outlets, and the reports since late last year of pay cuts and withdrawal of performance bonuses of officials in even the more prosperous provinces and cities like Jiangsu, Zhejiang, Guangdong, Fujian and Shanghai.

In a talk at the 14th Golden Kirin Forum on December 2, Tsinghua University economist David Li Daokui warned that the next five years could be the toughest in China's 40 years of reform and opening up. He listed weakening external demand, industrial chain restructuring, pressures of carbon reduction, and insufficient domestic demand as among the contributory factors.

In the run up to the conference, Chinese Premier Li Keqiang chaired a symposium of economic experts and business leaders on November 18, to get a feedback and suggestions from top advisors before setting the economic policy agenda for 2022 at the Central Economic Work Conference. Later, on December 6, Chinese President and CCP CC General Secretary Xi Jinping convened separate meetings of the Politburo Standing Committee and the

Politburo to discuss the economic challenges facing China and the proposed remedial measures.

Reporting (December 6) on the Politburo Standing Committee and Politburo meetings, *Xinhua* said apart from highlighting "the strong leadership of the Party Central Committee with Comrade Xi Jinping at the core", the meetings emphasised the need to focus on innovation-driven high-quality development, tackle the pandemic, continue to improve the people's livelihood, stabilise the macroeconomic market, maintain economic operations within a reasonable range, and maintain overall social stability. They called for enhancing "the core competitiveness of the manufacturing industry, enhancing the resilience of the supply chain and promoting construction of affordable housing to better meet the reasonable housing needs of buyers". The last flows from Xi Jinping's remark in August 2017 "houses are built to be lived in, not for speculation". Science and Technology received special attention, with the meetings resolving that implementation of science and technology policies should be accelerated, key core technologies tackled and national strategic science and technology forces strengthened. They called for realising "a virtuous circle of science and technology, industry, and finance".

The Politburo also "pointed out that it is necessary to do a good job in all aspects of the year-end" and "make overall arrangements for coal, electricity, oil, and gas transportation to ensure supply to ensure that the people live through the winter warmly. It is necessary to ensure the payment of wages for migrant workers". The reference to coal and electricity would be related to reports appearing from October that since August over 20 provinces in China have limited electricity usage causing blackouts in certain regions.

The lengthy almost 10,000-character statement issued at the conclusion of the Central Economic Work Conference flagged these problems while underscoring the severity of the difficulties. Significantly, it hinted at anticipated social unrest by mentioning "stability" 25 times. The *Global Times* (December 12) asserted that stability is a big theme. It said the meeting "prioritised stability, a word that was mentioned 25 times, for 2022, vowing to improve people's livelihood, stabilize the macro economy, and maintain social stability".

Equally significant was a Commentator's article in the *People's Daily* (December 16) which stressed the importance of Xi Jinping's leadership at this time. The article highlighted that "the Central Economic Work Conference pointed out that it is necessary to adhere to the centralized and unified leadership of the Party Central Committee, calmly respond to major challenges, and move forward in unison". It asserted that "Practice has fully proved that the decision and deployment of the Party Central Committee with Comrade Xi Jinping at the core are completely correct". The article did not minimise the difficulties and stated that China's economic development is "faced with the triple pressures of shrinking demand, supply shocks, and weakening expectations" and that "the external environment has become more complex, severe and uncertain". It urged cadres to work hard and focus on economic work.

Xinhua (December 10) stated that Chinese President Xi Jinping delivered an "important" speech at the conference where he described "2021 as a milestone for the Party and the nation". He reviewed the country's economic work in 2021, analysed the current economic situation and outlined the next year's economic work. Xinhua reported that the statement issued after the Conference cautioned that China's economic development is facing pressure from demand contraction, supply shocks and weakening expectations, and that "the external environment is becoming increasingly complicated, grim and uncertain". It said "We must face the difficulties squarely while staying confident" and remain "committed to China's own cause". The Central Economic Work Conference stated that China will continue to implement a "proactive fiscal policy and a prudent monetary policy and some infrastructure investment will be accelerated". This latter assertion could have been prompted by some estimates that 1.8 trillion yuan (US$ 283 billion) in unspent money is to be rolled over to 2022. The statement included long sections on 'common prosperity', unemployment, thrift and conservation.

The Central Economic Work Conference noted that China maintained a leading position in the world in economic development and epidemic control, with progress made in scientific strength, industrial chain resilience, reform and opening-up, people's livelihood and ecological civilization. It, however, urged proactive efforts to align with the highest international economic and trade rules, deepen reform via high-level opening-up, and boost high-quality development. *Xinhua* reported that the meeting "stressed the necessity to adhere to the centralized, unified leadership of the CPC Central Committee, promote highquality development and pursue progress while ensuring stability". It stressed the need "to safeguard macroeconomic stability, keep major economic indicators within an appropriate range and maintain social stability to prepare for the Party's 20th National Congress". Ning Jizhe, Deputy Head of the National Development and Reform Commission (NDRC), pointed out that the conference put "stable economic growth" at its core. He added "The huge potential of China's development lies in the vast rural areas and the central and western regions. We should tap into this potential and transform the potential into effective demand".

Articles published in the *People's Daily* (December 12) and the *South China Morning Post* (December 13) highlighted that Xi Jinping called for self-sufficiency in energy, food and minerals to meet global challenges. He said resource shortages could turn into a 'grey rhino' risk – an obvious yet ignored threat – for the world's No: 2 economy. Xi Jinping said China must establish a "strategic baseline" to ensure self-sufficiency in key commodities, from energy to soybeans, as the secure supply of primary products moves up China's long-term agenda. The Central Economic Work Conference identified the secure supply of primary goods such as agricultural products, minerals and energy as one of five "significant theoretical and practical issues" to prepare for amid the Covid-19 pandemic and changing international relations. It said the four other government priorities were "common prosperity", capital regulation, defusing major financial risks and carbon neutrality. The *People's Daily* quoted him as saying "[We] should fortify the national strategic materials reserve system to secure minimum needs at critical moments."

On grain security, Xi Jinping said China's "arable land area is reducing" and cash crops were being favoured over cereals and legumes. "The more food we have, the more we should think about the time of no grain." "I have repeatedly said Chinese people's rice bowls should be firmly held in our own hands, never let others take us by the throat on eating, which is a basic survival issue." The CCTV newscast on December 14 said Xi had pointed out that "seeds are the foundation for agricultural modernization. The ethnic seed industry must be promoted, and the security of seed sources must be raised to a strategic level related to national security". Separately, at another forum on December 11, Han Wenxiu, a Deputy Director of the CCP CC's Central Committee for Financial and Economic Affairs, said that "great shortages of primary commodities are likely to evolve into a grey rhino."

Xi Jinping also emphasised "stability" as the economic priority for 2022, ahead of the Winter Olympics and the 20th National Party Congress. He called on local cadres to adjust their approach in implementing national carbon emission targets and said "[We] should make the direction right, make the focus clear ... should prevent the 'devil in the details' hurting the overall situation."

The Central Economic Work Conference is undoubtedly gearing up for a tough year ahead. China's leadership is acutely aware of the deteriorating international environment and economic difficulties which will complicate China's 'rise'. Agriculture and food-grain production has been receiving noticeably elevated attention throughout 2021 as has been the maintenance of the supply chain, which becomes important in view of the growing strain in Sino-US relations. China's exports to the US were valued at US$ 452.58 billion in 2020. The Chinese leadership's apprehensions about the difficulties for China in the coming years were spelt out in June 2020 by Zhou Li, a former official of the CCP CC's International Liaison Department and career diplomat. Many of these are touched upon in the statement of the Central Economic Work Conference.

This was first published by the Centre for China Analysis and Strategy (CCAS) and Vivekananda International Foundation (VIF) in January 6, 2022.

30. China's Deteriorating Economy Has Created Instability for Xi Jinping

China's economy is in dire straits. While assessments of China's economic situation by foreign banks and economists is worrying, the views of some Chinese economists are even more pessimistic. They question the Chinese government's projected economic growth rate of five percent and say that growth is really negative and nearer minus two to three percent! Close scrutiny of China's official media too reveals a worrying picture with little prospect of an economic recovery in the near term. Chinese President Xi Jinping, who has focussed on dissemination of Xi Jinping's Thoughts through his books, has been slow in addressing the economy. It was only at the Politburo meeting on January 31 –two months after the 20th Party Congress – that the economy and development was discussed. It also discussed better coordination of development and security, but the priority accorded to security apparently continues to hinder development. The unchecked deterioration of the economy has contributed substantively to the revival of direct, overt criticism of Chinese President Xi Jinping amid indications that factions, or groups, opposed to his policies have become active.

A variety of factors like tough new regulations on the Fintech, real estate and private businesses, have contributed to the spreading dissatisfaction. The deleterious effects of the slowing economy were compounded by the disastrous zero-Covid policy. The latter caused sudden unanticipated disruptions in logistics supply chains from ports to production centres, in turn upsetting delivery schedules. Citizens were impacted because they couldn't get food supplies while under lockdown. The disruptions caused a drop in exports and forced tens of thousands of small businesses to shut down. China's National Bureau of Statistics on August 31, showed that manufacturing activity shrank for the sixth straight month in August. China's exports to the US too slumped by around

41 percent. Citizen's anger increased and was occasionally manifest in protests and public criticism of Chinese President Xi Jinping despite the critics risking punitive action. Because of the rising incidence of protests the government stopped publishing data on their numbers. This simmering anger was on display in October 2022 when, provoked by the death of some citizens because of stringent zero-Covid restrictions which prevented fire-fighters from reaching and rescuing persons trapped in a burning house, citizens spontaneously took to the streets in ten cities across China. Dubbed the 'White Paper' revolution, it shook the leadership and prompted Chinese President Xi Jinping to suddenly announce abandonment of the zero-Covid policy.

The increasing joblessness has affected entrepreneurs, fresh graduates, veterans, rural folk and aggravated dissatisfaction. China's National Statistics Bureau (NSB) admitted that unemployment among students and youth aged between 16 to 24 years was at an all-time high of 20.8 percent. Chinese sources estimate the figure is much higher and the NSB has since announced it would suspend release of this data. The impact is more than on just the individual as most of these youth belong to 'one child' families and their parents are dependent on them. Joblessness in the countryside is far higher. The lack of opportunities and pressure at the work place has also given rise to a social phenomenon of 'tangping' or lying flat. 'Tangping' means the youth stay at home doing nothing because they have lost all hope of getting a job commensurate with their qualifications, or have no worthwhile prospects. Another very recent trend visible on China's social media is that of youth resigning their jobs and hosting "quitting" parties because they feel under excessive pressure or that they are at a dead-end in their jobs. CCP cadres have expressed concern at the spread of the phenomenon as they have the potential to adversely impact national productivity and spread disillusionment about the CCP.

The campaigns to 'clean up', or regulate, the fintech and real estate sectors have contributed to the economic decline and unemployment. China's central authorities so far appear unwilling to bail them out. The real estate sector accounts for over 60 percent of the revenues of provinces and counties. The prohibition on the sale of land by the provinces and counties has meant severe budgetary constraints. An unusually candid and critical article in China's

Economic Observer on August 11, 2023, captioned "No mother can cook for her children with no rice" highlighted the acuteness of the problem. Its reporter interviewed four Finance Directors of different provinces and highlighted that each had admitted to the severe paucity of funds and consequent pruning of development projects. The Directors, whose real identities were not revealed by the newspaper, said they spent most of their long working days explaining to queues of applicants why they are unable to give funds. The balance of their 14-hour work days, they said, were spent standing outside the doors of senior cadres pleading for funds. In addition, they have to submit detailed explanations to inspection teams from the Central Discipline Inspection Commission (CDIC), provincial audit teams, County inspectors and inspectors from concerned Municipalities. Meanwhile, Provincial and county chiefs task them to ensure funds for key development projects, paying salaries of staff etc. The *Economic Observer* assessed it was only a short time before the real estate sector becomes bankrupt. The article was deleted within a couple of days.

Provincial and local governments are trying to implement central instructions to tackle unemployment among students and youth, veterans and rural folk and alleviate living conditions. The Ministry of Housing this month announced concessions and exemptions for public housing construction till December 2025. In addition to job fairs, State-Owned Enterprises are being urged to recruit youth and veterans. In provinces, students are offered travel concessions for 3 to 6 months and other financial incentives. Shaanxi province, for example, from mid-August began offering students 1500 Yuan per month to go and work in the countryside.

Chinese President Xi Jinping, however, continues to emphasise security and 'ideological' education. Books on Xi Jinping's thoughts are required reading for Party members who are mandated to read four books a month. Since June 2023, Party members are required to watch the 40-second video released each morning by CCTV's Xiaoyang Video. A spate of directives has been issued almost each month to Party members on issues like "absolute loyalty", avoiding corrupt practices, restraining their family and relatives from violating Party discipline, use of the internet etc. Xi Jinping has also strengthened the internal security apparatus to curb opposition and stamp out protests. The public security departments at the provincial level have trebled their manpower strength. Facial recognition and the social credit management systems have become widespread and angered the citizens. Academics and students are also subject to strict controls to ensure they adhere to the correct political line and don't succumb to, or disseminate, western liberal ideas. The administrative and financial powers of senior CCP cadres including members of the Politburo have been curtailed and they are under surveillance. CCP members and enterprises, including foreign-owned businesses, are mandated to attend Party education classes a couple of times each week. While Xi Jinping's acolytes portray that the Global Development Initiative (GDI) and Global Security Initiative (GSI) could be effectively implemented at the same time, there have been no substantive steps to revive the economy.

A major 3687-word article in the Jingji Ribao (*Economic Daily*; June 9) sought to explain the new development pattern with the new security pattern. Its focus, though, was on security. Authored by the National Defence University Party Committee Doctrinal Study Centre Group, among China's leading Party doctrinal centres, it stressed that "National security is the foundation of national rejuvenation, and social stability is the prerequisite for national prosperity. Adhering to the overall national security concept and guaranteeing a new development pattern with a new security pattern demonstrates our party's major strategic considerations in coordinating development and security, and achieving high-quality development and high-level security dynamic balance". Mentioning the role of security in every aspect, it said the 20th Party Congress report "for the first time proposed "guaranteeing a new development pattern with a new security pattern", emphasizing adherence to the principle of people's security, political security as the foundation, and economic security based on military, scientific, technological, cultural and social security, and relying on the promotion of international security, coordinate external security and internal security, homeland security and national security, traditional security and non-traditional security, self-security and common security, and maintain and shape the safety of the country as a whole". It justified the emphasis by saying "As the world enters a new period of turmoil and change, the instability and uncertainty of China's national security situation has increased, and various aspects and fields are facing many security challenges". The article's focus was on countering sanctions, restrictions hampering the country's development, safeguarding peace etc.

The difficult economic situation and discontent with Chinese President Xi Jinping and his re-election for a third term, has not only revived criticism of Xi Jinping but has encouraged factional politics in the CCP. Some factions are already clearly visible. China's official media continues to periodically report instances of cadres associated with senior cadres like former Politburo member Bo Xilai, Deputy Minister of the Public Security Department Sun Lijun, former Central Military Commission Vice Chairmen Xu Caihou and Guo Boxiong etc being punished. Some Party directives clearly warn cadres against "black-faced liars", "double faced cadres" and "factions, cliques and groups". The disappearance of Xi Jinping's protégé Qin Gang, who was divested by the National People's Congress Standing Committee (NPCSC) of his post of Foreign Minister in July this year, remains a mystery. Curiously Qin Gang has retained his higher post of State Councilor pointing to robust behind-the-scenes disagreements regarding Qin Gang. In this backdrop, conditions are suitable for factional infighting in the CCP.

In October 2022, coinciding with Xi Jinping's re-election for the third time, a 2015 essay by China's Rao Yi warning against "state eunuchizationcirculated on China's social media, with the warning: Today's China is mass-producing 'eunuchs'." Earlier this year, the photography department of a Beijing student press association organized by the Beijing Youth Daily, a Party-run media outlet controlled by the Municipal Communist Youth League, posted a requiem for the 2022 "White Paper Movement" to WeChat. The photograph was captioned: "I will remember November 26, 2022, I will remember the bravery of the Communication person." The post was quickly deleted.

Criticism has progressively become more direct. During the recent flood in Hebei Province, the authorities released water from the dams disregarding the plight of residents of Zhouzhou, who suffered heavy losses of life and property, to protect the Xiongan New Area. A CCP member called it "a typical 30 percent natural disaster and 70 percent man-made disaster". Many residents posted criticisms of Xi Jinping saying that unlike previous leaders he has never visited areas affected by disasters and natural calamities. Some alleged he was unaware of the extent of damage and had not despatched units of the People's Liberation Army (PLA) or People's Armed Police (PAP) to assist local authorities. The posts stayed for days.

Damaging in recent weeks, however, was the lengthy 2980-word article published by the pro-CCP Singapore newspaper *Lianhe Zaobo* on August 21, 2023. In classic Chinese style the article, a sharp criticism of Xi Jinping, but without actually naming him, was published outside China. Captioned 'The root cause of China's economic problems lies in political problems', the article did not name Xi Jinping but the target of its criticism was clear. It was authored by Lew Mon-hung, a Hongkong businessman and member of the 11th Chinese People's Political Consultative Conference (CPPCC) – China's top political advisory body. The author has taken considerable risk since outspoken critics in Hongkong have been arrested under the National Security Law. Its publication points to the beginning of factional infighting in the CCP.

Mentioning the contributions of past leaders like Deng Xiaoping and Hu Yaobang, the article discussed the distressing economic situation. It said China "is facing a wave of private enterprise closures, foreign companies evacuating, sharply shrinking investment, declining imports and exports, serious shortage of consumption, serial debt explosions, large-scale unemployment, and government facing losses in tax. Investment, export and consumption, all the three big economic engines are underpowered or even stalled". It said the joke in China is: "The three new engines of the economy are the National Bureau of Statistics, Central Propaganda Department, and Xinhua News Agency" and "the only toolbox to save the economy is blowing the trumpet"! The article regretted that decisions by consensus had been jettisoned. It asserted that the main reason for China's economic rise is that "the mainland government suspended class struggle in politics and insisted on economic construction as the centre, thus liberating productive forces". In contrast now there has been a "strengthening of ideology in politics, insisting that "Marx is right", eliminating private ownership, emphasizing the philosophy of struggle, and abusing the concepts of national security and anti-espionage". Consequently, it said, foreign businessmen and tourists are hesitant to visit China. It said that instead of implementing political system reforms for an effective anti-corruption process, various forms of political campaigns are successively initiated.

It attributed the economic downturn in recent years to the violation "by some people" of the centre's second historical resolution on "prohibiting any form of personality cult", advocating that "loyalty is not absolute, absolute is not loyal", and of "one authority determining the final say". It declared that the cult of personality had been raised to a new peak. It blamed the "wolf warrior diplomacy" and the boasting that accompanied it with claims that "China has surpassed the United States in terms of economy, technology, and comprehensive national strength" and that China "points the way for mankind". It regretted the lack of grace in international exchanges "and making enemies on all sides". It criticised the erroneous policy of support for Russia.

The article pointed out that "as a result of years of wolf warrior diplomacy, Sino-US relations have fallen to their lowest point since President Nixon's visit to China in 1972. Relations between China-Europe, China-UK, China-Japan, China-South Korea, China-Australia, and China-Canada have all fallen to their lowest point in decades. The result of the Belt and Road Initiative and the large-scale distribution of coins is only to ruin the hard-earned wealth of the Chinese people, and has not exchanged for real allies". It said if China "wants to realize modernization; the main target of opening up is the United States. Therefore, improving and developing relations with the United States is an inherent requirement of reform and opening up, and it is also a fundamental requirement for ensuring national security under the Cold War situation".

Saying "The example is right in front of you", it advocated reform of the political system, including the implementation of constitutional democracy, universal suffrage, declaration and publicity of officials' assets, judicial independence, freedom of speech and press and supervision by public opinion.

Unless the economic situation improves and unemployment comes down, confidence in the CCP will erode impacting its legitimacy. Opposition already exists within the CCP to many of Xi Jinping's policies – for example the intrusive security policies, on Russia, the US etc. – and have the potential to fuel factions. The next few years will be difficult for China and Chinese President Xi Jinping and be possibly marked by political instability.

This was first published by the Centre for China Analysis and Strategy (CCAS) and Vivekananda International Foundation (VIF) in September 2, 2023.

31. China's Central Finance and Economic Affairs Work Conference Reveals Emphasis on Security and Development

China's long awaited Central Financial Work Conference was held in Beijing on October 30- 31, 2023, and was the first held since the establishment of the Central Financial Commission and the Central Financial Working Committee. With the decline in China's economic growth and little prospects for its revival, there was expectation among Chinese economists, provincial government officials and others that the important once-in-five-year Central Finance and Economic Work Conference would take steps for stimulating and reviving the economy. They expected that measures to stimulate the economy would include infusing large sums into specific sectors, like real estate. While the conference did take some steps, it instead emphasised 'security' and 'development', which were the policy guidelines set for this term by the 20th Party Congress.

On October 30, Chinese President Xi Jinping and Chinese Premier Li Qiang delivered'important'speeches at the Central Financial Work Conference (CFWC), which was attended by Politburo Standing Committee members Zhao Leji, Wang Huning, Cai Qi, Ding Xuexiang and Li Xi . The *Xinhua* report on the Conference highlighted that "The meeting stressed that finance is the bloodline of the national economy" and "is an important part of the core competitiveness of the country". It emphasised the need to "comprehensively strengthen financial supervision, improve the financial system", "prevent and mitigate risks", and "unswervingly take the road of financial development with Chinese characteristics and provide strong support for the construction of a strong country with the Chinese-style modernisation and the national rejuvenation of the country in an all-rounded way". Emphasising that "The

CPC Central Committee has combined Marxist financial theories with the concrete realities of contemporary China and with the excellent traditional Chinese culture" it stressed "it is necessary to adhere to the centralised and unified leadership of the CPC Central Committee over the work of the financial sector, and to adhere to the people-centred value orientation." The meeting stressed "that in the current and future period, to do a good job in financial work, we must adhere to and strengthen the overall leadership of the Party, take Xi Jinping's thought of socialism with Chinese characteristics in the new era as the guide, fully implement the spirit of the 20th CPC National Congress....". It called for strengthening the policy financial institutions, and giving "full play to the functions of the insurance industry as an economic shock absorber and social stabiliser. "It called for doing a good job in the five major areas of science and technology finance, green finance, inclusive finance, pension finance and digital finance."

He Lifeng made the concluding speech. Representatives of the People's Bank of China, the General Administration of Financial Supervision, China Securities Regulatory Commission, Beijing Municipality, Liaoning Province, Hubei Province and Sichuan Province also spoke. Members of the CCP CC Politburo, CCP CC Secretariat, CCP CC and "leading comrades" of the National People's Congress Standing Committee, State Councillors, the President of the Supreme People's Court, and CPPCC were present at the meeting. Members of the Central Financial Commission, all provinces, autonomous regions, cities and municipalities with separate plans, Xinjiang Production and Construction Corps, relevant departments of the Central Government and State organs, relevant people's groups, relevant departments of the Central Military Commission organs, financial institutions managed by the Central Government, and the main comrades-in-charge of some enterprises, etc. also attended the meeting.

The 114-word resolution of the two-day Central Financial Work Conference established a new Party-led Central Financial Commission, a super-regulator that will oversee govt institutions such as the People's Bank of China and China Securities Regulatory Commission. Vice Premier He Lifeng, successor to Liu He, was appointed (October 30) the Office Director of the Communist Party's Central Financial and Economic Affairs Commission, which is being set up to strengthen the Party's control of the country's $61 trillion financial industry. A *People's Daily* (October 30) article captioned 'Do a solid job in financial work' said: "Finance is the lifeblood of the real economy, and serving the real economy is the inherent. purpose of finance. It is also the fundamental measure to prevent financial risks". The Beijing Daily (November 2) pointed out that supervision, risk and persistence are key words. It noted that this meeting once again emphasized the need to accelerate the construction of affordable housing, a theme articulated by Chinese President Xi Jinping.

The Conference generally adhered to the main points of the important, lengthy article in the *Jingji Ribao* (*Economic Daily*; June 9). It was authored by the National Defence University Party Committee Doctrinal Study Centre Group and titled "Guarantee the new development pattern with the new security pattern—Seriously study the first and second volumes of "Selected Readings of Xi Jinping's Works". It highlighted: 1. the importance of "a deep understanding of the great strategic significance of guaranteeing a new development pattern with a new security pattern"; 2. "National security is the foundation of national rejuvenation, and social stability is the prerequisite for national prosperity; 3. the report of the 20th Party Congress which devoted "a special chapter to make strategic deployments for maintaining national security and social stability, and for the first time proposed "guaranteeing a new development pattern with a new security pattern", emphasizing adherence to the principle of people's security, political security as the foundation, and economic security based on military, scientific, technological, cultural and social security, and relying on the promotion of international security, coordinate external security and internal security, homeland security and national security, traditional security and non-traditional security, self-security and common security, and maintain and shape the country as a whole Safety; 4. "Chinese-style modernization must be advanced on the basis of firmly guarding the bottom line of safety. The next period may be a period in which risks in all aspects of our country's development will continue to accumulate and even be exposed in a concentrated manner. The major risks we face include not only domestic economic, political, ideological, social risks, and risks from nature, but also international economic, political, and military risks.

5. National security is the basic prerequisite for the survival and development of a country, an important cornerstone for stability and stability, and a strong pillar for ensuring the development and growth of the country and the nation. 6. "Development and security must be dynamically balanced. Development and security, like the two wheels of a car and the two wings of a bird, complement each other and cannot be neglected. Looking at the history of the rise and fall of major powers in the world, we can find that when a great power rises, it is often able to coordinate development and security well, while its decline is closely related to the failure to coordinate development and security well. Coordinating development and security, enhancing the awareness of adversity, and being prepared for danger in times of peace are major principles of our party in governing the country"; and 7. "Adhere to the centralized and unified leadership of the Party Central Committee on national security work. Upholding the Party's absolute leadership over national security work is the fundamental guarantee for maintaining national security and social stability, and it is a fundamental political principle that must be followed. The *Jingji Ribao* also dealt with military security.

On November 6, China's *Nanfang Ribao* (Southern Daily) said that the conference for the first time proposed the goal of building a "financial power" and strengthening the centralized and unified leadership of the Party Central Committee on financial work. It asserted that the name was changed from the previous "National Financial Work Conference" to the "Central Financial Work Conference" to highlight the centralized and unified leadership of the Party Central Committee on financial work. Noting, however, that "financial chaos and corruption continue to occur, and financial supervision and governance capabilities are weak", it said the conference called for determination to fundamentally solve these problems. It emphasized the need to comprehensively strengthen financial supervision and effectively improve the effectiveness of financial supervision.

Discontent has been rising in China, among other reasons, because of the drop in people's living standards and steady rise in joblessness. This was highlighted when China's National Bureau of Statistics released figures on June 15, revealing that graduate unemployment had risen to 20.8 percent from 20.4 percent in May. Shortly thereafter the National Bureau of Statistics stopped publishing this data. Earlier, the authorities had prohibited release of data on the number of strikes and protests in China – another indicator of growing discontent. In this backdrop and despite some Chinese doubting his competence, there was expectation that Chinese Premier Li Qiang would take steps to revive the economy. The distribution of work among members of the Politburo Standing Committee, which seemed to expand Premier Li Qiang's remit, raised expectation that he would initiate the necessary steps. There was hope too that the Central Finance and Economic Work Conference would unveil measures to provide stimulus for private entrepreneurs and real estate sectors and address local government debt. None of this has happened. Instead, Chinese President Xi Jinping has further tightened his grip on economic policy and ensured priority to security over development.

Just weeks prior to the meeting of the Central Finance and Economic Work Conference, it was revealed that China's former economic tsar and Vice Premier, Liu He has retained oversight of the important Office of the Central Financial and Economic Affairs Commission, which is chaired by Chinese President Xi Jinping. Liu He, a close personal friend of Xi Jinping, apparently continues to be his economic adviser.

Another indication that Xi Jinping intends to maintain tight control over the financial sector were his visits — for the first time ever — to the People's Bank of China (PBoC) and the State Administration of Foreign Exchange (SAFE) on October 24. His visits came just a week before the Central Finance and Economic Work Conference. Chinese analysts are divided on whether Xi Jinping's visits imply that some policy palliatives are planned, or are a message to the PBoC and SAFE to further harden the financial system, while strengthening Party leadership and further cleaning up the financial system. A day earlier on October 23, Xi Jinping personally visited the Shanghai Stock Exchange and stated that A-shares are stable and improving, and there is no need for bailout policies.

However, the news is not all bleak for the provinces. China's financial magazine *Caixin* (November 2) reported that local governments in China are rushing to plan infrastructure projects to be funded by the new sovereign debt issuance worth 1 trillion yuan (US $137 billion) approved by China's National People's Congress the previous week to support disaster relief and construction. Hebei province held a meeting on October 29 to accelerate its plans to deploy funds from the special bond issuance. Several counties held subsequent meetings on implementation. This provided some relief to the cash strapped provinces, who depended on land sales for over 30 percent of their revenues till such sales were prohibited by the centre. Many provincial governments had to slash salaries of employees by 30 percent, withdraw bonuses etc.

While the Central Financial Work Conference did emphasise that Finance is the lifeblood of the real economy, its resolution avoided issues afflicting the Chinese economy namely, encouraging the private entrepreneurs, problem of debts of the provincial governments and the near bankruptcy of major real estate companies. The focus was more on security followed by development together with centralisation and supervision of financial work. The next few weeks and months will show whether the Chinese leadership unveil plans to separately address such specific issues.

This was first published by the Centre for China Analysis and Strategy (CCAS) and Vivekananda International Foundation (VIF) in November 14, 2023.

32. Quick Assessment of the Chinese Communist Party's Third Plenum

The Chinese Communist Party (CCP) Central Committee (CC) convened its Third Plenum after an unexplained delay of almost eight months. The failure to convene the Third Plenum despite China's steadily declining economy — which has over 23 percent graduate unemployment, high urban and rural unemployment, rising prices and cost of living, drastically reduced revenues of the provinces and widespread dissatisfaction resulting in strikes and protests — prompted speculation that the CCP leadership was divided on the prescription required for giving the economy the necessary fillip. Third Plenums are important as they set the country's economic policy for its 5 year term.

The 4-day (July 15-18), closed-door Third Plenum ended on July 18 with the release on the final day of a communique titled "Decision of the Central Committee of the Communist Party of China on Further Comprehensively Deepening Reforms and Promoting Chinese-style Modernization". The 199 members of the CCP CC and 165 Alternate Members attending the Third Plenum hammered out the 5020-character (Chinese) communique, which bore the definitive imprint of Chinese President Xi Jinping. Communiques issued by these Plenums do not contain details of the decisions taken, and this communique too did not announce any major decisions or reform measures. These are normally released in the succeeding days. It did state, though that Chinese President Xi Jinping delivered an "important" speech and that he explained the decision on further "comprehensively deepening reforms and promoting Chinese-style Modernisation". The Plenum document "unanimously" praised the CCP Politburo and CC for guiding the country "in the face of a severe and complex international environment and arduous and onerous domestic reform, development and stability tasks".

The communique also clearly suggested that the Chinese leadership is worried about the current state of the country's economy. Implying that there could be some policy interventions in the coming months, it said "The plenum analysed the current situation and tasks, and emphasized that [we must] unswervingly realize the annual economic and social development goals." It proposed 300 reform measures, but did not offer any special incentives to the engines of China's economy, namely China's private entrepreneurs. In May 2023, China's authoritative official news agency *Xinhua* said "The private sector contributes approximately 50 percent of China's tax revenue, 60 percent of its GDP, 70 percent of its technological innovation, and accounts for 80 percent of its urban employment". Instead, the Plenum appeared to continue policies favouring China's State-owned Enterprises (SoEs). It said "We must unswervingly consolidate and develop the public economy, unswervingly encourage, support and guide the development of the non-public economy, ensure that all types of ownership economies use production factors equally in accordance with the law, participate in market competition fairly, and receive equal legal protection, and promote the complementary advantages and common development of all types of ownership economies".

Suggesting a shift in economic policy to incorporate Xi Jinping's ideas, the plenum said plans had been made for "building a high-standard socialist market economy" and "promoting high-quality economic development". It said that "high-quality development is the primary task of building a modern socialist country in an all-round way. We must guide reform with the new development concept, based on the new development stage ....". It laid emphasis on "new industrialisation", developing the "digital economy" and "new energy". It stated that China "must remain committed to the basic state policy of opening to the outside world and continue to promote reform through opening up". Seeming to hint that China would strive to co-opt foreign partners for getting advanced technology, it said "[We must] improve the mechanisms for ensuring national security in foreign-related affairs".

The communique dwelt on ideology and the CCP's leadership role. A lengthy paragraph stressed that the "Party's leadership is the fundamental guarantee for further deepening reform comprehensively to advance Chinese modernization". It called for deeper "understanding of the decisive significance of establishing Comrade Xi Jinping's core position on the Party Central Committee and in the Party as a whole and establishing the guiding role of Xi Jinping Thought on Socialism with Chinese Characteristics for a New Era". Party cadres were exhorted to maintain political integrity, follow the leadership core, and keep in alignment with the central Party leadership; and uphold Comrade Xi Jinping's core position on the Party Central Committee and in the Party as a whole and uphold the Central Committee's authority and its centralized, unified leadership.

The document announced two important declarations, which sought to project confidence that China will be able to weather the difficulties caused by the imposition of sanctions by the US and West especially on technology. It said that "by 2035, a high-level socialist market economic system will be fully established, the socialist system with Chinese characteristics will be further improved, the modernization of the national governance system and governance capacity will be basically realized, and socialist modernization will be basically realized, laying a solid foundation for building a socialist modern power in an all-round way by the middle of this century". It added that by the 80th anniversary of the founding of the People's Republic of China in 2029 it will complete the reform measures proposed at the Plenum.

Of popular interest was the Third Plenum's decision pronouncing the fate of senior CCP and People's Liberation Army (PLA) officials who had disappeared from public view since 2023. The communique clarified that the request of former Chinese Foreign Minister Qin Gang, a protégé of Xi who still appears to retain his "protection", that he be allowed to resign from the CCP CC had been accepted. Confirming that he is not guilty of violating the CCP's disciplinary regulations and continues in the CCP, it referred to him as "comrade". Notable was the omission of any reference to former Defence Minister General Wei Fenghe who was also reported to be under investigation. Former Defence Li Shangfu, however, was charged with "serious violations of discipline and law" and expelled from the CCP. Interestingly, Li Shangfu and Xi were friends and their fathers had served together in the People's Army. The senior Vice Chairman of the Central Military Commission (CMC) General Zhang Youxia, a close associate of Xi who has been retained in the CMC past the retirement age, is reported to have recommended Li Shangfu's appointment as Defence Minister. The Plenum confirmed the expulsions from the CCP of former Rocket Force Commander General Li Yuchao and Chief of Staff of the Rocket Force Sun Jinming.

The Third Plenum communique had Xi Jinping's imprint and confirmed his authority on economic affairs. It affirmed Xi Jinping's concepts of a "high-standard socialist market economy" and "high-quality economic development" and maintained the emphasis on Party discipline and ideology. Specific mention was made of the Belt and Road Initiative. Though the communique has not revealed any incentives to boost the economy, it is possible that some initiatives may be disclosed over the coming weeks. China's private entrepreneurs who are major contributors to the country's economy, the students, urban and rural unemployed and others will, however, be disappointed.

This was first published by the Centre for China Analysis and Strategy (CCAS) and Vivekananda International Foundation (VIF) in July 20, 2024.

33. Fears of 'Colour Revolution' in People's Liberation Army (PLA)

China's People's Liberation Army (PLA) is the sword arm of the Chinese Communist Party (CCP). Its recruits swear an oath of loyalty to the Party. The evening that Xi Jinping took over China's top three positions of General Secretary of the CCP Central Committee (CC), Chairman of the Central Military Commission (CMC) and China's President, he convened an enlarged meeting of the CMC where he declared that henceforth the single determining criteria for promotion for PLA personnel would be their political reliability.

With the fading of 'Long March' veterans, all of whom commanded respect in the PLA because of their military experience, the CCP leadership comprised party apparatchiks with no military background and they began keeping a closer eye on the PLA. Particularly after Deng Xiaoping's demise, CCP CC General Secretary Jiang Zemin and his successor, Hu Jintao, began focussing on political discipline in the PLA and incrementally strengthened the authority of the PLA's Political Commissars. Chinese President Xi Jinping continued this trend and the Political Commissars today have a veto on the promotion of regular PLA field officers and even exercise disciplinary authority over troops.

The leadership closely monitors the PLA for any hint of wavering in political ideology and signs of dissatisfaction among the veterans and demobilised soldiers. They are apprehensive that dissatisfaction could easily spread to serving PLA personnel. Concern about diffusion in loyalty to the Party increased since 2012 following the calls by Chinese intellectuals, academics and "liberal" elements for separating the army from the Party and making the PLA an army of the State. Xi Jinping's view is that by placing the army under the State the Soviet Union had "disarmed" the Communist Party of the Soviet Union (CPSU) which was an important factor contributing to its downfall.

There are indications recently that the CCP leadership apprehends that attempts by "hostile" Western powers to instigate a "colour revolution" and delink the PLA from the Party could spread in the PLA.

An article in a publication of the Chinese Academy of Social Sciences (CASS), pointed to concerns about the ability of younger PLA officers and soldiers to withstand the online onslaught on ideology and efforts to separate the army from the Party. The South China Morning Post separately disclosed that PLA instructors and recruiters are finding it difficult to train the "newer breed of soldier", some of whom even dared to challenge superiors when they were not happy. It added that physical fitness is another tough challenge for the PLA since it began recruiting students.

An article by Ren Long and Lin Wenjie of the Political College of National Defense University and the Joint Logistics Support Force Longyan Comprehensive Warehouse Support Team respectively, was published in 'China Social Science News' (Issue 2169, May 20, 2021), a publication of the Chinese Academy of Social Sciences (CASS). In the article they disclosed that there are serious concerns about the PLA rank and file adhering to the policy of the Party's absolute leadership over the Army. Asserting that "the party's absolute leadership over the army is the fundamental principle of our party's army building and ruling the army", they wrote "at present, with the firm pace of strengthening the army and rejuvenating the army, grassroots construction has reached a new historical starting point, and profound new changes have taken place in mission requirements, construction connotation, daily operation status, troop organization, composition of officers and soldiers, and the external social environment. This has brought new challenges to the party's absolute leadership over the army taking root at the grassroots level".

The authors stressed that "Only by adhering to the party's absolute leadership of the army and extending it uninterruptedly down the line to the grassroots level can we ensure that the majority of officers and soldiers can align themselves in the face of severe tests, fulfil their missions in complex struggles, and continuously enhance the party's "direct power" of absolute leadership over the army." The article continued: "To be strong, the grassroots level must first be strong politically. The officers and soldiers of the new era generally lack the training in the severe and complex environment and the baptism of blood and fire on the battlefield. They often lack understanding and mastery of the party's absolute leadership over the military, and coupled with the extremely deceptive political propaganda of the hostile forces, they should be more effective. The soul of the disciplined army".

The article emphasised that it is important "to clear out the fog of thought". It quoted President Xi Jinping as pointing out that "some Western countries are stepping up to instigate "colour revolutions" in our country, stepping up the implementation of online "Cultural Cold War" and "political genetic modification" projects in an attempt to root out our military officers and soldiers and pull the military out of the party banner. The challenges we face in the field of ideology and political security are very serious. To this end, we must first strengthen positive publicity and guidance of public opinion. Consolidate and strengthen the mainstream ideological and public opinion, speak politically with a clear-cut stand, speak with reason, refute fallacies with rational argument and evidence, and guide officers and soldiers to grasp correct standpoints and viewpoints. Second, we must strengthen the system's self-confidence in the comparison between China and foreign countries. Looking at the world from the "Arab Spring" to the "Arab Winter".... The so-called process of "democratization" in the West has brought about long-term turmoil and war; this kind of hardship, from small to large, from weak to strong, from victory to victory, the most fundamental thing is to always uphold the party's absolute leadership over the army. Finally, we must stick to the main position of online public opinion. As young officers and soldiers of the "media generation", they will inevitably be involved in the struggle of public opinion. This urgently requires us to change our minds, carry out online struggles like a war, and continuously strengthen the ability of officers and soldiers to resist the erosion of social corruption and the infiltration and destruction of hostile forces."

Expressing doubts about the political reliability of the younger officers and soldiers in the PLA and recommending enhanced emphasis on 'educating' the personnel, the article particularly warns that they could be targeted by the adversary through online propaganda.

Such a candid article on ideological weakness in the PLA has not been noticed for quite some time. The last was a Liberation Army Daily article on June 17, 2012, which for the first time raised the issue of factional "sub-loyalties" in the PLA. Promptly thereafter consecutive annual political education campaigns have been launched throughout the PLA. These continue. Between 2011-2013, a number of intellectuals, university professors and "liberal" Chinese economists were noticed advocating "new liberalism", calling for political reform and arguing that the PLA should be an army of the State and not subservient to the CCP. The CCP and PLA leadership were troubled by such 'hostile' foreign-inspired propaganda.

Coincidentally, the *South China Morning Post* published a report (May 30) suggesting that the new, younger recruits were qualitatively different from their predecessors. It quoted Zhou Chenming, a researcher from the Beijing-based Yuan Wang military science and technology think tank, as saying "Military instructors found the strict and dogmatic training modes applied in the last century didn't work for the more individual young soldiers born in the 21st century. Some even dared to butt against and challenge superiors when they were not happy. The military was forced to adjust". It added that the PLA Daily had disclosed that after protests by young soldiers against a ban on mobile phones the PLA had to lift its restrictions in 2015!

A major reason for these concerns are that with the PLA moving towards becoming a technology-based armed force, in 2001 it introduced a focus on recruiting high school and college graduates. The number of such educated recruits have been steadily increasing. Data from China's Ministry of Education and *Xinhua News Agency* reveals that: in 2016, the total number of college students enlisted in the Army were 1.02 million; in 2017, the total number of enlisted college students was 1.07 million, an increase of 57,000 or 5.58 percent over the same period in 2016; in 2018, their number rose to 1.2 million; and in 2019, there were a total of 1.24 million college students enlisted in the Army. The PLA Military Academies also enrol students and in 2018 enrolled 30,500 students. Persons with a college background and high school graduates currently constitute the largest single source of recruits. Senior PLA echelons are concerned that these recruits might have got influenced or imbibed "liberal" ideas from their teachers and professors.

With the visibly rising concern since April about the US and West attempting to topple the CCP through a "colour revolution, the Chinese leadership has been taking steps to assuage any dissatisfaction among PLA soldiers and the veterans.

On May 20, the *Liberation Army Daily* published an article by a member of PLA Unit 31006 captioned *Party members must enhance their sense of honour*. It said "The sense of honour of a party member is a sense of pride and belonging to oneself as a member of the party organization, and is a concentrated expression of the party spirit of a party member". The unnamed author spoke of the inspiration gained from "the firm belief of the revolutionary ancestors" and urged soldiers to emulate "their infinite loyalty to the party" and the way they cherished "the honourable title of "communist".

As part of these efforts, Politburo member Sun Chunlan visited Shandong on May 25, when she met the veteran soldiers and praised their spirit. She pointed out that Shandong province has been "a large source of troops" and has "always had a glorious tradition of supporting military superiors". Praising the contributions of veterans, Sun Chunlan asserted that "it is necessary to give importance to the superior role of military personnel, combine the study and education of party history, tell the red revolution by instilling red genes and guide the majority of veterans to listen to and follow the party, and better cultivate and practice the core socialist values".

Guo Shengkun, Politburo member and Secretary of the powerful Central Political and Legal Affairs Commission which oversees China's security apparatus, also travelled to Shandong around the same time and visited the East China Revolutionary Martyrs Cemetery and Yimeng Revolutionary Memorial Hall. He insisted that "red resources should be used to carry out the study and education of party history, to inspire the powerful spiritual power of political and legal police officers to do their duty for the party and contribute to the people."

The appearance of such articles confirms the Chinese leadership's anxieties about efforts by the US and West to instigate a "colour revolution" and weaken ideological commitment in the PLA. It is likely that Xi Jinping could reinforce the "study campaign on Party History" underway in the PLA by sending teams to ascertain the political reliability and loyalty of PLA personnel.

This was first published by the Centre for China Analysis and Strategy (CCAS) and Vivekananda International Foundation (VIF) in June 3, 2021.

34. Initial Analysis of Leaked Video of Chinese War Preparedness Exercise in Guangdong

The timing of the 'leak' of the video of a 'War Preparedness Mobilisation Exercise' convened by the Guangdong Province Communist Party Committee on May 14, 2022 is interesting. It is yet unclear whether the video was deliberately 'leaked' by the Chinese as part of psywar, or it was an unauthorised recording of the meeting by a disgruntled People's Liberation Army (PLA) officer. It will nonetheless certainly be carefully analysed by China's neighbours and competitors.

The 'leak' also coincided with a People's Liberation Army Navy (PLAN) exercise (May 19- 23), US President Biden's visit to Japan and the Republic of Korea (RoK), and a joint China-Russia air exercise (May 24) when six strategic bombers of China's PLA Air Force (PLAAF) flew over the Mikasa Straits and Sea of Japan for the first time since 2021. China has maintained this military pressure on Taiwan with the multi-force exercises in the 'Eastern War Zone' on June 1.

The hour-long video reveals details of China's war planning, roles of the PLA Military Commander and Political Commissar, role of the Central and provincial CCP organisations and details of defence-related assets in Guangdong Province and the Region. It specified that the Provincial Party Committee Secretary is the General Commander of the provincial military-civilian joint command while the Governor, Provincial Military Region Commander and Political Commissar are commanders. The Governor is responsible for organizing implementation of mobilization and the provincial military district commander is responsible for organizing and 'commanding' the action before commencement of the war.

It disclosed that the Military-Civil Command comprises "elite" personnel from the provincial party committee, provincial government, provincial military district, provincial national mobilization committee, related enterprise units, the armed police Guangdong General Force, six mobile detachments of the armed police, and the 311 Sea Defence brigade. Analysis of the video will be useful for those of China's neighbours with outstanding territorial issues as the planning sequence and essential elements will be replicated in all provinces directly involved in military operations.

For India specifically, the provinces in the Western Theatre Command that will be mobilised are: Tibet (Xizang), Sichuan, Xinjiang, Chongqing, Gansu, Ningxia and Qinghai. Sichuan particularly has a concentration of defence manufacturers, including aircraft and drone companies. Lanzhou, Lhasa and Chengdu will be the mobilisation headquarters.

Chairing the meeting, Zhang Hu, member of the Standing Committee of the Guangdong Provincial Party Committee, Secretary of the Political and Legal Committee, Executive Vice Governor of the Provincial Government and Deputy Secretary of the Party Group, addressed the issues of morale and ideological awareness of troops. He described this as the key to winning and stressed the need to "unify" ideological understanding. Invoking Xi Jinping, he asserted "we won't hesitate to start a war, crush Taiwan's independence and strong enemies' plots, and resolutely defend national sovereignty and territorial integrity". He exhorted: "We must unify our thought and action according to the decision and deployment of the Party Central Committee and the Central Military Commission."

Civil-Military coordination was the next item on the agenda. Zhang Hu emphasised the need to "quickly set up a joint military-civilian command party committee. Second, pay a high degree of attention to our own defence, adhere to the bottom-line thinking, prepare for a rainy day, defend before the attack, and adhere to whole-process defence". He called for focus on the "Pearl River Delta super-dense cities and important military and livelihood targets in the region"; early and good coordination of air defence, target defence, and other preparations for war for maximum protection of people's lives and properties and maintaining the sustainability of mobilization.

The Guangdong General Force of the Armed Police, he elaborated, will take the lead and 7,000 local militia will participate. Ground defence operations in 17 cities outside eastern Guangdong will be led by local joint military-civilian commands. The Sixth Detachment of the Armed Police Second Mobile General, one mobile brigade, Sea Defence Brigade 311 and the second militia battalion comprising a total of 26,000 people (excluding forces in four cities in eastern Guangdong) were assigned ground defence operations in 17 cities.

Main defences were to be set up in Guangzhou, Foshan, Shenzhen, and Huizhou. The key defence areas identified were Guangzhou, Shenzhen, Huizhou, and Yangjiang. Important defence targets included the War Zone's joint warfare command centre, maritime operations sub-centre, Daya Bay Nuclear Power Station, South China Power Grid and other important civilian targets. The meeting noted that the Guangzhou area has capacities in radiation environmental monitoring, nuclear, biological, and chemical support, and biochemical medical testing.

PLA Major General Zhou He, Commander of the Guangdong Military Region and Major General Wang Shouxin, Political Commissar of the Guangdong Military Region, endorsed these decisions. They added: 1. provincial industry must obey the unified command of the joint command; 2. military-civilian departments at all levels should accomplish their respective duties and ensure that the 'party, government, military, police, and civilians work together to win'; 3. while transitioning from 'Normal to War state' the needs of the troops to support front-line operations must be fully ensured; 4. lives of the masses and stability of the rear [of the battlefield] must be ensured; 5. mobilization of the Taiwan Strait and the South China Sea must be simultaneously coordinated; 6. "traditional and new type forces", as well as resources from the province and overseas, need to be deployed for which all resources in the Taiwan Strait area need to be pooled; 7.since there are a large number of migrant workers and a large number of factories and enterprises, precautions require to be taken to prevent a run on banks, evacuations by factories, and exodus of migrant workers wanting to go home; 8. roads and targets must be well protected against enemy strikes and attacks; 9. because of China's proximity to Hong Kong and Macao and the long coastline, it is essential to prevent infiltration and sabotage of targets by the enemy; and 10. there was particular focus on Hong Kong to prevent it's use as a base by the enemy to create chaos to disrupt the war. They emphasised the need for multiple measures and a multi-pronged approach to ensure that people stay motivated and the rear areas and social order are stable.

The PLA officers revealed that the South China Sea area command post formed by its "elite" forces will be sent to the Zhanjiang area in due course and that twelve special command posts were established for people's air defence, traffic mobilization, national economic mobilization, public opinion propaganda, stability maintenance, chaos control etc.

The importance of communications using military and civilian links was underscored, with measures to establish an information data security and information room, a battalion-level information and communication force in the province, and company and platoon-level forces in municipalities and counties respectively. Four communications links were identified: 1. Military Commission Joint Command Centre to the War Zone Joint Command Centre, to the military joint command centres established in the province and cities. It disclosed that a 'confidential information remote delivery system' will be integrated into the joint command system; 2. CMC Mobilization Department to the provincial military district leadership, mainly relying on the 509 plus platform and the national defence mobilization task information command system; 3. command communication links from the provincial, city, and county level military-civilian joint commands to the task teams, relying mainly on the ultra-short wave, Tiantong-1 satellite phone to establish mobile communications; and 4. command and communication links from the army to the civilians, relying on the 'integrated confidential password system' on the 'Acer government intranet' and deploying the national defence mobilization information system to import civilian data to the military-civilian joint command.

1,358 detachments of various types with a total of 140,000 personnel, 953 ships of various types, and 1,653 units/sets of various unmanned equipment would be available. Other resources mentioned were 20 airports and docks, six repair and shipbuilding yards, 14 emergency transfer centres, and grain depots, hospitals, blood stations, oil depots, gas stations, etc.

The National Defence Mobilization Recruitment Office will recruit 15,500 new military service personnel, retired military personnel, and 'special talents' from Guangdong province.

The National Defence Commission will coordinate seven types of national level warfare resources, including sixty-four 10,000-ton roll-on/roll-off ships, 38 aircraft, 588 train cars and 19 civil facilities including airports, docks, housing and other civilian facilities.

'New-style' ocean-going forces will conduct reconnaissance, submarine search, search and rescue outside the first island chain; protect the forward deployment of rocket forces; and support troops to rescue the wounded and repair ships and aircraft. To ensure interoperability in the South China Sea, professional repair, and air and sea transport forces will be deployed to assist troops to repair and set-up towers and markers. Militia fishing boats will be organised to fight "the people's war" at sea and respond to infringements by Vietnam, Philippines, Malaysia and other countries.

Seven cities in western and northern Guangdong will have central roles in strategic decision-making, support and response for the South China Sea, while six major cities in the Pearl River Delta and the main deployment sites of the 74th Army Group will support strategic decision-making. It identified their five main tasks as: 1. Ground recruitment including recruitment of Reserve personnel and Retired military personnel from the rear region and the Pearl River Delta industrial clusters.;2. Maritime support mobilization involving 14 coastal cities. They will mobilise roll-on/roll-off ships, fishing vessels, salvage vessels, multi-purpose vessels and other vessels; 3. The core area of the Pearl River Delta will be responsible for 'New domain' and 'new system' resource mobilization, including aerospace reconnaissance, ocean warning, cyberspace, underwater detection, unmanned combat resources and other potential 'new domain and new system' resources; 4. economic centres at all levels, material insurance bases, comprehensive regional support centres, ship repair yards, grain depots, blood stations, oil depots, gas stations, etc will contribute to equipment and material mobilization, and 5. Ground Defense Force Mobilization assisted by all cities will recruit locally and locally deploy all militia detachments and defence mobilization professional teams.

Assuring that most tasks would be completed, the meeting said two aspects required special attention. These were: 2. to complete the recruitment of 15,500 troops within the short time of a month; and 2. the "big task" of maritime support coordination because of persisting problems with the quality of ship personnel, performance in wartime and fitness of equipment.

Among the several details revealed were: the war-time tasks delegated to Guangdong of retrofitting 365 ro-ro ships[35] within 45 days and responsibility for eight other ships and 64 'national resource ships.' It revealed that the Guangdong region has 90 enterprises capable of retrofitting ships. They can retrofit 113 ships altogether at the same time and 280 can be done within a month! These high-quality shipbuilding and retrofitting resources are concentrated in Guangzhou, Yangjiang, Dongguan, and other places. Enumerating the efforts to complete the retrofitting, the video said ship-repair personnel from Guangzhou, Jiangmen, and Zhanjiang would be recruited.

It disclosed that the monthly production capacity of the province's unmanned vessel centers, namely, Zhuhai Yunzhou, and Jianglong Shipbuilding, is 90.

Disclosing that 2,000+ pieces of hi-tech equipment, 480 drones and 70 unmanned boats are currently in place, it divulged that the province's drone mobilization center Shenzhen Keweitai at Dongguan can manufacture 80 drones a month. Drone production capacities of companies like Shenzhen Smart Drone (SMD), Dongguan, Guangzhou Hopong and another 9 companies, will be boosted.

The video disclosed that 'Network attack and control systems' will be deployed in this preparatory phase. Stating that of 21 'network attack and control' detachments, 15 had been mobilized, it revealed the shortage of six detachments, 60 people and 32 'attack and control system industry network' experts. Confirming the close ties between the PLA and China's IT and Technology companies, the meeting proposed mobilising Qianxin, Huawei, Tencent, and other hi-tech enterprises. Attack and control system industry network experts from the Southern Power Grid Guangdong Company, Guangzhou Metro Group, and other large enterprises would also be drafted. Southern Power Grid, incidentally, is closely tied to China's security apparatus.

Asserting that the Guangdong Region has a full industrial chain of commercial aerospace industries, the meeting decided to tap enterprises in Shenzhen to supplement the present reliance on Zhuhai Orbita, Shenzhen Aerospace, Dongfanghong Satellite Co., Foshan and Deliya.

The video revealed the Region has four satellite detachments and 16 low-orbit satellites with 0.5 to 10 meters global remote ultra-high optical resolution sensing and imaging capabilities. The provincial command would ensure these remain in play and improve security at the four ground receiving stations in Zhuhai (Guangdong), Mohe (Heilongjiang), and Gaomi (Shandong). The Zhuhai military-civilian joint command post was identified as an important defence target for inclusion in the joint defence system.

According to the leaked video, the meeting discussed the use of nuclear and chemical rescue forces. It noted that the province's nuclear rescue force is limited and relies on the resources of Shenzhen, Jiangmen and Yangjiang, and that professional forces need to be recruited from the Guangzhou area to form a nuclear and chemical rescue force.

In the actual preparatory phase posters for recruits, reservists and guidance of civilians will appear in the concerned areas. The advances in telecommunications, including quantum, could make Chinese traffic analysis very difficult, but there would be increased activity in the preparatory phase. Satellites and Radar should spot related military activity.

While the authenticity of the video is being verified, it nonetheless gives a fair idea of the resources each Theatre Command/War Zone can call upon. The War Time Preparedness Exercise does not imply preparations for an actual war against Taiwan, but does indicate that the PLA is preparing for this eventuality.

This was first published by the Centre for China Analysis and Strategy (CCAS) and Vivekananda International Foundation (VIF) in June 5, 2022.

35. Signs of Western Theatre Command's Importance Before Upcoming 20th Party Congress

As the sword-arm of the Chinese Communist Party (CCP), the People's Liberation Army (PLA) has enjoyed pre-eminent status as its third pillar since the founding of the People's Republic of China. However, as the old 'Revolutionary' leaders began fading and new leaders without links to the PLA began taking over, China's leadership began placing restraints on the PLA's political clout in order to maintain the CCP's supremacy and authority over the PLA. Its membership and, therefore authority, in the CCP's Politburo was gradually reduced to two.

Acutely conscious of the fate of the Communist Party of the Soviet Union (CPSU), Chinese President Xi Jinping is particularly concerned that the army remains 'an army of the Party' and to ensure this mandated a series of consecutive year long education campaigns in to instil ideology and the correct political orientation among the soldiers.

Xi Jinping's grip on the PLA is near absolute. He has used the CCP's anti-graft outfit, the Central Discipline Inspection Commission (CDIC), to weed out Generals of doubtful loyalty and, by September 2017 had dismissed over 4,885 officers, or nearly 40 percent of the PLA officer corps. Convening an 'enlarged' meeting of the CMC within two days of taking over as General Secretary of the Chinese Communist Party (CCP), Chairman of the Central Military Commission (CMC) and President of China in November 2012, Xi Jinping announced that political reliability and loyalty would trump all other considerations and be the sole determining criteria for promotions in the PLA. He also began taking steps to ensure that the PLA is "absolutely obedient" to the CCP and the Chairman of the CMC. Today, each of the

Generals in the PLA has been appointed by Xi Jinping. Xi Jinping has also donned an operational role and appointed himself Commander-in-Chief.

With the PLA maintaining its number of Delegates to the upcoming 20th Party Congress at 304 despite its downsizing by 300,000 personnel, it appears the PLA might continue to retain around 37 Full Members and 22 Alternate Members in the new 20th CCP Central Committee (CC) as it had in the outgoing 19th CCP CC. Its representation in the Politburo is also unlikely to be reduced. This makes the PLA's role and presence in the Party Congress and National People's Congress (NPC) important and would give Xi Jinping added leverage in the CCP CC.

Relevant for India is the attention being paid by Xi Jinping to the PLA Western Theatre Command (WTC). The largest of China's five Theatre Commands, it exercises operational jurisdiction over China's borders with Afghanistan, Pakistan, India, Nepal and Myanmar. Its tasks include protection of Chinese personnel and assets deployed on the China Pakistan Economic Corridor (CPEC). The Western Theatre Command is operationally responsible for the intrusions in the Ladakh region in April 2020. The entire 4057-kilometre Line of Actual Control (LAC) between India and China has got activated since then.

Interesting in this backdrop of continuing tension and deployment of approximately 60,000- 70000 troops in the high altitude eastern Ladakh is that the number of Delegates representing the PLA WTC at the 20th Party Congress is nearly double that of the other four Theatre Commands. The WTC has selected 30 Delegates to the 20th Party Congress compared to the 15-19 by the others. There are other signs of the leadership's attention to the WTC. Chinese President Xi Jinping visited and met WTC officers on three occasions in the past year. He met them in Lhasa on July 23, 2021, in Chengdu on July 9, 2022 and again on July 15, 2022 in Urumqi. The WTC receives advanced military hardware and latest jet aircraft ahead of all other Theatre Commands, except the Eastern Command. The 14th Five Year Plan approved last March sanctioned massive infrastructure construction plans scheduled for completion by 2030-35. These include three new railways, a new highway and upgrading of others and 30 additional airfields in the Tibet Autonomous Region (TAR) and surrounding areas. The timelines, interestingly, match those mentioned in the article published in June 2013 by the China-owned Hongkong-based Wen Wei Po, of the wars that China will fight in the next 50 years. It projected the third war with India, for the "reconquest of southern Tibet", as taking place between 2035-2040!

Furthermore, there is little sign of abatement of the considerable widespread discontent inside China, further inflamed by the 'zero-Covid' policy and unending lockdowns. A PLA Daily editorial had earlier warned that the United States could 'use the tense domestic situation in China to fan social upheaval and provoke social conflict'. "Colour revolutions" is a serious worry for the Chinese leadership. Significant for China's neighbours and India is the fresh warning issued just weeks before the 20th Party Congress scheduled for mid-October. This was through a Commentator's article, which conveys the views of the CCP CC.

Releasing the "Opinions on Strengthening and Improving Population-Wide (全民) National Defense Education Work", this Commentator's article in the *People's Daily* (September 2) stated that the world has become increasingly turbulent and more prone to change. In an unusually candid statement, it acknowledged that the "country's security situation has become increasingly unstable and uncertain." It also disclosed the CCP leadership's concern at the increasingly "prominent issues" related to maritime disputes and the "increased likelihood of chaos on our doorstep," thus making the task of "defending the country's political security and social stability more formidable."

The latest warning clearly implies that Xi Jinping is facing a difficult period and will be on edge. CCP cadres, the public security apparatus and the PLA, including the WTC, are certainly on high alert. In case the situation doesn't improve, or deteriorates, and the CCP's authority and legitimacy are perceived as beginning to erode, Xi Jinping will be tempted to divert attention and resort to military actions abroad. He would be tempted too if he assesses that Putin is inching towards victory in Ukraine. In this backdrop any expectations, including any prompted by disingenuous Chinese media comments or the tactical disengagement at the Gogra-Hot Springs (PP-15), that Xi Jinping will change his attitude or policy towards India will be unfounded and premature.

This was first published by the Centre for China Analysis and Strategy (CCAS) and Vivekananda International Foundation (VIF) in September 11, 2022.

36. The People's Liberation Army (PLA) and China's 20th Party Congress

The People's Liberation Army (PLA) is the sword arm of the Chinese Communist Party (CCP). It has been the strongest pillar of the Party and has had a presence and voice in the Party's highest echelons since almost the very founding of the CCP. This is reflected at the Party Congress held every five years where the Work Report of the Government approved by the Party also sets out the task for the PLA for the coming five years. For example, Xi Jinping set a timeline for China's defence modernization at the 19th Party Congress in 2017. It mandated that the PLA would accomplish its military modernization drive by 2035 and the country would strive for global military leadership by mid-century. The PLA's tasking has been revised at this 20th Party Congress. The separate section on National Defence in the Work Report titled 'Centenary goal of the People's Liberation Army (PLA) and further modernising National Defence and the Military', therefore, needs to be carefully parsed.

As the revolutionary Chinese Communist cadres began to fade from the scene, Deng Xiaoping realised that the Party apparatchiks who would be taking over leadership of the Party lacked military credentials and could find it difficult to enforce the CCP's leadership over the PLA. CCP cadres taking over as General Secretary of the CCP Central Committee (CC) were also aware of this shortcoming and this was visible during Hu Jintao's term. Xi Jinping's personal information, publicised in 2012 when he took over as CCP CC General Secretary, also pointedly revealed that when he was private secretary (mishu) to then Chinese Defence Minister Geng Biao he held 'active' military rank in 1979. In addition, Xi Jinping began exercising close control over the PLA including conferring on himself the 'operational' military rank of Commander-in-Chief.

To facilitate Party control over the military, Deng Xiaoping introduced a slew of reforms designed to reduce the influence of the PLA Commanders and abolish their power base. The PLA's representation in the higher echelons of the Party was brought down to the current two members in the Politburo. The process continued under Chinese Presidents Jiang Zemin, Hu Jintao and Xi Jinping who restored the authority of the Political Commissars and once again made their inputs important determinants for promotions of the field Commanders. The Political Commissars were also given additional operational responsibilities. In 2013, Xi Jinping brought the PLA within the purview of the CCP's anti-corruption watchdog body the Central Discipline Inspection Commission. By 2015-16, Xi Jinping pushed through and implemented the most far-reaching reforms ever in the PLA. The reforms are intended to restructure, reorganise and streamline the PLA. The reforms downsized the PLA by 300,000 personnel with the ground forces affected the most. In addition, Xi Jinping has been putting the PLA through consecutive year-long political education campaigns to ensure it's "absolute obedience" to the CCP. The Work Report of 2022 dwells extensively on ensuring the loyalty and "absolute obedience" of the PLA to the CCP, its CC and Commander-in-Chief.

Underscoring its importance and notwithstanding the downsizing, the PLA has retained its representation in the 20th CC of the CCP at the 20th Party Congress (October 16-22). In fact, its representation has marginally increased from the 37 members it had in the 19th CCP CC in 2017 to 43 members in the 20th CCP CC. Its representation in the Politburo remains at two. A surprise entry to the Politburo and the Central Military Commission (CMC) is General He Weidong who was neither a member nor alternate member of the 19th CCP CC. The service-wise representation is: PLA Army (Ground Forces) - 23; PLA Air Force -5; PLA Navy - 10; PLA Rocket Force - 2; and People's Armed Police Force - 3.

The section on National Defence in the Work Report presented to the 20th Party Congress was 926 words, somewhat lengthier than that presented to the 19th Party Congress in 2017 which contained 794 words. Quite apart from its length, the Work Report to the 20th Party Congress dwelt a lot on the efforts by foreign powers to "blackmail, contain, blockade, and exert maximum pressure on China" implying the role envisaged for the PLA. The Work Report also advanced the date for "more quickly" elevating the armed forces to "world class standards" to 2027 – the PLA's founding centenary. While Xi Jinping had stated this earlier in 2021, now with the 20th Party Congress approving the Work Report it has the stamp of approval of the entire Party. The pace of modernisation and strengthening of the PLA will henceforth gather momentum.

An important addition in this Work Report is the exhortation to "simultaneously carry out operations, boost combat preparedness and enhance our military capabilities". It did not clarify whether carrying "out operations" would mean simulation exercises, training or giving troops experience through actual manoeuvres along the borders. The Report later said: "our military will remain both steadfast and flexible as it carries out its operations" and "This will enable us to shape our security posture, deter and manage crises and conflicts, and win local wars". These two sentences together suggest that these operations will have a definite military objective with inherent implications for India, where they are attempting to "shape the security posture". This opens the strong possibility of China incrementally undertaking further actions along the 4057 kms long India-China border to protect its investments in PoK, Gilgit and Baltistan where China is building additional defence infrastructure. It would similarly initiate actions in Arunachal Pradesh. Shaping the security posture is, of course, equally applicable to Taiwan, which is witnessing frequent consecutive air and sea operations around it.

The Work Report additionally stated that mechanisation, informationisation, and application of smart technologies will be accelerated. Xi Jinping and the PLA have already been laying considerable emphasis on applying Science and Technology (S&T) to the military especially under the Civil-Military programme. The presence of 29 members with backgrounds in S&T in the 20th CC and the induction of General Li Shangfu, an aerospace engineer who is likely to be appointed Defence Minister, in the CMC will accelerate these efforts. China has invested huge amounts of capital as it has sought to synergise the efforts of private tech enterprises, state-run institutes and laboratories and the PLA. Artificial Intelligence is one important area. Unmanned Underwater Vessel (UUV), Drone swarm technologies,

Quantum communications etc are examples. The Centre for Security and Emerging Technologies estimated in 2019 that expenditure on Research and Development (R&D) alone for military-related technology was US$ 2.7 billion. S&T's priority has been appreciably elevated at the 20th Party Congress in the wake of recent US restrictions on the sale of microchips, microprocessors etc as well as hardware, technology and knowledge required for their fabrication or technology.

The section elaborating the 'Centenary goal of the People's Liberation Army (PLA) and further modernising National Defence and the Military' includes other important disclosures. Of import is disclosure of the decision to establish "a strong system of strategic deterrence, increase the proportion of new-domain forces with new combat capabilities". This confirms reports that China is increasing its nuclear arsenal and also that it intends to enlarge the PLA Strategic Support Force and PLA Rocket Force and enhance their combat capabilities. Hinting that the PLA is being prepared for multiple roles, Xi Jinping said the PLA will be flexible in its operations.

Of special significance to the region and China's neighbours are Xi Jinping's observations on Taiwan and the military. Language on containing Taiwan's independence was inserted and stronger phrases used to reaffirm "two countries, one system". Striking an uncompromising stance on Taiwan and "realising China's complete reunification", Xi Jinping asserted that "We will implement our Party's overall policy for resolving the Taiwan question in the new era". He added "complete reunification of our country must be realised and it can, without doubt, be realised." This assertion implied that it will be achieved during Xi Jinping's term in office and was greeted with resounding applause by the Delegates to the 20th Party Congress. Xi Jinping also said in the Work Report that while China will strive for peaceful reunification "we will never promise to renounce the use of force".

Important is the assertion in the Work Report that the PLA's modernisation will "enable us to shape our security posture, deter and manage crises and conflicts, and win local wars". The term "win local wars" is new and was not mentioned in the previous Report of 2017. It undoubtedly addresses the current 'live' tensions along the India-China border and around Taiwan. In the backdrop of China's plans for a massive border defence infrastructure build-up and naval capability, the reference to winning local wars is pertinent. It has immediate implications for India in the context of the ongoing tension on the borders in eastern Ladakh. The screening of the clip of the clashes in the Galwan Valley in mid-June 2020, certainly with the approval of the highest echelons, to all 2340 delegates to the Congress and the 83 senior veteran cadres on the opening day of the 20th Party Congress underscored the negative portrayal of India.

The section on National Defence in the Work Report approved by the 20th Party Congress suggests that the PLA's present deployment on India's borders in Eastern Ladakh should be viewed as one phase of a longer-term plan. It is probable that in order to "shape the security posture" preparatory to border, or territorial, negotiations with India, the PLA will initiate additional military actions including incursions. China is a long-term problem for India and the region.

This was first published by the Centre for China Analysis and Strategy (CCAS) and Vivekananda International Foundation (VIF) in November 5, 2022.

37. 'China's New Leadership is Preparing for A Military Threat'

Amid the flurry of documents submitted and appointments confirmed at the recent plenary sessions of the National People's Congress (NPC) — China's version of a parliament — and the Chinese People's Consultative Conference (CPPCC) — China's top political advisory body — there are indications that China's leadership is rather anxious at the adverse and deteriorating international environment that China faces. The failure of US Secretary of State Blinken to travel to China because of the Chinese spy balloon episode revealed not only the poor state of Sino-US relations but the deep suspicion of China in the US political establishment and Administration. While the recent NPC and CPPCC plenary sessions have given economic development unmistakable priority in a bid to reduce – if not eliminate – dependence on the US, national security has been given equal importance.

In all his "important" speeches since the 20th Party Congress last October, Chinese President Xi Jinping has been emphasising the "grim" international environment, unpredictable looming difficulties and growing probability of "black swan" or "grey rhinoceros" events that are likely to confront China. In his 29-page Government Work Report to the NPC, Chinese Premier Li Keqiang echoed these concerns. In an unmistakable focus on the economy, he mentioned development 123 times and national security 21 times. China's new Premier and former Party Secretary of Shanghai Li Qiang too, in his first press interview on March 13, focussed on the economy and sought to reassure China's private business entrepreneurs. He also justified the "around five percent" GDP growth target, but struck a cautious note saying that achieving it would be difficult as China will be starting from a high base.

There are other signs that the Chinese leadership is very worried at the domestic situation. In addition to the sustained, consecutive 'political education' campaigns, Politburo Standing Committee members have in recent speeches been warning cadres to strictly comply with Party discipline and implement the "Two Establishments". Pointing to inner-Party discontent they, and Xi Jinping, have sounded sharp warnings about the existence of "double-faced" cadres, political gangs, "black-faced" cadres and "political liars". The CDIC Chief Li Xi even warned senior cadres that they are being monitored.

There is suggestion of preparations for a military threat too. The NPC Standing Committee has approved the discussion of a law to accelerate approval and enactment of military laws in event of an emergency. People's Liberation Army (PLA) deputies to the NPC and CPPCC expressed the view that passing of laws for the military could take unduly long at times when China is confronted with an emergency. Discussions during the ongoing NPC plenary session additionally revealed that China plans to rapidly build six aircraft carriers. This will obviously mean a potent and heightened PLA Navy presence in the South China Sea and Indian Ocean with consequent implications for Taiwan, India and the Indian Ocean littoral states. China has also, after an interregnum of two years restored the hike in the national defence budget to over percent and brought it to 7.2 percent. Reports have separately mentioned that China is increasing its nuclear arsenal.

Significant in this context are the retention of 72-year old General Zhang Youxia as Vice Chairman of the Central Military Commission (CMC) and the "helicopter" promotion of General He Weidong as the second Vice Chairman of the CMC and member of the Chinese Communist Party (CCP) Central Committee (CC) Politburo. The retention of General Zhang Youxia and presence of General Li Shangfu, who has a background in space and the PLA Strategic Support Force since 2006, in the CMC as a member and appointment as Defence Minister point to the thrust on the technology modernisation of the PLA continuing till 2027. Indication that the new CMC is "battle-ready" is that five of the seven CMC members have experience of China's only 'live' front, namely the Western Theatre Command.

The promotion and appointment of General Liu Zhenli as Head of the PLA Joint Staff Department is important. 59-year-old Liu Zhenli has battle experience having participated in the war with Vietnam in 1986-87 and is also among China's youngest Generals. General Liu Zhenli's military philosophy includes: accelerated building of a joint combat command system; accelerating transformation of the military; adapting to evolving patterns of war under the conditions of informatization combat requirements; and advancing preparations for military struggle.

Yet another pointer to the CCP leadership's concerns are the recently stepped-up activities of the National Defence Mobilisation Office. Set up in 2016 and headed by Lt General Liu Faqing, who is also a member of the CCP CC, it reports directly to the Central Military Commission (CMC).

In an interesting article (March 4), an anonymous Chinese foreign affairs expert wrote that "With the situation in the Taiwan Strait tense, many provinces and cities of the CPC have recently set up national defence mobilisation offices one after another". Expert analysts point out that this is part of the CCP's efforts to improve its ability to transition from peacetime to wartime and will help strengthen the CCP's centralised control over grassroots recruitment, improve coordination between local state-owned defence enterprises, local governments and local military headquarters, as part of national defence mobilisation. The major War Preparation Exercise held by the Guangdong Military Regional Command in May last year is part of these efforts. Some military analysts, however, assess that China is still far from the establishment of a comprehensive wartime system that can support the attack on Taiwan.

A report by the Voice of America (VoA) disclosed that from December last year till recently, Beijing, Shanghai, Shandong, Fujian, Wuhan, Hunan, Sichuan, Hubei, Inner Mongolia, Tibet and other important provinces and cities and even remote counties and townships have established national defence mobilisation offices and held ceremonies to publicise this. A senior retired US military officer, who once served as the US Military Attache in China, was quoted as assessing that the failure of the Russian army's war mobilisation in the invasion of Ukraine sounded the alarm for the CCP. He said mobilisation is a means of mobilising the people politically and enhancing popular nationalist sentiments. Liu Zhongjing, a historian who worked in Xinjiang's public security system for many years, posted an analysis on Twitter, saying, 'The core of the wartime system is the integration of the military, military sources, military industry, military industry resource producers, and transportation departments'. But, he said, the CCP Military Commission and the State Council, like the Russian Ministry of Defence and the Ministry of Economy are divided, making the country incapable of engaging in long-term large-scale wars. He said, therefore, the work of defence mobilisation must be transferred to the party's management.

The report added 'With the turmoil in the Taiwan Strait, the Beijing authorities have been making constant moves in conscription and war preparations in recent days. On March 1, Xiamen launched the 'Civil Air Defense Navigation' mobile app platform, which contains the location information of nearly a thousand air-raid shelters in the city; the 'Reserve Personnel Law', which came into effect on the same day, will apply the age limit between 18 and 60 years old'. Stating that there are many obstacles before a truly effective wartime mobilisation system can be established, it quoted He Tianmu, a senior researcher for international security at the RAND Corporation. He Tianmu pointed out that a key persistent challenge of the Chinese defence system is the lack of integration of information systems between the civilian sector, the business community, and military commanders. This problem has plagued the PLA mobilisation system for many years, and has apparently not been resolved. Liu Zhongjing pointed out that the National Development and Reform Commission, which reports to Xi Jinping, can only cooperate and connect a small number of state-owned military industrial groups. He said it would be able to connect with most market-oriented resource production enterprises after the powers of the National Development and Reform Commission are further increased. Asserting that this has not yet started and, therefore, it is impossible for a war to break out within a year or two, he cautioned that the timetable starts when the two sessions end.

Reports show that China's national defence mobilization system has been undergoing continuous reform to strengthen the country's capacity to counter threats to the party and homeland, especially since Xi Jinping took over as China's President. According to the report issued by *Recorded Future* in March 2022, this includes cataloguing the thousands of military and civilian resources that the party-state and People's Liberation Army (PLA) can bring to bear to uphold China's sovereignty, unity, territorial integrity, and security at home and abroad. The first section of the report draws on a draft document authored by the CMC's National Defense Mobilization Department (NDMD) to present 'A New Mobilization Planning System', which enumerates the full range of resources available to military-civil fusion mobilization efforts. These resources include those in China and overseas and relate to weapons research, maritime transport, cyber capabilities, public opinion guidance, natural resources, and space-based technologies. It says another core part of national defence mobilization reform is the creation of increasingly specialized militia forces, an effort that began in the early 2000s but has accelerated under CCP CC General Secretary Xi Jinping's leadership. These forces are intended to carry out emergency response tasks, support the needs of modern warfare, and help extend China's military power into new strategic spaces such as cyberspace, outer space, and the polar egions.

The detailed "Party and State Institutional Reform Plan" jointly issued by the CCP CC and the State Council and published by *Xinhua* on March 16, specified that Reform tasks at the central level should be completed by the end of 2023, and reform tasks at the local level be completed by the end of 2024. These reforms envisage enhanced Party control and supervision over finance, security and other entities. It is relevant that there has been no easing in China's military posture since the 20th Party Congress last October.

This was first published by the Centre for China Analysis and Strategy (CCAS) and Vivekananda International Foundation (VIF) in March 17, 2023.

38. Indication of Disarray in PLA and Imminent 'Rectification Campaign'

The senior echelons of China's People's Liberation Army (PLA) appear to be in disarray. The unexplained long absences of Central Military Commission (CMC) Vice Chairman General Zhang Youxia and sudden removal of Defence Minister Li Shangfu, both with close family ties to Chinese President Xi Jinping, has added to the state of uncertainty. Many senior officers have also in recent months been removed on charges of corruption or violation of political discipline. In addition, a usually reliable report claims that the PLA has conveyed to Xi Jinping that it is not ready for an invasion of Taiwan. It is almost certain that the PLA will be subjected to a thorough 'cleansing' or rectification centering on corruption and political reliability.

Ever since China's former Defence Minister General Li Shangfu suddenly disappeared from public view in September last year, there has been persistent speculation as to why he disappeared and who would replace him. Speculation was heightened because of Li Shangfu's close family connections with Chinese President Xi Jinping and the equally sudden and, as yet, unexplained disappearance earlier in July of China's Foreign Minister Qin Gang – another protégé of Xi Jinping. There have subsequently been indications that they were probably guilty of corruption and violating Party discipline. Interestingly though, both retain their position as members of the Chinese Communist Party (CCP) Central Committee (CC). Li Shangfu was formally divested of his post as Defence Minister in October 2023, but it took another three months before former PLA Navy Commander General Dong Jun was appointed the new Defence Minister in December 2023. The appointment for the first time of a former PLA Navy Commander as Defence Minister has raised fresh questions about the PLA Ground Force and PLA Rocket Force. At the same time, because of the long absence of CMC Vice Chairman

General Zhang Youxia from April to September and again intermittently for long stretches there is speculation that his relations with Xi Jinping are under strain. Coverage of the study session on promoting high-quality financial development at the Central Party School in Beijing on January 16, by the state-owned CCTV also showed Zhang Youxia sitting on the third and last row behind General He Weidong, which is quite unusual.

While corruption is known to have been rampant in the PLA for decades, immediately after taking over as Chairman of the Central Military Commission (CMC) Xi Jinping had subjected it to successive year-long ideological and anti-corruption campaigns. The new, major, emphasis on modernisation and all-round technological upgradation of the PLA meant that huge sums of money would have been made available to the PLA. The PLA Rocket Force (PLARF) particularly has been the recipient of large sums because of the effort to increase its inventory of missiles, induct new types of missiles and build numerous underground silos. The removal of officers in defence scientific establishments associated with the PLA Equipment Development Department confirms that they too have been involved in corruption. Xi Jinping will have been angered that corruption on such a large scale persists despite his unprecedented anti-corruption campaign in the PLA, which by 2017 had resulted in the dismissal of over 40 percent of its officer corps on charges of corruption. It implies that the reporting and supervision mechanism put in place has not functioned and the PLA has resisted the Party's efforts to supervise it. The PLA Daily Editorial of January 1, 2024, gave priority to fighting corruption and mentioned 'corruption' three times.

Meanwhile, the Commander and Political Commissar of the secretive People's Liberation Army (PLA) Rocket Force, General Li Yuchao and General Xu Zhongbo respectively, were removed from their posts and placed under investigation for corruption. Reliable reports said that the amount involved an estimated US$ 2 billion. On December 29, the NPC removed nine senior PLA officers from their posts. Five of those removed were past or current commanders of the People's Liberation Army Rocket Force (PLARF). In June 2023, Rocket Force Commander Li Yuchao, who had earlier overseen exercises for launching a nuclear counter-strike after coming under nuclear attack, Rocket Force Commissar Xu Zhongbo, and his deputies Liu Guangbin and Zhang Zhenzhong were all removed from their positions. While no official cause was given, speculative rumours have pointed to embezzlement and espionage and leakage by Li Yuchao's son of government secrets to the United States while studying abroad. In July, a former deputy of the Rocket Force and head of the secretive Third Department Wu Guohua died under mysterious circumstances. In July 2023, Ju Qiansheng, Commander of the PLA Strategic Support Force (PLASSF) and member of the Third Department, went missing amid investigations of misconduct. In September, there was a major shakeup as Cheng Dongfang, head of the PLA Military Court and Li Shangfu, the Defense Minister, were removed from their positions. Former PLARF Commander Zhou Yaning, Head of the PLARF Armaments Department Lu Hong, and former PLARF deputy Li Chuanguang were all removed. Commander of the Southern Theater Navy Ju Xinchun and former PLAAF Commander Ding Laihang, who has pushed for pilots to get more realistic training, were also removed from their positions. Interesting was the dismissal of PLA Equipment Development Department officials Zhang Yulin, and Rao Wenmin. By early January 2024 nearly 15 senior PLARF officers had been removed from their posts and placed under investigation.

The names of the 15 PLA RF officers removed from their posts are given below:

Name	Title	Date of Public Removal
Zhang Yulin	Former deputy director of General Armament Department	Dec. 29, 2023
Rao Wenmin	Member of EDD	Dec. 29, 2023
Zhou Yaning	Former commander of Rocket Force	Dec. 29, 2023
Zhang Zhenzhong	Former commander of Rocket Force; deputy chief of joint staff department of Central Military Commission since at least 2022	Dec. 29, 2023

Li Chuanguang	Deputy commander of Rocket Force since at least 2018	Dec. 29, 2023
Lyu Hong	Member of Rocket Force	Dec. 29, 2023
Ju Xinchun	Worked as Li Shangfu's deputy in China's manned space program; navy commander of Southern Theater Command since February	Dec. 29, 2023
Ding Laihang	Former commander of Air Force	Dec. 29, 2023
Wu Yansheng	Chairman of China Aerospace Science and Technology Corp	Dec. 27, 2023
Liu Shiquan	Former executive at China Aerospace Science & Industry Corp; chairman of China North Industries Group Corp	Dec. 27, 2023
Wang Changqing	Executive at China Aerospace Science & Industry Corp	Dec. 27, 2023
Li Tongjian	Major-general of Rocket Force	Nov. 24, 2023
Li Shangfu	Former director of EDD; former defense minister; CMC member	Oct. 24, 2023
Li Yuchao	Former commander of Rocket Force	Jul. 31, 2023
Xu Zhongbo		

(The list has been compiled by Bloomberg on January 4.)

An analyst for Cercius Group, a Canadian geopolitical consulting firm, told *Asia Sentinel* that the numbers were considerably higher. He claimed "So far, we have been able to track down around 70 individuals who have been taken away within the larger frame of the Rocket Force investigation. As of yet, we believe, considering that procurement, and logistics are also involved, it is still too early to inquire about the results of the ongoing crackdown."

It is unusual for China's official media to report on misdeeds in the PLA, but a series of articles, some authored by PLA officers, appeared in China's official newspapers pointing to ideological and discipline problems in the

PLA. At least six such articles were noticed between mid-November and mid-January. On December 6, 2023, Chen Zuosong, Director of the Political Work Department for the Southern Theatre Command Air Force, published an article in the *Study Times*, the official newspaper of the Central Party School. In the *Study Times* article Chen Zuosong bluntly declared that "hostile forces" are exerting more influence in China, leading to the spread of misguided ideas in the military. Outlining the ideological risks facing the PLA, Chen Zuosong called for a culture of "absolute loyalty" to the ruling Communist Party and said "the changes in information technology have brought an increasing number of variables and hidden dangers to the ideological field"[36] and "Hostile forces have increased cognitive penetration and destruction, and various erroneous ideological trends and arguments have ... spread into military camps." He asserted that the military should be patient and confident, and loyal to both the party and Xi.

Soon thereafter the *Guangming Daily* (January 14) published an article by the 'Research Center for Xi Jinping Thought on Strengthening the Military', which emphasised that "Political army building is the primary and fundamental issue in the construction and development of the people's army". It added that Chinese President Xi Jinping has clearly stated that "political army building is the foundation of our army". The article explained the five points of political thought on army building. It listed them as: 1."The Party's absolute leadership over the military is an essential feature of socialism with Chinese characteristics, an important political advantage of the Party and the country, and the foundation of the people's military and the soul of a strong military. It said the PLA must stick to this most fundamental issue"; 2. "The Chairman's Responsibility System of the Military Commission is the fundamental system and form that upholds the Party's absolute leadership over the military. It solves the issue of the supreme leadership and command authority of our military. It must be observed as the highest political requirement and maintained by the highest political discipline"; 3. "Upholding the party's absolute leadership over the military is guaranteed by the party committee system, the dual-chief system, the political committee system, etc. These are an institutional arrangement and a political design that must be consistently adhered to"; 4. to meet the political standard of "absolute", the "army is armed with guns, and its loyalty to the party must be sole, complete, unconditional, unadulterated, and without any moisture"; and 5. "Political discipline and political rules must be strict and solid, and the four fundamental things of ideals and beliefs, party spirit principles, combat effectiveness standards, and political work prestige must be firmly established in the entire military. Building the party style and clean government and the fight against corruption must always be promoted".

Writing in the *PLA Daily* (January 17) Luo Jiale of the PLA Air Force 107th Regiment of the 36th Bomber Division of the Central Theatre Air Force, picked up on the theme of ideological and discipline problems in the PLA mentioned by the Director of the Political Work Department for the Southern Theatre Command Air Force in his article in the Study Times. Underscoring that there is increased pressure on the army and that officers and men need to work efficiently and hard, he regretted, "there are still some officers and soldiers who are unwilling to push, take their time, and either go with the flow, stepping on the watermelon rind and sliding wherever they go." He emphasised that PLA officers must develop a sense of purpose and urgency.

There were at least three, lengthy hard-hitting articles on corruption. The article captioned 'Seeing corruption and power-seeking as a great disgrace' by PLA officer Han Deming described corruption "as the biggest cancer that harms the vitality and combat effectiveness of the party", adding that the "abuse of power for personal gain and corruption" is a "great shame". It recalled that Xi Jinping at the 20th Party Congress and earlier Mao Zedong, Zhou Enlai and Peng Dehaui had all spoken out against corruption and privilege. The article warned "Greed is like fire, if it is not contained it will start a prairie fire; desire is like water, if it is not contained it will surge to the sky. For party members and cadres, especially leading cadres, if they break a rule once, they will leave a stain; if they do something special, they will lose a point of prestige; if they seek personal gain once, they will lose a piece of people's hearts." It regretted "there are still some party members and cadres who defy the rules and regulations for personal gain, engage in corruption by trying the law, cannot control themselves and their families, and ultimately lose in the battle between loyalty and betrayal". It said "Party members and cadres, especially leading cadres, must always be strict with themselves and guard the line of defense against corruption and degeneration. They must not indulge themselves by saying "little things are fine", forgive themselves by "not being an example", or be paralyzed by "no one knows"." It acknowledged that "Party members and cadres do not live in a vacuum" and "human interference, ideological infiltration, and "hunting" by people with ulterior motives are everywhere". It said "party members and cadres, especially leading cadres, must be particularly clear-headed and firm in attitude, and often compare themselves with each other."

Another article by Fan Jing of the 'Research Center on Xi Jinping's Thought on Strengthening the Military' titled 'The essence of corruption is the abuse of power…Promoting comprehensive and strict governance of the Party and the military' bluntly declared that "Corruption is the deadliest "source of pollution". It said it is "the biggest cancer that harms the party's vitality and combat effectiveness, the greatest threat our party faces, and the "number one killer" of combat effectiveness." Asserting that it is necessary to guard against the abuse of power, it cited examples of 'old comrades' who had not succumbed to the temptation of misusing power to benefit their families. Stating that "Power without supervision will inevitably lead to corruption", it insisted that supervision is imperative. Appearing to hint at resistance among some Party cadres to supervision, it said "Every party member and leading cadre should regard supervision as the greatest concern, the best protection, and the most sincere help … and be willing to accept supervision and develop the habit of working and living in an environment subject to supervision and restraint".

In apparent escalation of the level of warnings, the *People's Daily* (January 12) published a Commentary on eliminating corruption in the PLA. It emphasised that "The fight against corruption must be a protracted one." It warned that "Corruption is the biggest cancer that harms the vitality and combat effectiveness of the party, and is the biggest threat our party faces. If corruption is allowed to spread, the party and the country will eventually be destroyed. The fight against corruption is a "must answer" for comprehensive and strict governance of the party. It is a serious political task and a major political responsibility that we must grasp well." It indicated that the campaign against corruption has no time limit and said: "The anti-corruption struggle can only be ongoing and never completed; the anticorruption struggle must be accomplished over a long period of time and cannot be accomplished once and for all". It said this is necessary to "ensure that the party will never deteriorate and the red country will never change colour". Indicating that a rigorous anticorruption campaign is likely in the army, it said "The military is armed with guns, and corruption cannot have a place in the party, especially in our military. The more powerful the military is in fighting corruption, the purer and more effective it will be. The entire military must thoroughly study and implement the spirit of Chairman Xi's important speeches and Chairman Xi's important thoughts on the Party's self-revolution, continuously deepen the understanding of the laws of the Party's self-revolution, make the Party's self-revolution ideas and measures more rigorous, and solidly promote Strict governance of the Party and the military will be developed in an all-round way".

Earlier that day (January 12) at the annual meeting of the PLA's disciplinary inspectors, CMC Vice Chairman General He Weidong warned "[We must] always adhere to a strict tone, use stricter standards to scrutinise the key few, and show determination to get to the bottom of long-standing [corruption] problems". He also stressed the need for the CMC's Commission for Discipline Inspection to keep an eye on political loyalty and support for President Xi Jinping. He Weidong said it is essential to tighten the party's governance and political responsibilities, strengthen political supervision, deepen political rectification, firmly support the "Two Establishments," resolutely uphold the "Two Maintenances," and comprehensively implement Xi Jinping's responsibility system of the Military Commission. He said it is necessary to use stricter standards and have a zero-tolerance attitude to comprehensively promote the prevention of corruption, the incapability of corruption, and the unwillingness to be corrupt and establish a solid ideological dam.

Despite persistent efforts since 2013, Xi Jinping has been unable to eliminate corruption from the PLA and the supervision system put in place does not seem to have worked. More troubling for Xi Jinping would be that all the senior officers were promoted by him and even persons close to him, like Li Shangfu, are among the officers removed from their positions. It is almost certain that the PLA will be subjected to a rigorous campaign to eradicate corruption and reinforce the PLA's political reliability and ideological commitment.

This was first published by the Centre for China Analysis and Strategy (CCAS) and Vivekananda International Foundation (VIF) in January 21, 2024.

39. China's 14th National People's Congress Session Gives New Direction to PLA

The plenary sessions of the Chinese People's Political Consultative Conference (CPPCC), the top political advisory body, and the National People's Congress (NPC), China's version of a parliament, which opened in Beijing's Great Hall of the People on March 4, 2024 and March 5, 2024,respectively amid high security provided a fresh thrust to the People's Liberation Army (PLA). The observations by the NPC deputies and CPPCC delegates give some insight into the mood and thinking of the Chinese authorities. The NPC session (March 5-11) signalled that Xi Jinping had still further consolidated his stature as China's preeminent leader and more firmly stamped the Chinese Communist Party (CCP)'s imprimatur on the state. Equally importantly, it reaffirmed China's global leadership ambitions.

As in past years the Chinese leadership ensured that the PLA was adequately provided for. The National Defence budget was officially increased by 7.2 percent, or 1.67 trillion yuan (US$ 231.4 billion) making 2024 the ninth straight year to see a single-digit hike in the country's defence budget. The National Defence budget has doubled since 2013 when Xi Jinping took over. This increase, in spite of China's slowing GDP growth rate, confirms that China continues to build a modern, technologically-advanced world class army and harbours ambitions to 'recover' its so-called 'lost' territories. Noticeable too is the fresh thrust towards advanced technology and the emphasis on building the Navy. The focus on advanced and emerging technologies was emphasised by Chinese President Xi Jinping in an important speech to PLA and People's Armed Police (PAP) Deputies and Delegates attending the NPC and CPPCC sessions on March 7. This will mean greater attention to the PLA Strategic Support Force (PLA SSF) and PLA Rocket Force (PLA RF). The presence at the event of Politburo (PB) member and Central Military

Commission (CMC) Vice Chairman General Zhang Youxia, PB member and CMC Vice Chairman He Weidong and other CMC members Liu Zhenli and Zhang Shengmin ensures implementation of the instructions.

The PLA SSF is already at the centre of China's hi-tech military integration and modernisation plans as is evident from its organisational structure. Its Aeronautical Support Force (Satellite and Space), Network Systems Department (Cyber and SIGINT) and Aerospace Force (Space launch, Space Tracking, Telemetry and Control (Space TT&C), Space C4ISR, Counter Space and Strategic Intelligence) encompass almost the entire range of emerging technologies. In March 2024, in fact, the SSF sought to recruit majors in computer science, artificial intelligence and big data, and aerospace technologies, from top-tier universities for nearly 500 positions. According to a report published in 2021 by the Centre for Security and Emerging Technology at Georgetown University, US, the SSF accounts for more AI-related equipment contracts than any other PLA branch. The South China Morning Post (March 27) disclosed that the SSF held training exercises in February using countermeasures in response to simulated drone attacks and network penetration by "enemies" and that it had earlier conducted exercises involving "electromagnetic confrontation" in an exercise under the Central Theatre Command.

According to *Xinhua*, on March 7, Chinese President Xi Jinping "emphasised that the strategic capabilities in emerging fields are crucial components of the national strategic system and capabilities, which are related to the high-quality development of China's economy and society, national security, and the initiative of military struggle". He stressed the need to "promote the efficient integration and two-way stimulation of new productive forces and new combat forces". He emphasised the need to strengthen the sense of mission, deepen reform and innovation, and comprehensively enhance the strategic capabilities in emerging fields. Six PLA deputies from various military sectors presented their suggestions. The issues reflected the PLA's areas of interest. These were: advancing maritime situational awareness capabilities, enhancing cybersecurity defence capabilities, promoting the application of Artificial Intelligence, strengthening the coordination and management of space resources, standardizing the development of emerging field standards, and innovating the construction and application of unmanned combat forces.

Speaking to the 269 PLA and PAP deputies attending the meeting – of the 281 PLA and PAP deputies 12 were removed on charges of corruption etc. – Xi Jinping focused on the enhancement of strategic capabilities in emerging fields, the need to grasp the characteristics for developments in emerging fields, efficient integration of new productive forces and new combat forces, and achieving mutual promotion. He highlighted the importance of prioritizing breakthroughs in development and ensuring the implementation of strategies and plans for building strategic capabilities in emerging fields.

Xi Jinping stressed the importance of innovation and said that the development of emerging fields fundamentally relies on technological innovation and application. He advocated enhancing confidence in innovation, promoting independent and original innovation, and fostering a vibrant ecosystem for innovation. Xi Jinping also emphasized the need to prioritize reform in emerging fields as a key aspect for further comprehensively deepening reform. He called for building an innovative ecosystem that is self-reliant, open, integrated, and dynamic, and improving the overall efficiency of developing emerging fields. This, he pointed out, required establishing and improving systems and mechanisms for processing demand, planning coordination, and resource sharing, advancing standardisation, and enhancing the overall benefits of the development of emerging fields.

Additionally, he emphasised accelerating the development of new combat capabilities, deepening reform of the national defence science and technology industry system, optimizing the structure of the national defence science and technology industry, and establishing mechanisms for agile response and rapid transformation of advanced technologies to adapt to the development of emerging fields. Xi Jinping called for updating ideological concepts, boldly innovating and exploring new models of construction and application of new combat forces, and fully liberating and developing new combat capabilities.

Xi Jinping pointedly stressed it is important to "integrate preparation for maritime military warfare, safeguarding of maritime rights and development of the maritime economy". On the side-lines of the NPC session, Yuan Huazhi, Political Commissar of the PLA Navy and NPC Deputy, told the Hong Kong

Commercial Daily (March 5) that China will unveil its fourth aircraft carrier soon. He said there is no bottleneck in China's aircraft carrier technologies, and the development is progressing smoothly. The appointment of General Dong Jun, a PLA Navy officer and submariner, as Defence Minister will ensure adequate funds for the Navy.

Xi Jinping also underscored the need to build a network space defence system and enhance safeguards for national network security. Alluding to Civil-Military fusion, he called for strengthening the coordinated implementation of major projects in science and technology, promoting independent and original innovation, and fostering a vibrant ecosystem for innovation. Stating that State owned Enterprises (SoEs) are playing a key role, Zhang Yuzhuo, Chairman of the State-owned Assets Supervision and Administration Commission (SASAC) of the State Council, disclosed (March 5) that investment by central SOEs in strategic emerging industries increased 32.1 percent year on year in 2023. He said the SASAC's goal envisaged income derived from strategic emerging industries by central SOEs as accounting for 35 percent of their total income by 2025. He said it is important to increase investment in industries "especially in brain-like intelligence, quantum information and controlled nuclear fusion."

The leadership of the State Council's State-owned Assets Supervision and Administration Commission (SASAC), which controls the central State-owned Enterprises (SoEs), moved rapidly and met in Beijing on March 29. It called for reforms to enable SoEs to invest more on innovative and fundamental technologies over a medium-to-long-term rather than short-term. Consequent to the economic slowdown and US-led restrictions on critical technologies, Beijing is relying increasingly on central SOEs to drive technological innovation and industrial upgrading. In 2023, the combined investments of central SOEs in strategic emerging industries (SEI) surged by 45.3 percent year-on-year, reaching RMB 2.18 trillion.

Of particular importance was the attention given by Xi Jinping to strengthening the armed forces for multi-dimensional warfare (land, air, cyber, space and sea) by using advanced technology and to enhance the PLA Navy's maritime capabilities.

Indicating that the military was studying the new direction, soon after the NPC session concluded the (March 24) published two important articles on enhancing strategic capabilities and AI. The articles were authored by members of the Party Innovation Theory Research Centre, National University of Defence Technology, and faculty members of the Army Engineering University and Army Command College respectively.

The article by the Party Innovation Theory Research Centre, National University of Defence Technology, said "accelerating defence technological innovation is an urgent need to win military competition and maintain the initiative in warfare". It listed the following steps as necessary to precisely grasp the pulse of the future battlefield in emerging fields:

1. new concepts, new technologies, and new achievements emerge frequently in fields such as artificial intelligence, cyberspace, deep sea, and outer space, and generate new productive forces and also accelerate the generation of new combat capabilities. It is, therefore, necessary to target the forefront of technological development in emerging fields.
2. It is imperative to scientifically distinguish which are the new domains and qualities that will dominate the future battlefield, which are the long-term forces that can still influence the direction of modern warfare in traditional space, and which are the backward capacities that need to be eliminated.
3. We should comprehensively develop strategies for technological development in various fields, seize opportunities and advance with the times, adhere to the integrated development of mechanization, informatization, and intelligentization, and promote the overall improvement of technological innovation in all fields. The vitality of military-civilian collaboration in emerging fields must be exploited.
4. Strong grassroots talent teams should be built to upgrade combat effectiveness and achieve the "best solution" to defeat the enemy..
5. Technological innovation in emerging fields should focus on new quality productivity and high-quality development, focus on the generation of new quality combat power and new types of combat forces. It should attract cross-industry, cross-disciplinary, and cross-regional research and

development. Data and resources should be collected and integrated across industries, disciplines, and regions, to provide support for innovation.

6. Based on the generation of new quality combat power, we should improve cooperation between industry, academia, and research institutes, integrate resources from enterprises, universities, research institutes, and other parties, strengthen multi-party cooperation and joint research and development, form a strong synergy for tackling key core technologies, and achieve common promotion of military and civilian technological innovation resources, and jointly tackle key core technology challenges. This will ensure that technological innovation in emerging fields are shared between the military and civilian sectors, projects are jointly developed by the military and civilians, and the outcomes of technological innovation are shared between the military and civilians. It will accelerate the transformation of technological achievements in emerging fields into new quality combat capabilities.
7. Accelerating the enhancement of new quality combat capabilities relies on technological innovation and technological empowerment. Whether it is "future wars", "hybrid wars"[36] or "high-end wars" beyond conceptual distinctions, they share the common characteristic of being technological wars. It is necessary to use new technologies and new concepts to transform and enhance the efficiency of traditional achievements.
8. The tremendous potential of new quality combat capabilities must be transformed into actual combat capabilities through practical training. Emerging fields are often unfamiliar territories for many combatants, and new technological achievements must transition from the "laboratory" to the "battlefield" through countless "experimental fields" "training grounds", and "timelines".
9. To expedite the transformation of technological innovations into actual combat capabilities, it is necessary to reduce the time for transforming from "old" to "new" capabilities. This includes studying operational issues in emerging fields, innovating operational concepts and tactics, promoting the weaponization of emerging technological achievements, enhancing technological cognition, innovation, training by weapon development

personnel of various levels of combatants, and continuously achieving breakthroughs in combat capability quality.

The second article by the Professors at the Army Engineering University, and Army Command College focussed on AI and the likely changes in the mode of warfare. Interestingly, they argued that "in future intelligent warfare, the core functionality of combat force systems will not undergo fundamental changes" and the essential elements of personnel, weaponry, and organization for carrying out combat missions will still be indispensable. However, they will undergo reshaping with the support of artificial intelligence technology. The article said in "intelligent warfare" the focus will shift from widespread personnel casualties to effective control over enemy combat centres and even combat systems. Combat personnel will engage less in direct confrontations as "warriors" and increasingly serve as "strategists" monitoring and controlling combat actions, with closer connections to the entire warfare system. In future wars, simulated "human-like" robots, which surpass humans in certain functional areas, will be extensively deployed on the battlefield and become the primary combat entities tasked with various missions.

In "intelligent warfare", as the intensity and breadth of confrontations between systems continue to increase, the focus on forming open, integrated, and flexible combat systems is at the core of the construction of the intelligent warfare organizational structure. The integration of military forces is gradually becoming the trend. Intelligent combat force systems are usually constructed based on mission requirements, using intelligent algorithms to precisely calculate the composition of combat force units and optimize their organization through the precise allocation of modular forces, forming specialized and efficient systematic combat forces. This requires combining the requirements of intelligent selection for force modularization, and refining and quantifying the functions of existing functional module forces so that they form corresponding functional "menus" in terms of attack capability, protection capability, mobility, autonomy, and integration capability, ensuring that they can be accurately read, measured, and called upon during wartime.

Within days of the conclusion of the second session of the 14th NPC, Chinese leaders, scientific establishments, government and provincial government entities began discussing ways to implement Chinese President Xi Jinping's directions of March 7. In addition to the huge amounts already invested in science and technology, especially in AI and emerging technologies, China has now begun harnessing the financial and other resources of the mammoth central State-owned Enterprises (SoEs). With the Civil-Military Fusion programme in force there is now no difference between research for civil or military use or in the application of new emerging technologies.

This was first published by the Centre for China Analysis and Strategy (CCAS) and Vivekananda International Foundation (VIF) in March 31, 2024.

40. The People's Liberation Army (PLA)'s New Information Support Force

On April 19, Chinese President Xi Jinping announced that a new People's Liberation Army (PLA) Information Support Force had been established. At the same time he announced establishment of the PLA Aerospace Support Force and PLA Cyberspace Support Force and the disbandment of the PLA Strategic Support Force (SSF). Together this constitutes the largest reorganisation of the PLA since the one effected in 2016. The reorganisation comes a month after Chinese President Xi Jinping's speech to PLA and PAP Deputies attending the National People's Congress (NPC) session on March 7, 2024. In this speech he emphasised the importance of using emerging fields and building strategic combat capabilities. Details of the leadership or specialist functions of the Forces have, however, not yet been revealed.

Consequent to the reorganisation, the PLA now comprises 'Three Arms and Three Services'. The order of precedence for the new services, important for the hierarchy conscious PLA, was indicated in the order they were listed, namely: the PLA Aerospace Support Force, PLA Cyberspace Support Force, PLA Information Support Force and the Joint Logistics Support Force. Each of these services is now an independent entity at the Deputy Theatre Commander-level reporting directly to the Central Military Commission (CMC). They all have single missions and are focussed on one aspect of warfare, which would be intended to make command and control, as well as their performance, more effective.

There are various reasons for the reorganisation. The capital-intensive PLA Strategic Support Force encompassed a wide range of varied aspects of modern hi-technology warfare capabilities and this probably made it difficult for the PLA SSF Commander to pay adequate attention to the individual specialised forces under his command. At a time of rapid advances in military technology and battlefield tactics evolving on the battlegrounds in Ukraine and the Middle East, which the PLA leadership has been studying and analysing very carefully, this would be an impediment for the PLA in becoming a world class military capable of fighting and winning wars. As the conflicts in Ukraine and the Middle East have also shown, the battle of perception has become very important in present day warfare to win popular support and influence outcomes. Information warfare and shaping the scenarios have been noticeably prominent and, to a large degree, successful in both these conflict zones. The current reorganisation of the SSF will ensure focussed attention, proper allocation of resources, and better utilisation of funds for each Force. It will additionally ensure that trained officers are available for each Force. Since each Force is specialised, it can be expected that the separate Forces will formulate their own recruitment criteria and establish their own training establishments so that professionally competent personnel are available.

The composition of the PLA Information Support Force, as discernible from available information, indicates that its main functions would include communications, including satellite communications, analysis of the battlefield environment and target data, shaping the battlefield environment and the maintenance, disruption and monitoring of cyber and communications channels. Many of the entities integrated into the Information Support Force are from the Strategic Support Force.

Available information shows that the agencies integrated into the PLA Information Support Force include the Headquarters of the former Strategic Support Force and the Information and Communication Base, which used to be the primary unit responsible for command communication and informationsupport across the military. The Information and Communication Brigades of the Xinjiang and Tibet Military Districts comprising the 6th Information Support Brigade (Urumqi); 1st Communications Regiment (Urumqi); 2nd Communications Regiment (Urumqi); and the Tibet Military Region Communications Corps. The Target Data Battalion; Battlefield Environment Battalion; Communications Support Battalion; Spectrum Control Battalion; and the Intelligence Analysis Centre of the Joint Staff Department (JSD) of the Central Military Commission

(CMC). Certain functions and capabilities from the Battlefield Situation and Strategic Early Warning Sub-Centres of the Joint Operations Command Centre of the Central Military Commission, as well as the Battlefield Situation Battalion, Information Service Battalion, and Command Operations and Maintenance Battalion of the Theatre Command Joint Operations Centres, have also been integrated. Furthermore, some forces from the 35th Base and the Satellite Communications Centre of the former Strategic Support Force, along with the Battlefield Environment Research Institute and the Network Information Research Institute of the Systems Engineering Research Academy of the Academy of Military Sciences, are now part of the Information Support Force.

A military expert has suggested that among these, the 'Battlefield Environment Battalion' is probably the Central Military Commission (CMC) Joint Staff Department Battlefield Environment Support Bureau. This was formed in 2016 with the merger of the Mapping and Navigation Bureau, Meteorology and Hydrology Bureau, and other units.

The Communications Support Battalion and Spectrum Control Battalion could have originally been with the CMC. While under the CMC Joint Staff Department, the Communications Department was responsible for technical reconnaissance, electronic warfare, and electronic countermeasures. The Spectrum Management Brigade's role probably includes establishing electronic warfare doctrine and deconflicting theatre-level electronic warfare operations, to include satellite jamming.

The Systems Engineering Research Academy of the Academy of Military Sciences, established in 2017, is one of the eight research institutes within the Academy and focuses on various aspects of systems engineering and related technologies. It is involved incutting-edge research and development to support the strategic needs of the PLA. Directly affiliated to it are the Northern Electronic Equipment Research Institute (formerly the 54th Research Institute of the Network Systems Department of the PLA Strategic Support Force) (Unit 32802) and the Military New Energy Technology Research Institute. The Systems Engineering Research Institute is a key player in advancing military scienceand technology within China's defence framework.

It is probable that most personnel of these formations and units would have been retained and moved to the Information Support Force with the original units. The leadership elements would have largely been left undisturbed. The Commander and Political Commissar of the Aerospace Force and Cyberspace Force could similarly have been left in place. Unless selected from outside the erstwhile Strategic Support Force, among those likely to have been considered for appointment as Commander and Political Commissar of the Aerospace Force and Cyberspace Force are Lt. General Zheng Junjie, Lt. General Hao Weizhong and Major General Yi Jianshe and Major General Fei Jiabing. All are Deputy Commanders of the erstwhile Strategic Support Force.

According to *Xinhua*, speaking to the 269 PLA and PAP deputies – of the 281 PLA and PAP deputies 12 were removed on charges of corruption etc. While attending the National People's Congress (NPC) meeting on March 7, Chinese President Xi Jinping focussed on the enhancement of strategic capabilities in emerging fields, the need to grasp the characteristics for developments in emerging fields, efficient integration of new productive forces and new combat forces, and achieving mutual enhancement. He highlighted the importance of prioritizing breakthroughs in development and ensuring the implementation of strategies and plans for building strategic capabilities in emerging fields.

Six PLA deputies from various military sectors presented their suggestions at the meeting. The issues raised by them reflected the PLA's areas of interest. These were: advancing maritime situational awareness capabilities, enhancing cybersecurity defence capabilities, promoting the application of Artificial Intelligence, strengthening the coordination and management of space resources, standardizing the development of emerging field standards, and innovating the construction and application of unmanned combat forces. These subjects were all touched upon by Xi Jinping.

Xi Jinping stressed the importance of innovation and said that the development of emerging fields fundamentally relies on technological innovation and application. He advocated enhancing confidence in innovation, promoting independent and original innovation, and fostering a vibrant ecosystem for innovation. Xi Jinping also emphasized the need to prioritize reform in emerging fields as a key aspect for further comprehensively deepening reform. He called for building an innovative ecosystem that is self-reliant, open, integrated, and dynamic, and improving the overall efficiency of developing emerging fields. This, he pointed out, required establishing and improving systems and mechanisms for processing demand, planning coordination, and resource sharing, advancing standardisation, and enhancing the overall benefits of the development of emerging fields.

Additionally, he emphasised accelerating the development of new combat capabilities, deepening reform of the national defence science and technology industry system, optimizing the structure of the national defence science and technology industry, and establishing mechanisms for agile response and rapid transformation of advanced technologies to adapt to the development of emerging fields. Xi Jinping called for updating ideological concepts, boldly innovating and exploring new models of construction and application of new combat forces, and fully liberating and developing new combat capabilities.

Xi Jinping pointedly stressed it is important to "integrate preparation for maritime military warfare, safeguarding of maritime rights and development of the maritime economy". On the side-lines of the NPC session, Yuan Huazhi, Political Commissar of the PLA Navy and NPC Deputy, told the Hong Kong Commercial Daily (March 5) that China will unveil its fourth aircraft carrier soon. He said there is no bottleneck in China's aircraft carrier technologies, and the development is progressing smoothly. The appointment of General Dong Jun, a PLA Navy officer and submariner, as Defence Minister will ensure adequate funds for the Navy.

Xi Jinping also underscored the need to build a network space defence system and enhance safeguards for national network security. Alluding to Civil-Military fusion, he called for strengthening the coordinated implementation of major projects in science and technology, promoting independent and original innovation, and fostering a vibrant ecosystem for innovation. Stating that State owned Enterprises (SoEs) are playing a key role, Zhang Yuzhuo, Chairman of the State-owned Assets Supervision and Administration Commission (SASAC) of the State Council, disclosed (March 5) that investment by central SOEs in strategic emerging industries increased 32.1 percent year on year in 2023. He said the SASAC's goal envisaged income derived from strategic emerging industries by central SOEs as accounting for 35 percent of their total income by 2025. He said it is important to increase investment in industries "especially in brain-like intelligence, quantum information and controlled nuclear fusion." It is clear that Xi Jinping will lay considerable emphasis on technology in the PLA.

The reorganisation has implications for China's neighbours. The creation of the Information Support Force will mean increased attention to enhancing satellite, signals and electronic monitoring, interception and disruption capabilities. It will probably be responsible for disinformation campaigns and will enhance its cyber warfare capabilities. There will be enhanced emphasis on Civil-Military Fusion and the synergy between Chinese Information Technology companies and the PLA will be further elevated. The Information Support Force can be expected to be under pressure to show results and it should be apprehended that cyber-attacks and disinformation campaigns against India and targets in the region will increase. The Dalai Lama's set up would equally be a target in the present context. An important additional area of focus for the new Force will be the Maritime Domain and particularly the Taiwan Strait and South China Sea.

This was first published by the Centre for China Analysis and Strategy (CCAS) and Vivekananda International Foundation (VIF) in June 2, 2024.

41. Tibet Government Chairman Projects That Tibet is Headed for Major Changes

The *People's Daily* on March 25, 2021, published a lengthy 3975-character article authored by Che Dalha (in Chinese: Qi Zala), Chairman of the Tibet Autonomous Region (TAR). Che Dalha's important article, which included nine mentions of Xi Jinping, predictably focuses on activities in Tibet, but makes explicitly clear that the Tibetans are headed for a difficult period.

A central theme in Che Dalha's article, which comes in the wake of China's 'Lianghui', or National People's Congress (NPC) and the Chinese People's Political Consultative Conference (CPPCC) plenums that concluded on March 11, was the need for 'unity of the motherland' and that Tibet and China had inseparable cultural, historical and religious ties. Repeating that Princess Wencheng entered Tibet in 641 AD, it claimed she brought "Buddha statues, and Buddhist scriptures, and also introduced Buddhist culture such as temple construction methods and regulations". Other points stated that greater efforts will be made to: make Mandarin the main language of instruction in schools; "forge a sense of community of the Chinese nation" among ethnic cadres, especially the leading cadres; adapt "Tibetan Buddhism to socialism with Chinese characteristics" and secure acceptance of China's role in the recognition of 'Living Buddhas' especially the Dalai Lama and Panchen Lama; and ensure greater integration of ethnic Tibetans with other people.

One of the senior-most ethnic Tibetans active in the Chinese Communist Party (CCP), Che Dalha is an upward mobile cadre. He joined the Communist Youth League in 1979 and the CCP in 1982. He is from Shangri-La (formerly known as Zhongdian County) in Yunnan province. After working in various capacities in the Tibetan areas of Yunan, he was sent to TAR around November 2010 to head the Party's United Front Work Department. He was later promoted to the important post of Party Secretary of Lhasa Municipality replacing Qin Yizhi, a Han, who had held the post since September 2006. Che Dalha's appointment was welcomed by Tibetans. He is reputed to be pro-active on economic development. This was evident recently when he urged the early grant of approvals and construction of the large dam on the Great Bend on the Brahmaputra (Yarlung Tsangpo), which was approved at the recently concluded NPC plenum. He also advocated exploitation of the natural gas reserves in northern Tibet.

Che Dalha highlighted the benefits that would accrue from the projects approved for Tibet in the "14th Five Year Plan (2021-2025) and the Long-Range Objectives through the Year 2035 for National Economic and Social Development of the People's Republic of China" that was approved at the NPC and CPPCC Plenums which ended on March 11, 2021. Pointing to the imminent huge influx of engineers, technicians and labour from the Mainland, Che Dalha highlighted that the various projects would promote development and raise the incomes of the people of Tibet. He urged that major infrastructure and public service facilities be built around the Sichuan-Tibet railway construction and other projects to promote economic activity. The goal, he said, is for Tibetans to reach or come near the national average per capita disposable income of urban and rural residents by 2025.

Subtly hinting at the possible altering of ratio between Tibetans, Hans and other ethnic nationalities, he laid emphasis on the integration of Han and Tibetan ethnic minorities in towns, streets and the 'xiaokang' model border defence villages. Picking up on the NPC's decision to build 200 new border defence villages, his article called for equal stress on strengthening the border areas. Che Dalha emphasised the need to "vigorously promote population" as well as facilities, industries, and services in the border areas to support the population settled there. The implication is that, as is presently being done in the case of the 'model well-off (xiaokang) border defence villages', the number of people residing in these border defence villages will be increased from the average 1 or 3 families to about 20-30 people. This suggests that the resident population in these villages will be integrated with Tibetans from different parts of Tibet, and possibly different Tibetan Buddhist sects, with the aim of diluting cohesion. It is possible that other ethnic nationalities could also be settled in the 'well-off (xiaokang) border defence villages'.

Chinese President Xi Jinping told delegates from Inner Mongolia to the plenary sessions of the NPC and CPPCC, on March 1, 2021 that "cultural identity is the deepest form of identity. It is also the root and soul of ethnic unity and harmony." Following that message, Che Dalha gave particular stress on the need to "vigorously cultivate and practice the core values of socialism" and make people understand that the "Chinese nation is a community with a shared future". He wrote that multiple measures are necessary to cultivate and practice the core values of socialism, implement the 'project of the Chinese nation', and build a 'patriotism education base', so that "Chinese culture becomes the emotional bond and spiritual belonging of all ethnic groups in Tibet".

Implying that efforts to make Mandarin, instead of Tibetan, the primary language of instruction in schools in TAR would be energetically pursued, he emphasised the need to continue to promote spoken and written Mandarin (Putonghua) and disclosed that 18 Putonghua proficiency test stations would be established. Mandarin has been replacing Tibetan in schools in ethnic Tibetan areas outside TAR since 2015. The process has accelerated after January 20 this year when the Director of the Legal Affairs Committee of the National People's Congress (NPC), Shen Chungyao, announced during a meeting of the NPC Standing Committee that schools in "minority areas" were no longer allowed to teach their own languages. He declared such education to be "unconstitutional". In the report that he presented, Shen Chungyao emphasised that local regulations in some cases that allow ethnic schools to use ethnic languages in teaching are inconsistent with the Chinese Constitution's order to promote Putonghua in the country. Che Dalha's article makes clear that, as is being done in the Xinjiang and Inner Mongolia autonomous regions, Mandarin will now begin to replace Tibetan as the primary language in Tibetan schools inside TAR.

In anticipation of the influx of large numbers of engineers, workers and labourers, he advocated greater exchange and integration of all ethnic groups. Che Dalha invited Tibetan college graduates to work and start businesses in the Mainland, and Mainland enterprises and individuals to start businesses in

Tibet. Saying this would help build a "mutually embedded social structure and community environment" and a "multi-ethnic harmonious street (community, family)", Che Dalha revealed that TAR would implement the "Plan for the Establishment of a Model Area for Ethnic Unity and Progress in the Tibet Autonomous Region (2021-2025)". The time-bound plan envisages establishing all seven prefectures as 'demonstration areas of national unity and progress' by 2025. He claimed that Prefectures and 80 percent of the counties (districts) have already become autonomous region-level model counties for ethnic unity and progress.

This will be reinforced by efforts to superimpose Chinese (Han) history and culture on the Tibetan people. Che Dalha disclosed that work would begin on compiling the "Encyclopedia of Ethnic Unity and Progress (Tibet Volume)". China's version of the history of Tibet, mentioned in Che Dalha's article, can be expected to be taught in schools and colleges.

Asserting that "the people of all ethnic groups in Tibet share the same heart with the people of all ethnic groups in the country" and "cherish national unity", he said that "the consciousness of the Chinese nation's community is deeply integrated into the blood of the people of all ethnic groups in Tibet". Cadres in ethnic areas, especially ethnic minority leading cadres, were exhorted to strengthen the "four consciousnesses", strengthen the "four self-confidence", and achieve the "two safeguards", continuously improve political judgment, political understanding, and political execution ability. Che Dalha said they must "consciously assume the responsibility and mission of forging a sense of community of the Chinese nation". They asked them to "always maintain a high degree of consistency with the Party Central Committee with Comrade Xi Jinping at the core. Adhere to the party's strategy of governing Tibet in the new era, and do a good job of stability, development, ecology, and strengthening the frontier".

Che Dalha devoted an entire paragraph to the issue of 'sinicisation' of Tibetan Buddhism and recognition of the Dalai Lama's reincarnation. He called for the "extensive mobilisation of the masses to participate in the struggle against separatism" and to "form a copper and iron wall to maintain stability". He stated the need to "actively guide Tibetan Buddhism to adapt to the socialist society". Stressing the importance of the "Sinicization of Tibetan

Buddhism", he urged "religious rituals and historical customization of the reincarnation of the living Buddha", so that the reincarnation of the living Buddha "must adhere to the important principle of "domestic search, golden vase drawing, and central approval". Actively guide Tibetan Buddhism to adapt to the socialist society. Always be clear about your own responsibilities and positioning, and be a good cadre with a high degree of political understanding.

Che Dalha's article indicates that the recent plenary sessions gave some directives regarding China's ethnic minority nationalities. TAR now appears poised to see a more energised bid, as noticed in Xinjiang and Inner Mongolia, to superimpose Han culture and history on the Tibetan people. There will be special efforts to mobilise Tibetans against 'separatism' – a codeword for the Dalai Lama's supporters and influence – combined with even greater efforts to get Tibetans and Tibetan Buddhist religious personages to accept Beijing's authority in recognising the reincarnations of the Dalai Lama and Panchen Lama.

This was first published by the Centre for China Analysis and Strategy (CCAS) and Vivekananda International Foundation (VIF) in March 30, 2021.

42. 'China Intensifies Campaign to Assimilate Tibetans into Mainstream Han Culture'

Tibet appears poised to initiate a vigorous campaign aimed at assimilating the Tibetan ethnic minority into the Han national mainstream. An important speech by Tibet Autonomous Region (TAR) Party Secretary Wu Yingjie, at a meeting of the District Party Committee Ideology and Propaganda and Ideological Work Leading Group in Lhasa on June 21, signals that such a campaign is imminent.

TAR Party Secretary Wu Yingjie's speech at the meeting in Lhasa on June 21, during which he mentioned Xi Jinping twelve times, was reported in detail by the official Tibet Daily the following day. The 1772-word Tibet Daily report disclosed that the meeting was attended by Liu Jiang, District Party Committee Executive Deputy Secretary, District Party Committee Ideology and Propaganda and Ideological Work Leading Group Deputy Leader, District Party Committee Standing Committee, Secretary-General, District Party Committee Ideology and Propaganda and Ideological Work Leading Group Deputy Leader; Wang Haizhou, District Party Committee Standing Committee, Propaganda Department and Minister and Deputy Leader of the District Party Committee's Ideology and Propaganda and Ideological Work Leading Group; Duo Ji Cizhu, Vice Chairman of TAR and Deputy Leader of the Leading Group for Ideology and Propaganda and Ideological Work of the District Party Committee; Du Jiangong, Vice Chairman of the TAR's PPCC; and members of the Leading Group for Ideology and Propaganda and Ideology of the District Party Committee.

At the outset Wu Yingjie emphasised that "ideology and propaganda and ideological work is an extremely important work of the party" and that Xi Jinping's series of important speeches on ideology, propaganda and ideological work had "provided us with unswervingly doing ideological work in the new era" as well as a guiding ideology to follow. He emphasised that ideology and propaganda and ideological work provide a strong ideological guarantee and a strong spiritual force for the long-term stability and high-quality development of "Tibet in the new era".

Assuring that "Xi Jinping's new era of socialism with Chinese characteristics is deeply integrated into the blood of cadres of all ethnic groups", Wu Yingjie elaborated that "masses of all ethnic groups feel the party, the determination to listen to the party and follow the party is firmer, the ideological foundation for opposing split is firmer, the Chinese nation's sense of community is further strengthened".

Particularly significant is Wu Yingjie's assertion that "the religious masses have begun to transform from "pursuing the afterlife" to "living well in this life". This implies that the huge sums poured into Tibet's development and the consequent material benefits are beginning to have the desired outcome. It indicates that the older generation of Tibetans and particularly rural nomads have begun to accept the benefits. Use of this phrase by Wu Yingjie is intended to suggest that the hitherto unwavering belief of Tibetans in Tibetan Buddhism and especially the Dalai Lama is beginning to weaken. Earlier on February 8, 2021, the Head of the Chinese Communist Party (CCP)'s United Front Work Department (UFWD) You Quan, while meeting the Panchen Lama, had claimed that the 'sinicization of Tibetan Buddhism has made new achievements in promoting the adaptation of Tibetan Buddhism to a socialist society'.

Wu Yingjie declared that "important discourses on Tibet work are combined with the party's strategy for governing Tibet in the new era". He said it is imperative to combine the spirit of the eighth and ninth plenary sessions of the Ninth Party Committee of the District Party Committee with the actual working conditions in Tibet, to "Achieve integration, brain and heart".

Pointing to the work ahead to "educate and guide" the masses, he urged the "study and education of party history, deepen educational activities such as "Four Stresses and Four Loves", "Follow the Four Standards, Strive to Be Advanced Monks and Nuns" and the need to publicise the party with Comrade Xi Jinping at its core. Declaring that the Party attaches "great importance to

Tibet's work and special care for the Tibetan people", cadres were exhorted to "further strengthen the confidence and determination of the people of all ethnic groups to appreciate the party's favour, listen to the party, and follow the party, vigorously promote the core socialist values, take a clear-cut stand to eliminate the negative influence of the 14th Dalai Lama's use of religion, and educate and guide the masses to treat religion rationally." He emphasised the importance of downplaying "the negative influence of religion", reducing "religious consumption and live a happy life".

Wu Yingjie did not hesitate to touch on the subject of adapting Tibetan culture to that of the Han. He said it is necessary to "encourage "new wine in old bottles", and actively inject new era connotations into Tibetan traditional art forms such as Tibetan opera, Langma, and Duixie, and promote the creative transformation and innovation of Chinese excellent traditional culture development, so that traditional culture can better integrate into modern life". This effort is to be extended to agricultural and pastoral areas. The objective is to "guide people of all ethnic groups to integrate into modern civilized life" and oppose and resist feudal superstitions and stereotypes. He made no specific mention of the plans to replace Tibetan with Mandarin (Putonghua) as the primary language in ethnic Tibetan schools.

He emphasised the importance of the Chinese nation's community. He said the people of all ethnic groups must "understand the long history and splendid culture of the Chinese nation, and deeply realize that Tibet has been an inalienable part of the great motherland since ancient times. Tibetan culture is an important part of Chinese culture". Wu Yingjie pointed out that "culture has always become the emotional bond and spiritual belonging of all ethnic groups in Tibet" and has strengthened "a clear-cut stand against division, and consciously safeguarding the unity of the motherland and ethnic unity." Wu Yingjie asserted the importance of consolidating Marxism in Tibet and in its philosophy, social sciences and theoretical questions on stability and development.

Wu Yingjie also focussed on the students. Noticeably avoiding mention of a 'colour revolution', he said it is essential "to work hard to effectively prevent and resolve hidden risks" and be highly vigilant against not only the "black swan" incident, but also the "gray rhino" incident. He referred to enhancing supervision of the network media such as short videos and webcasts. But he did emphasise the need to "continuously improve the ideological risk prevention and control mechanism of colleges and universities" and "do in-depth and practical ideological and political work for young students".

It is significant that Wu Yingjie's speech includes certain features of an interview published in June 2013. Professor Jin Wei, a senior faculty member of the Central Party School in Beijing had given an interview to the Hongkong-based magazine *Yazhou Zhoukan* (Asia Week) in June 2013. In that interview, which created a stir including within the CCP's senior echelons, Professor Jin Wei was categoric that the reincarnation of the XIVth Dalai Lama must be found inside China and that China must "at all costs avoid a situation of two Dalai Lamas like that of the two Panchen Lamas". She had stated that Tibetan Buddhism is important to the Tibetans who revere the Dalai Lama as a God. Wu Yingjie noticeably sidestepped any derogatory reference to the Dalai Lama in his speech.

Wu Yingjie's assertion that "the religious masses have begun to transform from "pursuing the afterlife" to "living well in this life" also echoes Professor Jin Wei's remarks in 2013. She had said the Chinese leadership needs to: "Untangle religion and politics; carefully judge the psychological needs of the Tibetan people. Tibetan people have been influenced by religion for thousands of years, forming a 'heavily spiritual and light on materialism, heavy on the next life and light on this life' national identity. This is a huge difference with the main nationality of China, the Han. As the ruling Communist Party of China, it is necessary to understand this clearly."

The CCP's efforts to motivate the monks and nuns to adapt Tibetan Buddhism to socialism with Chinese characteristics and inculcate "gratitude" and "love" for the Party has been underway for some years, but picked up since the Seventh Tibet Work Forum in August 2020. Major monasteries like Nyima Ling in Nagchu and Tashi Lhunpo in Shigatse were among those who soon after the Seventh Tibet Work Forum organised 'study sessions' for monks and nuns. The National People's Congress (NPC) Plenum that concluded on March 11, 2021, provided further impetus to these efforts. Teams from the TAR Party Committee and government have been regularly visiting the monasteries in TAR to "educate" monks and nuns and meet the

Monastery management committees. Monks and nuns who conform to the CCP's instructions are conferred the title "model".

Gyaltsen Norbu, the Chinese appointed Panchen Lama, has been roped into these efforts. He visited Tibet from July to September 2020 when he travelled to 25 counties and 33 monasteries and for the first time visited Ngari (Ali), Nyingchi and Yadong. In the course of a seminar in Lhasa, he asked monks, nuns and heads of the religious sects, to accept and listen to the leadership of the party, and to "adhere to guidelines to sinicize Tibetan Buddhism and contribute to long-term stability". This was his longest ever stay in Tibet.

At a press conference on May 11, 2021, the Gyaltsen Norbu criticised "anti-China forces" for using Tibet and Tibetan Buddhism to "attack China's ethnic and religious policies". He added that "Foreign anti-China forces", specifically referring to USA, are "not truly concerned about the Tibetan people nor about Tibetan Buddhism but are using Tibet-related matters for their vested interest". China is simultaneously trying to project to the world the development that has taken place in TAR. Coinciding with the hundredth anniversary of the founding of the CCP, China's Ministry of Foreign Affairs is organising a Global Promotional Event on Tibet.

An intensified campaign to adapt Tibetan Buddhism to 'socialism with Chinese characteristics', replace Tibetan with Putonghua as the primary language in ethnic Tibetan schools and mould Tibetan culture and history to suit that of the dominant Han, will undoubtedly enhance resentment among the Tibetans. The campaign is part of Xi Jinping's directive, published by the UFWD in January 2021, which asserts that the Han and ethnic minorities are part of a "common community with a common destiny". Similar efforts being made in the autonomous regions of Inner Mongolia, Gansu and Ningxia Hui have triggered protests and demonstrations. At the same time, noticeable in Wu Yingjie's speech is the stress on preventing "splittism" and opposing the forces of the XIVth Dalai Lama, which confirm that the Dalai Lama's influence among Tibetans inside China remains strong. While TAR has thus far been peaceful, the new measures could see protests in TAR too.

This was first published by the Centre for China Analysis and Strategy (CCAS) and Vivekananda International Foundation (VIF) in June 27, 2021.

43. China is Replacing Ethnic Languages with Mandarin

Wary of efforts by the US and West to bring about the collapse of the Chinese Communist Party (CCP), particularly as memories of the disintegration of the erstwhile Soviet Union and collapse of the Communist Party of the Soviet Union (CPSU) still remain sharply etched, Chinese President Xi Jinping has been focussed on strengthening the CCP to ensure it retains its monopoly on power. Xi Jinping has also long had an interest in united front work and ethnic minority issues and in 2017 took over as head of the powerful Central Leading Small Group on United Front Work, which exercises direct control over the formulation and implementation of policies for China's ethnic minorities. Since then, there has been a noticeable uptick in united front activity concerning the ethnic minorities.

Recognising that the language of a people is the key to their retaining their culture, traditions and history, the united front, among its other policies, has centered on replacing ethnic languages taught in schools in ethnic areas with Putonghua (Mandarin). A factor would be the heightened apprehension among China's leaders, following the outbreak of the China US trade war and rapid deterioration in bilateral ties, that the US, West and 'hostile neighbours' would attempt to fan discontent among the ethnic minorities residing in China's border provinces. A pointer is the attention that Beijing pays to Nepal.

An indication that tough policies for accelerating the assimilation of ethnic minorities, instead of the more accommodative policies of Deng Xiaoping's era, would be implemented is the recent change at the helm of the body responsible for ethnic minority affairs. On December 14, 2020, Chen Xiaojiang, a 66-year-old Han cadre, was appointed to head the National Ethnic Affairs Commission, breaking a tradition followed since 1954 of having a member of one of China's 56 ethnic minority groups head the body. The change comes in the wake of the National Ethnic Affairs Commission being placed under direct Party control and bringing it under the CCP Central Committee's United Front Work Department in 2018. Till then it was under China's State Council.

The CCP has been making systematic efforts to replace the ethnic languages with Mandarin. It has sought to introduce Mandarin in place of the ethnic languages taught in schools in minority areas and regions. Efforts at assimilation of ethnic minorities into the Han mainstream includes selecting young students for education in schools and colleges in the Chinese Mainland. Many young students stay for decades at these schools and colleges with the more recent arrivals imbibing "Xi Jinping's thought on socialism with Chinese characteristics in the new era"! While these efforts have been observed in varying degrees in the Tibet and Xinjiang Autonomous Regions, since last year the policy is being enforced in the Inner Mongolia Autonomous Region too.

For example, in 1984 the CCP decided to establish schools for Tibetan students in Chinese provinces and cities as part of the so-called "Aid Tibet" programme. From the following year at least 16 Chinese provinces, like Tianjin, Liaoning, Shanghai, Jiangsu, Yunnan etc., began to annually admit 1,300 students, who had finished primary school, from the Tibet Autonomous Region (TAR). Radio Free Asia (RFA) reported that Chinese government websites and the Tibet Daily had publicised that by January 2019, a total of 141,900 Tibetan students were enrolled in these schools, colleges and universities. Tibetan students were enrolled in a total of 75 junior high schools and senior high schools in 20 Chinese cities; 29 schools in 12 cities with secondary vocational classes; and 196 colleges and universities with Tibetan students. In 2020, there were 4,472 students from TAR taking college entrance examinations. These special schools for Tibetans supplement the CCP's other efforts to assimilate Tibetans into the Han national mainstream and cultivate generations of Tibetans more comfortable with Chinese (Han) culture, language and 'socialism with Chinese characteristics'. Chinese authorities justify this educational system as intended to provide economic and social development in Tibet and benefit Tibet's long-term stability.

Efforts have now begun to gradually replace Tibetan with Mandarin in Tibetan schools. A start has been made with Tibetan counties outside the Tibet Autonomous Region. Outside TAR, more than 50 percent of the schools have converted to the new system where students are taught all subjects in Putonghua with Tibetan as just a language class. An exception is Rebkong County in Ngaba and some schools in Golok and Ganzi Dzong which still follow the earlier practice. In other Tibetan areas outside TAR, both primary and secondary schools have implemented the new system. Politburo Standing Committee member and Chairman of the Chinese People's Political Consultative Conference (CPPCC) Wang Yang's tour to the Golok Tibetan Prefecture in Qinghai Province on September 14-15, 2020, was intended to give a push to this process. The policy will be gradually extended into and across the TAR.

Active implementation of the new system began in TAR in 2015. Thus far, it is only Lhasa that has fully implemented the new system. Some primary schools in Nyingtri (Nyingchi) have begun implementing the new system. All the schools have nonetheless introduced a Putonghua promotion week each year in all prefectures in TAR.

A similar policy was crafted for the Uyghur ethnic minority in the Xinjiang-Uyghur Autonomous Region. From 2007, entrance exams at all levels of the Xinjiang education system began to change with the stress on minority students taking tests in their non-native language. Ethnic minority students were told to "master and use the nationally used language and writing system," in other words, Chinese. Uyghur students also began being segregated from the age of 15 on the basis of their grades under a "secondary vocational training enrollment plan" and sent to vocational schools. A primary goal was to send more minority students, or Uyghurs, to Han-majority schools. 5000 Uyghur students began being enrolled annually in 16 schools in the Chinese mainland from 2007.

In August 2020, the Inner Mongolian government mandated that primary and secondary schools must use Mandarin (Putonghua) and not Mongolian, as the language of instruction. The authorities implemented a unified Chinese language teaching plan. Hou Yuan, then Director of the Education Department, claimed that "textbooks reflect the will of the Communist Party and the State" and the use of unified textbooks was a "major decision" made by the CCP Central Committee. The policy triggered widespread resistance among Mongolians and more than 300,000 students staged protests and demonstrations in the Nei (Inner) Mongol capital of Hohhot in which government employees also joined. People worried that the unique Mongolian language and culture will be extinguished as a result of these policies.

Notwithstanding popular discontent, the Chinese Communist Party (CCP) has stepped up other efforts to accelerate assimilation of the Mongol people, possibly because they number only five million and are in a minority in the Autonomous Region. The Education Department of the Inner Mongolia Autonomous Region, in a notice to publishing houses dated January 8, 2021, stated that in compliance with the instructions of the China National Textbook Committee it had conducted an "Ideological Special Investigation" and an audit of textbooks such as *Inner Mongolian History and Culture*, *Mongolian History*, *Hulunbuir History and Culture*, *Hetao History and Culture*, and *Korqin History and Culture (Trial)*. The notice declared that the textbooks did not adequately highlight "the awareness of common roots", but instead emphasised individual "ethnic identity" and "ethnic awareness." The Department of Education of Inner Mongolia had consequently decided to ban the use of the textbooks of *Inner Mongolia History and Culture, Mongolian History,* and *Hetao History and Culture* from the Spring of 2021. It stated that the textbooks of *Hulunbeier History and Culture* and *Korqin History and Culture (Trial)* will not be used from the Fall semester of 2021.

On February 8, 2021, the 'Regulations of the Inner Mongolia Autonomous Region on Promoting National Unity and Progress', which had been approved by the Inner Mongolia Autonomous Region People's Congress on January 30, 2021, were publicised. Comprising 56 Articles, these stress the promotion of "traditional Chinese culture" and customs and assert that the Han and ethnic minorities are part of a 'common community with a common destiny'. They also mandate that "religious groups, venues for religious activities, and religious schools shall fully implement the Party's basic policy on religious work, adhere to the direction of sinicization of religion in China" and, in addition to actively promoting ethnic unity, will "support the leadership of the Communist Party of China, support the socialist system, adhere to the path of socialism with Chinese characteristics, and maintain national unity, the unification of the motherland, religious harmony and social stability". Other restrictive provisions are in Article 54, which states that "It is forbidden to deny the Chinese ethnic community, slander national customs and habits, damage national dignity, and harm nationality"; Article 55 which asserts "No organization or individual may spread speech that is not conducive to national unity"; and Article 56 which warns against infiltration, subversion, sabotage, violent terrorist activities, ethnic separatist activities, and religious extremist activities etc. that disrupt national unity, ethnic unity, and social stability.

Following the publication of new Rules for the United Front Work Department (UFWD) in January 2021, the CCP CC's UFWD convened a national meeting on January 18 in Beijing of UFWD Directors from all across China. Speaking at the meeting, Politburo Standing Committee member and CPPCC Chairman Wang Yang focussed on ethnic minorities and religious affairs and, implying the need to hasten the process of assimilation, said "we need to mobilize all active factors that we can mobilize."

On January 20, the Director of the Legal Affairs Committee of the National People's Congress (NPC), Shen Chungyao, announced during a meeting of the NPC Standing Committee that schools in "minority areas" were no longer allowed to teach their own languages. He declared such education to be "unconstitutional". In a report that he presented, Shen Chungyao emphasised the superiority of national laws over local laws in autonomous provinces and regions by observing that all local regulations violate "the country's major reform directions" and "the provisions of the higher-level law". He said some local regulations that allow ethnic schools to use ethnic languages in teaching are inconsistent with Chinese Constitution's order to promote Putonghua in the country.

Viewed along with the UFWD policies including the 'sinicisation' of religions, especially Tibetan Buddhism, and the sustained 'education' of monks and nuns in Tibetan Buddhist monasteries, it is apparent that the CCP's efforts to affect the assimilation of the ethnic minorities into the Han national mainstream have accelerated.

This was first published by the Centre for China Analysis and Strategy (CCAS) and Vivekananda International Foundation (VIF) in February 14, 2021.

44. 'CPPCC Chairman Wang Yang's Visit to Tibet Autonomous Region is Important'

The three day (August 18-21, 2021) visit to Lhasa by Wang Yang, Politburo Standing Committee member and Chairman of the Chinese People's Political Consultative Conference (CPPCC), at the head of a 22-member delegation is important. The visit follows that by Chinese President Xi Jinping in late July and, together, the two are intended to give a substantive push to the Chinese Communist Party (CCP) leadership's plan to affect a cultural and socio-economic transformation of Tibet.

Indications of the proposed changes were given at the National People's Congress (NPC) in March 2021, which approved the '14th Five Year Plan and Long-Range Plan-2030'. Tibet has received elevated attention from the CCP leadership since Xi Jinping took office and especially over the past year. Central Party organisations and the TAR leaders have been urging cadres to intensify the campaigns designed to bring about the changes.

CPPCC Chairman Wang Yang arrived in Lhasa at the newly opened Terminal 3 of Lhasa Gonggar Airport just after noon on August 18, 2021. The delegation, which had come to take part in the celebrations of the 70th anniversary of the so-called "peaceful liberation of Tibet" on August 19, was welcomed at the airport by TAR Party Secretary Wu Yingjie, Chairman of TAR People's Congress Lobsang Gyaltsen, Chairman of TAR People's Government Che Dalha and nearly 500 representatives of "ethnic groups in Tibet". The *People's Daily* marked the celebrations with a 20-page special pull-out.

Included in the delegation from Beijing were: You Quan, Politburo member and Head of the United Front Work Department (UFWD); Pema Trinley, presently Vice Chairman of the NPC Standing Committee and former Chairman of the TAR People's Government; Zhang Qingli, Vice

Chairman of the CPPCC Standing Committee and former hard-line TAR Party Secretary from 2006-2011; Sithar, former Executive Deputy Minister and Head of the UFWD Seventh Bureau who played a key role during the 2002-2010 talks with envoys of the Dalai Lama; and Admiral Miao Hua, Political Commissar of the Central Military Commission (CMC).

On arrival at the airport on August 18, Wang Yang was received by TAR Party Secretary Wu Yingjie and senior TAR officials. Soon after its arrival, the delegation attended the opening ceremony of an exhibition at the Tibet Museum on the theme "The Party's greatness shines on the borderland and the Tibetan Plateau — the 70th Anniversary of the Peaceful Liberation of Tibet!" The same evening the delegation had a meeting with leading cadres of Tibet including Pema Trinlay, Phakpa La Gelek Namgyal, Legcho, Pasang, Lobsang Gyaltsen, Che Dalha, Wu Yingjie and the family of Ngapon Ngawang Jigme.

The official celebration of the 70th Anniversary commenced at 10 am at the Potala Palace Square and was attended by more than 20,000 party cadres and masses. 24 officers of the People's Liberation Army (PLA) including seven lady officers and 10 representatives from the People's Armed Police Force (PAPF) were also present.

Wang Yang addressed the gathering and the Head of the UFWD, You Quan read out the congratulatory messages from the CCP Central Committee, NPC, the State Council, CPPCC and the CMC. TAR Party Secretary Wu Yingjie, Commander of the Tibet Military Region Lt. General Wang Kai, a representative of the people who currently works as Director of the Zangre Community Neighbourhood in Lhasa, Tenzin, and a representative of the Tibet Aid Cadres and Deputy Secretary of Shuanghu County Party Committee, Liang Nanyu, also delivered speeches. Commemorative messages and plaques were presented by Wang Yang to select persons and a representative each of the TAR, the Tibet Military Region, Headquarters of the PAPF, the Political and Legal Affairs Commission (PLAC) of TAR and the Tibet Branch of the Buddhist Association of China.

Phakpa La Gelek Namgyal, Vice Chairman of the CPPCC and Chairman of the TAR PPCC, and other TAR leaders like Lobsang Gyaltsen, Chairman of TAR People's Congress; Yan Jinhai, Party Secretary of Lhasa Municipal Party Committee, Zhang Xuejie, Tenkho, Jiang Jie, He Wenhao,

Pema Wangdui, Liu Jiang, Wang Weidong, Chen Yongqi, Wang Haizhou and old Party Cadres like Legcho and Pasang attended the celebration. Gyaltsen Norbu, the Chinese-appointed 11th Panchen Lama was also present. As he was not photographed or mentioned in the list of delegates arriving from Beijing, it is likely that he arrived in Lhasa separately. The Celebration was presided over by the Chairman of the TAR People's Government, Che Dalha.

Wang Yang's over 2500-word speech mentioned Xi Jinping at least seven times. Addressing the 70th anniversary celebrations of the so-called "peaceful liberation of Tibet" on August 19, Wang Yang asserted that "The peaceful liberation of Tibet in 1951 was a major victory in the cause of liberation of the Chinese people and China's reunification" and said "It marked a historic transition with epoch-making significance for Tibet". Asserting that serfdom had been abolished, he said Tibet presently has over 35,000 deputies of people's congresses and over 8,000 CPPCC members at various levels, 90 percent of whom are ethnic minorities. He claimed that "separatist and sabotage activities" committed by "the Dalai group and hostile external forces have been crushed". Wang Yang said that more than 1,700 temples in Tibet have full access to water, electricity, the Internet, fire-fighting and other facilities. All the 46,000 monks and nuns in TAR are covered by the government's social security scheme. He also expressed support for "a national demonstration zone for ecological civilization construction."

Wang Yang urged that officials and the general public of all ethnic groups should be mobilized to forge an "ironclad defence" against separatist activities. He also called for efforts to ensure "that religions in China are Chinese in orientation and guide Tibetan Buddhism in adapting itself to socialist society. And we should rally religious figures and believers around us in a joint effort to safeguard national security and social harmony. Tibet's development over the past seven decades demonstrates that unity and stability is a blessing, whereas separatist activities and chaos can only lead to disaster. No one outside China has the right to point fingers at us when it comes to Tibetan affairs. Any attempt or maneuver designed to separate Tibet from China is doomed to fail".

Referring to the project for assimilating Tibetan culture with that of the Han, he said "It is necessary to promote the cause of national unity and progress based on forging the consciousness of the Chinese nation as a community as the main line." Wang Yang explained that this entails "Efforts to raise public awareness of ethnic unity and progress should go hand in hand with efforts to raise awareness of core socialist values, of patriotism, of struggle against separatist activities, of contrast between old and new Tibet, and of the Marxist views of country, history, ethnicity, culture and religion. Such efforts will enable people of all ethnic groups to strengthen their faith in our great motherland, the Chinese nation, the Chinese culture, the CPC and socialism with Chinese characteristics, thus solidifying the cultural foundation for ethnic unity. A shared cultural identity underpins ethnic unity."

Continuing with this theme, he said "All-round efforts should continue to be made to teach standard spoken and written Chinese language. We should foster and share Chinese cultural symbols and images of the Chinese nation among all ethnic groups, and thus create a source of inspiration for the entire Chinese nation."

On August 20, the delegation split into two groups and left Lhasa for inspections to Nagchu, Shigatse and Lhoka. Wang Yang, Zhang Qingli, Miao Hua and some members from the delegation from Beijing went to Nagchu (Ch: Nagqu) and visited the Animal Husbandry Industry Demonstration Base (Green House), Kaima Village in Sernyed Chu District, and the Hangjie Middle Military School, which was established in 2017 as the single largest project of the 13th Five Year plan aided by Zhejiang Province and has more than 2000 students. The delegation visited the Nagchu City People's Hospital and inaugurated the Nagchu-Yangbachen Section of the Beijing-Tibet National Expressway. TAR Party Secretary Wu Yingjie, accompanied this delegation for their visits.

You Quan, Pema Trinlay and some of the other delegates who had come from Beijing left for visits to Lhoka (Ch: Shannan) and Shigatse (Ch: Xigaze). Lobsang Gyaltsen, Chairman of TAR People's Congress accompanied this group. At Lhoka the delegation visited Nyedong District's Ethnic Hand-knitting Professional Cooperative Society, the Lhoka City People's Hospital, the Lhoka No.2 Vocational and Technical School, and held a meeting with Lhoka Municipal Party Committee officials and local people. The delegation also visited the 'Exhibition Hall of the First Democratic Reform Village'.

In Shigatse, the delegation visited the Jianglou Khangsar Community in Samdrubtse District, and inspected the Tashi Lhunpo Monastery, Shanghai Experimental School and the Shigatse People's Hospital. Interestingly, there was no mention of Gyaltsen Norbu, the Chinese-appointed 11th Panchen Lama, being present at the Tashi Lhunpo Monastery, which is his traditional religious seat, though he had attended the 70th Anniversary celebration in Lhasa on August 19.

CPPCC Chairman Wang Yang's speech clearly outlined the thrust of the CCP's policy for Tibet in the coming years. The focus was on unity among Han and Tibetan ethnic groups, the oneness of their culture, harmony and stability in Tibet and the defence and security of the borders. Interesting were the repeated references to separatist and sabotage activities and the Dalai Lama and 'his clique', though in the same speech Wang Yang also asserted that separatism had been crushed. Important in this context was the indication of continuing resistance to the CCP's efforts, highlighted by the call to "rally religious figures and believers around us in a joint effort to safeguard national security and social harmony".

This was first published by the Centre for China Analysis and Strategy (CCAS) and Vivekananda International Foundation (VIF) in August 23, 2021.

45. China's Efforts to Erase The Dalai Lama's Influence and Promote Panchen Lama are Yielding Minimal Results

Chinese President Xi Jinping has increased efforts in recent months to try and erase the XIVth Dalai Lama's influence inside Tibet and among the growing number of adherents to Buddhism elsewhere in China. This suggests an apparent urgency to ensure that the exiled Dalai Lama's reincarnation, when the situation arises, will be nurtured by tutors compliant with the Chinese communist regime and later remain in the firm grip of the Chinese Communist Party (CCP). The spectre of two Dalai Lamas — one quite outside Beijing's control — like presently in the case of the Panchen Lama, though the one approved by the Dalai Lama has been secreted somewhere among China's 1.4 billion people, haunts the Chinese communist leadership.

Beijing's fear is that a Dalai Lama outside the CCP's control would continue to be revered by the Tibetans and other Chinese Buddhists as at present. The reincarnate could also persist in raising issues such as the freedoms and human rights of Tibetans and, as China's relations with the West and Europe get progressively strained, put China under increasing pressure. The Dalai Lama nominated by Beijing will also not be accepted by the Tibetan people, much as the Chinese-nominated Panchen Lama, Gyaltsen Norbu, is only now after 25 years beginning to be acknowledged, but just as a "learned monk"!

Beijing's apprehensions are reflected in the new regulations issued late this January and imposed across the Tibet Autonomous Region (TAR)'s seven administrative districts and Tibetan areas in adjoining provinces. On January 25, a directive to all districts and municipalities of the TAR mandated that workers employed in Tibetan government offices, schools or hospitals must be "trustworthy and reliable citizens" and remain loyal to the CCP. It instructed them to renounce the Dalai Lama and his followers and, referring to the group of supporters surrounding him, his "clique." Continuance in employment and promotions have been made conditional upon such a declaration.

The same month the TAR authorities reiterated warnings to officials to be loyal to the CCP. At a two-day symposium in Lhasa and Shigatse on January 13-14, officials and leaders, including those who had retired, were urged to always have a clear-cut and firm political stance especially in opposing "separatism," safeguarding national unity and in drawing a clear-cut line from the "Dalai Clique." They were told that the party will not tolerate "two-faced" people.

Efforts have been made at regular intervals to curb worship of the Dalai Lama, compel Tibetans to not keep photographs of the Dalai Lama in their homes, and weed out "double-faced" cadres — those working for the TAR government while concealing their loyalty to the Dalai Lama — and prevent Tibetans from crossing into India for an audience with the Dalai Lama. There was an uptick in warnings by TAR leaders against 'separatist' elements and "double-faced" cadres prior to Xi Jinping's visit to Tibet in July 2021. These efforts have met with negligible, or very limited, success. This year, however, the regulations, which threaten punishment, are likely to be more stringently enforced as they come in the politically sensitive run up to the 20th Party Congress scheduled for later this year.

At the end of January another new law "Measures for the Administration of Internet Religious Information Services" was promulgated. Due to take effect from March 1, this law prohibits, or severely limits, efforts to spread religion or disseminate religious teachings through online channels. Curbs on monks giving 'teachings' in Tibetan Buddhist are already in force in Zhejiang and other provinces. The latest regulation orders Tibetan social media groups affiliated to religion to disband or face punishment. It decrees "All online coordinating of religious activities and related events will be banned".

The Chinese leadership has simultaneously been striving to promote Gyaltsen Norbu, whom they appointed the Panchen Lama in 1995. The Panchen Lama has an important traditional role as the reincarnate Dalai Lama's Tutor. The Dalai Lama performs a similar function for the Panchen

Lama. Gyaltsen Norbu has been gradually sought to be introduced to the Buddhist clergy and believers. In 2006 he attended the China-sponsored World Buddhist Forum — his first international gathering — and gave a speech in Tibetan on Buddhism and national unity. In 2012 he travelled outside Mainland China for the first time to attend the World Buddhist Forum in Hongkong. It was only in mid-May 2019 that he made his first international trip and visited Thailand.

More important, though, is to have Gyaltsen Norbu accepted by the Tibetan people. The Tibetans inside China and in exile, however, continue to recognise Gedhun Choekyi Nyima, who was born on April 25, 1989 and recognized by the XIVth Dalai Lama as the 11th Panchen Lama on May 14, 1995. China's communist rulers took Gedhun Choekyi Nyima away on May 17, 1995 and there has been no word of him since. On February 3, 2010, Norbu was appointed Vice President of the Buddhist Association of China.

In 2018 he was brought to TAR for the first time since his 'enthronement' as Panchen Lama. During the three-month visit he travelled to Lhasa, Lhoka (Shannan) and the Panchen Lama's traditional religious seat of Shigatse and visited the sacred lake of Lhamo Lhatso. He met people in these three prefectures and conducted religious Buddhist activities. Gyaltsen Norbu visited Tibet again in 2019 and 2020 for a two-month sojourn on each occasion. In 2019, he travelled to Nagchu and Ngari for the first time and spent 20 days there. The number of Tibetans attending his religious teachings have grown each time, but are still considerably fewer than at the time of his predecessor the Xth Panchen Lama.

Gyaltsen Norbu's longest stay in Tibet thus far was in 2021 when he stayed for three months and conducted various Buddhist religious activities and visited villages, monasteries and entrepreneurial centres. He went to eleven monasteries of different sects, including Narthang monastery, Gyantse Palkor Chöde Monastery, Ralung monastery, Shalu monastery and Yungdrungling. He also attended the 70th Anniversary of the "liberation of Tibet" with the other dignitaries from Beijing, including Chinese President Xi Jinping. On October 26, 2021, in the presence of 800 representatives of monastic Teachers from various sects of Tibetan Buddhism he was conferred the title "Ka-Chen", equivalent to a doctorate in modern Education. He returned to Beijing at the end of October.

The China-appointed Panchen Lama Gyaltsen Norbu has also been used to propagate that Tibetan Buddhist monks and nuns should "love the nation" and "adapt Buddhism to socialism with Chinese characteristics". During his visits to monasteries, Gyaltsen Norbu has reiterated that "loving the party, the country, and the religion is the key to Tibetan Buddhism's continued inheritance and entry into the next century". He has emphasized that "the Communist Party of China has allowed all Chinese people to live a happy and peaceful life, and has given Asia and the world a better guarantee of peace. This is exactly what Buddhism has pursued for thousands of years, and the Chinese Communist Party has achieved it in 100 years. Without the Communist Party of China, there would be no peace and peaceful New China, nor would there be a happy New Tibet today."

Despite high security and the persistent efforts of the Chinese communist leadership, protests by the Tibetan Buddhist clergy and ordinary Tibetans in TAR and Tibetan areas in adjoining provinces continue to be reported. The successive campaigns against the Dalai Lama and campaigns to 'sinicise' Tibetan Buddhism have yielded negligible results as cadres have preferred to maintain peace rather than enforce these goals. The number of Tibetans in TAR being prosecuted for endangering "state security", which includes subversion, 'splittism', incitement to subversion or splittism, espionage, and violations of state secrets has also increased since 2018.The number ofTibetans in TAR prosecuted on charges of endangering "state security" rose from 37 in 2019 to 74 in 2020. Another 15 Tibetans were sentenced in the Ganzi Tibetan Prefecture in western Sichuan. Figures for other Tibetan regions in the Sichuan, Gansu, Ningxia, and Yunnan provinces are not known.

Matters are likely to become more complicated for China in the interregnum when the XIVth Dalai Lama's reincarnation, or 'emanation', is settling in. The Tibet Support Groups, Tibet Information Network and Friends of Tibet Parliamentary Groups etc., which have worldwide networks can be expected to become more active in projecting the XIVth Dalai Lama's successor and his policies. Additionally, the US has expressed support for the Tibetans in the Tibet Policy and Support Act, 2002, which, among other provisions, expressly 'opposes any effort by the Chinese authorities to identify, select, educate or install Tibetan Buddhist religious leaders, including any future Dalai Lama, in a manner inconsistent with the Tibetan Buddhist faith and community'. Tibetan youth in exile will probably also make a push for "full independence", giving a fillip to those inside China resisting the Chinese occupation of Tibet. A further complication will be in case, as is probable, the Dalai Lama's successor is discovered in India!

This was first published by the Centre for China Analysis and Strategy (CCAS) and Vivekananda International Foundation (VIF) in February 21, 2022.

46. Xi Jinping's Visit to Tibet is Important and Has Implications for India

Chinese President Xi Jinping arrived in the Tibet Autonomous Region (TAR) at Nyingchi's Mainling Airport on July 21 at the start of a two-day (July 21-23) visit, without prior public notice. The visit, which comes shortly before the 70th anniversary of the "peaceful liberation" of Tibet, is important. With this visit Chinese President Xi Jinping has given impetus to the initiatives on ethnic unity, promoting Mandarin as the primary language in ethnic schools in TAR, adapting Tibetan Buddhism to socialism with Chinese characteristics and combatting separatism, etc. The visit would encourage the People's Liberation Army (PLA) deployed on the borders with India and could be a response to the Prime Minister's wishes to the Dalai Lama for his 86th birthday. It could presage new initiatives by the PLA along the Line of Actual Control (LAC).

Xi Jinping's visit was kept a tightly guarded secret till his arrival in Nyingchi in Tibet on July 21. This would have been to prevent any demonstrations or protests during the visit or embarrassment to China's President. There has been an increase in warnings by TAR leaders against separatist elements and "double-faced cadres" in recent months. Privately recorded video clips showed that plainclothes security personnel around Xi Jinping, as he walked down Barkhor street waving to the sizeable crowds, were visibly tense. The video-clips suggested that security personnel, Party members and vetted people would have formed a large part of the crowd. Much of the crowd in Lhasa appeared to comprise ethnic Hans while at Nyingchi there were many Tibetans or other ethnic minority nationalities. Barkhor street was closed to the public on July 22. Clues are now available to indicate that planning for Xi Jinping's visit had started weeks earlier. The Drepung monastery, one of the three largest monasteries of the Gelug school of Tibetan Buddhism, held a "special counseling session" for its monks and nuns on June 21. The Potala

Palace announced on July 20, that it would be closed to the public on July 22 because its walls and electrical wiring were being checked, but would reopen on July 23.

China's official news agency Xinhua on July 23 reported the visit. Underscoring the importance of the visit was the presence of three Politburo members among several high-level officials who accompanied Xi Jinping as part of his entourage. The senior officials included Ding Xuexiang, Liu He, Yang Xiaodu, General Zhang Youxia, Chen Xi and He Lifeng. Their inclusion suggests the agenda for the visit.

It is significant for India that that Xi Jinping's visit to Tibet takes place in the midst of high military tension between India and China — presently in the Ladakh region. Xi Jinping's decision to start his tour of TAR from the Nyingchi Prefecture opposite India's Arunachal Pradesh is important. China's official maps depict the Nyingchi Prefecture's administrative boundaries as including most of India's state of Arunachal Pradesh within its boundaries. The visit follows the meeting between the Indian and Chinese Foreign Ministers on the side-lines of the Shanghai Cooperation Organisation (SCO) meeting at Dushanbe on July 6, where Chinese Foreign Minister Wang Yi reiterated that India is responsible for the current situation and that the PLA will not restore the status quo by withdrawing to its April 2020 positions. Chinese President Xi Jinping has, incidentally, not yet publicly commented on the state of India-China relations or the situation on the India-China border and neither have these been publicly reported as having figured on the agenda of meetings of the CCP Central Committee (CC)'s Politburo or Politburo Standing Committee.

Xi Jinping has visited TAR twice earlier. On each occasion he commenced his visit from Nyingchi, showing the importance that he personally attaches to this prefecture. Relevant in this context are Xi Jinping's insistent calls for the "great rejuvenation" of the Chinese nation and recovery of territories claimed to have been lost by the imposition of unequal treaties by hostile foreign powers. Xi Jinping's first visit to Tibet was in 1998 when as Party Secretary of Fujian, he had gone to inspect and be briefed on 'Aid Tibet' projects assisted by Fujian. At that time his visit was confined to Nyingchi. The second time Xi Jinping travelled to TAR was as China's Vice President in July 2011 for the

60th anniversary of the "peaceful liberation" of Tibet. Then too, he commenced his visit from Nyingchi and later visited Shigatse and Lhasa.

There are other factors that underscore the importance of the visit to Nyingchi. Nyingchi is of military importance and a number of PLA Units, militias, Border Defence Regiments and missile bases are situated there. There has recently been elevated Chinese military-related activity in the area. Nyingchi is also the gateway through which the strategic railway linking Chengdu, the capital of Sichuan province, with Lhasa, the capital of TAR, passes. Once the remaining section of the railway is completed, this will be the second railway connecting Lhasa and Shigatse to other provinces in the Mainland. It will reduce travel time between Chengdu and Lhasa to 10 hours from the present almost 30. The world's largest dam being built at the Great Bend on the Brahmaputra (Yarlung Tsangpo) is also in Nyingchi.

After arrival at Nyingchi, Xi Jinping drove to the Niyang River Bridge and received a briefing on the ecological environment protection efforts and the construction of nature reserves in the Yarlung Zangbo River and Niyang River Basin. The Niyang River is one of five tributaries flowing into the Yarlung Tsangpo (Brahmaputra) and the main water source for Nyingchi. Xi Jinping emphasised the importance of ecological environment protection, restoration of important river basins, and protection of lives, plants, and mountains. That afternoon he visited the Linzhi City Planning Museum for a briefing on the construction and development plans of Linzhi City. Later, Xi Jinping went to Gala Village, located in Linzhi Town, which is famous for its peach blossoms in spring. He walked to the village convenience service center, "green bank" exchange shops, health rooms, etc. and met the villagers. One villager, Dawa Jianshen said that last year his family's income exceeded 300,000 yuan and Xi Jinping responded that "the good life in Gala Village is a microcosm of the economic and social development achievements of Tibet since the peaceful liberation of Tibet over the past 70 years". Xi Jinping then visited Gongbu Park, located at the junction of the old and new towns of Nyingchi.

On the morning of July 22, Xi Jinping went to Linzhi Railway Station, an important hub station of the Sichuan-Tibet Railway which opened on June 25 this year, for a briefing on the overall plan of the Sichuan-Tibet Railway and the construction and operation of the Lhasa-Nyingchi section. He received a report on the progress of the construction of the Ya'an-Nyingchi section, and sat on a special train to observe Lalin. Xinhua stated that Xi Jinping attaches "great importance" to the construction of the Sichuan-Tibet Railway. He pointed out that the planning and construction of the Sichuan-Tibet Railway is a major measure to promote the development of Tibet and improve people's livelihood. Xi Jinping and his entourage then travelled by the FuXing (Bullet) train to Lhasa.

The same afternoon that he arrived in Lhasa, Xi Jinping visited Drepung Monastery in the western suburbs of Lhasa. He listened to a report on how Drepung Monastery strengthened innovative temple management, and affirmed Drepung Monastery's active contributions in "supporting the leadership of the Chinese Communist Party (CCP), supporting the socialist system, and safeguarding the unity of the motherland over the years". Xi Jinping emphasised it is necessary to fully implement the party's basic policy on religious work, respect the religious beliefs of the masses, manage religious affairs in accordance with the law and actively guide Tibetan Buddhism to adapt to socialist society. After a short walk down Barkhor street, Xi Jinping came to the Potala Palace Square and asked about the protection and management of the Potala Palace. Xi Jinping pointed out that Tibet was developed jointly by all ethnic groups, and the history of Tibet was written jointly by all ethnic groups. He said the development of Tibet is "at a new historical starting point. As long as we follow the Communist Party of China and firmly follow the path of socialism with Chinese characteristics, and work together to strengthen national unity, we will definitely be able to achieve the second centenary goal as scheduled, and realize the Chinese dream of the great rejuvenation of the Chinese nation". That evening Xi Jinping watched a national cultural performance with cadres and the masses of all ethnic groups in the Tibetan People's Hall.

In an unmistakable gesture to Tibetans, Xi Jinping called on Phakpa Lha Gelek Namgyal, who was born in 1940 and joined the CCP in 1950! He is also a 'living Buddha'.

On July 23 morning, Xi Jinping listened to the work reports of the Tibet Autonomous Region Party Committee and Government, and appreciated their achievements. He hoped that the Party Committee and Government of the Tibet Autonomous Region would unite and lead the cadres and the masses, do a solid job of mass work, improve social governance, and ensure national security, social stability, and people's happiness. He said "we must persist in integrating the education of national unity" and propagate the "socialist core values, education, patriotism education, anti-separatism education" and comparison of old and new Tibet. Stressing the necessity of blending ethnic groups, Xi Jinping highlighted the importance of the Chinese nation, Chinese culture, the Communist Party of China, and socialism with Chinese characteristics. He called for deepening reform and opening up, accelerating the construction of railways, highways and other major infrastructures, and national clean energy bases. He said development and security must be coordinated. Xi Jinping stressed the importance of "building border infrastructure, and encouraging people of all ethnic groups to take root in the border, guard the country and build their hometowns". Xi Jinping emphasised the study of party history and need to maintain the 'red blood'.

Reform and economic implementation issues appear to have been high on the Chinese President's agenda. Liu He is Politburo member, Vice Premier and Director of the Office serving the CCP's Central Financial and Economic affairs Commission headed by Xi Jinping. He Lifeng is Minister of the important National Development and Reform Commission (NDRC). The two can be expected to have discussed and reviewed the projects earmarked for TAR in the '14th Five Year Plan and Long Range Objectives of the People's Republic of China'. These include defence infrastructure-related projects like the twenty 'general purpose' border airports and the upgradation and extension of two additional highways along the LAC, the numerous smaller dams along the Yarlung Tsangpo (Brahmaputra), and massive dam at the Great Bend on the Yarlung Tsangpo (Brahmaputra). Various other developmental projects would also have been reviewed. The likely impact of the influx into sparsely populated Tibet of large numbers of workers and technicians from the Mainland for these projects would have been an agenda item.

The inclusion of Central Military Commission (CMC) Vice Chairman General Zhang Youxia in Xi Jinping's entourage further confirmed the military content of Xi Jinping's trip. The recently appointed Commander of the Western Theatre Command (WTC) General Xu Qiling, its Political

Commissar Wu Shenzhou as well as Lt. General Wang Qiang, promoted as Commander of the WTC Air Force in April 2020, and the officiating WTC Army (Ground Forces) commander are likely to have received Xi Jinping and General Zhang Youxia at Nyingchi and travelled to Lhasa with his delegation by train. General Xu Qiling and Political Commissar General Wu Shenzhou were seated next to Xi Jinping and Zhang Youxia at the meeting in Lhasa.

Xi Jinping met military officers, personnel and veterans at Lhasa. Xi Jinping separately addressed over at least one thousand military officers in Lhasa of whom more than 32 were above the rank of Major General and the rest were of the rank of Colonel and above. Greeting the officers and thanking them for their "large contribution to the nation in terms of security and unification along with ensuring peace and stability in Tibet", Xi Jinping said that "for all this, the Party and the people of China are thankful to them. He urged "the army to be committed to the Party and its ideology" and "have a strong military mind with a focus to become a formidable force. The officers have to become the source of military guidance to ensure their motto is kept alive. They need to follow the 'old Tibet spirit' which means they need to follow their ancestors and what they have done in Tibet in the past 70 years. They need to follow in their footsteps and take their work forward". He declared that "They have already passed the difficult challenge of Tibet's harsh climate and environment and protected the country and they have done a good job. However, they need to continue training hard and prepare for future wars".

The prevailing situation along the Line of Actual Control (LAC) in Ladakh and seeming current impasse would certainly have been discussed and approvals obtained for further action and future operations. Activation of the eastern segment of the border opposite Nyingchi and Shigatse could well have been discussed.

The presence of General Zhang Youxia indicates that he has not been adversely affected by the publicity earlier this month surrounding his nephew Zhang Tao's egregious assault on two distinguished elderly Chinese scientists and subsequent arrest by Beijing Police.

Politburo members Yang Xiaodu and Chen Xi's inclusion is interesting. It suggests that Party and disciplinary matters were discussed. Yang Xiaodu is a Politburo member and Director of the National Supervisory Commission.

He has served in Tibet during his early political career. Chen Xi is head of the CCP CC's powerful Organisation Department, which decides on cadre promotions and transfers, deputation of cadres to the Central Party School etc.

There has been an increase in references over the course of last year to "double-faced" or "two-faced" cadres, referring to cadres who are employed by the authorities but owe loyalty to the Dalai Lama. Yang Xiaodu would have discussed this and the punishment of 'tainted' cadres with TAR Party Secretary Wu Yingjie and TAR Chairman Che Dalha. The future prospects of cadres considered as promising would also have discussed. It is possible that Wu Yingjie, who is now 65 years old and has completed a term as TAR Party Secretary, might be moved to Beijing. If so, his possible replacements would have been discussed. It has been noticed in recent months that among cadres in TAR, Che Dalha, Danke and Yan Jinhai have been receiving enhanced prominence. Che Dalha has been visiting border counties for "consolidating security" and accompanied TAR Party Secretary Wu Yingjie to Beijing last year and again this year to the National People's Congress (NPC) session. He also wrote an important article days after the NPC session ended on March 11, 2021 which was published by the *People's Daily*.

Xi Jinping's visit would have given a definite impetus to the policies now being implemented in TAR. Xi Jinping has advocated: consolidation and security of Tibet's borders; he referred to the 'xiaokang' (well off) border defence villages; adapting Tibetan Buddhism to socialism with Chinese characteristics; building ethnic unity; consolidating the Party and ensuring the loyalty of members; making Mandarin (Putonghua) the primary language in ethnic schools and highlighting Han culture; accelerating development of the transport network including railways and highways as part of China's Belt and Road Initiative (BRI) and its westward push; and strengthening the PLA.

The visit is important and will give a major push to the changes already planned for TAR. It has implications for India too. India should anticipate increased military activity on the LAC and an acceleration in the construction of border defence infrastructure in Tibet. Most of these are planned to be completed by 2030.

This was first published by the Centre for China Analysis and Strategy (CCAS) and Vivekananda International Foundation (VIF) in July 25, 2021.

47. Tibet: The Fulcrum of China's Strategic Policy in the Himalayas

China is positioning Tibet as the fulcrum for its strategic policy in the sensitive Himalayan region thus directly and adversely impacting India. Beijing appears to have assessed that it has sufficiently calmed the Tibet Autonomous Region (TAR) to feel adequately secure in opening Tibet up wider for interaction with foreign countries. China's foreign policy objectives are aimed at enveloping the Himalayan states in the region, which are on India's northern periphery, into a China-dominated grouping. While it will be wrapped in the garb of preserving the ecology and environment, the main objective will be to advance Beijing's strategic agenda. Two recent events in TAR and the TAR Party Secretary's trip to Nepal, Sri Lanka and Singapore earlier this month need to be viewed in this backdrop. China appears to be preparing to enhance military, economic and diplomatic pressure on India in the Himalayan region along India's northern frontiers.

Activity in the Tibet Autonomous Region (TAR) and particularly in its Nyingchi (Nyingtri) Prefecture, which borders Arunachal Pradesh, has visibly increased over the past year and bears careful watching. These point to China getting ready to mount considerable and sustained pressure on India in the Himalayan region. The importance of the Himalayan region cannot be overestimated, especially at a time when the Tibetan Buddhists – predominant in this region — are entering a sensitive period with succession to the current XIVth Dalai Lama being the central issue. There have been a series of high-level visits by Chinese Communist Party (CCP) officials to the TAR and Nyingchi Prefecture. Their speeches included references to strengthening defence of the border, increasing the number of 'model' border defence villages, and completing the strategic G-219 highway on time. In initiatives timed to pressure India and intended also to blunt international criticism about China's repression of Tibetans, Beijing held two important, though less noticed, events in the TAR. These were the 'Third China-Tibet "Rim of the Himalayas" International Cooperation Forum for International Cooperation' in Nyingchi, TAR, from October 4-5, 2023, and the '2023 Annual Conference of the China South Asia Society' which held a seminar on the "Intersection and Integration of Regional Country Studies and Frontier Studies" in Lhasa on November 4, 2023.

The Nyingchi Prefecture, measuring 116,175 km square kilometres on the eastern edge of TAR, has a long un-demarcated border with India. Official Chinese maps depict Nyingchi's official administrative boundary as including most of the Indian state of Arunachal Pradesh, which the Chinese refer to as "Southern Tibet". In the 2023 edition of the Standard Map of China published on August 28, 2023, China claimed parts of Ladakh, Aksai Chin and Arunachal Pradesh as Chinese territories. The Yarlung Tsangpo, or Brahmaputra River, courses through the TAR for 2900 kilometres before it reaches the Great Bend in Nyingchi. The Great Bend, where the Brahmaputra turns south and flows into India and onwards through Bangladesh into the Bay of Bengal, is the site for China's proposed largest dam in the world. Construction of this mega dam will directly and adversely impact India and Bangladesh. An official announcement in December 2020 confirmed earlier reliable reports that China planned to erect a series of dams on the Brahmaputra and divert the river to irrigate it's arable, but water starved north. China claims that the proposed mega dam, which will be three times the size of the world's largest Three Gorges Dam, will supply adequate hydropower for China's entire southwest. Construction work related to the dam is already well under way and the Motuo road link, vital for the proposed mega dam on the Brahmaputra has been completed. Construction of the Dam also has military implications for India.

Military activity in TAR across the Line of Actual Control (LAC) including across Arunachal Pradesh has also increased in recent months. For example, the PLA's 71st Group Army — though its operational jurisdiction covers the Jiangsu province region — revealed an addition to its military capability earlier this November and used a tactical ballistic missile during a livefire exercise in the Gobi Desert. Another report disclosed the presence of

Red Arrow-12 missiles in the Xinjiang Military region. PLA Rocket Force (PLARF) and PLA Strategic Support Force (PLA SSF) units are present in the PLA Western Theatre Command close to the LAC. Satellite imagery of mid-October shows that China is constructing new underground military facilities at Shannan in TAR. Multiple underground facilities already exist at Shannan. Confirming reports that the Chinese are building major defence infrastructure projects and roads in the region, Satellite images on October 31, showed PLA construction activities in Seti Chu and Chupda Chu valley's opposite Tulung La sector in Arunachal Pradesh. Separately, the Telegraph (October 31) quoting an Indian Home Ministry security official reported, "A close analysis of recent satellite imagery suggests a massive troop deployment by the Chinese in several depth areas, especially Yangtze in the Tawang sector along the LAC". Also in October, a Light Combined Arms Regiment (CAR) of the Xinjiang Military Region conducted combined training in the Pangong Lake area.

There has similarly been increased PLA Air Force activity in TAR. Satellite images between October 23 and 25, 2023, showed a fleet of KJ-500s. On October 31, satellite photographs indicated that Golmud Airport was holding a larger training exercise the previous week. CCTV programmes have also revealed the deployment of drones on the front line against India and said the PLA is currently building such bases on the Sino-Indian border, with the frontline outposts and drones as the first-line force. The report said that the progress of infrastructure construction and other system construction in the river valley has "actually increased our confidence in future border negotiations, and further blocked the Indians from using military adventurous means and taking desperate risks on the Sino-Indian border".

An indication of Nyingchi's elevated importance for Chinese President Xi Jinping is that he has visited Nyingchi a total of three times. Once as China's President in July 2021 earlier in 2011 as Vice President and once in 1998 as Party Secretary of Fujian. He has travelled to Nyingchi each time he visited the Tibet Autonomous Region. The visits indicate his interest in acquiring Arunachal Pradesh or, what the Chinese now refer to as 'southern Tibet'.

On October 4-5, 2023 China convened its 'Third China-Tibet "Rim of the Himalayas" International Cooperation Forum for International Cooperation' in Nyingchi, TAR. Its theme was: 'Ecological Civilisation and Environmental Protection'. Significant among the 280 representatives from over 40 countries, regions, and international organizations attending the conference were the: Pakistan Acting Foreign Minister Jalil Abbas Jilani; the Interim Foreign Minister of Afghanistan Amir Khan Muttaqi; Vice Chairperson of the National Assembly of Nepal Urmila Ayal; Secretary of the Ministry of Energy and Natural Resources of Bhutan Karma Tshering; the Deputy Prime Minister of Mongolia S. Amarsaikhan, and Sri Lanka's Minister of Sports and Youth Affairs Roshan Ranasinghe. While many of the others have companies working on mining and other projects in Tibet, the presence of representatives from Pakistan, Afghanistan, Nepal and Bhutan indicates that Beijing intends to involve them in its policies for the Himalayan region. It will offer trade and connectivity. China has for some years been talking of a Trans-Regional Himalayan Corridor (THRC). The presence of Sri Lanka would be to draw another South Asian country that already has close ties with China even closer. Displaying Beijing's support for this foreign policy initiative, CCP CC Politburo member and Chinese Foreign Minister Wang Yi also attended and spoke. In fact, the invitations to foreign government representatives were issued by China's Foreign Minister.

The speech by TAR Party Secretary Wang Junzheng outlined China's aims for this Forum. He welcomed the leaders of central and state agencies, ministries and commissions, political figures from various countries, experts and scholars who attended the China-Tibet Forum, and expressed his gratitude for their long-term support for the development of various economic and social undertakings in Tibet. Wang Junzheng said that cooperation and exchange are the only way for the prosperity and development of the Himalayan region. He said 'Tibet is an important node on the Southern Silk Road and an important channel for China to open up to South Asia'. It has obvious location advantages in strengthening cooperation with neighbouring countries around the Himalayas. He hoped that "all guests, leaders, experts and scholars will actively provide suggestions and deeply discuss the cooperation mechanism between China and neighbouring countries in the Himalayas, expand cooperation areas, create cooperation opportunities, and contribute wisdom and strength to better promote the development of the Himalayan region".

Chinese Foreign Minister and Politburo member Wang Yi emphasized that the Himalayas "represent a land brimming with vitality and hope" and stressed that China has engaged in "extensive and profound cooperation with other countries in the Himalayan region, continually building consensus on cooperation, actively supporting green development, and enhancing capacity building". He pointed out that "the Asian century is on the horizon" and said the "Himalayan countries are geographically connected, share cultural similarities, and are intertwined by destiny. They hold highly similar views on ecological protection and are partners in the modernization process". Asserting that China is committed to amity, good neighbourliness, and neighbourhood diplomacy, he said China together with the regional countries, seeks to share historical development opportunities and "jointly build a community with a shared future in the Himalayan vicinity". Wang Yi added that this will contribute to the prosperity, stability, and green environmental protection of the region and the world at large. Two of the five suggestions he proposed envisage major connectivity projects, trade and cultural exchanges. He identified these as: strengthening connectivity, advancing regional integration, and establishing a more convenient Himalayan interconnection network; and enhancing exchanges and mutual learning, revitalizing ancient civilizations, and creating a model area for cultural exchanges around the Himalayas.

A month later on November 4, 2023, the 2023 Annual Conference of the China South Asia Society and the "Intersection and Integration of Regional Country Studies and Frontier Studies academic seminar were held in Lhasa, capital of TAR. It held its first meeting in 2018 in Linzhi, TAR. The annual conference jointly discussed changes in the political and economic situation in South Asia and the construction of the Ring-Himalayan Economic Cooperation Belt among other issues. Its aim was to provide " intellectual support for the high-quality development and high-level opening up of the Tibet Autonomous Region (TAR)". Attending the meeting Zhang Guanzi, Dean of the Institute of Information and Intelligence of the Chinese Academy of Social Sciences (CASS) described the annual meeting as an important channel for China to open up to South Asia, adding that the Tibet Autonomous Region has achieved results in communication and construction with South Asia in terms of policies, facilities, trade, and capital. Jiang Jingkui, Vice President of the Chinese Society for South Asia, said: "the political, economic, trade and cultural ties between China and South Asia have become increasingly close, and the importance of the unique location of the Tibet Autonomous Region has continued to rise".

Soon thereafter and seeming to operationalise these plans, TAR Party Secretary Wang Junzheng visited Nepal from November 8-12, 2023, before proceeding to Sri Lanka and Singapore. Unusual for China's Provincial Party Secretaries too, the TAR Party Secretary was accompanied by a cultural troupe which staged performances in Sri Lanka and Singapore. During his stay of five days in Nepal, Wang Junzheng met Nepal's President Ram Chandra Poudel, Prime Minister Prachanda, Vice President Yadav, Federal Council of Nepal Chairman Timirsina, and Deputy Prime Minister and Interior Minister Narayan Kaji Shrestha. The two sides spoke on the need to make concerted efforts to implement the proceedings of Xi Jinping's visit to Nepal in 2019 and the joint statement between China and Nepal. They also discussed and promoted the exchange of views on mutually beneficial cooperation between the TAR and Nepal.

Wang Junzheng stated, inter alia, that "The Tibet Autonomous Region , linked to Nepal through culture and longstanding friendship, will leverage its geographical and humanistic advantages to deepen exchanges and cooperation, jointly constructing a cross-Himalayan three-dimensional interconnection network." He said the focus will be on high-quality joint construction of the Belt and Road Initiative, expanding cooperation in port construction, economy and trade, tourism, and aviation, and assisting northern Nepal in building "small and beautiful, benefiting people's livelihood" projects. Wang Junzheng said efforts will be made to strengthen exchanges with Nepalese universities, academic institutions, and think tanks, and promote friendly cities and relations between the Tibet Autonomous Region and Nepal, fostering people-to-people communication and contributing to deepening practical cooperation between China and Nepal.

Nepal said it is eager to actively participate in the Belt and Road Initiative, further strengthen its relations with the Tibet Autonomous Region and promote pragmatic cooperation in agriculture, economy and trade, tourism, port construction, and other fields for common prosperity and development.

Wang Junzheng also discussed the joint venture between the Tibet Autonomous Region and Nepal, particularly the operation of Himalayan Airlines and witnessed the signing of a memorandum of understanding between the TAR People's Government and the Ministry of Finance of Nepal, as well as the agreement on the establishment of a friendly city relationship between Shigatse and Bharatpur. Almost coinciding with his visit, a new land port linking Letse in Drongba county of Xizang (TAR) and Nechung in Mustang county of Nepal was officially opened on November 13. It is the fourth land port in the region.

The invitation to Bhutan would be intended to entice Bhutan into accelerating progress in the China-Bhutan Boundary Talks. On the sidelines of the '3rd China-Tibet "Rim of the Himalayas" International Cooperation Forum for International Cooperation', Chinese Foreign Minister Wang Yi and Afghanistan's Acting Foreign Minister Amir Khan Muttaqi discussed (October 5) the opening of a strategic corridor to enhance trade ties between Beijing and Kabul. The two countries agreed to improve trade ties through the Wakhan Corridor, linking Afghanistan's Badakhshan province with Xinjiang in China.

The developments indicate that Beijing is intent on setting up a grouping of Himalayan states and drawing them into its economic, diplomatic and if possible cultural-religious sphere, and at the same time confront India. The construction of roads will facilitate Chinese exports and people to these countries, offer them alternate routes, and gradually overwhelm their economies. Though the plan will take some years to take shape, China will start focussing on growing its economic, political and military influence in these countries. The development implies, as indicated by the presence of the Deputy Prime Minister of Mongolia S. Amarsaikhan, that China will make strenuous efforts to ensure that its nominee succeeds the XIVth Dalai Lama.

This was first published by the Centre for China Analysis and Strategy (CCAS) and Vivekananda International Foundation (VIF) in November 26, 2023.

48. China Has Just Raised The Level of Threat for India

Capitals around the world have undoubtedly carefully monitored the recently concluded plenary sessions (March 4 - 11, 2021) of China's National People's Congress (NPC) and the Chinese People's Political Consultative Conference (CPPCC), popularly referred to as the 'Lianghui', or 'Big Two'. For India, among the documents approved by the NPC Plenary session, one merits especially close attention. Particularly significant is the 142-page, 70,000-character "14th Five Year Plan (2021-2025) and the Long-Range Objectives through the Year 2035 for National Economic and Social Development of the People's Republic of China" which sets out China's national strategic intent. This document identifies core areas of national security and development, strategic scientific programmes and projects, and a number of major strategic national science and technology projects in frontier areas such as artificial intelligence, quantum information, integrated circuits, life and health, brain science, biological breeding, air and space science and technology, and deep earth and deep sea.

The English translation of the "14th Five Year Plan (2021-2025) and the Long-Range Objectives through the Year 2035 for National Economic and Social Development of the People's Republic of China" has not yet been released. Approval of some projects mentioned in the document means they have now shifted from the realm of speculation, or potential concern, to imminent threats. These will put India under additional pressure, including military pressure, from China.

Approval of these projects assume greater significance in the backdrop of China's continuing and unprovoked military aggression in Ladakh and its massive military deployment — unprecedented for decades — along the entire 4057-kms Line of Actual Control (LAC). There is no sign yet of

Beijing thinning its troop-deployment or pulling back to its earlier positions. A relevant backdrop are the observations by Hu Shisheng, Director of South Asian Affairs of the Chinese Institutes for Contemporary International Relations (CICIR), one of China's most prominent think-tanks and directly subordinate to the Ministry of State Security (MoSS). He candidly stated that China-India relations were doomed to clash from the very start. He anticipated tense relations ahead with occasional military clashes. Separately, during a talk on February 27, 2021, Major General Jin Yinan, Professor in China's National Defence University (NDU), highlighted five flashpoints for China, namely Taiwan, Diaoyu (Senkaku) Islands, South China Sea, Korean Peninsula and the Sino-Indian border. He identified India as "the threat from the west".

Shedding China's earlier obfuscation on plans to build a major dam on the Brahmaputra (Yarlung Tsangpo), the 14th Five Year Plan and Long-Range Objectives -2035 confirmed that "building hydropower bases in the lower reaches of the Yarlung Tsangpo River will be a priority". It added that "major projects" such as "the development of hydropower downstream of the Yarlung Tsangpo River will be implemented" and that a major dam on the Brahmaputra (Yarlung Tsangpo) will be built.

Reports had confirmed, just prior to the NPC session that China will build the world's largest dam — larger than the Three Gorges Dam in Sichuan province — on the Great Bend on the Brahmaputra River. During the NPC session, Che Dalha, Chairman of the Tibet Autonomous Region (TAR), said (March 6) that authorities of the Tibet Autonomous Region (TAR) should "strive to begin construction [of the dams] this year" and that "comprehensive planning and environmental impact assessments for the project should be approved as soon as possible". China's popular guancha.com quoted hydropower industry insiders describing the decision to develop hydropower on the lower reaches of the Yarlung Tsangpo River as a rare "historical opportunity". They disclosed that the project is planned to generate nearly 60 million kilowatts, which is equivalent to "building three Three Gorges" and it will ensure national security in many areas and benefit the country and the people.

The massive dam on the Brahmaputra, and the estimated seventeen other dams along its lower reaches, will adversely impact approximately 1 billion people in the lower riparian countries who are dependent on the river and the tributaries feeding it. The huge influx of people and the large-scale construction activities in Tibet, including building border airports and 200 border defence villages, will certainly result in warming of temperatures. In turn, this will accelerate the retreat of glaciers and drastically reduce the flow of water in the glacier-fed rivers that irrigate the Indo-Gangetic plain where the majority of India's population reside. There will be attendant non-conventional security issues.

To give apparent impetus to the massive project, 58 year-old Li Guoying was appointed China's new Minister of Water Resources in February 2021. A hydropower engineer who has served mostly in the Ministry of Water Resources, Li Guoying has political heft as a former Alternate member of the 18th CCP Central Committee (CC) and member of the current 19th CCP CC. He is also a Deputy to the 13th NPC.

The 14th Five Year Plan and Long-Range Objectives -2035 outline the activities envisaged for completion in Tibet and Xinjiang by 2025 and 2035. The document confirmed plans for improving the "comprehensive transport corridors" and strengthening the "construction of strategic main corridors of leaving Xinjiang and entering Tibet, in the central and western regions, along the rivers, along the coast and along the borders". Plans that "orderly (sic) promote the upgrading and expansion of capacity-constrained corridors, and strengthen interconnection with neighbouring countries" were approved. The range of projects to be undertaken in the two Autonomous Regions can be expected to see a massive influx and deployment of labour, technical personnel and induction of People's Liberation Army (PLA) engineers.

Immediately prior to the NPC Plenary session, *Nikkei Asia* reported (March 4, 2021) that China has begun construction of a 319.8 billion yuan (US$ 49.4 billion)-rail line that would greatly improve access to Tibet. The 1,800 km railway will directly connect Lhasa to Chengdu and travel at speeds between 120 and 200 kph reducing travel time to a little more than 10 hours. Service is scheduled to start around 2030. Of strategic importance, this will be the second railway connecting TAR to the Chinese mainland.

Che Dalha, Chairman of TAR, had referred to the rail project at the TAR People's Congress held in January 2021. He laid out a medium- to long-term plan commencing 2021 that called for accelerating the building of infrastructure with the objectives of ensuring national security and raising the quality of life of the people. At the ground-breaking ceremony of the rail project in November, Xi Jinping had said "The railway project has great significance to maintaining national unity, promoting ethnic unity and consolidating stability in border areas." He also said that exploration of natural gas in northern Tibet should be one of the focus areas of national energy development goals over the next five years.

Earlier this year on February 24, 2021 *Xinhua* disclosed that the CCP CC and State Council had issued the "National Comprehensive Three-dimensional Transportation Network Planning Outline". The Outline planned to connect all county-level and above administrative regions, border ports, defense facilities, and major scenic spots across the country. It aims to build a national comprehensive three-dimensional transportation network with "railways as the backbone, roads as the foundation, and the comparative advantages of water transportation and civil aviation". *Xinhua* said that by 2035, the national comprehensive three-dimensional transportation network will total about 700,000 kilometres (excluding the overseas section of the international land corridor, air and sea routes, and postal routes). This would include about 200,000 kilometres of railways, about 460,000 kilometres of roads, and about 25,000 kilometres of high-grade waterways. There are 27 major coastal ports, 36 major inland river ports, about 400 civil transportation airports, and about 80 postal express hubs. It said the focus will be on building 7 international land transportation channels including the New Asia-Europe Land Bridge, China-Mongolia-Russia, China-Central Asia-West Asia, China-Indochina Peninsula, China Pakistan, China, Nepal, India, Bangladesh, China, India and Myanmar. It referred to strengthening the four maritime international transportation channels. These include (i) the Pacific Ocean to the Americas via Japan and South Korea; (ii) Southeast Asia to Oceania; (iii) Southeast Asia and South Asia across the Indian Ocean to Europe and Africa; and (iv) the Ice Silk Road across the Arctic Ocean "to protect crude oil, Iron ore, grain, liquefied natural gas and other national key materials". The report makes clear that China will continue to press ahead with plans for the CPEC, BCIM and the Trans-Himalayan Regional Corridor (THRC), which according to the Chinese plan will cut through the Himalayas to link China with India through Nepal.

Projects centering on Tibet are mentioned in the 14th Five Year Plan and Long-Range Objectives -2035 document. It asserts that "to serve major national strategies", major projects such as "the Sichuan-Tibet Railway, the New Western Land and Sea Corridor, the national water network, the development of hydropower downstream of the Yarlung Tsangpo River" will be implemented. Specific mention was made of "The construction of the Ya'an-Linzhi section of the Sichuan-Tibet Railway" and the "advance work on the railways from Rikaze (Shigatse) to Jilong (Guizhou province) and Hotan (Xinjiang) to Rikaze, the opening of the G219 and G331 lines along the border road, and the upgrading of the G318 line of the Sichuan-Tibet Highway". There was a suggestion that the G219 and G331 national highways would be extended to run along China's southwestern border. The document stressed the importance of "Tibet in building an important channel for opening up to South Asia".

It is significant that work, or requisite preparatory arrangements, on some of the projects began within days of the end of the 'Lianghui'. In addition to the massive dam on the Brahmaputra, directly relevant for India is the approval by the 14th Five Year Plan and Long-Range Objectives -2035 of plans for constructing airports in Tashkurgan and Longzi among others. Tashkurgan is the westernmost town in China's Xinjiang-Uyghur Autonomous Region and the first stop on the Karakoram Highway and falls within the PLA's South Xinjiang Military District. Longzi county is in the Shannan District of TAR. The airports are likely to be completed by 2025. The document mentioned that plans have also been approved for the "construction of about 20 general-purpose airports on the border" in addition to the relocation and construction of some others. These will obviously be dual-purpose airports.

The linking of Shigatse (Rikaze) in TAR with provinces in Mainland China would appear intended to make Shigatse a hub connecting Tibet with South Asia. It will additionally augment the PLA's capacity to rapidly transport troops, military cargo and hardware into Tibet thereby sharpening the threat to the LAC's middle sector especially Sikkim and Yadong. Upgrading the

G219 and G318 highways will further strengthen China's defence border infrastructure.

The projects listed in the preceding paragraphs are only a few of the strategic infrastructure and other development projects mentioned in the "14th Five Year Plan (2021- 2025) and the Long-Range Objectives through the Year 2035 for National Economic and Social Development of the People's Republic of China". Projects in TAR, incidentally, are invariably planned in consultation with the PLA. The railway, road and airports in TAR have definite military implications and work on many of them has begun within days of their being approved. By the time the projects are completed Tibet will have been militarised. These projects will further raise the level of threat to India from China within five years.

This was first published by the Centre for China Analysis and Strategy (CCAS) and Vivekananda International Foundation (VIF) in March 26, 2021.

49. Implications of Recent Developments in PLA's Western Theatre Command

The Western Theatre Command (WTC) is the largest of China's five Theatre Commands and exercises operational jurisdiction over the country's currently 'active' borders with India and Afghanistan. Particularly since the People's Liberation Army (PLA)'s military manoeuvre against India in early May 2020, which caught the Indian armed forces by surprise, and consequent onset of military tension along the Line of Actual Control (LAC), the Chinese leadership has been paying special attention to the Western Theatre Command (WTC). It has raised its inter-se grading among Theatre Commands and brought the WTC on par with the Eastern Theatre Command, which is ranked first, in terms of priority for receiving new aircraft and weaponry. Other visible indicators of the leadership's attention are the high-level visits; postings of new officers to the Western Theatre Command; the enhanced and qualitatively different exercises by PLA forces deployed in the Xinjiang and Tibet Military Regions subordinate to the Western Theatre Command; and the new, modern equipment that is now being supplied to them.

Since the middle of last year, there have been changes at the higher echelons of the WTC. In addition to the appointment of a new Commander of the WTC on September 6, 2021, the WTC also witnessed the arrival and appointments of other senior officers.

The recent rapid changes in WTC Commanders have, however, raised questions particularly since China's military leadership would normally be expected to select a competent, experienced officer to head such an important Command — whose operational jurisdiction includes active borders — for a full tenure. Instead, the WTC has witnessed the change-over of three Commanders within a year.

General Zhao Zongqi (DoB: 1955) was replaced as he had reached retirement age. In fact, he was retained for some months beyond retirement before his replacement, Zhang Xudong, was posted. General Zhang Xudong (DoB: 1962) took over on promotion from Zhao Zongqi in December 2020. Though only 59 years old, he developed health issues because of which he had to be moved. He was replaced in June 2021 by Xu Qiling (DoB: 1962), who was till then WTC Deputy Commander and Commander of the Army (Ground Forces) in the rank of Lt General from June 2020 till June 2021. Xu Qiling was promoted to General when he took over as Commander, WTC from General Zhang Xudong in June 2021.General Xu Qiling is just three months younger than General Zhang Xudong. Given his outstanding career record, it is anticipated that Xu Qiling may be appointed Chief of the PLA Ground Forces or to head the CMC Joint Staff Department. On September 6, 2021, Lt General Wang Haijiang was promoted to the rank of General and appointed Commander of the WTC.

Another new appointment of interest in the WTC is that of PLA Air Force (PLAAF) Lt. General Qiao Xiangji as a new, or additional, Deputy Commander of the PLA WTC in April 2020. News of Qiao Xiangji's appointment was confirmed on June 27, 2021. It is not yet clear whether he will take over from the current Commander of the WTC Air Force Lt General Wang Qiang, or whether he brings in additional expertise. His appointment could also suggest that the WTC's air assets have increased. Reports indicate that the number of China's latest fifth generation 'stealth' J-20 fighters, J-16, the upgraded J-16 D and other aircraft including drones in the WTC have increased.

Qiao Xiangji was born in February 1963 in Hebei Province and joined the PLAAF in July 1979. He has trained as a pilot. Qiao Xiangji received training in the Battle Command Class of the Air Force Command Academy of the PLA and attended the Advanced Training Class of the Military Academy of the Russian Air Force. In 2011, he was conferred the award of Model Division Commander by the PLA Air Force. He was also Division Commander of the 30th Aviation Division. In December 2013, he was appointed Assistant to the Chief of Staff of the PLA Air Force. In December 2014, he was appointed Commander of the Air Force Fuzhou Command Post. Qiao Xiangji was promoted to the rank of PLAAF Lieutenant General in April 2020.

Lt General Wang Qiang, who is the current Commander of the WTC Air Force and concurrently a Deputy Commander of the Western Theatre Command, was born in Rongxian County, Sichuan, also in 1963. Lt General Wang Qiang served as Deputy Chief of Staff of the Western Theatre Command and Chief of Staff of the WTC Air Force before being appointed Deputy Commander of the WTC and Commander of the WTC PLAAF in April 2020.

Interesting too, is the promotion and appointment of Lt. Gen. Liu Lin as Commander of Xinjiang MR. Liu Lin was, till his promotion, Major General and Commander of the 3 South Xinjiang Military District which includes operational supervision of the Hetian and Ngari (Ali) MSDs. He represented the PLA at 12 rounds of Army Commander-level border talks held at the PLA Moldo Garrison near Chushul. Liu Lin has extensive service in the Xinjiang MR and familiarity with this sector of the border.

Relevant too is the 'special' meeting that Xi Jinping, who combines the offices of General Secretary of the Chinese Communist Party (CCP), Chairman of the Central Military Commission (CMC), Commander-in-Chief of the PLA and Chinese President, had with PLA officers in Lhasa on July 23, 2021. Xi Jinping complimented the military officers for bravely facing the harsh conditions, their good defence of the borders and asked them to "prepare for future wars". A short video clip of the meeting telecast by the state-owned CCTV's military channel showed that nearly 400 PLA and PLAAF officers attended the meeting. All were of the rank of Colonel and above, indicating that it was a restricted meeting. The designations of officers identified seated in the conference hall is interesting. Seated in the front row with Xi Jinping were: General Zhang Youxia, Vice Chairman of the CMC; General Ju Qiansheng, who had just that month been promoted and appointed Commander of the PLA Strategic Support Force (SSF); General Xu Qiling, then Commander of the Western Theatre Command; Lt General Wang Kai, Commander of the Tibet Military Region; Lt General Zhong Shaojun, Director of the CMC General Office; and Lt General Zhang Xuejie, Political Commissar of the Tibet Military Region. The presence of the Commander of the SSF is significant as, among its other roles like combat support, it is the space-, cyber-, and electronic-warfare force of the PLA. The presence of the senior officers of the Tibet Military Region may suggest plans to activate other sections along the LAC. No officers from the Xinjiang Military Region could be identified.

Underscoring Xi Jinping's attention to the WTC, the CCP-owned Global Times on September 13, publicised that Xi Jinping had written a letter to a Battalion (Unit No: 77656) stationed in the border region of Tibet "at the northern foot of the Himalayas". The letter complimented them for guarding the "sacred territory of the motherland with youth and blood" and accomplishing their mission "brilliantly". The letter is obviously intended to encourage PLA personnel deployed in harsh conditions at high-altitudes and is confirmation that close attention is being paid to this border.

A number of Politburo members and senior CCP cadres have also visited the Tibet Autonomous Region (TAR) this year. Many of them visited Ngari (Ali), Shigatse (opposite Yadong) and Nyingchi (opposite Arunachal Pradesh). Central and TAR public security, propaganda and united front teams have visited the TAR border counties. They all emphasised loyalty to the Party, "eliminating the 14th Dalai Lama's influence" and to border defence.

In addition to the approval of major defence and dual-use infrastructure projects in the '14th Five Year Plan and Long-Range Objectives 2030', there has been a steady stream of reports of enhancement of defence infrastructure, induction of new aircraft, and equipment for troops, in the WTC. Apart from the 'combat support exercise' using "unfamiliar" airfields conducted by the WTC Air Force in June-July 2021, the WTC has been noticed holding a number of military exercises at the Battalion level and above. A total of 108 military exercises were noticed to have been conducted in the WTC between May 2019 to May 2020. Among them 31 military exercises were conducted in the Tibet Military Region (MR); 36 in the Xinjiang MR, and 24 military exercises by the PLA 76th Group Army, 9 by the PLA 77th Group Army, and 8 military exercises were conducted by unidentified Military Regions/districts of the WTC.

A total of 93 major exercises were conducted between June 2020 and June 2021. Of them, 53 military exercises were conducted in the Tibet MR and 22 in the Xinjiang MR, and 18 military exercises were conducted by unidentified Military Regions/districts of the WTC.

It is noticed that there has been a sharp increase in military exercises in the Tibet Military Region i.e. from 31 in May 2019-May 2020 to 53 in June 2020-June 2021. A reason for the reduced number of military exercises in the Xinjiang MR in the period June 2020-June 2021 would have been because of the military activity and volatile situation at the LAC after May 2020. The sharp and sudden increase in exercises in the Tibet MR between June 2020-June 2021, when viewed with the military deployments along the LAC and activities of the TAR authorities in the border counties, could suggest that the PLA is readying to 'activate' other sectors along the LAC in addition to Ladakh.

In this backdrop, the promotion and appointment of Wang Haijiang as WTC Commander is significant. Wang Haijiang is thoroughly familiar with the region and topography of the India-China LAC having served 22 years in the South Xinjiang Military District (overseeing the Hetian and Ngari (Ali) Military Sub Districts (MSDs) which includes the Depsang Plains, Pangong, Demchok and Chumar areas) and the Tibet Military Region. He is a veteran of the 1979 Sino-Vietnam War. His taking over as WTC Commander will facilitate any plans for military activity along the LAC.

Xi Jinping's visit to Tibet and meeting with PLA officers at this time are significant. He has reinforced his message with the letter to a Battalion posted in Tibet. Separately, the CCP's official *People's Daily* on September 16, reproduced a speech delivered by Xi Jinping last year, where he, inter alia, stated that "China has not yet achieved the complete reunification of the motherland, and has disputes over territorial sovereignty and maritime rights and interests with many neighboring countries. Solving these problems is a hurdle we must cross, and it is also a major risk and challenge that we must correctly handle .... The motherland must be unified. We must do our utmost to strive for the prospect of peaceful reunification, but we will not promise to give up the use of force... ." It is interesting that this speech has been published at a time when China faces an increasingly adverse international environment.

Far from any signs de-escalation by the Chinese, when seen in the context of the continuing build-up against India on the LAC, these developments in the WTC give cause for considerable discomfort.

The attached Appendix provides additional details.

Appendix

Brief profile of WTC Commander General Wang Haijiang:

Wang Haijiang was born in July 1963 in Anyue, Sichuan and has over 22 years of continuous experience in the erstwhile Lanzhou and Chengdu (Tibet) Military Regions. He is possibly the most qualified PLA officer at that level to serve as WTC Commander at this time. It is likely that the Central Military Commission had decided to promote Wang Haijiang earlier, but may have decided to wait till after Xu Qiling, initially as WTC Army Commander and later as WTC Commander, had brought about certain changes in the WTC.

Wang Haijiang is a deputy to the 13th National People's Congress. He was one of the first batch of students to enter the military academy after the national college entrance examination resumed in 1977. Early on in service he participated in the Sino-Vietnamese War in 1979 and served as Company Commander of the main attack company, earning First-Class Merit. He has served as Secretary (mishu) of General Li Qianyuan, former Commander of the Lanzhou Military Region. In January 2013, he was appointed Deputy Commander of the South Xinjiang Military District. In 2016, he was appointed Deputy Commander of the Tibet Military Region and on February 24, 2018, he was elected as a representative to the 13th National People's Congress. In December 2019, he was appointed Commander of the Tibet Military Region and in March 2021, was transferred as Commander of the Xinjiang Military Region. On September 6, 2021, he was promoted to the rank of General and appointed Commander of the WTC. Having joined the PLA at the early age of 17, he is among the very few PLA officers with 40 years of experience in the PLA.

Wang Haijiang was promoted to the rank of Major General in December 2013. In December 2019, he was promoted to the rank of Lieutenant General and in September 2021, was promoted to the rank of General.

When Wang Haijiang was posted as Commander of the Xinjiang MR, Zhou Chenming, a Beijing-based Chinese military analyst said Wang Haijiang was equipped to take on the difficult Xinjiang role given his experiences, including as former Commander of elite units of the PLA. "The 61st Division is one of the three top units, they are all heavily armed and they are used as models for the other troops in the PLA to learn from."

Major Accomplishments:

In 2017, Wang Haijiang spent 10 months on the border defense line at an altitude of more than 4,000 meters, and led the officers and soldiers in building the Panshan Highway under extreme weather conditions. He also contributed to the construction of the border well for a village. Wang Haijiang was commended by the PLA Daily for his contributions. On June 15, 2020, the Tibet Military Region under Wang Haijiang's command established the first-of-its-kind 'Snow Mastiff Plateau Resistance Team'. This militia team comprised the 20 best fighters from China's top fighting club. At the inauguration ceremony, he praised the Militia Team and said the fighters who have come from the ring to border defense will contribute to the construction of border defense with practical actions. This Militia Team is to assist the border defense Regiment and the Special Force Brigade in combat training.

Awards:

Wang Haijiang was awarded a 'first-class combat award' when he served as the Commander of the main attacking company in border Operations.

'Plateau Warriors', the official WeChat public account of the Tibet Military Region, on January 15, 2020, reported that the Tibet Military Region held the first award ceremony of the "Top Ten Models for Strengthening Frontiers and Stabilizing Tibet". TAR Party Secretary and First Secretary of the Party Committee of the Tibet Military Region Wu Yingjie, attended the award ceremony and presented awards to the 'pace-setters' together with the Commander of the Military Region, Wang Haijiang.

Brief profile of General Xu Qiling

General Xu Qiling was born in 1962 and is a member of the Chinese Communist Party (CCP). Xu Qiling was one of the first officers to be appointed Commander of a Group Army after the Group Armies were restructured and reorganised. Xu Qiling was appointed Commander of the WTC Army barely a few days prior to the deadly conflict between China and India in the Galwan

Valley where soldiers on both sides were killed. He was promoted as China and India prepared for the 12th round of military commander-level talks.

Like Zhang Xudong, Xu Qiling was promoted from the rank of Lt. General in December 2019, to PLA General in June 2021 after one and a half years, which is a 'fast track' promotion in the PLA. At the time of his promotion, Xu Qiling was one of the youngest Generals in the PLA.

Xu Qiling is one of the few PLA Commanders who has served in four Theatre Commands (except the Southern Theatre Command). He has a reputation in the PLA for emphasising 'combat preparedness' and for 'on site supervision' during training. Chinese military experts have suggested that Xu Qiling's youth and focus on military preparedness in the WTC might have appealed to the CMC leadership in the context of handling the border dispute with India. During his tenure as WTC Army Commander and later as WTC Commander, Xu Qiling introduced many changes in training in the WTC, amenities for troops, and upgraded its inventory of air assets and equipment.

MILITARY EXERCISES IN WTC (May 2020 – June 2021)

A total of 93 major military exercises were noticed to have been conducted in the WTC between May 2020 and June 2021. Of them, 53 military exercises were conducted in the Tibet MR, 22 in the Xinjiang MR, and 18 in unidentified MR/MD of the WTC.

The Military Exercises conducted in the WTC between May 2020- June2021 were varied and covered different fields such as:

Psychological Behaviour Training; Alpine Snow Mountain Training; Helicopter Rescue of border guards; Comprehensive support practice drill; large scale formation Parachute training; Live ammunition training for air defense capabilities; long range airborne training at night; military training at border radar station; coordinated strike drills; long range maneuver training; test of rapid strike capability; cable descent training; heavy equipment air drop; anti-hijacking drill; female soldier field trekking training; border defense drone pilot training; assassinations' exercise; and mass training led by political leaders (Political Commissars).

Some illustrative major activities/changes made in the WTC between May 2020 and June 2021:

Innovative Training Model implemented in May 2020; Poverty Alleviation Working Group was set up in May 2020; TMR builds mass education platform on May 21, 2020; Major General Tao Dapeng was appointed Director of Political Work Department of the WTC AF on August 16, 2020; NDU conducts Border Defense practical training activities in Tibet MR on August 25, 2020; tensions at the border area near Pangong Lake on August 31, 2020; incident at the border near Pangong Lake on September 7, 2020; HQ-9 surface to air missile was deployed on September 11; Digitalization of WTC completed on September 17, 2020; Replacement of outdated equipment in the WTC began on September 17, 2020; Frontier Troops in the WTC were given new patrol outfits on September 21, 2020; 10 UAVs allocated to the Tibet MR for the first time for logistics support on October 6, 2020; New recruits arrive in Tibet on October 9, 2020; new insulated cabins developed by PLA deployed to the WTC frontier defense troops stationed in the Plateau on October 9, 2020; WTC War Hymns released on November 5, 2020; Military-Local Cooperation Mechanism set up on November 10, 2020; WTC Recruiting Ceremony was conducted on November 11, 2021; Self Heating pot provided to soldiers stationed at altitudes of 4500m on November 20, 2020; Thousands of tons of food and rations arrived at the border areas in Tibet MR on November 25, 2020; J-16 fighter aircraft deployed in batches in WTC on November 25, 2020; a Dispatch Center in the WTC was set up for military supply network on December 20, 2020; Three female soldiers participated in patrol mission in Tibet MR on January 1, 2021; HQ-16B installed in Tibet MR on January 3, 2021; 5592 Observation Post of the highest PLA garrison in Tibet was publicly disclosed on January 3, 2021; PHL-11 New Modular wheeled rocket launcher inducted in Tibet MR on January 11, 2021; Sky Camouflaged Uniforms provided to frontier department of Tibet MR on January 18, 2021; brawl at Nakula occurred on January 18, 2021; Border Guard duty station in Medog Tibet MR connected to internet on January 27, 2021; fifth generation 'stealth' jet fighter aircraft J-20 stationed at Hotan Base on February 7, 2021; Off-Grid new energy microgrid power supply for border defense forces at Xinjiang MR reported on

February 7, 2021; reported on February 7, 2021 that Border troops stationed at Shenxianwan Post produce fresh vegetables; PLA increases military deployment in Pangong on February 8, 2021; deployment of Type-99A Main Battle Tank at Karakoram Mountain reported on February 9, 2021; PLA adjusts and deployed 200 tanks in a day on February 17, 2021; Tibet MR border posts connected to the state grid improves living conditions of border guards on February 18, 2021; PLA Xinjiang MR operationalises first Type-15 light tank on February 21, 2021; HQ-17A Anti-Aircraft Weapons inducted in WTC in May 2021. Psychological services for soldiers stationed at plateau in Xinjiang MR conducted on May 26, 2021; (Swarajya-September 13, 2021) latest satellite images (from September 2021) show a PLA helicopter base is under construction in Aksai Chin. It is located 130 km away from Galwan Valley.

MILITARY EXERCISES IN WTC (May 2019 – May 2020)

A total of 108 military exercises were noticed to have been conducted in the WTC between May 2019 to May 2020. Among them 31 military exercises were conducted in the Tibet MR; 36 in the Xinjiang MR, and 24 military exercises by the PLA 76th Group Army, 9 by the PLA 77th Group Army, and 8 military exercises were conducted by unidentified MR/MD of the WTC.

The Military Exercises conducted in the WTC between May 2019 to May 2020 were varied and covered different fields such as:

Soldiers running while carrying weights; Air Defense using UAVs; Reconnaissance Training; Transport training in Tibet; Coordinated training; education of border guards; use of information technology to standardise military training; actual combat assessment; regular high altitude training (manoeuvre training); air transport training in inaccessible areas; field training; participation of female soldiers in artillery 'live fire' exercises; tactical drills; battlefield manoeuvre operations; combined brigade 'live fire' exercises; patrolling in plateau areas; military drills with advanced weapons; integrated air-to-air and air-to-ground training; cross-day 'live fire' exercises; 'live fire' flight training exercises; joint anti-terror exercises; 'live fire' shooting training;

stationing of troops in Kunlun for two months; integrated tactical exercises; communication drills; cross-day high altitude heavy fire power assessments; combat confrontation drills; emergency transport and supply mission; Troops training in plateau for four months; night flights; plateau troops first aid skills; plateau combat drills etc.

Other Senior Appointments in WTC since June 2019

- WTC Commander – General Xu Qiling (徐起零) Appointed June 2021
- WTC Pol Com- Lt Gen. Xu Deqing (徐德清) Appointed in June 2018
- WTC Deputy Commander-Lt. Gen. Qiao Xiangji (乔相记) (Appointed in April 2020)
- Deputy Commander of the WTC & Commander of the WTC AF - Lt. General Wang Qiang (王强) (Appointed in April 2020)
- WTC AF Political Commissar- Lt. Gen. Jiang Ping (姜平) (Appointed in January 2019)
- Xinjiang MR Commander- Lt. Gen. Wang Haijiang (Appointed in April 2021
- Xinjiang MR Commander- Lt Gen. Liu Lin (Appointed on September 6, 2021) replacing Lt. Gen. Wang Haijiang who was promoted to General and appointed Commander WTC.
- Xinjiang MR Pol Com.- Lt. Gen. Yang Cheng (杨诚) (Appointed in December 2020); Xinjiang MR Deputy Commander- Major General Sun Huibing (孙会兵) (Appointed in September 2019)
- Tibet MR Commander- Lt. Gen. Wang Kai (王凯) (Appointed in April 2021)
- Tibet MR Pol Com.- Lt. Gen. Zhang Xuejie (张学杰) (Appointed in May 2018)
- South Xinjiang MR Commander- Maj. Gen. Liu Lin (柳林) (Appointed in March 2019.
- Commanders of Ali MSD- Maj. Gen. Gan Weihan (甘维汉)
- Commander of Lhasa Garrison- Maj. Gen. He Sheng (贺胜) (Appointed in May 2019)
- Commander of Shigatse MSD- Maj. Gen. Ma Yun (马赟)

New Initiatives

Some new initiatives appear to have been taken following Xu Qiling's appointment as first, the Commander of the WTC Army (Ground Forces) and later as WTC Commander. Illustrative listings are given below.

New Recruitments

China Military Net (Dec. 15) reported that after completing their three-month training on December 12, 2020, 1000 recruits were transported by air to Tibet.

China Military Online (Jan. 14) reported that 30 grassroots cadres and police officers from border cities (counties) in the Xinjiang Uygur Autonomous Region, passed the 'assessment' for border defense drone pilots on January 12. This border defense drone pilot training, jointly conducted by the PLA Army Academy of Border and Coastal Defense (Urumqi) and the Border Defense Commission of the Xinjiang Uygur Autonomous Region, aims to cultivate professional 'backbones' capable of drone operation, command, as well as maintenance for the frontier defense forces. The border defense drone training mainly includes four steps, namely, theoretical study, simulation training, actual flight operation, and assessment and certification. The trainees will obtain the national civil drone pilot certificate after passing the final assessment. At least six types of advanced drones (UAVs) are deployed in the WTC. The training suggests that drones will be deployed in WTC in larger numbers.

Unconfirmed reports claimed on 18 April 2021, that the PLA is building a Special Tibetan Army. PLA officers from Lhasa visited Rudok town in Ngari/ Ali Prefecture in the far west of TAR in the 3rd week of February to recruit Tibetans as soldiers.

Lt General Wang Haijiang, Commander of Xinjiang Military Region, accompanied the Chairman of TAR People's Government Che Dalha (Ch: Qi Zhala) for inspecting the borders of Ngari (Ch: Ali) from June 20-21, 2021. Speaking at a Forum held after the inspection, Lt. General Wang Haijiang thanked the TAR Party Committee and TAR People's Government for their support to the army and infrastructural developments to defend the borders. He assured the meeting that the Xinjiang Military Region would implement Xi Jinping's 'exposition' on strengthening the army, shouldering political responsibilities, protecting China-India borders, ensuring its security and stability, and strengthening military to military cooperation.

Xinhua (June 18) disclosed that on June 15, more than 4000 Spring recruits in three camps of the recruits' brigades of the Tibet Military Region lined up for their swearing-in ceremony in front of the military flag, and completed the transition from local youth to qualified military personnel.

New incentives are being offered to Tibetan high school and college students to join the PLA. Citing Tibetan sources, Radio Free Asia (RFA-August 11), reported that Tibetan students ages 18-21 are being offered reimbursement of their school fees in exchange for enrolling in a two-year course of military training. According to a recent Chinese government notice sent to students' phones by text, students in high schools and colleges enrolled in the program may continue their studies after their training has ended. Students already receiving state aid for their schooling are, however, required to enrol. The official notice states that the deadline for enrolment in the program is August 15. A high school student in Tibet told RFA in a written message that "Military training has been a part of our schools' curriculum in the past, but this is the first time that an official government notice has been sent out to all the schools promoting enrolment in programs of military training."

New Equipment

More rapid induction of new weapons and equipment in the WTC Army has been apparent after Xu Qiling's appointment.

According to the report issued in June 2018 by the China Aerospace Studies Institute (CASI), as of July 28, 2020, China has deployed 36 aircrafts and helicopters at the Hotan Air Base in Xinjiang, including 24 J-11 or J-16 fighters, six J-8 fighters, two Y-8G Transport Aircraft, two KJ-500 Airborne Early Warning Aircraft, 2 Mi-17 helicopters, Rainbow-5 attack/reconnaissance drones. The Type-15 Tanks were inducted to the Tibet Military Region (MR) in June 2020 and Xinjiang Military Region (MR) in January 2021.

According to the PLA Daily (August 17, 2020), two J-20 stealth fighters were seen at the Hotan Air Base. On October 6, 10 UAVs were provided for the first time to the Tibet MR for logistics support.

Dongfang.com (Dec. 13, 2020), reported that a brigade of the PLA Army Aviation Corps of the Tibet Military Region had the new Z-20 helicopter in its inventory.

An official WeChat (December 14) account of the WTC reported that an unidentified brigade of the Tibet Military Region had a certain type of infantry equipment based on the QBZ-191 rifle named as the QBU-88 sniper rifle.

A Chinese media report on December 16, 2020 disclosed that the PLA had deployed a long-range rocket launcher regiment in Xinjiang and Tibet. They have 122mm long-range rocket launchers and the latest Type 05 155mm self-propelled howitzers. The more advanced domestic artillery such as the Type 122 mm self-propelled howitzer, the Type 09 122 mm truck gun, and the 120 mm mortar are available in large quantities with the field troops in the Xinjiang Military Region and Tibet Military Region. The report claimed the deployment of these weapons in 'large quantities gave China an overwhelming advantage over India in terms of firepower'.

China's fifth generation 'stealth' fighter aircraft J-20 have been stationed at the Hotan Base on February 7, 2021.

China Military Online (February 9, 2021) reported that the PLA has deployed its most powerful tank, the Type 99A, in the high-altitude border frontier at the Karakoram Mountain.

China Military Online (February 21, 2021) disclosed that the PLA's Type 15 light-weight tanks were spotted participating in an exercise in a low temperature mountainous plateau region. It said this type of tank has significant advantages over other types of tanks or armoured vehicles in such regions. Sina.com (July 29, 2021) quoting an article in the 'North Xinjiang Guardian' reported that an artillery battalion of a combined brigade of the PLA 78th Group Army recently held a 'live ammunition' tactical exercise where it displayed the new four-wheel drive 122mm vehicle-mounted howitzer with which the combined brigade is now equipped. It said that this is the third unit that is known to have been equipped with this new type of vehicle-mounted howitzer after a combined brigade in the Tibet Military Region and a combined regiment in the Xinjiang Military Region.

A Chinese website reported (July 30, 2021) that the border defense forces of the Tibet Military Region have been equipped with many advanced weapons, such as the 'Red Arrow 12' anti-tank missile, and a new type of precision shooter rifle.

Reporting on the 'Western Joint 2021 Exercises', Sina.com (August 9, 2021) disclosed that the Army Aviation Combat Group in the Western Theatre Command uses helicopters as its main equipment, and uses low-altitude and ultra-low-altitude as the main battlefield to implement three-dimensional, full-depth, and mobile operations. It added that in the days before the upcoming "Western Joint-2021" exercise the WTC Army Aviation Combat Group was trying to improve its low-altitude joint operations capabilities.

Combat Exercises & Training

The frequency of combat exercises is noticed to have increased in the last one year in the WTC Army (Ground Forces) and particularly in the Xinjiang MR. The rapid changes in the training mode in the WTC appear to not only be to strengthen combat preparedness but, through frequent live-fire combined exercises and the use of AI-based technology, to create a strong deterrence force against India and in the Himalayan region. Illustrative examples are listed below:

SCMP (January 6, 2020) quoting the state media reported that the People Liberation Army (PLA) has begun a major military exercise in the high-altitude border areas of Tibet, deploying latest weapons including a new lightweight tank and anti-aircraft missiles to check combat readiness of its troops and the efficiency of its weaponry.

China's state-run broadcaster CCTV reported on June 3, 2020 that a PLA scout unit had in 'recent days' mobilised towards a target in the Tanggula Mountains at an altitude of 4,700 metres (15,420 feet) using night vision devices on their vehicles to avoid drone surveillance from the "enemy side".

On December 15, 2020, the China News Service reported that officers and soldiers of a brigade (unidentified) of the Tibet Military Region carried out practical and tactical drills in an "unfamiliar" area with an altitude of more than 4,700 meters in the cold winter plateau to improve their response to diverse battlefield environments.

The China News Network on June 4, 2021 disclosed that 24 representatives of the Tibet Military Region, 1028 officers and soldiers gathered at a comprehensive training base at an altitude of more than 3,700 meters to participate in the "Top of the Snow 2021" record-breaking "mass training event".

Female Soldiers - Exercises & Trainings

Female soldiers have also for the first time been reported participating in military exercises in the Tibetan Plateau. China News Service (January 29, 2021) reported that an Army Aviation brigade of the Tibet Military Region organized more than 200 officers along with 18 female soldiers and other soldiers to carry 30 kilograms of luggage on a 40-kilometer winter trekking exercise.

In July 2021, 'live ammunition' training was conducted for a women's artillery squad at an altitude of 4,600 m in "southern Tibet".

A brigade of the Xinjiang Military Region stationed on a snow-covered plateau at an altitude of 4,500 meters was reported on May 30, to have conducted highland exercises with three "special" female soldiers in a brigade heavy firearms training team. It said the three "special" female soldiers are all about 1.6 meters tall and weigh more than 50 kilograms.

New Facilities Provided for the Soldiers at Plateau

China News Service (January 27, 2021) reported that a border defense regiment in the Tibet Military Region, on duty in the Medog No Man's Land at an altitude of more than 3,900 meters, has recently been connected to the internet.

In March 2021, new equipment was distributed to individual soldiers of the Xinjiang Military Region plateau garrison troops including camouflage tactical vest, assault backpack and life backpack.

China Military Online (February 5, 2021) disclosed that the first batch of military identification tags developed by the Logistics Support Department of the CMC were distributed to plateau field training units assigned to the PLA's Xinjiang Military Command for trial use. It described the move as of great significance in building systematic operational support capabilities based on an information system, as well as promoting battlefield logistics and medical support. The military identification tag is an intelligent carrier that records basic personal and medtag information, which could be used for identity authentication, treatment of the wounded, identification of remains and wartime support.

China Military Online (February 7, 2021) reported that the Shenxianwan border defense company, located at an elevation of over 5,000 meters, was finding it extremely difficult to meet the troops' demands for fresh vegetables in a stable manner. It stated that the PLA Xinjiang Military Command has now introduced advanced biological and opto-electronics technologies, and made use of intelligent computers and electronic sensing systems to monitor and manage the environmental factors, such as temperatures for vegetable plant growth, humidity levels and light intelligently.

China Military Online (February 19, 2021) — The Kunmujia sentry post located at an elevation of 4,960m in the middle of the no-man zone in the westernmost end of the Tibet Military Command, faces an annual average temperature of 5°C, -37°C at the lowest, and a 5-month-long period of snow when there is no access at all. The sentry post is now covered by the national power grid. Electric blankets and the other electric appliances, such as the humidifier, shoe dryer, radiator, and water heater, now help keep the soldiers warm and comfortable.

This was first published by the Centre for China Analysis and Strategy (CCAS) and Vivekananda International Foundation (VIF) in September 20, 2021.

50. Some Chinese Assessments of India's Geo-Economic and Foreign Policies

A good indication of Chinese thinking on India is discernible from the Chinese print and social media. While China's English-language publications, like China Daily and Beijing Review, are intended for the English-speaking foreign audience, the Chinese-language media especially caters to the domestic readership. Articles published in Chinese-language publications usually do not appear in the English-language publications and are intended for specific professional audiences and academics. In this context, articles commenting on India —published now as a steady daily criticism — in the Global Times target the Indian audience. Owned by the Chinese Communist Party (CCP)'s official mouthpiece *People's Daily*, the Global Times also transmits the 'official line' and conveys messages that the Chinese authorities want to, but cannot in as blunt and sensational a manner.

Important to note, however, is that China's media is strictly monitored by the Chinese Communist Party (CCP) Central Committee (CC)'s Propaganda Department. Editors receive 'guidance' thrice a day telling them what they can report, prominence it should be given and, in controversial matters, advising them to adhere to the version disseminated by the official news agency Xinhua. Failure to abide by this 'guidance' attracts punitive action. Nonetheless, a careful reading of the Chinese media does yield useful information, especially as Chinese President Xi Jinping more liberally censors information and imposes progressively stricter controls thereby increasing opacity.

Three recent articles in the Chinese-language media give an insight into Chinese officialdom's thinking on Indian geo-economic and foreign policies. Each has appeared in a specialised Chinese academic publication. The third article has been published in Chinese and English by the think-tank to get wider readership.

China's Nanya Yanjiu (South Asian Studies Quarterly - Issue No. 2, 2021), a bimonthly brought out by the University of International Studies at Beijing Foreign Studies, published an article by two academics, Li Tao and Yuan Xiaojiao. The article assessed the theory and practice of the Modi administration's economic diplomacy. They assess that under the Modi administration, India's economic diplomacy seeks to attract FDI, build relationships with the global Indian diaspora, and elevate India's status in regional and multilateral forums. Li Tao and Yuan Xiaojiao argue that India's economic diplomacy is grounded at a theoretical level in a mixture of neoliberal institutionalism and nationalism. On the one hand, Modi has pursued a pragmatic strategy of cooperation via bilateral and multilateral agreements. Through "selective multilateralism," India can participate in global multilateral forums while placing some limitations on the impact of globalization and India's integration into a free and open global economy. At the same time, Modi's economic diplomacy reflects 'Hindu nationalism', urging citizens to limit their material consumption and protect the domestic economy. In this view, India's economic development is a "duty" of both the Indian individual and the Indian government. According to Li and Yuan, this mixture of 'neoliberal institutionalism' and 'Hindu nationalism' is evident in India's economic diplomacy.

The two academics say that at the core are India's interests. India's relations with its South Asian neighbours reflect "defensive economic nationalism," as India uses its influence to protect its national economic interests, and its economic diplomacy is characterized by 'asymmetric interdependence'. As the largest economy in South Asia, India seeks to increase its neighbours' economic dependence on India by encouraging the adoption of a common market and offering commercial aid. In its relations with great powers such as China, the United States, Russia, and Japan, India mixes neoliberal institutionalism with economic nationalism; it balances and free rides in an attempt to maintain strategic autonomy and assert regional leadership. For example, India has accepted the US "Indo-Pacific" strategy as a way to fend off pressure from China's Belt and Road Initiative.

With regard to China, India's policy has shifted from "soft checks and balancing" to "comprehensive decoupling" in the wake of the 2020–2021 skirmishes in the Galwan valley. At these peripheral and global levels, India adopts liberal economic policies by seeking to expand economic partnerships. Modi has focused on building relations with Asian countries to attract foreign capital and provide employment opportunities for India's vast working-age population. Farther afield, Modi has pursued military, energy, and trade deals with Australia and countries in Western Europe and promised credit lines and aid to much of the African continent. Modi has also affirmed India's commitment to multilateral economic institutions by pursing leadership roles and seeking to reshape global economic governance to reflect a multipolar world order.

Another article published in Guoji Luntan (International Studies - No. 5, 2021) of the China Institute of International Studies, commented on US-India-China relations. Li Qingyan, Associate Research Fellow at the Department for Developing Countries Studies at the China Institute of International Studies, explored US efforts to incorporate India into its Indo-Pacific strategy, which he said is motivated by the US desire to contain China, and Indian motivations for pursuing closer ties with the United States, and the inherent limits to US–Indian relations.

He said that under Modi, India has shifted from its traditional "non-alignment" policy to a "multi-alignment" approach that emphasizes building strategic relations with multiple great powers. Politically, the United States, operating under what Li criticises as flawed zero-sum Cold War thinking, views India as a key pillar of its Indo-Pacific strategy. India is happy to acquiesce to the Indo-Pacific strategy because it views cooperation with the United States as a way to achieve its great power ambitions. Consequently, India has increased its dialogues and cooperation with the members of the Quad. In the security field, the United States regards India as a "defense partner" and treats it much as it would treat a formal ally. The two countries share technology and some intelligence, have worked to integrate military operations, and participate in joint military exercises.

Li Qingyan contends that India and the United States have teamed up to oppose the Belt and Road Initiative, painting its projects as "debt traps" and "neocolonialism,"and promoting their own initiatives as an alternative. Despite the strengthening of US–Indian relations, however, Li Qingyan asserts that geopolitical, security, and economic differences will hinder the development of formal alliance relations. US–Indian relations are limited by conflicting objectives and a lack of mutual trust. India participates in the Indo-Pacific strategy not because it wants to take the United States' side in the US–China strategic competition, but because India views cooperation with the strategy as the best way to achieve its great power ambitions and establish its regional significance as the world transitions to multipolarity. He points to India's continuing purchase of weapons from Russia and trade frictions that are undermining Indian–US relations. Li Qingyan anticipates continued tension between US policies first developed under Trump's "America First" approach and those promoted by Modi's "Made in India" strategy of domestic protectionism. He argues that the "China factor" is not enough to push the United States and India toward alliance relations: India remains unwilling to sacrifice its strategic autonomy for US interests.

Stating that India's willingness to cooperate with the United States is motivated by India's perception that China poses a threat to India's regional dominance and its global influence, Li Qingyan argues, this analysis is completely flawed. He said if India "abandons 'strategic autonomy'" and aligns with anti-Chinese elements in the West, it will lose its opportunity to become a great power. He contends that over the long term, China and India as emerging markets with enormous populations have many common interests and face similar development challenges, which might push the two countries closer together. The two countries have extensive trade relations. They also share the view that the Global South should have a far greater say in global economic governance than it currently does and anticipate that their countries will play increasingly significant roles as the world transitions toward a multipolar order. Furthermore, Li Qingyan expects India's decision to pursue closer relations with the United States for geopolitical reasons to shift over the longer term. He expects that the United States and China will eventually learn to coexist in a multipolar world, decreasing India's opportunity to advance its own interests by playing off China and the United States against each other, and strengthening the value of strategic autonomy. Li Qingyan predicts that the Indo-Pacific strategy ultimately will fall away as China and India rise together.

Ouyang Wei, a 'princeling' who retired from China's National Defence University (NDU) as Professor and Senior Colonel and is presently Deputy

Director of Academic Committee, Director of Border Studies Center, at the Grandview Institution — ostensibly a private think-tank — authored a lengthy nearly 6700-word article on the situation along China's borders. A border affairs expert, Ouyang Wei assessed that China faces increasingly serious challenges at its land and sea borders on almost every side and must urgently reinforce its defences in these regions. In his report titled 'Current Situation in the Building and Development of China's Border and Coastal Defense' posted on the Grandview Institution's site in mid-October, he noted that the US has stepped up its military presence in the South China Sea and the Taiwan Strait, and uncertainties grow on China's land borders with India, Afghanistan, Myanmar and North Korea.

Ouyang said the country was facing encroachment, secession and terrorism in some border areas. In his India-specific comments, he stated that "India takes China as a strategic contestant and adopts an approach of "defending the north and advancing eastward". It has "deployed forces of comparative advantage against China in the disputed land border areas, intensifying its encroachment on China's territory". At the same time, it has increased its budget for the naval forces and implemented the "Act East Policy" to push into the Pacific Ocean. Joining the "Indo-Pacific Strategy" system, India vigorously interacts with the United States, Japan and Australia. It keeps monitoring and preventing China from expansion into the Indian Ocean. Countries like the Philippines and Vietnam that have unresolved disputes with China over maritime rights and interests are trying to leverage the endorsement of major countries from outside the region so as to counterbalance China's increasing control over the South China Sea and to grab their own vested interests. Apart from that, the instability and uncertainty in the Korean Peninsula, Myanmar, Afghanistan and other regions has direct impact on China's border and coastal defense". He assessed that the possibility of intervention by the major powers from outside the region is on the increase.

In a subsequent paragraph he added that China has signed boundary treaties with Myanmar, Nepal, Laos and Vietnam (with India and Bhutan) successively and established the ASEAN Free Trade Area, which has stabilized the security in the southwest border area as a whole. "Keeping a negotiation mechanism and announcing the political guidelines for the settlement of the boundary issue,

China has inked the border defense cooperation agreement with India in 2013 in an effort to reduce border friction. However, out of its strategic coveting in the Indo-Pacific region and encouraged by the US Indo-Pacific Strategy, India has readjusted its strategy towards China in recent years, taking a hardline anti-China stance on the Belt and Road Initiative and territorial disputes". He added "It has built up military deployment in border areas and encroached on China's territory. The 2017 Doklam Standoff in the Sikkim sector of the China-India border, the 2019 Ladakh clash, and the 2020 border conflict in the Galwan river valley that resulted in casualties, show that the task of defending and managing the Sino-Indian land border is far more demanding than in other directions. As strategically both China and India have clear intention to avoid military conflict, and besides, the reorganization of China's military forces acts as a counterweight to India's deployment of border forces, the Sino-Indian border disputes are held under control for the time being. It is very unlikely that local clash and war harming the overall stability of the border areas and bilateral relations should occur". He also discussed the situation with Myanmar and maritime territorial issues in detail.

Around almost the same time the English-language version of the *Global Times* published a toughly-worded article.

The *Global Times* (October 11) article, second in as many days, referred to the PLA Western Theatre Command statement released the same day, which claimed "China has made tremendous efforts to ease and calm the border situation, while India insisted on unreasonable and unrealistic demands, adding difficulties to the negotiations". It quoted the PLA Western Theatre Command statement that "China's determination to safeguard sovereignty is unwavering, and China hopes India will not misjudge the situation". It said the "status quo" that India referred to is to legitimise their continuous encroachment on Chinese territory. India's statement said the "resolution of the remaining areas would facilitate progress in the bilateral relations. This shows the Indian side's current attitude of linking border disputes with overall China-India relations and trying to coerce the Chinese side to make concessions". "It said the border issue between China and India remains stuck because the "Indian side still hasn't developed a correct attitude in the negotiations. It always makes unrealistic demands not in line with the real situation or its strength". It added that "New Delhi anticipates Beijing softening its stance over the border issue and yielding to its demands to prevent New Delhi from aligning itself with Washington against Beijing" and that "such an opportunistic attitude has lowered India's status in international politics as a major power, because this tactic will not work between great powers. The border issue is related to the dignity of all nations. So, when border conflicts occur between two major countries, it needs to be managed based on major power relations. And for any of these countries, trying to coerce the other side to make concessions not in line with the real situation and detrimental to its national interests creates a problem for itself. This is because its goal is impossible to achieve, and will only create trouble for itself".

The *Global Times* warned, "The Chinese people know that both China and India are great powers with enough national strength to sustain a long-time border standoff with each other. Such mutual attrition is regrettable, but if India is willing to do so, China will keep it company until the end. New Delhi needs to be clear about one thing: it will not get the border the way it wants. If it starts a war, it will definitely lose. Any political maneuvering and pressure will be ignored by China". It said "India is indulging itself this way. It has lackluster abilities, but has turned itself into a "superpower of patriotism." In addition to border disputes with China, India also often raises unreasonable demands over other issues". In conclusion the article said "In handling the border dispute with India, it is of the utmost importance for China to do two things. First, we should stick to the principle that no matter how India makes trouble, China's territory belongs to China and we will never cede it. The second is to be patient and be prepared for a military struggle in the event of a deteriorating scenario, but do our best to maintain peace in the China-India border area. India is still sleepwalking on the border issue. We can wait for it to wake up".

The contrast in styles and aggression between the *Global Times*' reporting and other articles is evident, but the content is similar! All emphasise that China is in a stronger position, but chooses not to take tougher measures. There is also the suggestion that the US and China will, over time, possibly reach some sort of modus vivendi.

This was first published by the Centre for China Analysis and Strategy (CCAS) and Vivekananda International Foundation (VIF) in November 29, 2021.

51. 'Xi Jinping's Upgrading of The PLA and Implication for India'

China's perception of its external environs has been changing incrementally since Xi Jinping took over as General Secretary of the Chinese Communist Party (CCP), Chairman of the Central Military Commission (CMC) and China's President, in 2012. Recent descriptions in official documents and statements by Chinese leaders reveal growing concern that China's external environment is becoming unpredictable and no longer as peaceful as earlier. India has begun to figure in these statements. The changing perception, which coincides with Xi Jinping's declared ambition of making China a strong and powerful nation, will shape the People's Liberation Army (PLA)'s preparedness.

A commentary in the official *PLA Daily* (January 13) by Chen Hanghui of the PLA Nanjing Army Command College, anticipated that "the military game of great powers will become more intense" in 2022. It said "major powers such as Russia, the United States, the United Kingdom, France, Germany, and India have accelerated their military transformation, focusing on key areas to enhance their "high-end warfare" capabilities." Notable is the inclusion of India as one of the countries that the PLA is paying attention to. While the US, Russia, Japan and, to a lesser extent France and Germany were the focus of the commentary, it mentioned that India "will continue to promote the actual combat deployment of its first domestic aircraft carrier". It added that "The militaries of France, the United Kingdom, India and other countries have also strengthened research on artificial intelligence technology, trying to apply this technology more widely in the fields of intelligence reconnaissance, auxiliary decision-making and network security".

Chinese military commentators have similarly stressed that the risks to China's security are growing as it comes under pressure from a number of countries. Chinese military commentator Liu Yantong said "Right now, we are facing the threat of war. The army needs to be urgently aware that a war may happen overnight ... We should be fully prepared and combat ready at all times". Zhou Chenming, a researcher from Beijing's Yuan Wang Military Science and Technology Think Tank, said "the country's overseas interests are expanding, with major security threats coming from the sea, then the air, and even the cyber world".

These concerns were reflected in the report titled *Current Situation in the Building and Development of China's Border and Coastal Defense* by Ouyang Wei, a border affairs expert and retired PLA Senior Colonel of the National Defence University. Posted on the official website of the ostensibly private Grandview Institution on October 12, it said China faces "increasingly serious challenges at its land and sea borders on almost every side and must urgently reinforce its defences in these regions". Ouyang Wei assessed that "China was facing encroachment, secession and terrorism in some border areas".

He specifically referred to India and indicated that the present military tension is unlikely to ease for quite some time. He said "India takes China as a strategic contestant and adopts an approach of "defending the north and advancing eastward"." He added that India had deployed large numbers of forces against China in the disputed land border areas, "intensifying its encroachment on China's territory". He anticipated that clashes could occur, but would not damage the overall stability of the border. Ouyang Wei noted that India had increased its Navy budget and implemented the "Act East Policy" to push into the Pacific Ocean and, together with the United States, Japan and Australia, is monitoring and preventing China from expanding into the Indian Ocean. He concluded that "the possibility of intervention by the major powers from outside the region is on the increase".

The changing Chinese perceptions make the extensive military reforms more relevant for India as is the attention paid by Xi Jinping to the People's Liberation Army (PLA). China's official media regularly publicises Xi's visits to PLA establishments and units during his visits to provinces and cities outside Beijing and attendance at major military conferences. Xi has been monitoring the progress of professionalisation and modernisation in the PLA with special focus on making it a hi-tech scientific force with a thrust on the application and use of Artificial Intelligence (AI). Preparing for war under realistic battle conditions is now routine in PLA training exercises.

The *PLA Daily* (November 1) publicised that Xi Jinping had signed a new set of regulations on military equipment procurement, focusing on war preparedness and combat capabilities, to facilitate rapid acquisition of the best weapons and equipment most needed on future battlefields.

Pointing to the likelihood of more military reforms, a book of commentaries published by the CCP's official newspaper *People's Daily* in mid-November mentioned the existence of structural problems. Military commentator Zhong Xin was quoted saying "The military's command system is not systematic, the army's structure is not sound enough, and the policy system lags, seriously limiting the PLA's defensive operations. If these problems are not resolved, plans to build a world-class modern military are just empty talk."

Meanwhile, there are indications that the PLA plans to modify and upgrade training programmes as well as improve its policy regarding the placement of soldiers. The *PLA Daily* (November 28) disclosed that Battalions face the problem of finding the appropriate jobs for recruits, or slotting the right person in the right job. It observed that this had become more important with the rapid development of military weaponry and equipment technology, the increasingly complex system, the increasing degree of knowledge intensiveness, and the increasingly higher requirements for specialised posts. A growing percentage of recruits in recent years are technically qualified or college graduates and this would relate to their job assignment. Other articles in the *PLA Daily* have referred to 'adjustment' and discipline problems with the younger recruits, many of who are graduates or generally better educated.

The Central Military Commission's Order No. 1 of 2022 signed by Xi Jinping on January 4, which is a Training and Mobilisation order, emphasises training and requires the entire Army "to comprehensively promote the transformation and upgrading of military training, and to train elite soldiers who can fight well". It specifies that these "elite soldiers must be trained and toughened during the winters". A Commentator's article in the *PLA Daily*

(January 5,2022) explained that the Central Military Commission's Order "sounded the clarion call of the times for military training and preparation for war". Introducing a sense of urgency, it quoted Xi's remark that "In today's world, power politics and the "law of the jungle" still prevail, and various foreseeable and unforeseen risks and challenges have increased significantly, and the danger of war is a reality."

The mention of "elite soldiers" in the Mobilisation Order is new and suggests not only specialised training and equipment for such soldiers but also a specific, and as yet undisclosed, role. The instruction that they "must be trained and toughened during the winters" implies they will probably be deployed in the PLA Western Theatre Command along the border with India. Viewed in the backdrop of earlier reports that the authorities were stepping up recruitment of Mongolians from the Inner Mongolia Autonomous Region for posting in the high-altitude Tibetan Plateau, the instruction also appears to hint that the adaptability and performance of troops already deployed on the borders needs to be improved.

Alongside the intensified training programmes, Xi is paying attention to the salary and allowances of serving soldiers and the living conditions of the 56 million retired soldiers and veterans. The Chinese leadership is aware that dissatisfaction among the latter could spill over into the PLA. On January 4, 2022 in addition to the regular pay hikes, China's Ministry of Veterans Affairs issued the "Measures for Retired Soldiers' Monthly Retirement Payments and Resettlement Measures". This introduced a new system for the placement of retired soldiers and a monthly payment of pensions together with other measures to give them "respect" in society.

The PLA's task is spelt out in the Chinese Defence White Paper, 2019 which, for the first time, states that China is "the only major country yet to be completely reunified", thereby confirming that reunification is a political and military aspiration. In this context, the interview by retired PLA Col Liu Mingfu to Asahi Shimbun in May 2019 is especially relevant for India. Asked about China's territorial ambitions and what its limits would be, Liu Mingfu replied that the map used by "the current Chinese government is the clear standard for national sovereignty and territory". The reference to current Chinese government maps implies Chinese ambitions in the East Sea or Sea of Japan, the Senkaku Islands or Diaoyu Islands, South China Sea, Taiwan, and India's Ladakh, Jammu & Kashmir (J&K) and Arunachal Pradesh. He also hinted at the possible use of force, probably in the context of Taiwan, by stating that "as time passes, the gap in national power with China will become less for the US".

This was first published by the Centre for China Analysis and Strategy (CCAS) and Vivekananda International Foundation (VIF) in January 20, 2022.

52. 'Border Security is Receiving Higher Salience in Tibet'

Over the past year, the Chinese authorities have increased emphasis on border security along the Sino-Indian Line of Actual Control (LAC). There have been a number of visits by senior Tibetan Autonomous Region (TAR) officials and TAR Security and Propaganda teams to villages in the border areas. This has become more pronounced after the visits by Chinese President Xi Jinping and Politburo Standing Committee (PBSC) member and Chairman of the Chinese People's Political Consultative Conference (CPPCC) Wang Yang to Tibet in July and August 2021 respectively. Xi Jinping's meeting in Lhasa with officers of the People's Liberation Army (PLA) of the Tibet Military Region posted in Tibet underscored this. The number of references to strengthening border defence also appear to have increased after the appointment of the new TAR Party Secretary Wang Junzheng.

Apparently to compensate for the limited capabilities of aircraft at the high altitudes of the Tibetan plateau, a number of airports are now being rapidly built across the region. Already, thirty airports are reportedly under construction on the Tibetan Plateau and Xinjiang. Now, a late January report reveals that Qinghai province — part of the original Tibet — plans to construct 10 new airports by 2025, with at least one airport in each county. In addition, the construction of 9 new airports, which began in 2017, is to be completed by 2030. Some of these are strategically located like those in Medok, Nyingtri (opposite Arunachal Pradesh); Dromo County, Shigatse (across Yadong); Purang County, Ngari (bordering Uttarakhand); and Kyirong (on the border with Nepal). The others too are in Lhasa and near the borders with India. Construction of an additional five airports is planned to begin in 2022.

Construction of the 'xiaokang' model well-off border defence villages was accelerated and has been completed. On January 7, 2022 while presenting the

Report on the Work of the Government in 2021, to the Fifth Session of the 11th TAR People's Congress, the recently-appointed Chairman of the TAR People's Government, Yan Jinhai announced that all 624 'xiaokang' villages had been completed.

Later, when meeting the delegates from Lhasa and Ngari (Ali) a day prior to the fifth session of the 11th TAR People's Congress, he emphasised the importance of defending the borders. He specifically told the delegates from Ngari that they must focus on improving the overall situation of the region by paying close attention to protecting the "soil and the border", industrial development and the people's livelihood for "high quality development in Ngari".

More recently, the *Tibet Daily* (January 28, 2022) publicised TAR Party Secretary Wang Junzheng's recent visit to the Tibet Entry-Exit Frontier Inspection Station in Kyirong (Ch: Geelong) in Shigatse (Ch: Xigaze) to inspect border strengthening work, border stability maintenance and port control work. During the visit, in addition to giving political directions, Wang Junzheng told officials and border guards to thoroughly study the 'spirit' of the Sixth Plenary Session of the CCP Central Committee (CC), and consolidate border defence work, border security and resolutely defend the "southwestern border of the motherland." He told them to "build indestructible steel like border barriers" and make new contributions for long term and comprehensive stability in Tibet.

Wang Junzheng also visited the main command centre station at Kyirong port, the Everest Border Police Station and the Pangong lake Border Police Station, where he asked the border guards to "stick to their post in the ice and snow", but also take care of their health. He stressed that social stability in Tibet is related to national stability, and border security in Tibet is related to national security. Wang Junzheng exhorted "put the cause of the party and the people first, loyalty to the core, support to the core, maintain the core and defend the core to ensure security and stability on the border."

Interesting in this context is that China's official media publicised a meeting of the Tibet Military Region Party Committee in Lhasa on January 17. The report disclosed that Lt. General Yin Hongxing is the new Political Commissar of the Tibet Military Region (TMR) subordinate to the Western

Theatre Command. Lt General Yin Hongxing was earlier the Political -Commissar of the 71st Group Army in the Eastern Theatre Command. Born in 1965, Yin Hongxing was promoted to the rank of Lt. General in December 2021 when he was appointed Political Commissar of the Tibet Military Region (TMR). This is his first tenure in Tibet.

The Tibet Daily (January 19) reported that Lt General Yin Hongxing chaired the Seventh Plenary meeting of the Tibet Military Region Party Committee held in Lhasa on January 17 and presented a report. TAR Party Secretary Wang Junzheng and Lt General Wang Kai, Commander and Deputy Secretary of the Party Committee of the Tibet Military Region attended the meeting and gave speeches. Meetings of the TMR Party Committee are not regularly reported.

In his speech, TAR Party Secretary Wang Junzheng "expressed his gratitude and respect to the officers and soldiers who have been fighting in the snow-covered plateau for a long time." He acknowledged that in the past year the Party Committee of TMR had 'vigorously implemented the decisions and work deployments of Xi Jinping and the Central Military Commission, united and led the officers and soldiers, strengthened their political stance, their ability to prepare for war and their proactiveness in working for long term stability and high-quality development in Tibet'. Wang Junzheng stressed that Xi Jinping attaches great importance to army building and work in Tibet, and that the President visited Tibet in person on the occasion of the 70th anniversary of the "peaceful liberation of Tibet" and met the representatives of officers and soldiers stationed in Tibet, and had personally replied to all officers and soldiers of the "Plateau Frontier Guard Model Camp". He urged that "all levels of the TMR must always bear in mind the heavy trust of General Secretary Xi Jinping, resolutely implement Xi Jinping's thoughts on strengthening the army and the Party's strategy for governing Tibet in the new era" and deeply understand the significance of the "two establishments".

He asked the soldiers and officers to "faithfully perform their duties of defending the country and guarding the borders well and to strive to create a new situation of high-quality development of the army on the new journey of governing borders, stabilizing Tibet and strengthening the army". Wang Junzheng reiterated Xi Jinping's "orders to prepare for war, his insistence on placing military training in a strategic position, to combine combat training with scientific technology, to strengthen civil-military joint training in key areas such as disaster relief and emergency rescue purpose". He stressed that the Party Committees and Governments at all levels will fully support the consolidation of national defense, the army, and in solving the challenges and problems of the officers and soldiers including their work and life problems, welfare of the retired military personnel, and fostering a good atmosphere of caring for the soldiers from the society.

A couple of days later on January 19, the Metok (Medog) County Party Committee held its Economic Work Conference where Metok County Party Secretary Wei Changqi delivered a speech. Metok county is strategically located on TAR's border with the Indian state of Arunachal Pradesh. It is also the site of the proposed dam — envisaged to be the world's largest — on the Great Bend of the Brahmaputra River. Apart from stressing strong support to the "two establishments", rural revitalisation etc., the Metok County Party Secretary laid considerable emphasis on border defence. Two of the four agenda items for the meeting focussed on national security and strengthening the border.

The Metok County Party Secretary said it is important to firmly establish an overall national security concept and constantly build a national security barrier. He emphasised the importance of maintaining stability, carrying out the struggle against separatism and promoting ethnic unity. Focussing on strengthening the border and making the border regions and people prosperous, he said, "the emphasis should be on securing and strengthening the border and vigorously promoting border defense". Along with the stabilisation of the border, he said it was important to promote "the anti-encroachment struggle and implement a "push forward strategy". In this context he urged, "the transfer of people in the central areas to the front line", and the need to speed up "construction of settlements in the border areas, and ensure that the people move into new homes as soon as possible". He stressed that it was "necessary to deepen the development of militarycivilian integration", implement policies for supporting the army giving priority to their families, and do a good job in socialized logistics support services. He reiterated the importance of "strengthening the control of border areas, keeping an eye on the front line of the border, and building a steel Great Wall that guards the border".

The uptick in activity in TAR's border areas points to accelerated construction of defence-related infrastructure and improvement in living conditions for troops. This has been accompanied by stepped-up activity of the TAR's Propaganda and Security Bureaus in TAR's border areas and villages. These indicate plans for long-term, or permanent, presence of the People's Liberation Army (PLA) in the border areas along the LAC and possibly further military operations by the PLA.

This was first published by the Centre for China Analysis and Strategy (CCAS) and Vivekananda International Foundation (VIF) in February 2, 2022.

53. Indications of Elevated Military Preparations in Tibet

Monitoring developments in the Tibet Autonomous Region (TAR) has become even more important after India's 4057-kms Line of Actual Control (LAC) with China became active along its entire length since at least July 2021, when the clash at Galwan Valley resulted in the deaths of Indian soldiers. Activities of the TAR authorities increase noticeably as they sensitise their population while preparing for any initiative or periods of tension, whether military or otherwise. Over at least the past month the higher TAR authorities have been noticed paying unusually increased attention to the border prefectures and counties.

On April 2, 2023, China's Ministry of Civil Affairs announced a "Standardised" list of 11 geographical names of places within the Indian state of Arunachal Pradesh while referring to it as "Southern Tibet". These were published in Chinese, Tibetan and Pinyin. This set off a wave of nationalism on China's social media with Chinese netizens applauding the announcement and calling on China to 'retake' the 90,000 square kilometres of "Chinese territory" comprising almost the entire territory of India's Arunachal Pradesh sooner or later. China claims this territory has been under India's illegal occupation for 70 years. Predictably the posts mentioned Tawang's religious and cultural significance as the birthplace of the Sixth Dalai Lama and claimed that the culture and religious beliefs of the people in Tawang and Tibet were very similar. Another post blamed Britain's colonisation of India as the root cause of the current India-China dispute over Arunachal Pradesh. China had made similar announcements in 2017 and 2021 when it renamed six and 15 places respectively in Arunachal Pradesh.

A day after the so-called "standardisation" of names in "Southern Tibet" by China's Ministry of Civil Affairs, the TAR People's Government announced that Milin County of Nyingtri (Ch: Linzhi) and Tsona (Ch: Cuona) County of Lhoka (Ch: Shannan) would be upgraded to the City level. Elevating these two critical border counties to the level of Cities is strategic as it places them under the direct administrative control of the TAR government at Lhasa. The population of both these places is under 27,000 and does not normally justify this administrative upgrade.

Tsona County is located just 34 km north of Bum La Pass, close to the Line of Actual Control between India and China and adjacent to Bhutan. After its upgradation to City level, Tsona's Administrative Government was moved to Marmang Ethnic Town in Lekpo Gorge (Ch: Lebuguo). This was the site from where People's Liberation Army (PLA) Commander Lieutenant General Zhang Guohau launched attacks against India during the Sino-Indian War 1962.

Marmang Ethnic Town, the new Administrative unit of Tsona City, is 2,800 meters above sea level and almost 1500 meters lower than the previous Tsona County Headquarters at 4300 meters. Observers assess that shifting the headquarters has socio-economic and political advantages as the relatively warmer environment would attract people to relocate and be conducive to large-scale infrastructure development. Chinese netizens have said that shifting the headquarters of Tsona to the new location at Marmang Ethnic Town, close to the LAC, shows China's determination to "not give up an inch of land" and its will to strengthen, control and manage the eastern sector of the Sino-Indian border.

The seat of government of Milin City remains unchanged and is still in the original Milin Town.

With their elevation to the level of a City, the TAR government will exercise direct administrative jurisdiction over Milin and Tsona. This will accelerate the expeditious building of logistics infrastructure and other facilities including for the 'xiaokang' (model border defence well-off villages) and facilitate the mobilisation of troops and conduct of routine border patrols.

Senior TAR officials have also been noticed visiting TAR border counties since early this month. TAR Party Secretary Wang Junzheng, accompanied by four other officials from TAR inspected (Lhodrak, Tsome, Tsona, Lhuntse, Nakartse, Nedong) and other counties of Lhoka from May 4-9. The officials were: Wang Haizhou, Member of the Standing Committee of the TAR Party Committee and Director of the Propaganda Department; Dawa Tsering, Vice Chairman of TAR People's Government; Xu Chengcang, Deputy Director of the Standing Committee of TAR People's Congress and Secretary of the Lhoka Municipal Party Committee; and Lang Fukuan, Vice Chairman of TAR People's Government and Director of the National Language Work Committee of TAR. In addition to meeting the local people, farmers and grassroot Party cadres, the TAR Party Secretary particularly urged local officials to promote and implement the 'Three-in-One' management system, i.e., grassroots party building, grid-style social management and digital governance, to achieve long-term stability. He, accompanied by his team, went to the frontlines of border defence and interacted extensively with border officers, soldiers, police and border residents. He spoke of strengthening border defence and infrastructure and making border residents prosperous.

The TAR Party Secretary's visit to Lhoka was followed by a nine-day (May 4-13) inspection tour by Zhuan Yuan, Executive Deputy Secretary of the TAR Party Committee and Secretary of the Party Group of the TAR People's Political Consultative Conference (PPCC). He inspected the border counties of Lhoka. In addition to meeting Monastic Management Cadres and inspecting monasteries to resolve potential and "hidden dangers to stability", Zhuan Yuan met the River Chief of Yarlung Tsangpo (Brahmaputra) to oversee the protection, management and government of the river and implementation of the work designated by the TAR Party Committee.

Almost coinciding with Zhuan Yuan's inspections in Shigatse and Lhoka, the Head of the TAR United Front Work Department (UFWD), Karma Tsetan, inspected Nyingtri for three days from May 4-7, 2023. He inspected Lunang Town in Drayibchu (Ch: Bayi), Lamaling Monastery, Meche Temple, Karla Village (Ch: Gala), the newly upgraded Minling City, Minling Airport, Qionglin New Village, Lhoba Ethnic Town and Kongpo Gyamda County. Incidentally, a new airport has recently been built at Karla Village (Ch: Gala). Karma Tsetan also went to the 'Little Red Pastoral House' and Patriotic Re-education base in Qionglin village in Minling City, which the Party considers significant for military, national unity and border protection measures. All these places are located close to the LAC.

Chen Yongqi, Deputy Secretary and Executive Vice Chairman of TAR People's Government, also inspected the border counties of Lhoka and Shigatse in the second week of May. He visited Lhuntse, Nakartse, Samdrubtse, Gampa and Khangmar. He emphasised the importance of maintaining a "solid" border, the need to give equal attention to the troops stationed there and welfare of people residing on the borders, improving the livelihood and social security of border residents and improving the infrastructure. He also spoke of developing traditional industries conducive to the local environment, the need to actively integrate the 'One Belt, One Road', and construct a South Asian Grand Corridor. Chen Yongqi stressed that maintaining a "strong border is a political responsibility and, therefore, must be fulfilled."

From May 9-12, 2023, the Chairman of the TAR People's Government, Yan Jinhai conducted parallel inspections in Drayib-chu, Minling, Metok and Pome counties of Nyingtri. He checked the progress in construction of border defence villages, traditional industries, rural tourism and grassroots social governance. He also met frontline party cadres.

Additionally, there are reports of infrastructure construction and military activity along the LAC. On April 6, the Tashigang/Demchok Border Police Station of the Ngari (Ch: Ali) Border Management Detachment organised a patrolling exercise for police and border guards to go to the first border village, i.e. Demchok village's Guge Duty Patrol Point. Guo Yuanjing, an official at the Tibet Frontier Inspection Station, emphasised the importance of patrolling and said that patrolling helped the border guard police keep abreast of the situation on the front line of the border to ensure its safety and stability.

Reports on March 24 revealed that China's Strategic Support Force (PLASSF) had recently established a new electronic warfare base in Nyingtri, 30 km from Arunachal Pradesh (India). A photograph of the base was available on a Twitter site on March 24.

Earlier in December 2022, satellite imagery showed that China is constructing a new Radome facility at Pangong Tso near the disputed China-India border. Reports suggest it is now ready. In case it is a PLA SSF facility it would be used for SIGINT collection, satellite communications, or radar. five kms east of the PLA's Sirijap Fort post, there is a larger size Radome at a higher altitude.

Another report on April 24 stated that the PLA has increased patrolling activities in the Metok region (opposite Upper Siang District, Arunachal Pradesh). Among the possible reasons could be: 1. Mining activities (for Rare Earth Elements); 2. Proposed construction of 60GW Metok HPP (Hydropower Plant); and 3. Chinese claims along the Eastern Sector of the India's China border. A possible explanation was provided in a post (May 10, 2023) on the Chinese portal Weixin, which highlighted the importance of the Metok Hydropower Station. It said in addition to contributing to the creation of arable land in the water-starved Taklamakan Desert, the Metok hydropower station can generate up to 300 billion kWh per year, which is equivalent to saving 120 million tons of standard coal or 60 million tons of oil for all human beings every year. Calling it a great contribution to environmental protection, it declared "Whoever dares to block the construction of the Metok Hydropower Station is destroying the great goal of carbon neutrality for mankind, and whoever does so is an enemy of entire Europe and the United States. India is so well-behaved, presumably, it is definitely unwilling to do such a thing as a public enemy of mankind, right?" Metok, which is just across the border opposite Arunachal Pradesh, is the scene of considerable construction activity related to the Dam – claimed by China as the world's largest — that China is building on the Great Bend on the Brahmaputra (Yarlung Tsangpo).

Activities to support the troops posted in the high altitude region of Ladakh were also noticed during this period. The People's Liberation Army (PLA) Western Theatre Command General Hospital at Chengdu issued a recruitment notice on May 9, 2023, stating that, "the hospital plans to recruit 107 professional and technical personnel in medical treatment, nursing, pharmacy, medical technology, engineering, and scientific research assistants"... Separately, the PLA authorities on May 10, announced bidding for the construction of oxygen supply systems in Shigatse, Nyalam and Chamdo in TAR. The project is estimated to cost around 3 billion yuan and is expected to be completed in 50 calendar days. The oxygen supply will help the troops stationed in remote areas of TAR to easily access oxygen without travelling back to Lhasa or other big cities.

In addition to these developments, a number of posts critical of India have been noticed during April-May 2023, on Chinese social media, like Weibo.

One post claimed that Indian Foreign Minister Jaishankar's insistence that Beijing make efforts to resolve the border first as a precursor for cooperation in other arenas should be interpreted as reflecting India's "opinion that the Sino-Indian border issue is not as serious as the 'Taiwan issue' and hence New Delhi regularly tests the patience of Beijing at the border'. It added that, "China has already demonstrated her highest levels of 'benevolence' towards India. New Delhi has already experienced the might of PLA during the 2020 Galwan Valley clashes and it appears that Modi would like to bring back the 1962 memories alive". It said, "with the induction of J16 fighter aircraft and Type 99A Tank in Tibet, it has already become a norm in the border region. Chinese PLA should get ready to fight against India again". An earlier Weibo post of October 2022 advocated building bridges in the Galwan Valley area. It said the, "Galwan River Bridge has made us strategically active than instead of passively waiting for the enemy's provocation and launching a counterattack".

These activities by China along the LAC need to be viewed in the backdrop of Beijing's overall unfriendly attitude towards India and its unyielding stance at the 19 rounds of the border commanders' conference. It has at this time again signalled its support to Pakistan and terrorism by rejecting the listing of Pakistan-based Jaish commander Abdul Rauf Azhar as a terrorist at the United Nations Security Council (UNSC). These developments suggest a heightened level of alert by the PLA along the LAC.

This was first published by the Centre for China Analysis and Strategy (CCAS) and Vivekananda International Foundation (VIF) in May 23, 2023.

54. 'China is Unbending on Improving Relations with India'

There is negligible prospect of improvement in India-China relations in the near future. The absence of communication at high leadership levels and China's recent protest against economic assistance to projects in Arunachal Pradesh, on the thin pretext that it is disputed, are brazen examples. In fact, they point to China expanding the areas of pressure on India.

The bilateral relationship has been subjected to considerable strain ever since Beijing decided to make it clear that it will attempt to forcibly take the territories it claims and India will have to acquiesce to China being the leading power in the region. China has simultaneously redoubled efforts to establish its dominance over Asia. These developments have coincided with the view in the Chinese Communist Party (CCP) leadership that India has drawn uncomfortably close to the US. Additionally, Beijing sees India as adopting a tougher, unyielding stance, which includes standing firm and building defences along the border as well as initiating steps to close-off the burgeoning Indian market to China. Beijing views these as unwelcome steps, but considers that India does not yet pose a serious challenge.

In a cosmetic attempt to show that China wants to improve ties but it is India that is playing spoil sport, Beijing put out reports that it had sent its Ambassador, Xu Feihong, to India to improve ties. Xu Feihong arrived in India almost 20 months after his predecessor Sun Weidong departed in October 2022. Reports that Xu Feihong was being sent to India were in circulation for at least the past 3-4 months. Xu Feihong has no prior history of engagement with India or its neighbours. His arrival was preceded by disinformation peddled in Delhi that it is a move by Beijing to enhance communication and improve bilateral ties. This 'line' has been echoed by a number of Indian journalists, academics and others. Taking advantage of India's open, democratic system, from the time he arrived Xu Feihong has virtually been holding court and meeting Indian politicians, officials including former diplomats, and opinion makers calling on him. He has also met Indian businessmen and travelled to rural areas in India. The reality is, however, different. China has no intention of taking substantive steps to ease tensions on the border, but is interested in maintaining commercial and economic access to India's market. At the same time, it is determined to keep India under protracted and sustained pressure.

There are other signs of China's belligerent attitude. A clear recent indicator of Beijing's intentions was the failure of Chinese President Xi Jinping to observe even basic diplomatic niceties and congratulate Modi on his election as India's Prime Minister for the third term. Xi Jinping has till today not congratulated Modi. In fact, Xi Jinping has initiated no direct contact or meeting with Indian Prime Minister Modi since April 2020! Chinese Premier Li Qiang did send a routine message of congratulations, but only after Modi's swearing in on May 5, as if there were any doubt that he would be sworn in! China's Ministry of Foreign Affairs explained it would have been 'premature' to convey greetings prior to the swearing in. There was, however, no such apparent hesitation in inviting Indonesia's President-elect on an official visit prior to his swearing-in! There is no doubt that Xi Jinping's failure to send a message of congratulations was deliberate. Whether it is Beijing's ploy to restrict interactions between China and India at the level of the Chinese Premier remains to be seen.

China's prickliness was on display also when Taiwan's President Lai Ching-te congratulated Prime Minister Modi. Lai Ching-te's greetings mentioned expanding ties and Prime Minister Modi responded with similar sentiments. China objected, as expected, and elicited an appropriate reply from India's Ministry of External Affairs.

These steps are in conformity with Xi Jinping apparently not wanting to meet Prime Minister Modi or visit India. He skipped the G-20 Summit and Shanghai Cooperation Organization (SCO) meetings. A senior CCP cadre had divulged a couple of months prior to the G-20 Summit that China had decided that Xi Jinping would not attend the G-20 Summit and calculated it would, therefore, be a failure. However, these decisions were blunders and, in reality, India scored a coup! Xi Jinping's absence ensured there would be no distractions. The G-20 communique was successfully drafted and unanimously approved and, importantly, India brought the Global South within the G-20s fold!

The situation on the border has not changed and both countries have between 60,000 to 70,000 troops deployed on the front lines. Accommodation has been built by the Chinese on the border to billet additional reinforcements. The Chinese continue to induct new advanced weaponry and new military units to the border. Border defence infrastructure continues to be built at a frenetic pace. China has plans to build 35 military or dual-use airports by 2035. China is also building major arterial railways and roads along the border in Tibet and connecting China's border provinces of Qinghai, Gansu and Sichuan to Tibet.

Xi Jinping signaled his attitude towards India on the opening day of the 20th Party Congress in October 2022, at the start of his third term as China's President, General Secretary of the Chinese Communist Party (CCP) and Chairman of the Central Military Commission (CMC). A video of the fateful Galwan clashes of July 2020 was screened on the opening day of the 20th Party Congress in the Great Hall of the People in Beijing for the over 2000 senior Chinese cadres comprising the past, present and future leadership of the CCP. Foreign affairs does not figure prominently at the Party Congresses and this was an undiluted message to those present of Xi Jinping's views on India. Since April 2020 when he authorised China's PLA to conduct a major military manoeuvre and intrude in Ladakh, Xi Jinping has sought to ignore India. He has not initiated any communication with the Indian leadership. In these past four years he has not had a conversation with Prime Minister Modi. The seniormost Chinese leader to communicate with Indian leaders has been Chinese Foreign Minister Wang Yi. This effort to isolate India could presage an attempt to downgrade communications with India to the level of the Chinese Premier, who has no authority on Foreign, Military or Border Affairs. In recent years China's main interlocutors with South Asian countries have been the Foreign Minister or the head of the CCP CC International Liaison Department or, at a higher level, the Prime Minister.

China's real attitude towards India is now clearer. The Chinese foreign ministry's remark on July 10 that "South Tibet is China's territory," and India's development activities in the area are "illegal and invalid" underscored its adamant attitude on border issues and its approach. The same day Chinese Foreign Minister Wang Yi, who is also China's Special Representative for border talks, congratulated Ajit Doval on his reappointment as National Security Advisor and Special Representative observing he is ready to "properly handle" issues related to the situation on the ground in border areas. Use of the phrase "properly handle" indicates that discussions would be in accordance with China's stated position on the border since April 2020.

China's attitude will undoubtedly colour its position on Pakistan and in border negotiations with India. China will also explore other avenues for applying pressure on India, especially in international financial organisations. India needs to factor this in while considering any proposals by Beijing to coordinate positions in international bodies or give China a free pass on issues like human rights, Tibet, Xinjiang etc. Beijing will additionally try to increasingly use and activate Indian businessmen and chambers of commerce to exert pressure on the Government to facilitate travel by Chinese personnel to India and imports from China. Such concessions by the Government would be at the cost of the public exchequer while further increasing the already galloping trade deficit and severely undermining the effort to 'make-in-India'. Indian businesses have other options, though more expensive, to acquire technical knowhow and machinery. India must not be taken in by Chinese propaganda or pressure, but must further tighten controls on imports from China. Indonesia, for example, has recently imposed 200 percent duties on all Chinese goods.

This was first published by the Centre for China Analysis and Strategy (CCAS) and Vivekananda International Foundation (VIF) in July 20, 2024.

55. Slowing Economy Has Prompted China's Conciliatory Posture Towards India

The Chinese leadership has stepped up efforts for unfettered access to the large, and as yet untapped, Indian market since last year. This has come amid the incremental decline in imports from China by the US and EU and growing tension between the US and China. While China has not altered its aggressive policy towards Japan, the Philippines and Taiwan, it has tactically adopted a more accommodative tone towards the US and India. The tensions have aggravated the Chinese leadership's concerns caused by its failure to arrest the steady decline of the Chinese economy.

In implicit acknowledgement that the economy was continuing to slide, Chinese President Xi Jinping finally approved a stimulus package. The Chinese Communist Party (CCP)'s Third Plenum held in July this year had indicated that some measures would be taken to help the economy. China's leadership and the official media have also been highlighting China's importance in the global supply chain and asserted it will encourage and facilitate investments by foreign financial entities and businesses. Earlier, to offset the sliding economy and drop in imports from China by the US and Europe, the CCP leadership authorised the over production of solar panels and steel for export in disregard of international trade norms.

For example, China's Economic Observer disclosed on August 17, 2024 that the price of lithium carbonate plummeted from above 120,000 yuan/ton, to below 70,000 yuan/ton. It said, "Since 2024, the price of lithium carbonate has been experiencing a 'Waterloo'." Stating that the main lithium carbonate contract LC2411 of the Guangzhou Futures Exchange has fallen by more than 40 percent in the past year, it mentioned that Lithium carbonate is a core raw material for new energy vehicles and energy storage. The newspaper added that in the past two years, due to the continuous relaxation of production capacity, the oversupply of lithium carbonate in China has continued to intensify. In August alone the price of lithium carbonate fell by more than 10 percent in just half a month. It said on August 15, the price of lithium carbonate LC2411 hit a new historical low, reaching 71,800 yuan/ton which is a new low in more than three years. Pointing out that the price of lithium carbonate has fallen sharply, it said many industry insiders remain pessimistic about the future market: the situation where lithium carbonate supply exceeds demand is difficult to alleviate, and the downward trend is expected to continue in the short term.

As China sought to explore ways to access the large Indian market, it's Ambassador and diplomatic missions in India commenced actively propagating that Indian industry needed Chinese equipment and technicians if the economy is to grow. In discussions Chinese interlocuters bluntly said that: India needs to ease restrictions on visas and travel by Chinese nationals, permit imports of Chinese goods, resume air flights, and allow the posting of journalists. That China has only the limited tactical interest of gaining access to India's market is evident from its actions on the border where there has been no let-up in military activity, indicating that there is no likelihood of China restoring the status quo of April 2020.

The Chinese leadership has also as yet taken no substantive steps to repair the relationship. In addition to continuing efforts to exert pressure on India in international forums and financial institutions, the PLA continues to build border defences and induct new weaponry and additional personnel along the LAC. This includes building a bridge at Pangong Tso opposite Chushul, and defences at Depsang, Demchok and Rudok. Leaders of the Tibet Autonomous Region (TAR) have also in the last few weeks been visiting the counties bordering India. In the last month TAR leaders, for example, visited: Tsada Dzong, Ngari (Ali), which borders India's Himachal Pradesh in the west, Uttarakhand in the south, and Ladakh to the northwest; the Border Defence Company and villages of Tashigang in Demchok village; Nedong Dzong (Ch: Naidong), Gonggar Dzong, (Tsona), Lhodrak (Ch: Lhozhag) Dzong and Nagarze Dzong (Ch: Langkazi) of Shannan. During their inspection they exhorted the troops on the borders to strengthen defences. They also explained the extent of China's borders to the residents and urged those residing in the 'Xiaokang' model border defence villages to put down roots in the county.

At the same time, the parlous state of China's economy and spreading dissatisfaction among the populace, which has the potential to spark widespread unrest, has been causing serious concern to the Chinese leadership. This is reflected in the rise in public security expenditure which in the past two years has again exceeded the national defence budget. The Governor of the People's Bank of China (PBoC) Pan Gongsheng announced the long awaited stimulus package on September 24. In a noticeable departure from past practice, this time the CCP Politburo, which should have met earlier to discuss the economy and approve the stimulus, most unusually met only on September 26 — two days after Pan Gongsheng's announcement. Since 2018, Politburo meetings to discuss the economy have usually been held in April, July and December. There was also no 'study' session where an expert briefed the Politburo members. The State Council too met after announcement of the stimulus package.

Pan Gongsheng unveiled a strong stimulus package aiming to take the economy closer to its growth target in 2024. The package included a raft of monetary stimulus, property market support and capital market strengthening measures to boost the country's 'high-quality economic development'. Key measures include accelerating investment projects of about 200 billion yuan, focussing on revitalising cities, and infrastructure. It proposed that the government will continue to issue ultra-long special treasury bonds and encourage local governments to make all efforts to use special bonds for project construction. To support the enhancement of domestic consumption, the upgrade of electrical appliances and automobile trade-in and purchase was strengthened. The government also promised to ensure strict regulation of business enforcement and stated that it would adopt "inclusive, prudent, and flexible" approaches. This aims to avoid unlawful practices such as arbitrary fines and excess inspections, making the environment friendlier for business. The measures promptly saw a rebound in car and home appliance sales. The stock market registered an immediate 10 percent rise with share prices of most registered companies going up.

Pan Gongsheng said, "The new policy, which is conducive to further reducing borrowers' mortgage interest expenses, is expected to benefit 50 million households, or a population of 150 million". This move is expected to reduce the total interest expenses for households by approximately 150 billion yuan per year on average, which will help boost consumption and investment. Earlier in May, the People's Bank of China (PBoC) issued three major new real estate policies, including reducing down payments to 15 percent. The down payment ratio for the first and second homes was lowered to no less than 15 percent and 25 percent respectively.

China's official Economic Observer, quoting Chinese analysts and observers however, suggested that the present stimulus is inadequate and that share prices will crash by early 2025. It said the interest rate of existing mortgage loans should be lowered again in one step. It pointed out that new home buyers in first-tier cities such as Beijing, Shanghai, Guangzhou and Shenzhen, especially those who bought homes between October 8, 2019 and May 14, 2022, did not enjoy the policy dividends and still stood at a high interest rate, becoming the "sandwich layer" of the policy. Most of these people are born in the 1980s and 1990s, who are starting families and raising children. They have become the backbone of society and the main consumer group. Taking Beijing as an example, although the loan market benchmark rate (LPR) has been lowered many times, the first mortgage rate for this group is still as high as 4.75 percent (five-year LPR + 55 basis points), while the latest first mortgage rate floor in Beijing is 3.4 percent (five-year LPR - 45 basis points). In other words, the interest rate spread between new and old mortgages has reached 1.35 percentage points.

Though Chinese officials expressed confidence in reaching the annual goal of around five percent growth, there have been a series of indicators of the difficulties confronting China's economy. On September 15, China's National Bureau of Statistics (NBS) published data which showed that China's industrial value-added, retail and real estate sector had further weakened and that China's economy continued to be sluggish in August. This prompted observers to ask whether the Chinese government will introduce bolder stimulus measures in the 4th quarter.

On September 27, 2024 the Chinese financial magazine Caixin Global disclosed that China's construction industry is reeling from a wave of defaults and financial turmoil as delayed payments and rising bad debts cascade through the sector. It said once fuelled by a booming real estate market, construction firms are now struggling with unpaid bills and shrinking liquidity. It identified

Xi'an Construction Engineering Group Co. Ltd., a state-owned construction company in Northwest China, as the latest victim of this crisis after defaulting on a 263-million-yuan (US$ 37 million) bond in August after a series of credit downgrades over the previous six months.

Chinese provincial authorities have also been struggling with reduced revenues following the central ban on land sales which accounted for nearly one-third of their revenues. Consequently, wages of provincial government employees have been slashed by at least 25 percent and bonuses withdrawn. Added to this, Caixin (September 27) citing government data revealed that more than half of the 31 provincial-level regions in China lagged behind their annual fiscal revenue growth targets in the first seven months of the year, sending worrying signs for the fiscal health of local governments. During this period, 16 provincial-level regions failed to keep up with their annual targets for general public budget revenue growth. Only six surpassed their targets, while data for the other nine regions were incomplete. The six who surpassed their targets were: Chongqing, Fujian, Liaoning, Hubei, Xinjiang and Shandong. Each surpassed the target by between 0-5 percent. Last year too, most provinces had failed to achieve their growth targets. The special report submitted to the National People's Congress (NPC) on September 10, also revealed that by the end of 2023, the government's debt exceeded 70 trillion RMB, or 56.1 percent of GDP.

The provincial governments independently took intermediate relief measures without waiting for the stimulus package. China's official Securities Daily (October 9) reported that Shaanxi, Jiangsu, Zhejiang, Shandong and other provinces had announced measures to support high-growth technology-based small and medium sized enterprises working in fields like biotechnology and artificial intelligence. Called "gazelle enterprises", they were offered financial aid, like subsidies for R&D, to promote their expansion. The Shaanxi Provincial Department of Science and Technology, for example, recognized 305 enterprises as 'gazelle' enterprises and 57 others as potential gazelle enterprises and announced an R&D subsidy of 300,000 yuan (US$ 42,129.51) for these enterprises.

The economic difficulties faced by the people and the real potential for discontent sparking protests saw the central authorities taking direct remedial measures. The *People's Daily* (September 25, 2024) announced that the State Council, the Ministry of Civil Affairs and the Ministry of Finance had jointly issued a "one-time living allowance to extremely poor people, orphans and other needy people on the occasion of the 75th anniversary of the founding of New China". It said the Ministry of Civil Affairs and the Ministry of Finance directed concerned departments to attach great importance to the issuance of this one-time living allowance and ensure that the one-time living allowance is issued to the needy before October 1, and to promptly convey the Party and government's care and concern for the needy. Reuters reported that China would issue Bonds which will "provide a monthly allowance of about 800 yuan ($114) per child to all households with two or more children, excluding the first child".

The slowing economic growth coupled with enforcement of the stringent anti-corruption laws, which also felled those not ideologically or politically aligned with Chinese President Xi Jinping, has resulted in a drop in public confidence. Quoting data supplied by the United Nations High Commissioner for Refugees, Nikkei Asia (October 2) said the number of Chinese citizens seeking political asylum overseas climbed to 120,000 in 2021, a more than twelvefold increase since the time of Xi Jinping's predecessor, Hu Jintao. The US border patrol separately registered 24,314 Chinese citizens entering the borders of southern California and Texas illegally in 2023, and the number climbed to 35,399 in the first seven months of 2024. These numbers represent a 15-24 times increase from a meagre 1,500 during the Hu Jintao era. The Voice of America (September 2) reported that UN data showed that since Xi Jinping came to power the number of Chinese applying for asylum in the UK citing political and social freedoms as the reason rose from 798 in 2012 to 2,384 in 2023. Nikkei Asia also added that according to an estimate from the Council on Foreign Relations, despite capital controls, the amount of private capital that has left China through legal and illegal means has risen significantly to a staggering $738 billion in the third quarter of 2022.

Other indicators suggest that notwithstanding a number of international companies like IBM and Apple shifting operations to other countries, China has continued to toughen social controls and surveillance. A Bloomberg report of September 12, said that the CCP is increasing its supervision of the country's 8,700 investment bankers and many securities firms require investment bankers to hand in their passports, apply for permission for all travel plans, and obtain approval for resignations. China's official media regularly reports the detention on charges of corruption of officials in banking and financial organisations.

With the economy in such poor shape China, which is an export-led economy, cannot afford to lose access to the world's largest untapped market, namely India. Persistent efforts were, therefore, initiated by the Chinese Ambassador and Chinese diplomatic missions in India and China's United Front to activate business and other pro-China lobbies in India. These efforts were reinforced by official and other Chinese interlocuters at Track 1.5 and Track 2 meetings. Chinese businesses including automobile companies, the majority of who receive subsidies between 60 and 93 percent, have also sought to penetrate the Indian market. Chinese-made cars like MG and BYD are now available in India and competing with Indian companies. Similarly Chinese-made consumer products like umbrellas, lamp shades, lighting and figurines, for example, occupy a large percentage of the Indian market because of their lower prices made possible by subsidies etc. Till the situation on the borders is completely resolved, it is essential for India to deal with trade and other issues cautiously.

While the meeting between Prime Minister Modi and Chinese President Xi Jinping is a sign of Beijing's maturity, it is equally an indication that China needs to keep its southwestern border relatively quiet at this time. China's posture and recent agreement on the border negotiations reached on the sidelines of BRICS must be viewed as tactical. They hold no promise that Beijing will not revive its territorial claims. Until China takes steps to rebuild trust and disengage, de-escalate and de-induct on the ground it will remain a threat. From present indications it seems unlikely that Xi Jinping will restore the status quo of April 2020. China's media too has been cautious in its comments regarding the agreement.

This was first published by the Centre for China Analysis and Strategy (CCAS) and Vivekananda International Foundation (VIF) in October 23, 2024.

56. Chinese Foreign Minister Highlights Main Features of China's Foreign Policy

The latest (May 16, 2023) issue of the Chinese Communist Party (CCP)'s leading theoretical fortnightly magazine 'Qiu Shi' (Seeking Truth) included a lengthy article by Chinese State Councillor and Foreign Minister Qin Gang. In it Qin Gang quite explicitly, but without naming, criticised the US and West and outlined China's global foreign policy agenda. Qin Gang is a close associate and protégé of Chinese President Xi Jinping and for years was in charge of managing Xi's foreign policy schedule. Just 57 years old, Qin Gang's rise has been rapid and he is well positioned to make it to the Politburo at the next Party Congress in 2027.

The over 4000-word article authored by Qin Gang, which contained at least five mentions of Xi, was titled *Provide new opportunities for the world with Chinese-style modernization*. Qin Gang has attempted to portray China as a benign economic power that has made major contributions to global progress. The article touched on topics of current interest and specially folded them within the policy initiatives associated with Xi. These include Chinese style modernisation, Global Development Initiative, Global Security Initiative and the Global Civilisation Initiative. China's official media propagates these global initiatives almost daily with articles by Chinese researchers exploring and explaining different aspects of a specific initiative. Qin Gang additionally folded 'common prosperity' and the Belt and Road Initiative, both also closely associated with Xi, into Chinese-style modernisation. Both these initiatives have had reduced mention in the official media over the past year. Qin Gang has credited Xi for all these initiatives by asserting that "Xi Jinping is the core of the Party Central Committee and the core of the whole party is at the helm to guide the navigation". This suggests that they will be important items in China's foreign policy agenda during Xi's third term.

Qin Gang called "Chinese-style modernization", China's most recent and prominent initiative to which references by Chinese leaders and in the official media noticeably increased over the past year, a major long-term achievement of the Party and people which came after 100 years of perseverance and "the birth of the Communist Party of China" and "did not fall from the sky, nor did it emerge from the ground". He clarified it was "under the leadership of the Party Central Committee with Xi Jinping at its core that the "accelerator button" has been pressed"! Describing Xi as "the chief architect and leader of Chinese-style modernisation", Qin Gang emphasised that Chinese-style modernization is essential for "the great rejuvenation of the Chinese nation". He attributed China's growth from a poor country to the world's second largest economy, largest trader in goods and manufacturer and with the largest foreign exchange reserves, to it.

Advancing China as an example for other countries, he sought to emphasise that the "Chinese-style modernization path that China has found through independent practice is deeply rooted in the excellent traditional Chinese culture ... showing a new picture different from the Western modernization model and creating a new form of human civilization". Stressing it was not a case of imposing another model of development, he also cautioned that "blindly copying foreign models will not only lead to the opposite direction but may even lead to disastrous consequences".

He sought to reinforce this argument by recalling that China had "always envisioned a world of great harmony". Asserting that food and clothing alone are not adequate, he asserted that in proposing the 'Global Civilisation Initiative', Xi had advocated the importance of 'civilisation inheritance' and respect for the diversity of world civilisations. Modernisation, he pointed out, does not mean the decline of civilisations, but would, in fact, promote the rebirth of traditional culture. Since the past few weeks, the Chinese Communist Party (CCP)'s official newspaper *People's Daily* has placed it in a prominent position on the front page and refers to it as "Xivilisation"!

Presenting the 'Global Development Initiative', the Chinese Foreign Minister stressed that China's development is not to seek hegemony and that in China's vocabulary "there is no such thing as a strong country must seek hegemony". At the same time, he said "the strength of Chinese diplomacy is not to be afraid of hegemony". He called the Initiative a people-centred philosophy that had lifted more than 400 million people into the middle-income group. He claimed that, "Every day, 320 million US dollars of Chinese direct investment goes to the world, and more than 3,000 foreign-funded enterprises settle in China every month. In the past 10 years, China's contribution to global growth exceeded the sum of the contributions of the G7 countries". He said this Initiative had been widely welcomed across the world. Alluding to efforts by the US and West to build "trusted" global supply chains to which China would not be central, he countered by saying that most people opposed "decoupling" with China and, instead, looked forward to partnering with it.

Wrapping 'common prosperity' and the 'Belt and Road Initiative' within the Global Development Initiative, Qin Gang said, "The common prosperity of people all over the world requires the common development of all countries". He pointed to "the joint construction of the 'Belt and Road' initiative and the global development initiative as public goods provided by China to the international community". He said in the past 10 years since the Belt and Road Initiative was put forward, "more than 3,000 cooperative projects have been formed, which have stimulated investment of nearly one trillion US dollars, and created 420,000 jobs for countries along the route". He urged countries to "uphold the correct direction of globalization and oppose the construction of walls and barriers, decoupling, unilateral sanctions, and extreme pressure... make every effort to maintain the stability and smooth operation of industrial and supply chains". Addressing the growing concerns around the world and especially of nations in China's debt, he assured that China will do its "best to help developing countries alleviate their debt burdens. This will enable international finance to break free from the nightmare of speculation, sanctions, and pressure, and return to serving the real economy and promoting modernization"

Discussing the 'Global Security Initiative', Qin Gang said it had been proposed by General Secretary Xi Jinping and pointed out the correct direction of common security and universal security. Stating that "Enemies should be resolved rather than knotted", he cited China's intervention that prompted Saudi Arabia and Iran to resume diplomatic relations as an example.

He referred also to the protracted crisis in Ukraine and China's efforts to promote talks for "decompressing" the crisis and "cooling down" the situation. He claimed "facts have proved that China's modernization is the growth of the force for peace and the growth of the force for justice".

Reflecting the importance of Taiwan's reunification with Mainland China to the CCP leadership, Qin Gang dealt with it in a separate sub-section captioned "more resolutely safeguard the international order". Qin Gang asserted that the UN charter is the cornerstone of the stability of the international order, but reiterated that China will "unswervingly promote the establishment of a new type of international relations". On Taiwan, he said that "Taiwan's return to China was an integral part of the post-World War II international order". He stated that "The "Taiwan independence" separatist forces and a small number of countries attempting to use "Taiwan independence" to undermine international rules and the stability of the Taiwan Strait are, in essence, trying to set aside the one-China principle, subvert the post-war order, and trample on China's sovereignty". Qin Gang declared "More than 1.4 billion Chinese people will never agree! Once China's land is recovered, it will never be lost again". Introducing a degree of apparent ambiguity, he announced "Once the international order has been established after the war, it will never be allowed to be subverted. Safeguarding national sovereignty and territorial integrity is justified. We will never be ambiguous about whoever wants to make a fuss about the one-China principle; whoever wants to make moves on China's sovereignty and security, we will never back down". Qin Gang does not clarify whether he refers to the existing international order or the one to be established in the future after Taiwan's reunification with Mainland China.

Equally direct was Qin Gang's assertion that "modernisation is the inalienable right of every country" and countries should not set up roadblocks and obstruct others from modernising. He announced that "China does not engage in competition between major powers" and opposes creating ideological confrontation, engaging in a "new cold war" and interfering in other countries' internal affairs.

Qin Gang's article clearly seeks to present China to the world as an alternative to the US and West. At the same time the article is critical of the US and West and their efforts to contain China. It affirms that China will not back down from contestation with the US and West, while also suggesting that Beijing wants to avoid confrontation. Qin Gang's article confirms the importance of all the initiatives mentioned indicating it is probable that they will be pushed during Xi's current term. It can be expected that they will increasingly figure in statements by Chinese diplomats and be advocated in official and media interactions. The inclusion of the Taiwan issue in the article is deliberate in the backdrop of rising US-China tension. The paragraph emphasises Beijing's resolve. It is an implicit warning to the US and underscores the importance of Taiwan for Xi and the Chinese leadership while hinting at some urgency.

This was first published by the Centre for China Analysis and Strategy (CCAS) and Vivekananda International Foundation (VIF) in May 20, 2023.

57. Chinese Reactions to US President Trump's Policies on Taiwan

Recent US pronouncements regarding Taiwan have annoyed Beijing and the US's plans to send its Ambassador to the UN, Ms. Kelly Craft, to Taiwan provoked a sharp response. Hers would have been the first trip at this level since 1968. Though Craft's visit, which was scheduled to start on January 13 was abruptly cancelled at the last minute, she did later have a virtual meeting with Taiwan President Tsai Ing-wen. The Chinese government is now closely watching whether Taiwan President Tsai Ing-wen or another Taiwanese politician is invited to attend President-elect Joe Biden's virtual inauguration on January 20.

Reacting earlier to US Secretary of State Pompeo's announcement of January 9, 2021 easing restrictions on contacts with Taiwan, a hard-hitting *Global Times* (January 10) editorial captioned "Pompeo may have started the count-down of Taiwan's final days," stated that "Pompeo once again is frantically digging holes and placing mines for Sino-US relations and the Taiwan issue. This is a criminal, structural sabotage to cross-strait peace and the bottom-line stability of Sino-US relations. The extent of its severe consequences is unpredictable." The editorial asserted that "Beijing needs to send a strong signal that the United States must stop before it is too late. It must let the United States and Taiwan's Democratic Progressive Party authorities know that if they dare to let Pompeo visit Taiwan before the end of his term, Beijing's response will be overwhelming." It warned: "The last few days of the current US administration may also be the last few days of the existence of the Taiwan Democratic Progressive Party."

Giving an indication of Beijing's anger, the Straits Times (January 15) quoted an unnamed Chinese Communist Party (CCP) official as cautioning that "US support for Taiwan to re-join the UN is our red line". Other CCP insiders, it said on January 11, had warned that if the US was to simultaneously establish diplomatic relations with Taiwan, Beijing would sever ties with Washington and China would be in a "state of war" with Taiwan.

A CCP official, who retired from a Chinese government reform think-tank and is critical of Chinese President Xi Jinping, offered a different perspective. Separately writing under the pseudonym Liang Jing in the Ziyou Yazhou Diantai (Radio Free Asia) on January 12, 2021, he described the easing of restrictions on Taiwan as Trump's "most positive legacy". Saying that "Trump's four years in power has irreversibly normalised US-Taiwan relations", he said the Biden administration might well revert to restoring some of the earlier restrictions, but will do so in a low-key manner as otherwise it would not be politically wise for them. Observing that some people feel normalising ties with Taiwan is dangerous, including for the world as it raises the risk of a US-China war, he said what would be absolutely unacceptable however is a policy of "appeasement" that runs contrary to the wishes of the majority of Taiwanese. He added that at one time he apprehended that Trump would use Taiwan as a bargaining chip to "make a big deal" with Xi Jinping.

Liang Jing said that many factors contribute to the freedom of a country and a small country like Taiwan could especially "end up with tragic results just like that currently of the Hong Kong people and the Tibetans and Uyghurs on the mainland". Adding a note of caution, he said that while the Taiwanese people are optimistic about defending their freedom notwithstanding the huge differences in the strengths of Mainland China and Taiwan – "particularly as the world economy is highly dependent on China's"— he said this asymmetry actually increases Xi Jinping's propensity to take risks.

At the same time, he assessed there had been a major shift in the entire international community's perception and attitude towards the CCP's regime due to the global COVID-19 pandemic. As a result of this change, the international community suddenly realised in 2020 that defending the freedom of Taiwan is in their own interest and their own freedom.

He explained that "two technical factors" not directly related to Trump's Taiwan policy have played a very positive role in the "historical development" of US-Taiwan relations. One technical factor is the Taiwan Semiconductor Manufacturing Co. Ltd. (TSMC)'s technological monopoly on high-end chips. Because of its key role in next-gen military and AI tech for the US and the free world, Taiwan's freedom will directly affect the balance of power between the 'democratic camp', or the West, and the CCP.

The second technical factor is the new vaccine technology against COVID-19, which allows the US and developed countries to proactively combat the epidemic and has turned China's current advantage into a disadvantage. The importance of this change will affect the future development of US-Taiwan relations. It, of course, also creates a valuable time window and room for tolerance for both sides. He argued that while Trump's Taiwan policy may not be a positive legacy and could have been the fuse causing the conflict to spin out of control, nevertheless strong leaders pursue the politics of great risk.

The retired CCP official expressed the view that Trump's Taiwan policy did not lead to catastrophic results, but was rather a positive legacy. At the same time, apparently hinting to the incoming US Administration to keep up the trend, he conceded that facing a complex world makes it difficult to take moral judgments and political choices especially for those unwilling to engage in "strongman politics".

This was first published by the Centre for China Analysis and Strategy (CCAS) and Vivekananda International Foundation (VIF) in January 18, 2021.

58. Views of Chinese Experts on Sino-US Relations

As China's economic situation becomes more difficult and its aggressive policies increase tensions in its neighbourhood, the Chinese leadership is concerned at the turn that its relations with the US are taking. This has generated renewed discussion on ways to try and mend the relationship, still acknowledged as the most significant of China's bilateral ties and one that has immensely facilitated China's rise. Chinese companies raise their valuation by listing on the New York stock exchange, enjoy a bilateral trade volume which in 2020 was US$ 615.2 billion and includes Chinese exports to the US valued at US$ 452.58 billion, and the US remains the prime source of hi-technology for China. The relationship is, however, fraught and its continuing deterioration is of considerable worry to China's leaders who apprehend that a further slide would at the least stall, if not reverse, China's 'rise'.

The Chinese leaderships concern has undoubtedly been accentuated with the plateauing of China's economic growth, rising prices, growing levels of unemployment, closure of many businesses, and the reports circulating since last month about pay cuts of officials in even the more prosperous provinces and cities like Jiangsu, Zhejiang, Guangdong, Fujian and Shanghai. The annual Central Economic Work Conference held in Beijing in December also pointed to the economic difficulties confronting China.

Of particular interest are the views expressed in the media and at two important conferences by senior influential Chinese officials and 'America experts' of the Chinese Communist Party (CCP). Interestingly, these views surfaced around the fortnight of the 'virtual' Summit between US President Biden and Chinese President Xi Jinping held in mid-November 2021. An interview given by Yuan Peng, acknowledged as one of China's Americas experts and President of the influential Chinese Institutes of Contemporary

International Relations (CICIR) directly subordinate to China's External Intelligence arm, the Ministry of State Security (MoSS), is especially of interest. It was published by a Chinese media just days prior to the Summit.

The *South China Morning Post* (December 23) drew attention to an article published by Yang Jiemian, former President of the Shanghai Institute of International Studies (SIIS) and younger brother of Politburo member and former Foreign Minister Yang Jiechi, in the Shanghai-based The Paper. The article hinted at the importance of the US to China while implying that the US remains powerful. In the article, Yang Jiemian said China's US strategy is "confrontational where it must be and collaborative when it can be" and suggested that China should make better use of the US factor in its burgeoning ties with Moscow while maintaining "a sense of crisis" about the limits of its own influence. Defending China's hawkish stance on the US, however, he cautioned about a possible deterioration in Beijing's ties with Europe in the coming months. Yang Jiemian cautioned too that, despite warming political and economic ties, China and Russia did not always see eye to eye, observing: "Of course there are problems. Even brothers will have their own problems, not to mention [Russia] is our neighbour." He added "It is clear that China and Russia are not exactly in the same position on specific foreign policy issues. But we need to bear in mind that those are a secondary aspect of Sino-Russian ties." While Yang Jiemian described Russia's turn towards the East, especially China, as "a qualitative change" in President Vladimir Putin's diplomacy, he said Beijing must remain on the alert and "We cannot afford to completely abandon the sense of crisis. [Communist Party] General Secretary Xi Jinping said we cannot make subversive mistakes on key issues. The same goes for Sino-Russian relations""

With reference to China's diplomatic strategy in Europe, he described the European Union as one of the four pillars of global affairs, along with China, Russia and the US, but warned that with Angela Merkel's departure "it would be unrealistic to expect Sino-German relations to remain the same." He pointed out that "Europe is an ally of the US and they share similar ideals and objectives. They have differences, but only up to a point." In a separate article published on the SIIS website in November, Yang Jiemian cautioned that Beijing should take into account Russia's vigilance towards China's expansion of its influence in Eurasia, and remain alert about Washington's attempts to split China and Russia and expand its Indo-Pacific strategy.

Significant too are the views expressed by China's longest serving Ambassador to the US, Cui Tiankai. Ideologically one of the more conservative 'Left' cadres, Cui Tiankai's term in Washington was extended by Chinese President Xi Jinping because of the good access he had built to the family and inner circle of US President Trump. Speaking at the Diaoyutai State Guesthouse in Beijing on December 21, to Chinese diplomats and academics at an annual seminar hosted by the China Institute of International Studies, a Beijing-based think-tank directly administered by China's Ministry of Foreign Affairs (MoFA), Cui Tiankai asserted that China must be very vigilant while dealing with the US.

Cui Tiankai said, "Every bit of the people's interest is hard-earned and we must not allow anyone to plunder it or make it suffer through our own carelessness, slackness and incompetence"" He added that tensions between the two powers continue to grow despite the first virtual summit in November between Chinese President Xi Jinping and US counterpart Joe Biden, during which they agreed to try to avoid conflict. He assessed that Sino-US relations were unlikely to improve in the near future. Cui Tiankai also said "The current stage of history in US-China relations will continue for quite some time, and the US will not willingly accept the rise of a power with a very different social system, ideology, cultural traditions and even ethnicity"" He pointedly mentioned that there had been "a very strong element of racism" in Washington's China policy. Cui Tiankai asserted "The US will inevitably try every possible means and spare no effort, even without a bottom line, to suppress, contain, divide and besiege China." His views appear to have sharpened since his article in July 2012 prior to his being appointed Ambassador to the US.

Speaking at the same event, Chinese Foreign Minister Wang Yi said China welcomed mutually beneficial cooperation and healthy competition with the US, but was not afraid of confrontation. Outlining China's diplomacy priorities for the next year, Wang Yi said China and the US should work together to improve their relations in 2022, which marks 50 years since former US president Richard Nixon's historic visit to Beijing that paved the way for normalising relations between China and the US in 1979.

A somewhat contrary viewpoint that seemed to have left the door open for compromise, was expressed by 73-year old Zhang Baijian, former deputy chief of the Party History Research Centre and the son of Zhang Wenjin, a former Chinese Vice Foreign Minister who took part in Premier Zhou Enlai's talks with Henry Kissinger during the latter's secret visit to China in 1971. Addressing a panel on Sino-US relations at an economic development forum in Sanya, Hainan, in December, Zhang Baijian stressed the need for China to balance 'opening up' and 'safeguarding national interests.' He said the US is capable of strongly overcoming all challenges and recommended that China should not bet against it. He said "The US's role as a global leader is declining but, from historical experience, the US is also a country with a strong capacity for self-regulation. So, it needs to be seen whether there will be an adjustment in the United States in the future." He added "It is important that we do not pin the hopes for our development on the inability of the United States to solve its own problems" Zhang Baijian pointed out that as the world's No. 2 economy, China's policy decisions could have a huge impact on economies big and small, as well as every element in global supply chains. He added that Beijing needed to make its goals, intentions and policies clearer when dealing with other nations.

About a fortnight prior to the Xi Jinping-Biden 'virtual' Summit, Yuan Peng, President of CICIR, gave a wide-ranging interview on Sino-US relations to Sina Finance. CICIR is among the more influential Chinese think-tanks and Yuan Peng has been noticed in the last two years occasionally briefing the Politburo. Sina Finance published the interview in Chinese on October 21.

In the interview Yuan Peng said "There is a deep-rooted tradition in the United States in dealing with international relations 'from a position of strength'. As a country that pursues realism, the United States has always pursued 'power is truth' since it became the world's number one power in the 20th century". He explained "there are two special reasons why the United States" has repeatedly emphasized 'starting from strength and status': "One is to emphasize that the United States is still the world's number one power". It is constantly emphasising 'starting from the status of power' to counter China's 'theory of the east is rising and the west is falling', and to prove that the world is still in the hands of the United States. "The second is to reflect the deep-seated worries of the United States about its own strength and status. Faced with domestic and foreign problems (and even worse domestic problems), the United States is less confident in its own strength than in the past. The phrase 'starting from strength and status' is said every day to cover up the anxiety in his heart, but to highlight the deep-seated worries about the problem of his own strength and status".

Stating that "China is looking at a general trend over a century or even a few hundred years, and it is not confined to a specific thing", Yuan Peng added that "the United States does not see the historical trend and does not respond to it through deep-level reforms; it still uses absolute strength to handle the relationship between major powers, which is going against the trend of history". He said, 'the 'September 11' incident in 2001 caused the United States to encounter a security crisis. The subprime mortgage crisis in 2008 caused the United States to encounter an economic crisis. Trump's victory in 2016 was regarded as a political crisis. It may also face a social crisis that has not been seen in decades". He asserted that on the other hand, China, "joined the World Trade Organization in 2001, it has been dedicated to development and adhered to the path of peaceful development, and its development is changing with each passing day. But what really worries the United States is not the extent of China's economic strength or GDP growth, but the rise of science and technology, the rise of the military, and the development of its own system which motivated the economic rise". He stressed that what particularly worries the US is that "China's rise is supported by the socialist system with Chinese characteristics and the leadership of the Communist Party of China, not the Western one. It turns out that some people in the United States predicted that China's continued rise must rely on the implementation of the Western system, and that economic freedom will eventually lead to 'Western-style democracy'. However, it is precisely through the improvement of its own system that China has achieved great development. This makes Americans completely unable to sit still, and even 'sleeping and eating'".

Yuan Peng said: "from a strategic point of view, China and the United States have undergone strategic changes simultaneously in the past 20 years. From 'Asia-Pacific rebalancing' to 'Indo-Pacific', the United States shifted its strategic focus to China's doorstep to deal with China, and implemented the so-called global strategic contraction and Asia-Pacific strategic offensive. As a result, the two powers namely, China and the United States, have 'head-on collision' and 'hand-to-hand contact' in the Asia-Pacific region for the first time in a century. Therefore, they often look at each other's every move in a strategically suspicious manner". He next assessed that China and the United States have lost the strategic foundation they relied on in the past. As two countries with completely different social systems, ideologies, civilizations, and stages of development, China and the United States used external factors as a solid strategic basis to support and maintain their relations. During the Cold War, he said, the US relied on the Soviet Union and after the end of the Cold War, it relied on economy and trade, and after the '9.11 incident' relied on anti-terrorism. Referring to the hurried withdrawal of the United States from Afghanistan, he assessed that was because, "It would rather lose its face and realize a strategic shift from counter-terrorism to better respond to China".

Observing that the two heads of state have spoken again and cooperation in climate change between the two sides has been steadily advancing, Yuan Peng said, "Sino-US relations have eased under tension. Ms. Meng Wanzhou returned to the motherland after a lapse of three years. It was achieved in this atmosphere. All this has at least produced positive and good results in the minds of the Chinese people and laid the foundation for promoting peace and stability in the relations between the two countries". However, he said, "we have also seen that the United States has created regional tensions through dangerous methods such as the formation of the US-UK-Australia Alliance (AUKUS) and has not loosened its containment and confrontation with China. The fundamental reason for the settlement of the Meng Wanzhou incident is that the Communist Party of China, the Chinese government, and the Chinese people have worked together and persisted throughout the struggle. It is the result of struggle and does not mean a major change in the United States' strategy towards China. If the Sino-US game is a protracted battle or strategic stalemate, then phased relaxation or tension will be a normal state. The current easing is only intermittent and partial".

Yuan Peng explained that "China's 'world view' is mainly manifested in three aspects. The first is the 'Hundred-Year Change Theory'. The big changes in the world and the 'great rejuvenation strategy' of the Chinese nation are like the horizontal and vertical coordinates, which determine the world situation and the overall stage of China. The second is the 'historical opportunity theory', that is, whether compared with itself or others China is still, and will be, in a period of strategic opportunity for a long time and whether there will be an even longer period of historical opportunity. The third is the 'development risk theory', which is that the more China is in a period of strategic opportunity, the more are the various risks". He underscored that "The current stage is precisely the stage with the highest risk coefficient". He added "Whether the Sino-US game is moving towards full confrontation or striving for peaceful coexistence will test our wisdom" and that for China, "the great rejuvenation of the Chinese nation is the overall situation, and the Sino-US relationship is a small situation". Yuan Peng said, in conclusion, that, "regarding the concerns of the outside world, China needs to maintain a calm mind. It must be good at repaying morality with virtue, and it must also be good at reporting grievances directly, and it must also dare to fight at critical moments. The rise of great powers in history is often achieved through war. We are determined and confident not to achieve the rise by war, but struggle is indispensable".

The appearance of these views in the public domain around the period of the 'virtual' Summit between the Chinese and US Presidents suggests that active discussions on Sino-US relations are underway in the CCP. Divergent views regarding Sino-US relations and Beijing's approach towards it have existed for some years within the CCP. These recent comments by senior Chinese communist cadres suggest they are aware that the US is still powerful and that China will have to prepare to confront the US over the long term. The tenor of their comments and insistence that China is focussed on its own development, however, hints that they favour reaching some compromise with the US in the near term to facilitate China's development. With Xi Jinping pursuing an assertive hard-line policy, however, a major issue will be to prevent any "loss of face". This will be very difficult at least till the 20th Party Congress.

This was first published by the Centre for China Analysis and Strategy (CCAS) and Vivekananda International Foundation (VIF) in January 2, 2022.

59. Chinese Assessments of The US and West and Sanctions on Russia

After the February 4 summit between Chinese President Xi Jinping and Russian President Vladimir Putin in Beijing on the side-lines of the Beijing Winter Olympics, where Putin briefed Xi Jinping — or certainly gave him at least a fair insight into his plans for Ukraine — China has been unwavering in its support to Russia. This despite the US repeatedly urging China, including as recently as March 5,2022, to join the US and West in their sanctions against Russia's invasion of Ukraine. The Chinese official media, which doesn't use terms like 'invasion' to describe Russian action in Ukraine, and has strongly supported Russia, however, it appears to have modulated its reporting on developments concerning Ukraine to some extent since around February 27-28. This will be to avoid attracting the adverse notice of the West and potentially sanctions against Chinese companies and entities trading, or doing business, with Russia.

The Chinese leadership's views — and certainly those of Xi Jinping and his close confidants — are reflected in assessments in the Chinese media including those posted on China's social media. A commentary published immediately after the visit highlighted that the joint statement can "be called a joint declaration against hegemony". China's social media is awash with posts criticising Ukraine, abusing and making offensive remarks about Ukrainians, and disparaging the West. Many project the xenophobia among the Chinese heightened by the nationwide national security campaigns promoted by Xi Jinping. The support for Russia is echoed in assessments of the impact of the West's sanctions on Russia.

On March 1, the popular Chinese portal *guancha* (Observer) published an analysis of the war in Ukraine by Professor Wen Yang of Fudan University and the Chunqiu Institute. He argued that 'in order to understand current tensions in the world, one should look no further than Afghanistan in Central Asia, Ukraine in Eastern Europe, and Taiwan in East Asia'. Citing Huntington's *Clash of Civilisations*, Wen Yang said though the three appeared different, each is actually at the crossroads of Western civilization's sphere of influence and other major civilizations. Stating that the 'war in Ukraine was unavoidable because its identity belongs to Russian Orthodox "civilization", whereas Western "civilization" dared to "provoke and dismember their civilization through economic and political annexation', Wen Yang suggested that a war over Taiwan between China and the US-led West is similarly inevitable. He attributed Western dominance over the international media as a major factor on 'par with a nuclear weapon'.

Professor Zhang Wenmu, a well-known political scientist, naval strategist and leftist scholar who is a Professor at Beijing's elite Beihang University's Center for Strategic Studies and Executive Director of the World Socialism Research Center of the Chinese Academy of Social Sciences (CASS), published a commentary on Ukraine on the PLA-maintained Kunlun Online on March 7, 2022. It was titled, *Why has Ukraine become Jewified, and why has Israel put up with it?* "It's because Wall Street wanted to plant a quasi-Israel in this problematic European region". Zhang Wenmu explained, briefly, that "the reason behind Ukraine's Nazification" was "designed to sow the seeds of a world war in Europe. In the previous one, The Jews did not anticipate Hitler, whom they had helped to power, to turn on them. However, Jews as a people, as well as the great bulk of humanity, are merely tools for Wall Street's profits"."

Chinese Foreign Minister Wang Yi too, in his press interview (March 7, 2022) on the side-lines of China's ongoing annual National People's Congress session, while responding to questions on Ukraine was careful to stress China's ironclad relationship with Russia. He said that "In order to maintain their hegemonic status, some major powers regained the Cold War mentality and created factional confrontations, which further aggravated the turmoil and division, and made the already troubled world even worse". Earlier, on March 6, the *People's Daily* quoted him saying "China believes that to resolve the Ukrainian crisis, it is still necessary to act in accordance with the purposes and principles of the UN Charter. The first is to respect and protect the sovereignty and territorial integrity of all countries, and the second is to insist on peaceful settlement of disputes through dialogue". The statement inherently had Beijing's support for Moscow.

On March 1, 2022, Ma Xue, Associate Researcher at the China Institutes of Contemporary International Relations (CICIR), published an assessment of the impact that Western sanctions will have on Russia. The CICIR is an influential think-tank of China's foreign intelligence establishment, the Ministry of State Security (MoSS). Its President occasionally briefs the Chinese Politburo. Bloomberg News claimed (March 1) that Ma Xue assessed that the sanctions levelled against Russia will ultimately cause more damage to the US and its allies. He said that Russia has largely adapted to dealing with punitive financial measures since 2014, when it was penalized for seizing Crimea. Ma Xue, concluded that the US and European allies will wind up suffering for supporting Ukraine. "If the Ukraine refugee crisis is not properly handled, this will be conducive for Russia to sow hatred and sabotage NATO. The fierce debate on refugee problems inside Europe could also damage its unity at crucial moments."

Two senior researchers of the Institute of World Economics and Politics of the Chinese Academy of Social Sciences (CASS), China's largest government think-tank, separately published a report entitled 'An assessment of the impact of financial sanctions on Russia'. Released on March 1, it was published by Regional Frontier Watch, a think-tank of China's Caijing financial magazine. It noted that since the outbreak of the Russian-Ukrainian conflict on February 24, the number of sanctions imposed by the United States and its allies against Russia have increased but the magnitude of their impact is yet to be assessed. It observed that between 2014 and 2021, the US has always imposed financial sanctions and export control lists against Russia and that the targets have invariably been the three major industries of finance, energy and defence.

The main points in this article by Xu Qiyuan, Researcher and Deputy Director of the Institute of World Economics and Politics, Chinese Academy of Social Sciences (CASS) and Hou Lei, Associate Researcher of the Institute of World Economics and Politics, Chinese Academy of Social Sciences are, very briefly:

1. European and American financial sanctions against Russia are constrained by the following three points: With trillions of dollars in assets owned by foreign capital in Russia, Russia is a commodity "superpower", and the global supply chain is already very tight.
2. The substantial impact of financial sanctions on Russia's energy exports has begun to emerge. Russia can still bear the price difference between Russia's crude oil exports and the international market.
3. Russia's fiscal situation faces four major challenges: the possible reduction of energy exports, the decline of the sovereign credit rating, the loss of liquidity of foreign reserves, the war itself and its impact on the domestic macro economy.
4. The sanctions on foreign exchange reserves will have the biggest impact, which will affect the stability of the Russian foreign exchange market, inflation and other macroeconomic order, and may even affect the domestic public opinion environment.
5. Russia has taken three measures to deal with the pressure on the foreign exchange market, but these measures also show that the liquidity of its foreign exchange reserves may already be under greater pressure.
6. For Russia, the progress of the current war itself is still the main aspect of the contradiction, and the progress of the war is of great significance to the stability of Russia's economy and finance.

The CASS researchers noted that the US has included more than 120 entities (including Belarusian entities with close ties to the Russian defense and financial industries) in its "most stringent financial sanctions list", as well as individuals and a ban on debt and equity transactions in 13 Russian state-owned and large private financial institutions. It said the scope of the sanctions had widened with the West joining. It identified the decision to ban Russian banks from SWIFT as a serious measure, but pointed out that not all 300 of Russian banks had been affected and it "does not target Russia's oil and gas industry". It claimed that restrictions on the Russian central bank's use of its international reserve position are also vague.

The report described Russia as an all-round commodity "superpower" and highlighted its reserves of energy, minerals and grain, which make it a major factor in the global supply chain. The assessment said that the progress of the current war is Russia's main concern and of great significance to Russia's economic and financial stability. It concluded that while Russia will be able to resist the sanctions in the near to medium term, if the war drags on for a long-time then the global energy supply situation will improve and will affect the fiscal balance of payments. This will make financing national debt financing difficult. Finally, after a period of time, the constraints of financial sanctions imposed by Western countries will be significantly reduced.

While these assessments are not conclusive, they do emphasise the importance of Russia ending conflict soon. A prolonged conflict will make it increasingly difficult for the Chinese communist leadership to maintain its support for Russian President Putin while avoiding Western sanctions. They also reflect China's view that there is room for peace negotiations which, it hopes, could see the sanctions against Russia being eased.

This was first published by the Centre for China Analysis and Strategy (CCAS) and Vivekananda International Foundation (VIF) in March 9, 2022.

60. Assessment of US Secretary of State Blinken's Two-Day Visit to China

The Western media, in sharp contrast to China's tightly controlled official media, seems to have gushed at the apparent success of US Secretary of State Anthony Blinken's visit to China on June 18-19. China's official media, in contrast, afforded low-key coverage to the visit, which they pointed out had been sought by the US. Successive articles in China's official media have cautioned that the US was advertising a so-called desire to improve ties when in reality it wanted to contain China. The special, warm welcome accorded to Indian Prime Minister Modi and the speeches during his recent visit to the US will have reinforced Chinese suspicions. A closer look at the official accounts of Blinken's meetings in China reveal the differences in the content and tone of the respective statements issued after the meetings, suggesting that the outcome of this and similar future contacts are likely to be at variance with popular expectations.

The tone for Blinken's visit was set with his reception at the airport by a mid-level Foreign Ministry official. Just two days earlier signalling an attempt to bypass the government and establish direct links with US hi-tech, Chinese President Xi Jinping and Bill Gates discussed cooperation in AI in a televised meeting. During his two-day halt in Beijing, Blinken had a five and a half hour meeting on June 18 with Chinese State Councilor and Foreign Minister Qin Gang at the Diaoyutai State Guest House. This was followed by a 35-minute meeting with Wang Yi, the senior most Chinese diplomat who is currently a Politburo member and Director of the Central Committee Foreign Affairs Office. The Chinese official statement issued after the meeting with Blinken showed that during the meeting Wang Yi sternly enunciated the issues of concern to China. Finally, giving barely 45 minutes notice — reminiscent of the style of the late Chairman Mao's style of functioning — Blinken was informed that he would be received by Chinese President Xi Jinping. Official statements released by both sides after Blinken's meeting with Xi Jinping indicated that Xi Jinping appeared satisfied with the visit describing them as "substantive" and "constructive".

While Xi Jinping has met all earlier visiting US Secretaries of State since Henry Kissinger, like Pompeo and John Kerry, given that US-China relations are currently at an all-time low, his meeting with Blinken undoubtedly sent out a couple of messages. These were tailored equally for the foreign as well as domestic audiences. To the foreign audience the message Xi Jinping sought to convey was that it was the US that had damaged the bilateral relationship and was now trying to contain China's growth with its sanctions on hi-tech sales and exports and attempts to create an alternative "trusted" secure supply chain. By raising issues like that of Taiwan, the US was attempting to pressurise it and place obstacles in the improvement of relations.

Chinese Foreign Minister Qin Gang in his meeting with Blinken pointed out that "the Taiwan question is at the core of China's core interests, it is the most significant issue in China-US relations, and it is also the most prominent risk". Qin Gang put forward specific demands on issues concerning China's core interests and major concerns, including the Taiwan question. Qin Gang pointed out that the Taiwan question is at the core of China's core interests, it is the most significant issue in China-US relations, and it is also the most prominent risk. He urged the US to adhere to the various agreements and truly implement its commitment not to support "Taiwan independence'. The two agreed to effectively manage differences, and promote dialogue, communication, and cooperation. They agreed to maintain high-level exchanges and Qin Gang accepted Blinken's invitation to visit the United States.

Wang Yi, presently the senior most Chinese diplomat, was more direct in his discussions with Blinken. Stating that the priority is to stabilize China-US relations, he emphasized that the "root cause of the current downturn in China-US relations lies in the US side's erroneous understanding of China, which has resulted in misguided policies toward China". He said the two countries need to "work together to find the right way for China and the US to coexist in the New Era" — a phrase that many Chinese have interpreted as China placing itself on par with the US. Listing China's demands, Wang Yi insisted that the US "stop hyping up the 'China Threat Theory', lift its illegal unilateral sanctions against China, abandon the suppression of China's technological development, and refrain from interfering in China's internal affairs at will". Wang Yi also gave Blinken a detailed analysis of the Taiwan question. He emphasised that "safeguarding national unity is always the core of China's core interests, and it is related to the destiny of all Chinese people and the unwavering historical mission of the Communist Party of China". Laying down a clear Red Line, he asserted that "On this issue China has no room for any compromise or concession". He called on the US to "truly adhere to the One-China principle".

The message to the domestic audience in China was similarly clear. There has been criticism inside China since the 19th Party Congress in 2017 of Xi Jinping's handling of the policy towards the US. In recent months and accompanied by official admissions of high graduate unemployment, rising unemployment in the rural and other sectors, and continuous reports of closure of businesses of Chinese entrepreneurs, China's official media has published articles pointing to the need for improvement in China-US bilateral ties. The latter are crucial for the revival of China's export-dependent economy and the country's economic development. China's exports to the US dropped by 17 percent last year and are likely to decline further this year. By meeting Blinken, Xi Jinping indicated that he favoured an improvement in relations thereby addressing domestic criticism that he was to blame for the deterioration in ties. At the same time, he conveyed to the more 'nationalist hard-line' elements that he will not yield ground and make no concessions. This he did by reiterating the clear 'Red Line' on the Taiwan issue drawn by Wang Yi. This message was underscored by China's blunt refusal to establish a crisis hot line between the two militaries. China's controlled official media has especially since the past couple years been consistently blaming the US for the deterioration in bilateral ties and raising tensions in the region by its actions.

Within a day of Blinken's departure, the authoritative *Xinhua* news agency published (June 21) a report titled US needs to honor commitments with actions to improve ties with China to avert the downward spiral of their relationship and bring it back on the track of stable development'. This was republished by China's official English-language *Beijing Review*. It seemed to strike a somewhat conciliatory tone and quoted Blinken's remarks that "the United States stands by the commitments made by President Joe Biden, namely that the United States does not seek a new Cold War, it does not seek to change China's system, its alliances are not directed at China, it does not support "Taiwan independence", and it does not seek conflict with China". The *Beijing Review* assured: "China respects US interests and does not seek to challenge or displace the United States". Restating China's concerns though, it added in the same vein that "the United States needs to respect China and must not hurt China's legitimate rights and interests. The US should stop playing up the so-called 'China threat'," lift illegal unilateral sanctions against China, stop suppressing China's scientific and technological advances, and stop interfering in China's internal affairs". In an apparent attempt to keep the dialogue going, the Chinese Foreign Ministry deleted (June 22) from the official transcript its spokesperson's sharp riposte to US President Biden calling Xi Jinping a "dictator".

Though the Chinese media, including the *People's Daily, Guangming Daily* and the state-owned China Central Television gave low-key coverage to the visit, it was anticipatedly closely watched by the Chinese. A number of comments were posted on China's social media platforms. There were many posts that expressed doubts about the outcome and an almost equal number that were more optimistic. For example, Hu Zhanhao, a well-known nationalist Chinese 'influencer' who also serves on the Hubei Provincial Committee of the Chinese People's Political Consultative Conference, observed that the meeting between the "Chinese head of state and Blinken is a pleasant surprise!" Saying that the meeting would not have occurred unless the US made significant political commitments, he questioned the US's intentions and asked whether "the US will not truly turn away from evil and pursue a better path?"

Chinese experts also commented on the visit: Yan Xuetong, Director of the Institute of International Relations, Tsinghua University, said (June 20): "As long as the US maintains its 'small yard, high fence' policy, the relationship between China and the US will essentially be characterised by 'more conflict than cooperation'. Zhu Feng, Director of the School of International Studies, Nanjing University said (June 20): "Based on the official statements made by both sides, I think Blinken's visit has been, generally speaking, very positive ... [However,] it is unrealistic to expect any substantial improvement in Sino-US relations in the short term." Wu Xinbo, Director of the Institute of International Studies and Director of the Center for American Studies, Fudan University: "Blinken's visit to China has been positive, but no breakthroughs were achieved." Ms. Shao Yuqun, Director of the Institute for Taiwan, Hong Kong and Macao Studies and researcher at the Centre for American Studies, Shanghai Institutes for International Studies (SIIS) said: "While the outcomes of Blinken's visit to China exceeded expectations, leading to temporary bilateral tension easing, US strategic goals, policies, and approach to China are still characterized by a zero-sum mentality. This mindset is expected to continue causing various disturbances in China-US relations." Zhang Zhixin, Associate Researcher, Institute of American Studies, China Institutes of Contemporary International Relations (CICIR), said (June 19): "This visit may go some way to reducing tensions between both countries. However, as long as the hostility between them does not subside, the situation will remain the same, with good talks across the table, but confrontation when away from it."

Blinken's visit is transparently an attempt to reduce tensions, but without offering any substantive proposals. It might have been intended to assuage US business, but by itself it will not alleviate the deep suspicions of the Chinese leadership. While Xi Jinping's meeting with Blinken is being interpreted as a positive sign, it has not been accompanied by any move by the Chinese to ease the strain in the relationship. On the contrary, China has yielded no ground, offered no concessions, reasserted its national ambitions, and placed the entire blame for the deterioration in relations on the US. Beijing has additionally indicated that the US should treat it on an equal footing. Chinese leaders, including Xi Jinping, are convinced that the US is intent on containing China and bringing about the downfall of the Chinese Communist Party (CCP) and this will complicate relations. The special welcome accorded to India's Prime Minister Modi and the major bilateral agreements signed during his recent visit to the US will reinforce Chinese suspicions.

This was first published by the Centre for China Analysis and Strategy (CCAS) and Vivekananda International Foundation (VIF) in June 23, 2023.

61. China-US: Limited Rapprochement Afoot?

Chinese Foreign Minister Wang Yi arrived in Washington on a two-day (October 26-28, 2023) visit after a telling interval of five years. Official readouts of the visit indicate some progress during Wang Yi's visit. Of importance were the disclosures that consultations on maritime affairs and arms control would resume and Chinese President Xi Jinping would visit San Francisco this November for the APEC Summit — this will be the second meeting between the two since US President Biden assumed office.

In the interim, China's leadership and official media has maintained a steady rhetoric critical of the US. Beijing has persisted with aggressive actions against India, the Philippines, Japan and Taiwan and Chinese President Xi Jinping continues to confidently push his global agenda offering the world an alternative model with his Global Security Initiative, Global Development Initiative and Global Civilisation Initiative. Speaking on October 30, at the ongoing 10th Beijing Xiangshan Forum, the Vice Chairman of China's Central Military Commission General Zhang Youxia again stressed that "China will never tolerate and will be relentless against anyone who dares to split Taiwan from China in any way".

That China decided to send Wang Yi, who as member of the Politburo and Director of the CCP's Central Foreign Affairs Commission is the senior most diplomat and foreign policy advisor to Chinese President Xi Jinping, to Washington for talks and to discuss Chinese President Xi Jinping's meeting with US President Biden on the side-lines of the Asia Pacific Economic Cooperation (APEC) Summit in San Francisco next month is significant. It points to the US and China both deciding to arrest the deterioration in their relations beginning with a meeting between US President Biden and Chinese President Xi Jinping at the APEC Summit. In view of the capital intensive policy initiatives taken by China in the past five years to become an advanced technology power, counter the US and West's efforts at 'reshoring', and the growing US military presence in the region, it is unclear as yet whether and what concessions either side made.

US-China relations slid downhill considerably since Chinese President Xi Jinping, quite unlike his predecessors or the usual world leaders, openly challenged Washington's global leadership role at the 19th Party Congress in November 2017. It predictably triggered a severe and sustained US reaction beginning February 2018. While the US has consistently insisted that China is its biggest concern and economic competitor, it continues to target China's hi-technology sector in a bid to effectively diminish its ambitions to become a leading world technology power by 2025. Days prior to Wang Yi's arrival in Washington, US President Biden announced further restrictions on hi-tech exports and sales to China. The objective has been to degrade China's ability to pose a military challenge to the US. Measures to steer US and Western companies away from doing business with China, euphemistically called 'de-risking', or 'de-risking', were simultaneously initiated. While Europe has been reluctant to disengage from China because of its deleterious effects on Europe's economy, some US companies have begun to move away. According to official Chinese data, US and EU imports from China have dropped substantially in the last two years. This has made recovery of China's export-led economy more difficult.

The US has meanwhile steadily deployed its forces in the Indo-Pacific region around China. Washington has simultaneously been consolidating and strengthening its relationships with countries in the region with a focus on military cooperation. It announced arms sales and military training programmes for Taiwan and President Biden on four occasions affirmed US support to Taiwan in case of Chinese aggression and, though the US State Department issued clarifications each time, this has added to the US policy of strategic ambiguity. The US and China have both released reports alleging assertive and, at times, risky, actions by the other. Tension is high in the region and the South China Sea with China's tense relations and manoeuvres against Taiwan keeping alive the real possibility of clashes.

Wang Yi's visit comes amid China's efforts to assess US strength and capability to interfere in the Indo-Pacific while engaged in the war in Ukraine and effort to contain Israel's war on Hamas from spreading to the larger Middle East region. A backdrop to Chinese calculations is its firm friendship with Russia and the strengthening ties with Iran. Inside China there is widespread lack of trust, including among officials, in the pronouncements of the US and West that they do not desire to 'contain' China. The statements by General Zhang Youxia and other leaders also address this audience.

Notwithstanding the negative official Chinese media rhetoric though, there have been reports of meetings between US and Chinese officials in third countries to try and ease tensions. Meetings have been held in Italy, Switzerland, Indonesia and Malta. The US made the first substantive move with US Secretary of State Blinken visiting China in June this year, his first since assuming office in January 2021. This was followed by a series of visits by senior members of the US Administration. The first was by US Treasury Secretary Janet Yellen early this July. US Special Presidential Envoy for Climate John Kerry visited later in July and was followed by US Commerce Secretary Gina Raimondo in August. During this period only one Chinese official, namely Chinese Commerce Vice Minister Wang Wentao, visited the US to attend an APEC meeting in May 2023.

In September, the Chinese Foreign Ministry Spokesperson said that Chinese Premier Li Qiang had a brief exchange with US President Biden at the G-20 Summit in New Delhi, when Li Qiang emphasized to Biden that China's development is an opportunity rather than a challenge to the United States, and China and the United States should strengthen exchanges. They reported President Biden as replying that "the United States hopes that China's economy will continue to grow and will not prevent China's economic development".

Negative rhetoric in China's official media has also recently yielded to more conciliatory coverage. Noticeable were the *People's Daily* (October 27, 2023) reporting that Xi Jinping and Biden had sent congratulatory messages to the annual Gala Dinner of the National Committee on US-China Relations. Widely covered by the official Chinese media was Xi Jinping's meeting with California Governor Gavin Newsom in Beijing on October 26, 2023. Newsom also met the Beijing Party Secretary. Earlier on October 9, Xi Jinping received a bipartisan group of US senators led by Senate

Majority Leader Chuck Schumer at the Great Hall of the People in Beijing. Schumer had earlier met: Politburo Standing Committee member and head of the National People's Congress (NPC) Zhao Leji; Politburo member and Foreign Minister Wang Yi; and Shanghai Party Secretary Chen Jining. *Xinhua* reported that Xi Jinping had told Schumer he wants to work together and avoid conflict. He said, "China maintains that the common interests of the two countries far outweigh their differences" and that "The 'Thucydides Trap' is not inevitable." According to Xinhua, Schumer responded that "The US side does not seek a conflict with China, nor does it seek to decouple" and "The United States is willing to enhance dialogue and communication with China in an open and candid manner...and stabilize and strengthen US-China relations."

The readouts issued by the Chinese and US also indicated progress during Wang Yi's current visit to Washington. Important was the disclosure that Chinese President Xi Jinping would visit San Francisco this November for the APEC Summit. This will be the second meeting between the two since Biden assumed office.

Official and media reports confirmed that Wang Yi had two rounds of closed-door meetings with US Secretary of State Blinken on October 26 and 27 before meeting US National Security Advisor Jake Sullivan and US President Biden on October 27. Wang Yi struck a positive note prior to meeting Blinken, and said China and the United States need to have dialogue. "Not only should we resume dialogue, the dialogue should be in-depth and comprehensive so that with dialogue we can increase mutual understanding, reduce misunderstanding and misjudgement, constantly seek to expand common ground and pursue cooperation that will benefit both sides so that we can stabilize China-US relations and return it to the track of healthy, stable, and sustainable development".

The US State Department spokesperson said the two discussed a range of bilateral, regional, and global issues, including addressing areas of difference as well as exploring areas of cooperation. Blinken, it said, reiterated that the United States will continue to stand up for our interests and values and those of our allies and partners. Blinken also expressed his condolences on the passing of former Premier Li Keqiang. Details of the issues discussed have not yet been revealed and it would be pertinent to see the areas of convergence and differences in the views of the US and China.

According to US media reports, Blinken told Chinese Foreign Minister Wang Yi that he wants to enlist Beijing's help in keeping the Israel-Hamas war from widening. The US State Department said that they discussed "a range of issues," including both "areas of difference" and "areas of cooperation." It again emphasized the need for "open lines of communication" with Beijing to "responsibly manage" tense ties. The White House reported that National Security Advisor Sullivan and Wang Yi had "candid, constructive, and substantive discussions on key issues in the US-China bilateral relationship, the Israel-Hamas conflict, Russia's war against Ukraine, and cross-Strait issues, among other topics". Sullivan discussed concerns over China's dangerous and unlawful actions in the South China Sea and raised the importance of peace and stability across the Taiwan Strait. Both sides reaffirmed their desire to maintain this strategic channel of communication and to pursue additional high-level diplomacy.

Reports of these meetings will be carefully scrutinised as they begin to emerge to assess whether compromises have been made. The US has been visibly and repeatedly pushing for contacts and dialogue, including a Summit level meeting. It has dropped confrontational words like 'containment', uses 'de-risking' instead of reshoring, and has striven to maintain ambiguity regarding Taiwan. Biden has on four occasions expressed US support to Taiwan in case of a Chinese military adventure but each time the US State Department has walked back on Biden's remarks.

Far from making any such gestures, China has stayed firm on its policy of becoming a major world power and dominating the Indo-Pacific region. It continues to follow an aggressive policy with continuing military build-up on the borders with India, the People's Liberation Army Navy (PLAN) damaging a Philippines vessel ferrying supplies to its personnel on Scarborough Reef, and almost daily intrusions of Taiwan's waters and Air Defence Identification Zone (ADIZ) by air and sea. At the same time, there are adequate indications of rising domestic dissatisfaction in China. Among the contributory factors is that people blame Xi Jinping for mishandling the relationship with US and accentuating economic hardship. As the window of opportunity for Xi Jinping to defuse tensions or divert the people's attention by attempting a military adventure shrinks, Wang Yi will try and assess US resolve and willingness to 'contain' China. The window for the US is shrinking too. As Washington pursues a policy of only economic competition with China, it risks allowing China to overtake it in global influence, economic and military power.

This was first published by the Centre for China Analysis and Strategy (CCAS) and Vivekananda International Foundation (VIF) in October 2023.

62. Initial Assessment of Chinese President Xi Jinping's Three Nation European Tour

Chinese President Xi Jinping, accompanied by his wife Peng Liyuan, Politburo Standing Committee (PBSC) member and Director of the CCP CC General Office Cai Qi and Politburo member and Foreign Minister Wang Yi, arrived in Paris on May 5,2024, on the first leg of his carefully crafted three-nation 5-day European tour. He was received at Orly airport by French Prime Minister Gabriel Attal. It was Xi's first trip to Europe in five years. The countries to be visited were carefully chosen with France, the most difficult, first on Xi's itinerary. Xi would have been encouraged by German Chancellor Scholz bending his knee in Beijing in April this year, and would have thought he could build on French President Macron's visit to Beijing in April 2023. The main aim of Xi's tour was to tempt EU and European countries with the financial benefits of partnering with China, weaken the EU, and further its decades old effort to drive a wedge between the EU and the US. The spokesperson of China's Ministry of Foreign Affairs called Xi Jinping's visits as "vitally important for China's relations with France, Serbia, Hungary and the EU at large'.

Nearly 4000 Tibetan and Uyghur activists from across Europe staged a protest in Paris. They unfurled a large banner across the expressway reading "Free Tibet — Xi your time is up!" French President Macron was aware of the Tibetans' plans. A small group of Tibetans also travelled to Budapest and staged a protest in May, outside the venue of the meeting between Hungarian Prime Minister Viktor Orban and Xi. The protestors clashed with some Chinese supporting the Chinese Communist Party (CCP) and the Hungarian police did not interfere.

Macron extended all courtesies to the Chinese President including taking Xi to his grandmother's home in the Hautes-Pyrénées to demonstrate reciprocated warmth and ensure a good atmosphere for the visit so that the considerable French business and economic interests are not jeopardised. A variation was that the formal reception and guard of honour were not held in the Versailles, but in the Elysee Palace where, just a week earlier, Macron had presented a former French Senator active in Tibetan affairs the Legion of Honour and met the head of the Central Tibetan Administration, or Sikyong, Penpa Tsering.

Macron's thinking has also changed since his visit to China last year. He now views Russia as an existential threat to Europe and has set up a 200-million Euro special fund to help Ukraine directly obtain weapons from the French defence industry. This was subsequently hiked by another 200 million Euros. In February this year France and Ukraine also signed a bilateral security agreement which provides for military support of up to three billion Euros. Macron's views now make the issue of Chinese military and dual-use assistance to Russia more important. His views are now more aligned with those of the US. French President Macron also took the precaution of showing that the EU and France are in close alignment and invited EU President Ursula von der Leyen to participate in the talks with Xi.

Timed to coincide with his arrival in Paris, Xi published a signed article in the French newspaper Le Figaro on May 6, 2024, where he sought to subtly flatter Macron by comparing his policy with that of the late French President Charles de Gaulle. He recalled that "six decades ago, General Charles de Gaulle, with a strategic vision based on the trend of the time, resolved to establish diplomatic relations with New China. It wasn't easy to make this independent decision at the height of the Cold War, but it has proven to be right and foresighted". Quoting Confucius that "History is our best teacher", Xi wrote that "China is ready to work with France in the spirit that guided the establishment of our diplomatic ties to forge a stronger comprehensive strategic partnership between our two countries and make new contributions to stronger cooperation of the global community".

The discussions had contentious issues on the agenda. These included: a French-backed anti-subsidy investigation into electric vehicles from China; complaints about Chinese overcapacity; and concerns over Beijing's indirect support of Russia's war in Ukraine.

Xi and Macron had 80 minutes of bilateral discussions. Xi said "As the world goes through transformation and turbulence not seen in a century, China and France should uphold independence and jointly prevent a "new Cold War" or "bloc confrontation" and "stay committed to the spirit that guided the establishment of their diplomatic ties, namely, independence, mutual understanding, long-term vision and mutual benefit, and enrich it with new features of the new era". He said they should "stick to taking a long view and work together for an equal and orderly multipolar world" and "and jointly oppose decoupling, cutting off supply chains." Xi asserted that "China is willing to maintain strategic communication with France, respect each other's core interests, and consolidate the strategic stability of bilateral relations, tap the vast potential of mutually beneficial cooperation and facilitate growth and balance in bilateral trade".

Holding out the prospect of commercial opportunities, he added "China is willing to import more quality products from France, push for more practical results from the "French farm to Chinese dining table" mechanism, and hope that France will export more high-tech and high value-added products to China". He mentioned the need to "deepen cooperation in traditional areas such as aerospace and aviation, strengthen cooperation in nuclear energy, innovation and finance, and expand cooperation in emerging areas such as green energy, smart manufacturing, biomedicine and artificial intelligence" as well as artificial intelligence governance and reform of the international financial system. These areas have become a subject of concern for Beijing since February, after the European Union imposed trade restrictions on three Chinese technology and electronics companies selling dual-use military goods. The EU has also used a new, French-backed anti-subsidy law to launch an investigation into electric-vehicle imports from China.

The *People's Daily* (May 7, 2024) quoted Macron as saying at the Elysee palace that, "The world now faces many pressing challenges, and the profound and rich France-China relationship is at a critical juncture" and "will play an important and positive role in addressing global challenges and opposing any logic of bloc confrontation". According to it, Macron said France hopes to export more agricultural products to China, will continue to open its market to China, will not adopt discriminatory policies against Chinese companies, and welcomes investment and cooperation by more Chinese companies, including high-tech firms. He said France is ready to step up cooperation with China in such areas as aerospace and aviation, and nuclear energy for civilian use, biodiversity protection, and AI, and jointly uphold multilateralism, the UN Charter and international law".

The China-France-EU trilateral meeting with Xi and Ursula von der Leyen on May 6, also at the Elysee Palace, lasted double the allotted time stretching over 100 minutes. Macron said "The future of our continent will clearly also depend on our ability to continue developing a balanced relationship with China". Xi, who throughout the two meetings read from his prepared script, brushed off concerns about Chinese goods overwhelming European markets. He told Macron and von der Leyen that China's production of renewables is helping the global energy transition and, according to China's foreign ministry, added, "There is no so-called problem of Chinese overcapacity". In a proforma response to Macron and von der Leyen's concern about Chinese military assistance to Russia, Xi said that China would closely monitor the export of dual-use goods. He stressed that "China is not at the origin of this crisis, nor is it a participant" adding that the crisis should not be used to tarnish China's image or start a new Cold War. Interestingly, in all the meetings Xi referred to the war in Ukraine as a "crisis".

After the meeting, EU President Ursula von der Leyen said she had pressed Xi on all the contentious points and urged him to rein in Chinese subsidies and manufacturing overcapacity and give European companies more access to the Chinese market. She said she was counting "on China to use all its influence on Russia to end Russia's war of aggression against Ukraine," and urged Beijing to stem the supply of dual-use goods helping Russia's military. She pointed out that "Given the existential nature of the threats stemming from this war for both Ukraine and Europe, this does affect the EU-China relations".

At a joint press briefing after the talks, where no questions were permitted, the two sides issued four joint statements on the situation in the Middle East, on AI and global governance, on biodiversity and oceans, and on agricultural exchanges and cooperation. Nearly 20 bilateral cooperation documents were signed in areas such as green development, aviation, agri-food, commerce and people-to-people exchanges.

On the evening of May 6, Macron and Madame Brigitte Macron hosted a welcoming banquet for Xi and Madame Peng Liyuan at Elysee Palace. Among the more than 120 guests invited to the state dinner were actress Gong Li – famous for her roles in films including Raise the Red Lantern and Farewell My Concubine – and her husband, the musician Jean-Michel Jarre, cinematic luminaries like Salma Hayek and nearly 60 corporate leaders including Louis Vuitton-Moet-Hennessey (LVMH) CEO Bernard Arnault, the owner of the French Cognac Hennessey, and his daughter Delphine Arnault, CEO of Christian Dior Couture. At the start of the dinner, Xi Jinping told the assembled French and Chinese guests that the two countries are "special friends", who have a "special relationship among world powers". Xi said "As important representatives of Eastern and Western civilisations, China and France have always appreciated and attracted each other. The ideas of Confucius profoundly influenced Voltaire and others, and provided inspiration for the French Enlightenment."

Macron presented Chinese President Xi Jinping two bottles of Cognac – a Hennessy XO and a prized Louis XIII by Remy Martin – along with rare volumes by Victor Hugo, the first French-Chinese dictionary and a sculpted glass vase from the town of Amboise. Xi Jinping presented French President Macron French-language books published in China as well as a painting.

The next day Xi arrived at Macron's grandmother's home in Tarbes, Hautes-Pyrenees, where he was welcomed by Macron and his wife, Brigitte Macron, at the airport. The Zhongguo Qingnian Bao (China Youth Daily; May 8) said the "two heads of state and their spouses sat by the window, overlooking the mountains, tasting local delicacies, discussing world affairs, and having strategic communication on some important issues in a relaxed and pleasant atmosphere". It said Xi asserted that "China will surely achieve the great rejuvenation of the Chinese nation".

Xi and his entourage arrived in the Serbian capital Belgrade on May 7,2024, which was also the anniversary of the bombing of the Chinese Embassy in Belgrade 25 years ago. This was Xi's second state visit to Serbia. Two Serbian Air Force fighter jets escorted Xi's plane after it entered Serbian airspace and he was greeted at the airport by Serbian President Aleksandar Vucic and his wife, Tamara Vucic. In a written statement upon arrival, Xi said "the two countries are bound by rock-solid political mutual trust, and have seen fruitful results in high quality Belt and Road cooperation" and that "our ironclad friendship has taken deeper roots in the heart of the two peoples". He added that "China and Serbia have rendered each other firm support on issues concerning their respective core interests and major concerns".

In a signed article in the Serbian newspaper Politika, published a day prior to his arrival, Xi wrote, "Whatever changes in the international landscape, China and Serbia remain true friends and good partners" and "Our ironclad friendship has withstood the test of blood and fire, and shines even brighter in the new era". Xi said, "We should deliver on the mid-term action plan for Belt and Road cooperation, and build more flagship projects. We should expand cooperation in technological innovation, advanced manufacturing, green energy, digital economy, artificial intelligence and other emerging areas". Stating that China and Serbia hold similar positions on many major international and regional issues, Xi said they "should step up coordination and cooperation in the United Nations and other international organizations, and advocate an equal and orderly multipolar world and a universally beneficial and inclusive economic globalization". Referring to the bombing of the Chinese Embassy in Belgrade 25 years ago in which three Chinese journalists were killed, Xi declared the Chinese people "will never allow such tragic history to repeat itself."

Xi met Serbian President Aleksandar Vucic on May 8, and later signed a joint statement on the "building of a China-Serbia community with a shared future in the new era", making Serbia the first European country to partner China in building such a community. The joint statement said the two countries had also decided to elevate the China-Serbia comprehensive strategic partnership. Serbia was the first Central and Eastern European country to become China's comprehensive strategic partner eight years ago. At the joint press conference that followed, Xi Jinping announced six measures to support the building of a China-Serbia community with a shared future. One of them was to invite a total of 300 Serbian youths to study in China in the next three years. He also announced that China will aid 50 young Serbian scientists in exchange programs with China for the next three years. Twenty eight documents were signed during the visit, including on economic, space and lunar and media cooperation.

China-Serbian relations have been very good and are poised to receive a boost after Xi's visit. The visit is an indication to Serbia, which is not a member of the EU, that partnering China would bring far more financial and other benefits more quickly. Two-way trade in 2023 surged to US$ 4.35 billion and in 2022, China became the largest source of direct investment for Serbia. Under the framework of the China-proposed Belt and Road Initiative are flagship projects such as the Smederevo Steelworks and the high-speed railway between Belgrade and Budapest, which has transported some 6.83 million passengers over the past two years.

In Budapest too, on May 8, Xi arrived to a warm welcome with two Hungarian Air Force aircraft escorting him from the time his aircraft entered Hungarian airspace. He was warmly welcomed at the airport by Hungarian Prime Minister Viktor Orban and his wife. In a written speech upon his arrival, Xi said "As a good friend and a comprehensive strategic partner", China rejoices over Hungary's achievements". He observed that Hungary was one of the first countries to recognize and establish diplomatic relations with the People's Republic of China in 1949. They elevated their relations in 2004 to "a friendly and cooperative partnership" and further to a "comprehensive strategic partnership" in 2017.

The *People's Daily* (May 8) reproduced the full text of Xi's signed article published in the Hungarian newspaper Magyar Nemzet where Xi said this was his second visit to Hungary and he had "forged a deep friendship" in meetings with Hungarian leaders. He said over 75 years, China and Hungary have developed a high degree of political mutual trust. Our bilateral relationship is at its best in history, and has embarked on a golden voyage". He added that the two had focussed "on high-quality Belt and Road cooperation" and today Hungary is China's top investment destination as well as its important trading partner in Central and Eastern Europe. He said the China Cultural Center in Budapest will soon be officially inaugurated and that Confucius Institutes and Confucius Classrooms are gaining popularity. Xi added, "as comprehensive strategic partners", China is ready to work with Hungary "to deepen and substantiate China's cooperation with Central and Eastern European countries and to ensure steady and sustained growth of China-Europe relations". He reiterated that "We should advocate an equal and orderly multipolar world and a universally beneficial and inclusive economic globalization, endeavour continuously to build a community with a shared future for mankind, and inject more positive energy into safeguarding world peace and promoting common development".

At the joint press conference on May 9,2024, Hungarian Prime Minister Viktor Orban announced that China and Hungary will expand cooperation in several areas, including in the nuclear power industry. Orban said, "China is one of the pillars of the new world order"." He added that Chinese investment in Hungary had burgeoned and by last year three-quarters of all foreign investment in Hungary was by China and it had provided jobs for tens of thousands of Hungarians. Orban also said Hungary would support China's peace plan for Ukraine. Speaking alongside Orban at the Budapest press conference, Xi said China will deepen economic, trade, investment, and financial cooperation with Hungary. Xi also said that "China supports Hungary in playing a bigger role in the EU and promoting greater progress in China-EU relations".

An article in the *People's Daily* (May 5) publicised the extent of Chinese investment in the Balkans and highlighted the Hungary-Serbia railway, a flagship project of the China-proposed Belt and Road Initiative (BRI). Stating that once fully operational, this railway will reduce the journey between their capitals to just three hours and enhance freight transport, promote trade, and invigorate the two economies, it claimed "the railway is among a range of Belt and Road projects that have delivered tangible benefits to Europe and beyond, and such achievements are not possible without visionary leaders who are keen to harvest shared benefits from win-win cooperation". It added that Hungary has been China's primary investment destination in Central and Eastern Europe for consecutive years and that China-France relations have long been at the forefront of China's relations with major Western countries and "the two serve as crucial stabilizing forces in the increasingly volatile China-Europe relations". It said there is ample evidence that "China and Europe are partners, not rivals; they offer opportunities to each other, not threats; their common interests far outweigh their divergence". Chinese investment in Hungary is exemplified also by the China-based Contemporary Amperex Technology building a US$ 7.8 billion electric-vehicle battery plant in Hungary and BYD similarly building a manufacturing plant in the Hungarian city of Szeged.

Xi's agenda in all three countries was primarily dominated by economic cooperation. Equally important, though, were strengthening ties with political elites and enhancing media collaboration. Beijing sees closer ties with the EU and European countries as important for its objective of weakening their ties with the US. It is also crucial for adoption of China's Global Civilisational Initiative, Global Development Initiative and Global Security Initiative, seen as vital for its agenda of fashioning a fairer,morefair and equitable world order.

The list of MoUs, Agreements etc signed during Xi's visit are appended.

This was first published by the Centre for China Analysis and Strategy (CCAS) and Vivekananda International Foundation (VIF) in May 13, 2024.

63. Brief Review of The Recent Xi-Putin Summit

The tension building on Ukraine's border, where approximately 130,000 Russian troops are poised for a possible military offensive and the US and West are arrayed against Russia, provided an ideal setting for the Russian and Chinese Presidents to display their close ties. It ensured that world attention would be focussed on their first meeting in person in slightly over two years. The Beijing Winter Olympics, which the US, UK, Australia and many European nations boycotted to protest the human rights violations of Uyghurs in the Xinjiang-Uyghur Autonomous Region thereby putting China under pressure, provided the perfect opportunity.

Russian President Vladimir Putin and Chinese President Xi Jinping, both nurtured within the apparatus of the respective communist parties, not only emphasised the close Sino-Russian economic and strategic ties but also introduced an ideological dimension.

Before he left for Beijing, Putin gave a written interview to Shen Haixiong, Director and Editor-in-Chief of China Central Radio and Television and Vice Minister in the Chinese Communist Party (CCP) Central Committee (CC)'s Propaganda Department. Shen Haixiong is an Alternate Member of the 19th CC of the CCP. The interview was publicised by the CCP's official mouthpiece *People's Daily* (February 4, 2022). While the interview focussed mainly on sports, Putin said that China ranks first among Russia's trading partners with preliminary figures showing that bilateral trade had reached a record high of $140 billion last year. He emphasised that "China is our strategic partner on the international stage. On most issues on the global agenda, we are aligned or very close" and that the two coordinate closely in major multilateral organizations such as the United Nations, BRICS, the Shanghai Cooperation Organization, G20, Asia-Pacific Economic Cooperation, and the East Asia Summit, which has "a stabilizing effect on the current complex world situation".

He said, "the Russia-China Treaty of Good-Neighbourliness, Friendship and Cooperation have brought the partnership between our two countries to an unprecedented high level".

Probably the event that attracted the most international attention was the Summit meeting between Putin and Xi Jinping on February 4. The meeting was prominently covered by *Xinhua* and the state-run China Central Television (CCTV) as well as China's other official media. *Xinhua* and CCTV (February 4) both reported that Chinese President Xi Jinping had an "in-depth and full exchange of views on Sino-Russian relations and a series of major issues concerning international strategic security and stability in a warm and friendly atmosphere" with Russian President Vladimir Putin at the Diaoyutai State Guesthouse in Beijing. Incidentally, Putin was one of only three visiting dignitaries who stayed at the Diaoyutai State Guesthouse. The other two were Kazakh President Kassym-Jomart Tokayev and Pakistan Prime Minister Imran Khan while other foreign dignitaries were accommodated in hotels.

Xinhua quoted Xi Jinping as saying that "the world has entered a new period of turbulence and change, and human society has encountered many challenges and crises". He added that "China and Russia have adhered to their original aspirations and have always maintained their bilateral relations to move forward steadily. The two sides firmly support each other in safeguarding their core interests. Political and strategic mutual trust is increasingly consolidated, and bilateral trade volume has hit a new record high". He asserted that "China and Russia are committed to deepening back-to-back strategic cooperation and safeguarding international fairness and justice side by side. This is a strategic decision that has far-reaching influence on China, Russia and the world, and will not be shaken in the past, present and future". Xi Jinping said they should continue to maintain close high-level exchanges and "strongly support each other in safeguarding sovereignty, security and development interests, effectively respond to external interference and regional security threats, and maintain international strategic stability".

Putin replied, "Russia-China relations are a model of international relations in the 21st century. The joint statement we issued today reflects the highly unanimous position of Russia and China on major international issues. The strategic nature of Russia-China relations is unprecedentedly prominent and has attracted worldwide attention. The deepening of comprehensive strategic coordination between Russia and China is conducive to the realization of the respective development of the two countries and the maintenance of the common interests of the two countries. It is also of great significance to safeguarding world strategic security and stability. The Russian side is willing to further intensify strategic communication and coordination with the Chinese side, firmly support each other in safeguarding sovereignty and territorial integrity, firmly uphold the core coordination role of the United Nations, firmly uphold international law and international fairness and justice, and promote the building of a more just and reasonable international order".

Xinhua said that the two heads of state had an in-depth exchange of views on the current international and regional situation and major hotspot issues of mutual concern.

After the talks, Xi Jinping hosted a banquet for Putin. The two sides thereafter issued the "Joint Statement of the People's Republic of China and the Russian Federation on International Relations and Global Sustainable Development in the New Era" and signed a series of documents for cooperation in key areas. A day earlier, Russia's Gazprom agreed to a 30-year contract to supply China's CNPC with natural gas from a new pipeline connecting Russia's Far East with China's northeast. An agreement was separately concluded for Russia to supply 100 million tons of oil to China over five years. Ding Xuexiang, Director of the CCP CC General Office, Politburo member and senior Chinese diplomat Yang Jiechi, State Councillor and Foreign Minister Wang Yi, Head of the National Development and Reform Commission (NDRC) He Lifeng, Commerce Minister Wang Wentao and Vice Foreign Minister Le Yucheng also attended the Xi-Putin meeting.

While the *People's Daily* (February 5) published a commentary titled *Inject more vitality into the development of Sino-Russian relation*', CCTV (February 4) reported on the 'China and Russia joint statement on international relations and global sustainable development in the new era' issued in Beijing the same day. CCTV said: The statement pointed out that at present, the world is going through great changes, and the international community has a stronger voice for peace and sustainable development. A few international forces continue to stubbornly pursue unilateralism and harm the legitimate rights and interests of other countries. The international community will never accept this". It listed the main points of the Joint Statement as:

- The two sides call on all countries to safeguard the common values of peace, development, fairness, justice, democracy and freedom for all mankind, defend the international system with the United Nations at the core and the international order based on international law, practice genuine multilateralism, and achieve world peace and stability and sustainable development.
- The two sides agreed that the people of all countries have the right to choose the form and method of democratic practice that suits their national conditions. Whether a country is democratic or not can only be judged by its people.
- The two sides believe that development is the key to realizing the well-being of the people, and are willing to continue relevant work on advancing the global development initiative proposed by China.
- The two sides reiterated that they firmly support each other's core interests and oppose external forces interfering in the internal affairs of the two countries and undermining the security and stability of the common surrounding areas of the two countries.
- As world powers and permanent members of the UN Security Council, the two sides will uphold responsibility and morality, promote world multi-polarization and democratization of international relations, and work together to build a new type of international relations.
- The Russian side spoke positively of China's concept of building a community with a shared future for mankind, believing that this concept will help strengthen the solidarity of the international community and work together to tackle common challenges.
- Russia supports China in successfully hosting the Beijing 2022 Winter Olympics and Paralympics.

The language in the joint statement appears to be centred on the Chinese sphere of interests, namely the Indo-Pacific, Taiwan, the Asia-Pacific region and Europe. The coordination between the CEE and BRI, for example, is of concern to China and much less so to Russia. Ukraine is neither explicitly mentioned and nor does the joint statement make any mention of mutual support in Russia's tensions over Ukraine. This would point to the limits of the growing Sino-Russia partnership. The joint statement does neither mentions this with respect to China's with Taiwan, but it does state, "The Russian side reaffirms its support for the One-China principle, confirms that Taiwan is an inalienable part of China, and opposes any forms of independence of Taiwan". The following paragraph asserts, "Russia and China stand against attempts by external forces to undermine security and stability in their common adjacent regions, intend to counter interference by outside forces in the internal affairs of sovereign countries under any pretext, oppose colour revolutions, and will increase cooperation in the aforementioned areas". The specific mention of 'colour revolutions' reflects the concerns shared by Russia and China and signals China's unease over the developments in Ukraine.

An interesting article was published on China's popular web-portal Weixin on February 6, 2022. This described the Sino-Russian joint statement more as an anti-hegemonic struggle, saying, "China and Russia still have not formed a military alliance, but a strategic alliance has been established in fact". Titled *China-Russia strategic alliance has reached a new level—— Comment on the Sino-Russian Joint Statement for a New Era*, the author, Zhang Zhikun, observed that the "Joint Statement of the People's Republic of China and the Russian Federation on International Relations and Global Sustainable Development in the New Era" was issued at a critical moment in the global strategy and that it is "a major strategic measure jointly adopted by China and Russia"". The article said the joint statement marks a new level of strategic cooperation between China and Russia. Stating that the "Joint Statement made a clear statement on a series of major international strategic and political issues, directly naming the United States, the United Kingdom, Australia, Japan and other relevant countries", it claimed the document "comprehensively criticizes and denies the dominance of hegemony" and can, therefore "be called a joint declaration against hegemony". The article added that "the joint targeting of third parties by China and Russia is an important sign that the China-Russia comprehensive strategic partnership of coordination has reached a new level" and that after this joint statement, "the military alliance between China and Russia will also be further strengthened". It points out though that they have still "not formed a military alliance, but a strategic alliance has been established".

The article claimed the joint statement demonstrates China and Russia's common views on democracy, civilization, development, history and security to the world and sounds "a new clarion call for the struggle against hegemony in human society, which will definitely impact the world order dominated by hegemonic countries and the Western Cold War bloc". It said the US and West had argued that the outbreak of a war between Russia and Ukraine would not benefit China and would have a huge impact on the global economy and energy supply and that China should exert influence in "some constructive way" on Russia and advise it not to resort to force. Instead, it said "China and Russia are leaning even more closely". It claimed that, "China and Russia have formed a firm strategic core and political backbone" to a number of countries in the middle zone, including in the BRICS, SCO etc. and given them other options for development thus laying the basis for "a worldwide peaceful united front" that will surely grow. Asserting that "the Sino-Russian Joint Statement for a New Era has a solid strategic foundation", it cautioned that a lot of work has still to be done such as "adjustment and follow-up of domestic and foreign policies, including currency settlement, technical exchanges, trade and investment and other specific issues".

The article underscored that it is important for Russia and China to jointly oppose "all kinds of sabotage and interference" in particular from the "huge pro-American and pro-Western forces in both China and Russia", which are "deeply rooted and powerful, and penetrates into all aspects of society, especially in the media and academic circles". It said these forces will resist Russia-China cooperation and "when it comes to specific projects, they will do everything they can to interfere and destroy". The author emphasized that the domestic struggle against hegemony is closely related to the international struggle against hegemony. In conclusion, the article claimed China-Russia "strategic cooperation has reached a new level and will provide a reliable guarantee and support for global strategic stability and balance, and will promote the arrival of a new era of global strategy".

The Putin-Xi meeting was as much for promoting bilateral economic cooperation as to project solidarity between the two countries, both of which are being subjected to pressure by the United States. They also share the apprehension that the US may resort to imposing tough economic sanctions, which will also adversely impact China since many Chinese companies are engaged with Russia. This could, in turn, adversely impact China's BRI. The omission in the joint statement of any reference to Ukraine is an indicator of this apprehension.

This was first published by the Centre for China Analysis and Strategy (CCAS) and Vivekananda International Foundation (VIF) in February 9, 2022.

64. Chinese Criticisms of China's Support to Russia's Invasion of Ukraine

After the February 4 Summit between Chinese President Xi Jinping and Russian President Vladimir Putin in Beijing and 18 days after Russia invaded Ukraine, China has not wavered in its support of Russia's invasion of Ukraine despite urgings by the US and West. Differing views are, however, now beginning to surface internally.

The Chinese Communist Party (CCP) Central Committee (CC)'s powerful Propaganda Department has ensured that the Chinese media complies with its policy. The Chinese social media, which doesn't use terms like 'invasion' to describe the Russian action in Ukraine, is awash with posts criticising Ukraine, abuse and offensive remarks against Ukrainians, and criticisms of the West. It has simultaneously got pro-Beijing elements, or those with ties to business interests in China, to spread reports that imposition of sanctions against China will not succeed, or that the EU is talking to Chinese Foreign Minister Wang Yi to mediate between Europe, Ukraine and Putin etc. Wang Yi, however, is reported to have made clear that China will not mediate until Europe lifts all sanctions against Russia.

At the same time, while doing business with Russia, Chinese officials are trying to ensure that they do not attract US and Western sanctions. Chinese companies operating in Russia are being careful. While Lenovo and Huawei continue to do business in Russia including with Russian government entities, the China National Petroleum Corp. is operationalising the plan — agreed during the Summit — to establish a new pipeline with an annual capacity of 10 billion cu. meters while Russia's Gazprom announced (March 1) it had begun work toward construction of the 'Power of Siberia 2' pipeline, which would have an annual capacity of around 50 billion cu. meters. China's coal companies and some banks have, however, temporarily ceased operations for fear of attracting sanctions.

But concern about China's stance is apparently mounting in China among its academics and officials. The prospect of US and Western sanctions being enlarged to encompass Chinese entities doing business with China would be worrying. US Commerce Secretary Gina Raimondo has issued a clear redline to Chinese technology firms that might plan to do business and supply services to Russia, warning that they will be cut off from the services and supplies they need to continue operating.

First to be noticed was the statement protesting the Russian invasion of Ukraine issued on February 26 by five Chinese Professors of prestigious Chinese Universities. The statement, which was posted on the Chinese social media was promptly deleted by Chinese censors, but is circulating among Chinese academics in the form of a petition. The five Professors are: Professor Sun Jiang, Nanjing University; Professor Wang Lixin, Peking University; Professor Xu Guoqi, University of Hong Kong; Professor Zhong Weimin, Tsinghua University; and Professor Chen Yan, Fudan University. Their statement said "The international community was shocked that a permanent member of the United Nations, a major power with nuclear weapons, would fight against a weaker brother" and that "Great catastrophes in history often started with local conflicts". It said, "We strongly appeal to the Russian government and to President Putin to stop this war and settle the dispute through negotiations. Power politics will not only destroy the achievements of civilization and the principles of international justice, but will also bring great shame and disaster to the Russian nation. Peace begins with the desire of the human heart. We oppose unjust wars". While the statement does not directly criticise Chinese President Xi Jinping, it is an implicit criticism of Chinese support to Russia and the Professors are likely to be penalised.

More such negative sentiments were expressed soon thereafter in an 'open letter' circulated on WeChat on March 3. Over 200 alumni of China's prestigious Tsinghua University, most of whom live in China, called on the university to strip Putin of an honorary doctorate awarded in 2019.

Interestingly, two recent articles expressing contradictory views on China and the ongoing war in Ukraine suggest that deliberations are underway in the

CCP's upper echelons. Prominent are those by Hu Wei and Wang Xiangsui. In his article Hu Wei, Vice Chairman of the Public Policy Research Center of the Counselor's Office of the State Council, Chairman of the Shanghai Public Policy Research Association, Chairman of the Academic Committee of the Charhar Institute and a Professor and doctoral supervisor, expressed strong reservations about China's present policy. By March 7, the original post had been viewed 185,834 times and been recycled by numerous outlets. The second is by Wang Xiangsui, retired People's Liberation Army (PLA) Air Force Colonel and co-author of the best-selling book *Unrestricted Warfare.* Published in Ouzhou Yanjiu [European Studies] under the title *Interpreting the Ukraine crisis from dual perspectives – the interweaving of geopolitics and geo-currency politics* on March 6, it topped Aisixiang's daily ratings before slipping to second position by March 11.

In his article titled *The Possible Outcome of the Russia-Ukraine War and China's Choice*, Hu Wei, argued that China needs to safeguard its own national interests and cease supporting Russia. He emphasised 'The bottom line is to prevent the United States and the West from jointly sanctioning China'. Stating that Putin's plans for a blitzkrieg have clearly failed, Russia is fast getting isolated, and events are leading towards a World War, he unequivocally recommended that China needs to cut ties with Putin in the "next one or two weeks" and "give up neutrality".

Hu Wei assessed there is a "high probability" that the Russian-Ukrainian war may escalate beyond Ukraine to become a World War and even include the possibility of a nuclear strike. Stating that the only way out for Putin is to have peace negotiations where Ukraine makes concessions, he said this will be difficult unless Kyiv is captured. More importantly, he said, it is not in Putin's character to withdraw and this will make it impossible for the US and West to stay out of the war. He anticipated that the US and Russia will also have a final confrontation, and since Russia's military strength will not be able to match that of NATO, Putin will lose even more. Even the capture of Kyiv would not mean the end of the war since a Government-in-exile would be formed regardless of whether Zelensky is alive or not.

Hu Wei said a protracted war would have major strategic repercussions. As the Russian people face increasing hardships with Western sanctions reaching an unprecedented level and impacting the domestic economy and people's livelihood, the anti-war and anti-Putin forces will get mobilised raising the possibility of a mutiny. He assessed that if Putin is removed due to civil strife, coup d'etat or other reasons, Russia will succumb to the West, or even be further dismembered. Russia's status as a great power will come to an end.

He anticipated an 'Iron Curtaain' again, dividing the Western-dominated camp and its competitors. With the West drawing the line between democracies and dictatorships, confrontation with Russia will be defined as a struggle between democracy and dictatorship. This will have an effect on other countries: "the US Indo-Pacific strategy will be consolidated and Japan and other countries will draw even closer to the US. The power of the West will increase significantly, NATO will continue to expand, and the influence of the United States in the non-Western world will also increase, more third world countries will embrace the West and the West will have more 'hegemony' in terms of military, values and institutions, and its hard power and soft power will reach new heights". The United States and Europe will "form a community of shared future more closely", and US leadership in the Western world will be paramount.

Disagreeing with the view that the US will not focus on China because of preoccupation in Europe, he warned that in such an eventuality China will be more isolated. He reiterated that if China does not take measures to actively respond, it will face further containment from the US and West. China will become the main target for strategic containment and Europe will cut itself off from China even more. He added that, "Japan will become the vanguard of anti-China, South Korea will further fall to the United States, Taiwan will join the anti-China 'chorus' and China will face not only the military encirclement of the United States and NATO, QUAD (US-Japan-India-Australia Quadrilateral Alliance), and AUKUS [Australia, United Kingdom and United States trilateral alliance], but also challenges from Western values and systems".

Retired PLAAF (People's Liberation Army Air Force) Colonel Wang Xiangsui traced the background of the 'major geopolitical' dispute in Ukraine. He said Ukraine is important as the main energy link between Russia and Europe and is a major safeguard for Russia as a European and world power.

He ascribed the current conflict to the rivalry between the West and Russia over Ukraine, contention in Ukraine between pro-Western and pro-Russian forces, effort by Western European powers to squeeze Russia's strategic space, and repeated US efforts to challenge Russia's hegemony which have left Russia with no choice but to retaliate. Wang Xiangsui discerned the appearance of three major economic circles in the world economic system: 1.the Eurozone with internal trade exceeding 70 percent; 2.the US-dominated North American; and 3.the East Asian, mainly comprising China and ASEAN states. This, according to him, challenges US global hegemony.

Stating that it is the scene of big power rivalry and all the powers have made mistakes and underestimated their opponents, he said the Ukrainian crisis will 'remain in manageable tension constrained by multiple factors, thus becoming a lasting 'ulcer surface' affecting Europe'.

Wang Xiangsui explained that, "the Ukraine incident undermines the foundation of Europe-Russia cooperation, returning a marginalised NATO to Europe's centre stage and giving the US an important political-economic lever there". Assessing that Europe faces long-term chaos in Ukraine, he said it will need to invest more resources to meet new security challenges. This will cause long-term harm to its economic development and security. He assessed that the crisis had further promoted Sino-Russian cooperation, describing it as 'hugely significant' for "curbing global hegemony and promoting multi-polarisation". He also listed various new areas of cooperation. Underscoring that China is a big manufacturing country, while Russia is the most resource-rich country in the world in need of a stable market, he identified long-term guarantee for China's energy supply as one important area. Asserting that the US Asia-Pacific strategy will be constrained by the Ukraine issue, he described the Asia-Pacific region as the economic center of the future world. He said US policies will inevitably lead to the intensification of the contradiction between Europe and the US, but the US national strength is not as before. If the US confronts Russia, China and Europe, it will make a "strategic mistake of making enemies everywhere".

In conclusion, Wang Xiangsui said America's performance in the Ukraine incident shows that it is no longer the "'solitary superpower, but only one of several major power centers in the world". He did not expect that the

Ukrainian crisis will be resolved as per the wishes of the US, but as a result of multilateral deliberation.

The publication of the two articles by prominent Chinese citizens, points to discussion gaining ground inside China regarding the merits of China aligning itself so closely with Putin and Russia. China's leadership seems to have allowed expression of the divergent views. The statements of protest by the academics suggest that a wide section of Chinese academics, including probably businessmen, feel the US is more powerful than Russia and are apprehensive that the US and the West may target China with sanctions. Millions of CCP members and their families will be similarly apprehensive. Large swathes of China's academia have blamed Chinese President Xi Jinping since 2017 for the policy towards the US. Uncontrolled public discussion of China-US relations, or in case China is targeted by sanctions, could make things very difficult for Xi Jinping at the upcoming 20th Party Congress.

This was first published by the Centre for China Analysis and Strategy (CCAS) and Vivekananda International Foundation (VIF) in March 14, 2022.

65. Russia-China: Implications of the Unequal Relationship

A brief background of world events will help set the context for assessing this relationship. Without delving into why Russia did what it did in Ukraine, over the past few years we have witnessed major powers attempting to consolidate or expand their territory – as in the case of China – or their areas of influence.

This prompts recall of the rather prescient remarks made by former British Prime Minister Tony Blair in October 2001. He said, "The starving, the wretched, the dispossessed, the ignorant, those living in want and squalor from the deserts of Northern Africa to the slums of Gaza, to the mountain ranges of Afghanistan: they too are our cause. This is the moment to seize. The kaleidoscope has been shaken. The pieces are in flux. Soon they will settle again. Before they do, let us reorder this world around us."

The remark not only reveals the lingering imperialist mindset, but gives an insight into the thinking of the major powers who are reluctant to yield power and influence to the emerging new global power centres. In this backdrop AUKUS can be seen as a pre-emptive attempt to retain and spread Western – in reality Anglo-Saxon — military power into Asia. It also sets the stage for big power competition.

China and Russia have a deep partnership in terms of economy, energy, trade and military supplies and, importantly, a shared ideology. The arrangement, which got steadily consolidated since 1990, suits a financially weaker Russia which receives payments in USD and consumer goods. But even deeper is the close relationship between Xi Jinping and Vladimir Putin. Xi has invested heavily in this relationship. This has trumped long abiding mutual suspicions.

Both are autocrats with unchallenged decision-making authority. They are creatures of their respective Communist Parties, their thinking has been moulded by their Party, they are both committed to their ideologies, and they share similar global ambitions. Additionally, both share a strong suspicion and dislike of the US and West which, they assess, exercise hegemony over the international world and trade order. They also see the US as intent on weakening them through 'colour revolutions' and by encroaching into their periphery. Putin's justification for the war in Ukraine and the Joint Statement issued after the Xi-Putin Summit in Beijing on February 4, 2022, are cases in point.

More importantly, the former Soviet Union and its successor state Russia and China have stood together for decades on the international stage. As two 'communist', or socialist, countries they have an adversarial relationship with many of the world's democracies and the West. China, for years the junior partner and treated as such by the CPSU and Soviet Union, witnessed the decline of the latter from the mid-1980s. Their roles got reversed as the Soviet Union became economically weaker and the shelves in its stores became bare, more so after disintegration of the Soviet Union. As China grew stronger and economically more powerful it still, however, took comfort from Russia being another large 'communist' power – in fact if not in name! The recent developments in Ukraine and prospect of Russia being defeated, therefore, are a cause of serious worry for Chinese communist leaders.

Xi especially has closely watched developments in Russia and, like virtually the entire Chinese Communist Party (CCP) leadership, was particularly disturbed at the downfall of the Communist Party of the Soviet Union (CPSU) and disintegration of the Union of Soviet Socialist Republics (USSR). Like most CCP members brought up on communist ideology, Xi admires Stalin and views Khrushchev disparagingly as a 'revisionist' and Gorbachev as the 'traitor' who brought about the dissolution of the Soviet Union. A 100-minute movie made by China's central Propaganda Department and screened in late March for Party members throughout China eulogised Stalin and Mao, implying of course that Xi was of similar stature!

These close historical ties are reflected in China's categorisation of its levels of partnership with various countries. The highest formulation "Comprehensive strategic partnership coordination relations" is used only to describe its relationship with Russia. The only other country with a separate stand-alone relationship is Pakistan. Describing the depth of Sino-Russian relations, a senior Russian diplomat said that the two sides consult each other on each issue before taking a step. More recently, the joint statement issued after the Xi-Putin Summit in Beijing on February 4, 2022, reiterated that there are "no limits" to China-Russia friendship.

While Russia lost the propaganda war from the very start as the Western media dominates print, radio and TV, it is nevertheless difficult to form a definitive assessment of the situation in Ukraine. What is clear is that the protracted war with no outer time horizon is certainly not to Beijing's liking. It has made Beijing very uncomfortable. Recent articles in the official Chinese media, while justifying Russia's invasion of Ukraine and enumerating its benefits for China, also candidly itemised some of the failures responsible for the lack of progress by the Russian Army. Chinese military planners have envisaged as doctrine a short sharp conflict using overwhelming cyber and firepower and ending in decisive victory. None of this is happening. On the contrary, the long-drawn-out war has — to China's surprise — seen the US and the West shed their differences and come together very quickly and has raised the worrying prospect of Western sanctions against Russia being extended to China. Such a development would have enormous repercussions for China's economy and Xi's continuance in office.

China, which is more integrated with US and Western markets, will be far more severely impacted than Russia in case it is hit by sanctions. For example, 75 percent of China's goods trade is still invoiced in dollars. Being barred from the dollar-clearing system and SWIFT would have unfathomable consequences for both Chinese banks and the global economy. The Chinese leadership has now seen how rapidly almost 600 leading multinationals and western consumer goods companies (like Starbucks, Mc Donald's, Louis Vuitton etc) exited Russia. China has not yet been able to boost domestic consumption and reduce dependence on exports – its exports to US exceed USD 600 billion annually. Importantly, the children and relatives of over 70 percent of the CCP's Department Heads study in the US and West. All this will end. The CCP is thus far holding firm on its support to Russia. China's official media and traffic on its heavily censored social media continue not to allow use of words like "invasion" or "war" and quickly remove articles anticipating Russia's defeat. Its social media is awash with posts criticising the US, West and Ukraine and denigrating Ukrainians and Ukrainian women.

The conversation between US President Biden and Xi on March 18, 2022, showed no change in China's position. Just days earlier Chinese Foreign Minister Wang Yi spoke to EU's Borrell and said China will not mediate until Europe lifts all sanctions against Russia. The same day that Xi and Biden spoke, a *Global Times* Commentary (March 18) in English asserted China's position. It described "China-Russia relations, the most strategic asset that cannot be damaged by US provocation" and emphasised that leaning on Moscow will only "undermine the China-Russia relationship and sabotage mutual trust". It stressed that the "Russia-China comprehensive strategic partnership of coordination has stood the test of time and is rock solid".

Chinese officials are being very careful not to attract sanctions and are mindful of US Commerce Secretary Gina Raimondo's redline to Chinese technology firms that might plan to do business and supply services to Russia, warning that they will be cut off from the services and supplies they need to continue operating. Chinese companies like Lenovo and Huawei continue to operate in Russia including with Russian government entities, and China National Petroleum Corp. is operationalising the plan — agreed during the Summit — to establish a new pipeline with an annual capacity of 10 billion cu. meters. China's coal companies and some banks have, however, temporarily ceased operations for fear of attracting sanctions.

But dissenting voices are being heard and, in some cases, possibly allowed. A number of comments critical of China's support to Putin and Russia are being posted on the social media and being rapidly deleted. The first indication of dissent noticed was the statement protesting the Russian invasion of Ukraine issued on February 26, 2022 by five Chinese Professors of prestigious Chinese Universities, which was posted on China's social media but promptly deleted by Chinese censors. More negative sentiments were expressed soon thereafter in an 'open letter' circulated on WeChat on March 3 by over 200 alumni of China's prestigious Tsinghua University, mostly living in China, who demanded that the university divest Putin of an honorary doctorate awarded in 2019.

Prominent, however, was the article by Hu Wei, Vice Chairman of the Public Policy Research Center of the Counsellor's Office of the State Council, Chairman of the Shanghai Public Policy Research Association, Chairman of the Academic Committee of the Charhar Institute and a Professor and doctoral supervisor, who expressed strong reservations about China's present policy. By March 7, the original post had been viewed 185,834 times and been recycled by numerous outlets. The article was deleted after a week, suggesting possibly that others in the Party apparatus supported it, and Hu Wei could face punitive action because of his criticism of Xi's policy.

In his article titled 'The Possible Outcome of the Russia-Ukraine War and China's Choice', Hu Wei, argued that China needs to safeguard its own national interests and cease supporting Russia. He emphasised 'The bottom line is to prevent the United States and the West from jointly sanctioning China'. Stating that Putin's plans for a blitzkrieg have clearly failed, Russia is fast getting isolated, and events are leading towards a World War, he unequivocally recommended that China needs to cut ties with Putin in the 'next one or two weeks' and 'give up neutrality'.

Hu Wei said a protracted war would have major strategic repercussions; the Russian people will face increasing hardships with Western sanctions reaching an unprecedented level; and the anti-war and anti-Putin forces will get mobilised raising the possibility of a mutiny. He assessed that if Putin is removed due to civil strife, coup d'état or other reasons, Russia will succumb to the West, or even be further dismembered. Russia's status as a great power will come to an end.

Spelling out the impact on China, he said the confrontation with Russia will be defined as a struggle between democracy and dictatorship and this will have an effect on other countries. 'The US Indo-Pacific strategy will be consolidated' and Japan and other countries will draw even closer to the US. 'The power of the West will increase significantly, NATO will continue to expand, and the influence of the United States in the non-Western world will also increase, more third world countries will embrace the West and the West will have more "hegemony" in terms of military, values and institutions, and its hard power and soft power will reach new heights'. The United States and Europe will 'form a community of shared future more closely' and US leadership in the Western world will be paramount.

He emphasised that if China does not take measures to actively respond, it will face further containment from the US and West and become the main target for strategic containment. The "anti-China" coalition comprising Japan, South Korea and Taiwan will coalesce and China will face military encirclement of the United States and NATO, QUAD (US-Japan-India-Australia Quadrilateral Alliance), and AUKUS, as also challenges from Western values and systems.

Most recently on May 10, former Chinese diplomat to Ukraine, Gao Yusheng, posted an article on the Phoenix website frankly anticipating Russian defeat in its war against Ukraine. It was taken down within hours.

The authorities have reacted to the criticisms which, in effect, challenge Xi Jinping's policy. Two lengthy articles by the Head of the People's Daily Sichuan Branch and Zhang Zhikun, Senior Researcher of the PLA-affiliated Kunlun Policy Research Institute, published on April 24 and 29 respectively sought to explain China's position and support for Putin. They described Putin's action as resistance against US and Western hegemony over the world order, a confrontation between democracy and other systems of governance and highlighted the advantages of the conflict to China. Nonetheless both expressed concern about the protracted war in Ukraine and imposition of sanctions. The appearance of these articles indicates that while the CCP leadership is presently unwilling to alter its policy towards Putin and Russia, this is being debated within the CCP echelons. The two articles also underscore the solid nature of Sino-Russia relations and the bond between Xi and Putin.

Quite apart from calls to Xi to dilute support for Russia, there are other factors that could compel such a decision. Among them is that Russia's usefulness as the supplier of military hardware and technology will be diminished. Russia already faces shortages of microchips and other vital components etc, which are all imported, for its weapons systems. Despite its problems with Ukraine, Russia was till now able to meet China's requirements. China, however, hedged its bets and forged ties with Ukraine by signing its first ever security agreement with a foreign power. China remains dependent on Russia for military supplies and technology, but will try to lure more Russian scientists.

Russia is also China's most secure source for Oil and Natural Gas. Much of China's purchases are paid for in US Dollars and consumer goods and there are large numbers of Chinese workers in Russia's Far East. But Russia's most useful, though intangible, role remains that of being the largest ideologically compatible state with China. The most worrying scenario for Xi Jinping is the Ukraine conflict ending in defeat for Russia – either because of internal unrest or inability to seize the objectives – or Putin being removed and the Russian Federation disintegrating, leaving China as the lone communist state standing against the West.

This evolving relationship is a matter of concern for India too. China will not change its policy towards India unless it obtains sizeable concessions. Russia is already China's junior partner. This will become more obvious after the Ukraine war, which will probably leave Russia exhausted, considerably weakened and diminished. As the sanctions take effect and it is unable to obtain critical parts, Russia's ability to manufacture and supply military hardware and equipment will be adversely impacted. Russia will become even more dependent on China. Pakistan Prime Minister Imran Khan's visit to Moscow on February 24 displayed the extent of forward movement in their bilateral relations at a time when Sino-Pak ties are already extremely close. These warn of unwelcome developments for India.

India needs an urgent comprehensive and objective review of its relations with Russia. They can certainly no longer continue as before. The recent announcement sharply reducing defence imports point to promotion of 'Atmanirbhar Bharat' but this needs to be enlarged to include other products and areas of cooperation to compensate for dependence on Russia and China. India needs to take advantage of the world's most advanced hi-technology, capital available for investment and huge markets available only in the US and West. They also have neither borders nor seriously clashing interests with India, which can be a reliable partner. India has a short window to ramp up indigenous production in critical sectors if it wants to be independent and rise to be a major power. A readily discernible deadline is 2035.

This was first published by the Centre for China Analysis and Strategy (CCAS) and Vivekananda International Foundation (VIF) in May 12, 2022.

66. Portends of the Xi-Putin Summit in May 2024

Summits between Russian President Putin and Chinese President Xi Jinping are invariably closely monitored in world capitals, especially since the onset of Russia's war with Ukraine in 2022 and the two having declared a "no limits friendship"! China is the largest country to sustain Russia's effort to withstand Western pressure. The Summits also incrementally advance their common agenda of changing the existing world order to make it "more fair" and "equitable". Xi Jinping has already articulated the principal features of the world order envisioned by him, namely a community of common destiny, and the Global Civilisational Initiative (GCI), Global Development Initiative (GDI) and Global Security Initiative (GSI). By initiating the war with Ukraine, Putin has fired the first salvo in the bid to replace the existing world order and US dominance.

The rapidly strengthening China-Russia ties have aroused concern in the US and Europe as it comes in the backdrop of growing and persistent reports that China is supplying weapons, ammunition and other military hardware to Russia for its war with Ukraine. China's long, porous border with Russia's Far East, over which huge quantities of grain and consumer goods have been transported for decades, will facilitate the subterranean shipment of military and dual-use goods. In the past few months US and European official interlocuters have made it clear to Beijing that there will be consequences if they are able to confirm that China is supplying weapons and ammunition to Russia. The US and Europe are also distracted by the war in Ukraine and this coincides with China's visibly escalated military actions around Taiwan and consequent increase in tension in the Taiwan Strait.

Despite the obviously close ties between Russian President Vladimir Putin and Chinese President Xi Jinping and their two countries, there are thinly concealed suggestions that mutual suspicions continue to linger. This was evident in China's recent interactions with the US and Europe where Russia appears to have contrived to display its close ties with China. Most recent was the announcement on May 14 that Russian President Putin would visit China. The visit came within a week of Xi Jinping's visit to France and Hungary. This was Putin's second visit to China in six months. Earlier, Russian Foreign Minister Lavrov too, interestingly, arrived in Beijing on the final day of US Treasury Secretary Yellen's visit to China and, barely a week prior to Xi's departure for his 3-nation European tour.

In a briefing to reporters on Putin's visit to China, Chinese Foreign Ministry spokesman Wang Wenbin said, "President Xi Jinping will exchange views with President Putin on bilateral ties, cooperation in various fields, and international and regional issues of common interest". The Kremlin said the two leaders would discuss their "comprehensive partnership and strategic cooperation" as well as "define key areas of development of Russian-Chinese cooperation and exchange views in detail on international and regional issues". The Kremlin said the two leaders would sign a joint statement after the meeting and that during the visit the two leaders will take part in a gala evening celebrating 75 years since the Soviet Union recognised the People's Republic of China. This was Russian President Putin's fourth in person meeting with Chinese President Xi Jinping since the start of the war in Ukraine. Setting the tone, on May 15, the *People's Daily* published the full text of Xinhua's interview with Russian President Putin.

On arrival at Beijing airport on May 16, Putin was received by Mme. Shen Yiqin, State Councilor in charge of Women's Affairs. Xi Jinping held a grand welcome ceremony and guard of honour for Putin at the east gate square of the Great Hall of the People. Signalling that economic issues would dominate the agenda, included in Putin's entourage were at least five Deputy Prime Ministers and almost all the important members of his cabinet.

On May 16 morning itself, Chinese President Xi Jinping held a "restrictive" meeting with Russian President Vladimir Putin at the Great Hall of the People. Xi noted that this year marks the 75th anniversary of the China-Russia diplomatic ties and that during this period the China-Russia relationship has withstood the test of international changes and "set an example of mutual respect, sincerity, peaceful coexistence, and mutual benefit between major countries and neighbouring countries". He said the "stable development of China-Russia relations serves the fundamental interests of both nations and their peoples and contributes to peace, stability, and prosperity in the region and the world. China is ready to work with Russia to stay each other's good neighbour, good friend and good partner that trust each other ... and uphold fairness and justice in the world". Xi emphasized that China and Russia must "always promote the Five Principles of Peaceful Coexistence, respect each other, trust each other equally, care for each other's concerns, and truly support each other's development and revitalization". Putin replied that he was pleased to visit China again after his inauguration as the new President of Russia. He said, "the development of Russia-China relations is not a temporary expedient and is not targeted at any third party. It benefits international strategic stability. Russia is willing to continuously expand bilateral cooperation, closely communicate and cooperate within the frameworks of the United Nations, BRICS, and the Shanghai Cooperation Organization (SCO), and promote the establishment of a more just and reasonable international order".

The two later presided over extensive talks between both full delegations. They listened to reports from the chairs of various intergovernmental cooperation committees of the two countries on cooperation in investment, energy, trade, "Northeast-Far East", humanities, and international fields. They expressed satisfaction with the progress made and affirmed suggestions for future cooperation. Xi said that They should enhance communication and coordination in international multilateral platforms such as the UN, BRICS, the SCO, and regional affairs, demonstrate international responsibilities, and promote the establishment of a fair and equitable global governance system. Putin said, ""the two sides have signed a series of cooperation documents, indicating their determination to further deepen and expand mutually beneficial cooperation. Russia is willing to work with China to implement Pre-2030 Development Plan on Priorities in China-Russia Economic Cooperation".

An unprecedentedly lengthy 12,000-character joint statement titled *Deepening China-Russia comprehensive strategic partnership of coordination for a new era* was subsequently issued. There was implicit criticism of the

US throughout the document, which mentioned the US 13 times, and expressed "serious concern over the United States's attempts to undermine strategic stability to maintain its absolute military superiority". Japan was mentioned once. Xi and Putin witnessed the signing of many bilateral cooperation documents spanning various sectors including economy and trade, environmental conservation, inspection and quarantine, media, etc. Interestingly, however, it made no mention of the 3,500 kms-long Siberia 2 gas pipeline despite Russia pushing hard for it. A Russian spokesman later said it would be announced soon, but there has been no comment yet by the Chinese.

At noon that day, Xi hosted a welcoming banquet for Putin in the Golden Hall of the Great Hall of the People. Chinese Politburo Standing Committee members Cai Qi and Ding Xuexiang, Politburo members Wang Yi, He Lifeng and Zhang Guoqing and State Councilor Shen Yiqin, among others, attended these activities. Chinese Premier Li Qiang also held talks with Putin.

Among the highlights of the Joint Statement are:

1. "that China-Russia relations have withstood the test of international vicissitudes, highlighting their stable and resilient qualities, and are at their best historical level". It affirmed that the comprehensive strategic partnership of coordination for the new era is not an expedient measure and has strong intrinsic motivation and independent value. The two declared they would "resolutely defend their legitimate rights and interests" and "oppose any attempts to obstruct their development or interfere in their internal affairs";
2. Russia reaffirmed "its adherence to the One-China principle, recognizing Taiwan as an inalienable part of the People's Republic of China. Russia opposes any form of "Taiwan independence" and said it "firmly supports China's efforts to safeguard national sovereignty and territorial integrity and achieve national reunification". In turn, China supported "Russia in maintaining its national security and stability, development and prosperity, sovereignty, and territorial integrity, and opposes external forces interfering in Russia's internal affairs;
3. It endorsed "China's concept of building a community with a shared future for mankind" and its "series of global initiatives";

4. It mentioned the very close cooperation at the political level between the offices at the highest level i.e. the Chinese Communist Party (CCP) Central Committee (CC) General Office and the Presidential Executive Office of the Russian Federation, the armed forces and security services;
5. Strengthening bilateral economic and social development, including in the banking and insurance sector, over the long term;
6. It established a Sino-Russian Arctic Route Cooperation Subcommittee under the framework of the Sino-Russian Prime Ministers' Regular Meeting Committee, to conduct mutually beneficial cooperation in the development and utilization of the Arctic as an important international transportation corridor, and deepen cooperation in polar ship technology and construction.
7. It promised to align the "Belt and Road" Initiative with building of the Eurasian Economic Union, and the Greater Eurasian Partnership";
8. It mentioned the SCO, BRICS and AUKUS; and expressed "serious concern over the United States attempts to undermine strategic stability to maintain its absolute military superiority."

Putin concluded his trip to China with a visit to Harbin, capital of Heilongjiang province, where he attended the opening ceremony of the Eighth China-Russia Expo in Harbin. Interestingly, on arrival at Harbin he was not received by the Heilongjiang Party Secretary, but the lower ranked Mme. Liang Huiling, Governor of Heilongjiang province. It is curious that Putin was received by women CCP cadres at Beijing and Harbin and, though senior, they were not Vice Premiers. At the gala event in Harbin, where Xi and Putin both spoke, Putin spoke in Russian and apparently forgot that he had to pause for the interpreter to translate. When this was pointed out at the end, Putin said he was so at home that he forgot he was speaking in a foreign language! While seeing-off Putin at Harbin, in a very unusual gesture Xi Jinping hugged Putin.

After Putin's departure, the *People's Daily* (May 21) published a lengthy article titled *China, Russia set prime example of new form of international, good-neighborly relations between two major countries*. It stressed that this meeting highlighted the importance of the two countries "always promoting the Five

Principles of Peaceful Coexistence, respect each other on an equal footing, trust each other, accommodate each other's concerns, and truly provide mutual assistance for the development and revitalization of both sides". It observed that the two presidents have held over 40 meetings, and this time had a candid and fruitful discussion. It attributed the "notable progress in China-Russia relations" to the commitment of both countries to five principles: 1. China and Russia are committed to mutual respect as the fundamental principle of relations, and always render support for each other's core interests; 2. China and Russia are committed to win-win cooperation as the driving force of relations, and work to foster a new paradigm of mutual benefit; 3. China and Russia are committed to lasting friendship as the foundation of relations, and carry forward the torch of Sino-Russian friendship; 4. China and Russia are committed to strategic coordination as an underpinning of relations, and steer global governance in the right direction; and 5. China and Russia are committed to fairness and justice as the purpose of relations, and dedicated to the political settlement of hotspots.

The article said the two countries need to make further structural improvements to their cooperation, and consolidate the good momentum in trade and other traditional areas of cooperation. It added that they need to look for areas where their interests converge, tap into their comparative strengths, deepen the integration of interests, and enable each other's success.

Though short, Putin's visit to China was important. It came amid Russia's growing dependence on China for consumer goods, military-related supplies and support in the international arena. It is in Xi Jinping's interest, at this time when he is under considerable pressure from the US, to ensure that Russia remains undefeated and China is not left as the sole major communist power facing the West. The lengthy, expansive Joint Statement revealed the commonality in their concerns and wide range of cooperative endeavours the two envisage. Both have also clearly endorsed their respective positions on security, sovereignty and opposition to interference by foreign powers in their internal affairs.

This was first published by the Centre for China Analysis and Strategy (CCAS) and Vivekananda International Foundation (VIF) in June 30, 2024.

67. Will China's Ambitions with Iran Materialise?

Given the rising US-China tensions, Beijing and Washington are both trying to consolidate their relationship with other important countries. China receiving Russian Foreign Minister Lavrov just prior to Chinese Foreign Minister Wang Yi embarking on a tour to the Middle East exemplifies this. The efforts have gained momentum after the meeting between Chinese Politburo member Yang Jiechi and Foreign Minister Wang Yi and US Secretary of State Anthony Blinken and National Security Advisor Jake Sullivan at Anchorage, Alaska, earlier this year.

The 90-minute meeting did not go as well as China had hoped though, in keeping with China's uncompromising stance on foreign policy issues, Chinese Politburo member and Director of the Central Foreign Affairs Commission, Yang Jiechi appeared to have come with a prepared text to give Blinken a dressing down.

China's recent moves in Africa, the Gulf and the Middle East point to China's efforts to build a constituency at this time of serious tension with the US. Chinese Foreign Minister Wang Yi's visit to Iran has come under special focus. The visit to Iran attracted special attention because of the ongoing tension between the US and Iran and because it coincides with the talks in Vienna to revive Iran's compliance with the 2015 Joint Comprehensive Plan of Action (JCPOA). Although Beijing has urged the US' new Biden administration to rejoin the 2015 Joint Comprehensive Plan of Action (JCPOA), which regulate Iran's nuclear activities, the visit by China's Foreign Minister Wang Yi at this juncture potentially provides China an opportunity. Especially the signing of the long speculated 18-page, 25-year "strategic partnership" deal between the two countries, not only ensured global attention to Wang Yi's visit to Tehran, but reveals China's underlying ambition to increase influence in the region. An opinion published by China's state-owned China Global

Television Network (CGTN) on March 29 endorsed this. It said that the China-Iran deal would "totally upend the prevailing geopolitical landscape in the West Asia region that has for so long been subject to US hegemony".

Though the Middle East has not been a priority on China's foreign policy agenda, China's interest in Iran stretches back to February 1979 when it quickly recognised the new Islamic regime and began assisting it to develop its military — and clandestinely — its nuclear capabilities. China was careful, however, not to get involved in the Iran-Iraq War although it had ties to both sides. It was similarly careful not to antagonise either the US or Israel with both of whom it was trying to improve relations.

Since mid-2010, China reduced and restricted economic interactions with Iran largely because of pressure from the United States. Following a series of UN and multilateral sanctions restricting financial dealings with Iran's central bank, China curtailed its imports of oil and gas from Iran. Beijing, however, kept up relations with Tehran and Iran was admitted into the Shanghai Cooperation Organization with the status of an 'observer' in 2005. Scholars in China described China's policy towards Iran as "actively expanding China's circle, within international norms, to not only gain the benefit of overseas energy supplies, but also to protect China's overseas financial interests in the United States and elsewhere."

On March 26, 2021 Chinese Foreign Minister Wang Yi and Iranian Foreign Minister Mohammad Javad Zarif signed the China-Iran Strategic Comprehensive Agreement expressing a desire to increase cooperation and trade over the next 25 years. The signing of the agreement was aired live on state-run TV. However, the text of the agreement has not yet emerged and is unlikely to be published, although a draft was leaked last summer. The 25-year deal has the potential to give China enhanced influence with Iran and in the region.

The deal has been under negotiation since 2016, when Chinese President Xi Jinping visited Tehran. Iranian Foreign Minister Javed Zarif has also visited China numerous times in recent years, testifying to the high importance that Tehran attached to the negotiations that culminated in the formal signing of the deal on the 50th anniversary of the establishment of diplomatic relations between the two countries.

The New York Times had in 2020 reported on a draft version of the agreement, which, it claimed envisaged Chinese investments totalling US$400 billion! The report said the deal would include a wide range of sectors spanning energy, banking, telecommunications and infrastructure. It would also offer military cooperation, including joint training, as well as research and cooperation in their defence industries. The New York Times said that, in return, China would receive heavily discounted supplies of Iranian crude oil for the next 25 years.

This is the first time that Iran has signed such a lengthy agreement with a major world power. By doing so, Iran hopes to balance Washington's clout over the country by building closer ties with China. The agreement also offers significant benefits to China. By anchoring itself in the region, China aims to integrate Western Eurasia – as Beijing calls it - deeper into its Belt and Road Initiative.

The day after the signing, Chinese Foreign Ministry spokesperson Zhao Lijian said the agreement "neither includes any quantitative, specific contracts and goals nor targets any third party, and will provide a general framework for China-Iran cooperation going forward". On the Iranian side, Foreign Ministry spokesman Saeed Khatibzadeh said the agreement was a "road map" for trade and economic and transportation cooperation, with a special focus on both countries' private sectors. Chinese investments in Iran's energy and infrastructure sectors were expected. Following criticism regarding why the details of the agreement were not published, the Foreign Ministry's Assistant for Asia-Oceania Affairs, Reza Zabib, claimed that it was "not customary" to publish agreements that were "unenforceable". The Agreement is yet to be presented to the Iranian Parliament.

While the agreement is likely to lead to increased investment and linkages between the two countries, it can best be described as an aspirational document. No specific commitments have been made, no figures mentioned, and no indication given of unprecedented military cooperation or Chinese troops being stationed in Iran. Rather, the agreement appears to be a roadmap with general plans for cooperation in ventures in areas ranging from banking and mining to infrastructure and space exploration between banks and infrastructure projects related to the "New Silk Road" and the Belt and Road

Initiative. A major gain for Foreign Minister Wang Yi personally and possibly for China was the official Chinese news agency Xinhua's report on March 28 that Tehran expressed interest in signing on to Belt and Road Initiative (BRI) projects and other projects in the region, with possible finance from Chinese banks.

Iran sees China as a vital lifeline for its economy that has been weakened by sanctions and diplomatic isolation. The partnership with China — its top oil importer — gives Iran a stable market for oil, allowing it room to posture and negotiate, especially with regard to resuming the nuclear deal with the US. The Diplomat stated that after eight years of courting the West with nothing to show for it, China represents a change of course for Iran – whether as a potential new partner or as a "China Card" to leverage in Iran-US negotiations. Former Iranian diplomat and columnist for several Iranian newspapers on diplomacy, Fereydoun Majlesi observed that "Every road is closed to Iran. The only path open is China. Whatever it is, until sanctions are lifted, this deal is the best option".

If implemented, Iran will be able to break the wide-ranging Western sanctions embargo which estimates claim, has cost it almost half its oil exports, a large drop in GDP, and sharp rise in the cost of living — by supplying oil and gas to China. In the press releases announcing the agreement, Beijing also indicated its willingness to invest in "the up-and-downstream projects of the energy industries" in Iran. This conforms to the Chinese Communist Party (CCP)'s leadership's keen interest in securing reliable, long-term supplies of oil from the Middle East. According to the South China Morning Post (April 3) Wang Yi also tried to erode "petrodollar hegemony" by persuading his Middle Eastern hosts to accept oil payments in renminbi.

While the deal has significant support among Iran's business community and at multiple levels of government, others do not consider China a stable partner, since it has pulled out of many deals with Iran in the past. China's track record of actual investments in various countries is barely six percent of the committed amounts. Closer relations with China also remain unpopular with segments of the Iranian population who are often reluctant to buy Chinese goods because of their perceived lower quality.

The official Fars News agency described the agreement as "somewhat ambiguous…with pros and cons". Regarding technology transfer, it urges that "if Iran wants to make progress… it should not wait for the other side" and needs to develop "a long-term plan" before entering into specific agreements. It says that while Chinese investors are "encouraged" to invest in Iran's various free economic zones, such as along the Turkish border, on an island in the Strait of Hormuz, and in a strategic Free Zone near Shatt al-Arab, the infrastructure that exists has not "been able to actively attract even domestic investment". Former President Mahmoud Ahmadinejad, in a speech in late June, called it a suspicious secret deal that the people of Iran would never approve.

Meanwhile, rumours on social media say that the deal will lead to nuclear waste being dumped in the desert and islands in the Gulf will be sold to China. Others claim that Iran will be flooded with Chinese workers and crime-ridden Chinatowns.

An Iranian news agency reports that protests broke out in Tehran, Karaj, and Isfahan against what they perceive as selling out their country to China. Social media showed people chanting "Iran is not for sale" outside parliament, while in Isfahan signs said, "China get out of Iran" and "we want the 25-year agreement cancelled". Wall graffiti also denounced the accord.

Unconfirmed sources wrote that China will invest 280 billion dollars in Iran's oil and gas industry, and 120 billion dollars in Iran's transportation industries. In exchange, Chinese projects will be prioritized, and 5,000 Chinese soldiers will be sent to Iran to oversee the "security" of their projects.

Considering China's plans for projecting power — especially maritime power — in the Indo-Pacific and beyond, cognisance needs to be taken of reports leaked by senior sources close to the Iranian government to OilPrice.com in early September 2020. These claim that China could seek to build an espionage hub in Iran under the 25-Year Deal. They state that electronic espionage and warfare capabilities would be centered around the port of Chabahar. In their estimation, in 25 years Iran will be an irreplaceable geographical and geopolitical fulcrum of Beijing's 'One Belt, One Road' project.

Oil Price.com also cited these sources as saying that China planned to use the end of the global arms embargo on Iran on October 18, to begin fast-tracked preparations for its increased military presence in Iran as part of the 'China-Iran Integrated Defence Strategy'. One of its priorities will be to ensure that the military hardware and personnel that China, and Russia would deploy in Iran are not vulnerable to attack. To protect Chinese and Russian firms working in Iran despite the US sanctions on Iran, counter-measures to be deployed would include three key EW areas namely, electronic support (including early warning of enemy weapons use); electronic attack (including jamming systems); and electronic protection (including of enemy jamming). Iran will host a range of Chinese and Russian technology, equipment, and systems for proactive intelligence-gathering. The defensive equipment will include Russia's S-400 anti-missile air defense system and the Krasukha-2 and -4 systems. The report claimed that dual-use facilities will be built next to the existing airports at Hamedan, Bandar Abbas, Chabahar, and Abadan and that dual-use facilities will be created at Iran's key ports of Chabahar, Bandar-e-Bushehr, and Bandar Abbas. At Chabahar port, China plans to build one of the world's largest intelligence gathering listening stations with a staff of nearly 1,000, and a near-5,000 kilometer radius range.

Whether China genuinely intends to fulfil these expectations, or do just enough to ensure its oil supplies and get ports to extend the operational reach of the People's Liberation Army (PLA) Navy warships, is uncertain. It is definite, however, that many countries will keep China's activities in Iran under very close watch especially as its ports are close to the Gulf of Oman and the Strait of Hormuz. Beijing will need to tread carefully as any sign of Chinese military-related activity or joint Russian-Chinese activity will invite a sharp and swift response.

This was first published by the Centre for China Analysis and Strategy (CCAS) and Vivekananda International Foundation (VIF) in April 14, 2021.

68. China-Pakistan Strategic Nexus: Implications for India

The growing China-Pakistan nexus raises the threat to India. Their strategic and territorial interests have been cemented by the China Pakistan Economic Corridor (CPEC). With the flow of Chinese military power into Pakistan, China veritably straddles India, with its armed forces present on India's northern, eastern and western borders. This not only raises the real spectre of a 'two-front' war, but positions China to play a role in Kashmir and the region. Both countries must therefore be viewed as potential threats.

It needs to be kept in mind that, since 2010, Pakistan is the only country with which China has an "all-weather strategic partnership". The relationship is also the only one described as: "higher than the highest mountains, deeper than the deepest ocean and sweeter than honey!" The only other country with which China has a special category of strategic partnership is Russia.

Since 2015, the CPEC has brought China and Pakistan even closer. It was the first leg of Chinese President Xi Jinping's flagship Belt and Road Initiative (BRI) to get operationalised, knitting their economic development and fusing their military capabilities.

In this context, the remark made privately in late 2015 by a Chinese academic and expert, who is often called to brief the Chinese Communist Party (CCP)'s Politburo on Pakistan and Afghanistan affairs, is especially relevant. His remarks give an insight into Beijing's view of the relationship. Asked what Beijing hopes to gain from the CPEC considering that Pakistan is not in sound financial condition, he replied, "You know, till now we have been purchasing the Pakistanis. Now, we are going to buy Pakistan!" Later, in another private discussion about China's internal situation and the pressure being exerted by the United States, a senior Chinese cadre confided that as long as Xi Jinping is China's 'leader' the BRI will remain a priority for the country.

Since April 2015, when the CPEC was announced, China's animus towards India has increased. The newfound assertiveness of Xi Jinping's foreign policy has meant that China's earlier practice of 'managing' contentious issues, or setting them aside for being dealt with later, has been discarded in favour of a more direct and aggressive approach. This assertiveness is becoming more apparent as China's comprehensive national strength grows.

From the onset of Sino-US tensions in 2018, China has visibly become more confident and willing to confront the United States in pursuit of its national agenda. Xi Jinping's calls for "rejuvenation of the great Chinese nation" and advocacy of the concept of 'a common destiny for mankind' as well as the 'Chinese model of governance', especially in the midst of the Covid pandemic, are almost reminiscent of Mao's policy of exporting revolution!

The 'Rejuvenation of the great Chinese nation' impacts India more directly than is commonly understood. It essentially means "the recovery of territories that China feels it has lost through the imposition of unequal treaties by hostile foreign powers". China's constant refrain while commenting on the border issue — that it is a colonial legacy left behind by history — flows from this narrative.

For India, the implication is that China is negotiating to 'recover' Indian territories that it claims namely, Aksai Chin, Ladakh, Jammu and Kashmir, Arunachal Pradesh and Sikkim. The issue of 'stapled visas' to residents of Jammu and Kashmir and Arunachal Pradesh despite India's protests reinforces this. As its national strength grows, China is becoming more aggressive on the border issue, indicating that these are areas of potential conflict. Had India been alert to this, China's military aggression and the pressure it has put on India since May 2020 could have been thwarted.

At China's 18th and 19th Party Congresses in 2012 and 2017, Xi Jinping announced ambitious goals for his country. His declaration that by 2025, China would enter the ranks of the world's most technologically advanced nations and by 2049 it would be "a power with pioneering global influence", put the United States on alert that it plans to rival, if not surpass, the world's leading power! The US reaction was swift. It specifically targeted China's technology sector, setting it back by at least five years. Some senior Chinese cadres said in confidence that it would have been better had Xi Jinping not made these declarations publicly.

Despite mounting US pressure on multiple fronts, Xi Jinping and the Chinese Communist Party (CCP) remain undeterred. Successive nationwide campaigns have been launched to infuse the people with nationalism, reinforce party ideology and self-confidence and ensure the CCP's monopoly on power. China's stress on self-reliance in the technology sector is pronounced. The 14th Five Year Plan and Long Range - 2035 documents – approved by the Fifth Party Plenum in October 2020 and plenary sessions of the National People's Congress (NPC) and the Chinese People's Political Consultative Conference (CPPCC) in March 2021 – clearly indicate that China is not scaling back its ambitions. These are expansive programmes which include a focus on innovation and the development of cutting-edge technology in frontier sciences and the modernisation of the People's Liberation Army (PLA).

It is clear that China's ambitions far outweigh those of Pakistan. Pakistan's interests are comparatively narrow. The Pakistan army unequivocally supports the CPEC, indicating its close collaboration with China's security and military establishments, which is why the opposition has been unable to dent it. It is because of the Pakistan Army's direct support to CPEC, most of whose projects are located in the Pakistani heartland where the more conservative elements of its Islamic society reside, that friction has been contained. Little enclaves of Chinese workers whose consumption of pork, alcohol and other proclivities go against the tenets of Islam, are a constant source of tension. Video clips and reports of clashes between the two have been suppressed; but resentment lingers.

China clearly sets the agenda. It probably views Pakistan as a junior partner, but certainly one that is important enough for its strategic ambitions to make huge investments and secure its enduring influence. As China's strategic and financial investments in Pakistan have grown, so too has its influence and interest in the country. Having staked his personal prestige on the BRI and CPEC, Xi Jinping will not allow Pakistan to sink beyond a point.

China and Pakistan both share a common objective: to prevent India's rise. A paper published in October 2020 by Hu Shisheng, who heads the South Asia Affairs Department of the Chinese Institutes of Contemporary International Relations (CICIR), an important think tank that is directly subordinate to China's Ministry of State Security — its foreign intelligence arm — is revealing. This unusually frank appraisal of Sino-India relations appeared in CICIR's official publication and was soon followed up in mid-December by another article in the CCP-owned Global Times. Both articles certainly had high-level official approval. Hu Shisheng stated that ever since China got 'liberated' and India became independent, a military showdown between the two was inevitable. He said India's rising international status since 2014 was a major contributory factor for the present crisis. He anticipated an uneasy and tense period ahead in Sino-India relations with occasional, even major, clashes between the armed forces — including exchanges of fire — till they reach their respective 'red lines' and settle on a Line of Actual Control (LAC). He expected that India would attempt to frustrate China's rise, including by disrupting groupings like the SCO and BRICS from within.

Since April 2015, when Xi Jinping announced the CPEC in Islamabad, there has been a pronounced shift in China's policy towards India. This is particularly evident on the issue of Jammu and Kashmir on which Beijing had maintained ambiguity for decades. By pursuing the CPEC and making enormous investments in it, China ignored India's sovereignty claims on PoK Pakistan Occupied Kashmir), Gilgit, Baltistan and the Shaksgam Valley and accorded de facto acknowledgement to Pakistan's claim over these territories. In a bid to secure its military and strategic interests Beijing began urging India at official and unofficial meetings, including with opinion-makers and think-tanks, that it should 'ease tensions with Pakistan, resume talks with Pakistan, resolve the Kashmir issue and then look to improving ties with China'. This stance has persisted. After India revoked Article 370 in August, 2019, China raised the issue in the UNSC on three occasions and could well do so again, indicating its willingness to strain ties with India.

That China is prepared to intervene militarily if it perceives a threat to the CPEC or its assets became clear in 2016, with the establishment of the

People's Liberation Army (PLA)'s Western Theatre Command, as part of the restructuring and reorganisation of its army. The Western Theatre Command is the largest of China's five Theatre Commands and merges the two former military regions of Lanzhou and Chengdu. It incorporates the Qinghai region, which facilitates the training of troops in high altitudes and acclimatizing them for rapid induction into Tibet. The operational tasks allotted to it are significant. They include "protecting China's borders, eliminating threats in Xinjiang and Tibet, as well as in Afghanistan and other states that host training bases for separatists and extremists and protecting the Chinese workers and assets of the China-Pakistan Economic Corridor". The Western Theatre Command is a very real and potent threat for India.

The military component of the CPEC has been clear from the beginning. These include the fibre-optic cable linking the headquarters of the PLA's South Xinjiang Military District in Kashgar initially to Rawalpindi, now being extended to include Islamabad, Karachi and Gwadar. The uninterrupted pace of development of the Gwadar port, after China was granted "sovereign rights", highlights its importance to China. China has an electronic eavesdropping station near Gwadar to monitor naval and shipping activities in the Arabian Sea as far as the Gulf of Aden. China's military media already refer to Gwadar port as a "logistics base" and Karachi as a "naval base"! China's Naval Base at Djibouti elevates the maritime threat. Plans also provide for linking the Punjab Railway with the South Xinjiang railway, providing seamless military transport capability supplemented by the proposed railway line and highway from Karakoram to Gwadar.

The Intelligence establishments of China and Pakistan have developed very close ties over the decades. This was observed during the clandestine flights in connection with the nuclear technology-for-missiles deal between North Korea and Pakistan, brokered by China. These ties have been raised with the posting of a Pakistan ISI Colonel in the PLA General Staff Department in Beijing. Chinese intelligence collaborates closely with its Pakistani counterpart to detect, identify and, at times just spirit away, Uyghurs residing in Pakistan into Xinjiang. On occasion, they request Pakistani assistance. Collaboration obviously extends to other areas, like the clandestine development of tactical nuclear weapons.

While close Sino-Pak ties in the diplomatic, economic, military and nuclear fields and the development of weapons systems is fairly well documented, their cooperation in the maritime domain is becoming a greater and lethal concern. In addition to collaborating in building frigates, there is now mention of collaboration on submarines and Unmanned Underwater Vessels (UUVs). If China supplies these to Pakistan they will be based at Gwadar, Karachi and Jiwani, increasing the vulnerability of India's western coast and the Arabian Sea. Reflecting official level thinking, China's military media in 2019 mentioned that China might sell its first aircraft carrier, Liaoning, to Pakistan, once its fourth aircraft carrier is ready. They have also mentioned that Chinese air force fighter aircraft could be given to Pakistan in event of the outbreak of hostilities with India.

China's efforts to isolate India, restrict its rise, and expand Chinese influence in our neighbourhood will continue. India must expect increased Sino-Pakistan collusion on issues like Kashmir, blocking its demand for the designation of persons like Masood Azhar, Zaki-ur-Rahman as international terrorists, etc. The convergence of Sino-Pak interests on strategic and territorial issues points to increased and enduring Chinese military pressure on India, as presently seen in Ladakh. China could well open hostilities through Pakistan, creating a "two-front war" situation for India.

This was first published by the Centre for China Analysis and Strategy (CCAS) and Vivekananda International Foundation (VIF) in April 14, 2021.

69. Rising Tensions in the Taiwan Strait

As January 2024 — the date for Taiwan's national elections — draws closer, it is certain that China will be a factor in the elections. Taiwan President Tsai Ing-wen's stop-overs in New York and Los Angeles and meeting with US House Majority Leader McCarthy on April 5, 2023, amid steadily escalating Cross Strait tensions has also provoked "robust counter-measures' by China.

Ever since the Democratic Progressive Party (DPP)'s Tsai Ing-wen took over as Taiwan's President in May 2016, Beijing has been upset at the turn Taiwan's politics have taken. Tsai Ing-wen herself has been cautious, but deliberate, in her moves to preserve Taiwan's distinct political entity. She has, at the same time, adhered to the DPP's principles on Taiwan's status and not yielded ground on the '1992 Consensus'. Her Southbound policy, for instance, is non-confrontational and farsighted and seeks to broad-base Taiwan's diplomatic and trade interactions while diversifying its economy and reducing dependence on the People's Republic of China. These are long range moves, which will benefit Taiwan and its business community, but they are unlikely to yield political dividends in the short term. She has simultaneously been firm in preserving the identity of Taiwan and it's people as a separate entity.

Tsai Ing-wen's caution has not met with an equally calibrated response from Beijing. Beijing has railed against her for not agreeing to the '1992 Consensus' and its warnings have ranged from intemperate threats of direct action against individual leaders — including their decapitation — to pressure on Taiwan's economy and Taiwanese businessmen residing in China. The growing warmth in Taiwan's relations with the US, at a time when Sino-US relations are deteriorating, are agitating Beijing and adding to tensions. There is concern in Beijing that the US may change its policy on China. Chinese President Xi Jinping has also pursued a more aggressive policy towards China's neighbours, including Taiwan, since becoming President in 2012.

At the 20th Party Congress last October and again at the National People's Congress (NPC) plenum last month, Xi Jinping reiterated his pledge for the reunification of China 'in the new era'. This has been accompanied by a strong implication of the use of military force.

China's new Premier Li Qiang, in his first remarks to the press after his appointment at the NPC, however, made no reference to the reunification of Taiwan with China. Instead, he focussed on people-to-people and business contacts. This would imply a re-energising by the Chinese Communist Party (CCP) of United Front tactics against Taiwan. An example is the ongoing visit of former Taiwan President Ma Ying-jeou — the first by either a serving or retired Taiwanese leader — to China. Other visits by KMT and other politicians can be expected to follow. It is anticipated that as part of China's two-pronged effort at reunification, there will be a pronounced uptick in the CCP Central Committee (CC)'s United Front Work Department (UFWD) activities in Taiwan.

There has been noticeably greater attention to activities of the United Front Work Department (UFWD) under Xi Jinping. After he took over as Chairman of the Central Small Leading Group on United Front in 2016, the UFWD's budget and personnel strength have doubled. The UFWD added four new bureaus responsible for 'overseas Chinese affairs' and absorbed the Overseas Chinese Affairs Office and the State Administration for Religious Affairs. As Mariah Thornton pointed out in her recent paper 'Countering United Front Work: Taiwan's Political Warfare System' published in 'China Foresight' of the London School of Economics, the UFWD's activities now target overseas Chinese, civil societies, governments, and economic operations of other countries. Taiwan has been a prime target for decades with successive Chinese administrations trying to effect Taiwan's reunification with the Chinese Mainland and Xi Jinping has reinforced these efforts. Despite these efforts, however, the large majority of the people in Taiwan now identify themselves exclusively as 'Taiwanese' as opposed to 'Taiwanese-Chinese' or 'Chinese,' and a vast majority of Taiwanese oppose unification with China. Alongside the strong consensus among Taiwanese that Taiwan and China are separate states, Taiwan has also become more entrenched in its commitment to democratic norms and values since its transition from authoritarianism to democracy in the 1990s.

US House leader Nancy Pelosi's visit to Taipei in 2022 marked a critical moment in China's relations with the US and Taiwan. Within days of her leaving Taiwan, China organised a massive air-sea military exercise to demonstrate the People's Liberation Army (PLA)'s capabilities including to show it can effectively blockade Taiwan. Almost each day since then PLA Air Force (PLAAF) fighter jets and PLA Navy (PLAN) warships have entered the Taiwan Strait and often crossed the median line. As stated by Xi Jinping in the Work Report presented to the 20th Party Congress, the PLA "will enable us to shape our security posture, deter and manage crises and conflicts, and win local wars". The PLA has obviously begun "shaping" its security environment.

The PLA officer who planned and supervised the operations, General He Weidong, was "helicoptered" by Chinese President Xi Jinping into the Chinese Communist Party (CCP) Politburo — he wasn't even a member of the CCP Central Committee — and appointed one of the two Vice Chairmen of the Central Military Commission (CMC). There are other indications of China preparing for a military offensive against Taiwan, like the Theatre and provincial level war preparedness, military amphibious exercises and accelerated construction of amphibious landing craft.

Xi Jinping's declaration at the recently concluded 14th National People's Congress (NPC) asserting the importance of effecting the reunification in "the new era" points to a time horizon. The retention of 67-year old Song Tao as Director of the Taiwan Affairs Office — similarly signals that the CCP, rather than the State Council, will play a dominant role in crafting China's policies towards Taiwan. China has also stepped up its cheque-book diplomacy and in recent weeks won over the Honduras, which had diplomatic ties with Taiwan. But a major impediment to Beijing's plans is the US. Whether Beijing will launch an offensive against Taiwan depends on its assessment of whether the US will intervene on Taiwan's behalf.

Meanwhile, though US President Biden has said that the US will intervene if Taiwan is attacked, Washington continues to maintain strategic ambiguity. There is bipartisan consensus in Washington that China is a major threat and that any Chinese military action against Taiwan needs to be thwarted. Last month the US approved the potential sale of new weapons worth US$ 619 million despite Beijing's protests. At least two bipartisan delegations from the US Congress have visited Taiwan in the last six months. US Navy ships occasionally transit through the Taiwan Strait and US aircraft carriers stay in the vicinity. A recent report by a Chinese think-tank, the 'South China Sea Strategic Situation Probing Initiative' (SCSPI) said the US had intensified military operations in the South China Sea in the past two years to promote its political and diplomatic agenda. The South China Sea Strategic Situation Probing Initiative (SCSPI) predicts forces targeting the Taiwan Strait. According to SCSPI statistics, there were about 1,000 sorties by large US recce aircraft into the South China Sea region with some as close as 13 nautical miles from the baseline of China's mainland territorial waters.

According to a South Asian Advanced Persistent Threat (APT) hacking group, the nuclear energy sector in China is being targeted in a recent cyber-espionage campaign. A group called "Bitter" was identified to have used updated first-stage trojan payloads in the recently observed espionage campaign. The group reportedly added an extra layer of script obfuscation and employed additional decoys for social engineering and obtaining critical systems information and gaining access to the infrastructure networks. US military commanders have recently made statements indicating that they assess a military showdown between the US and China is likely by 2025.

Aware of the deteriorating relationship with China, Tsai Ing-wen is taking precautions. She has increased Taiwan's military budget by 13.9 percent over the previous year and projected US$19 billion in defence spending for 2023. She has announced that Taiwan will extend its compulsory military service from four months to a year starting in 2024, and plans to send Taiwanese troops to the US for training. Taiwan has also stepped up construction of warships and has plans to build a nuclear-powered submarine. Japan has extended support and its Deputy Prime Minister Taro Aso stated in July 2021 that "If a major incident happened (over Taiwan), it's safe to say it would be related to a situation threatening the survival (of Japan). If that is the case, Japan and the US must defend Taiwan together". This is the first such categoric statement by a senior Japanese official.

Meanwhile, tensions escalated sharply with Tsai Ing-wen's trip to the US. The Chinese announced three day Combat Readiness Patrol and "Exercise United Sword" war games around Taiwan from April 8-10. The exercises included "sealing off" the island. Forty two Chinese aircraft and eight warships crossed the strait's median line on April 8 and the first footage from the military exercises on April 8 around Taiwan, telecast by the state-owned CCTV mentioned that Ground Force rocket launchers, PLA Navy destroyers and missile speedboats, PLA Air Force fighters, bombers, interference, and refueling aircraft, etc were involved. Taiwan's Defense Ministry said 42 Chinese planes and 8 ships crossed the strait's median line on April 8. Taiwan's Ministry of Defense said on April 11 that at least 8 PLA naval vessels are still operating in waters near Taiwan. On April 9, Taiwan's defence ministry said that they had spotted 58 Chinese aircraft, including Su-30 fighters and H-6 bombers, as well as nine ships, around Taiwan. By late April 9, 71 PLAAF fighter aircraft and 9 ships were engaged in military exercises for what the Chinese military said was the "encirclement" of Taiwan.

The Chinese aircraft carrier Shandong was operating south of Miyako, one of Japan's southernmost islands, and was accompanied by three warships over the past three days. Japan said (April 10) that fighter aircraft took off and landed 80 times on the Shandong in waters east of Taiwan and south of Japan as of April 9 night, while helicopters conducted an additional 40 flights from the ship. The Joint Staff of Japan's Self-Defence Forces said "In response to the take-off and landing operations, the Air Self-Defense Force scrambled fighter jets". CMC Vice Chairman General He Weidong, who is credited with planning and conducting the large PLA exercises immediately after US House Leader Nancy Pelosi's visit to Taiwan last year, would have supervised these exercises.

Taiwanese analysts and citizens are aware of the deteriorating Sino-US relations. They, along with many international observers, are apprehensive that this raises the chances of conflict between the two. The Taiwanese don't want to see Taiwan become another Ukraine and countries in the region would prefer not to have to take sides — at least till they are sure of the winning side! Meanwhile, with the rapid deterioration in China-US ties there is growing probability of a clash at sea between the navies of the US and China in the near future.

This was first published by the Centre for China Analysis and Strategy (CCAS) and Vivekananda International Foundation (VIF) in April 10, 2023.

70. China Is Raising Tensions in the Taiwan Strait

Tension across the Taiwan Strait has increased since Taiwan's pro-independence Democratic Progressive Party (DPP) won the Presidential elections for the third consecutive time in January 2024. The victory of the DPP's Lai Ching-te clearly signalled that the people of Taiwan do not want to reunify, or more correctly, be merged with the communist People's Republic of China. After a silence of over 25 hours during which Beijing made no comment on Lai Chingte's victory, it started flexing its military muscle and began sending large numbers of Navy warships and Air Force aircraft in the Taiwan Strait and around Taiwan, thereby signalling it was keeping open its military options for the reunification with Taiwan. Many of the Chinese aircraft crossed the median line in the Taiwan Strait.

At the same time, Beijing has been opening defence mobilisation offices in all 31 provinces. These offices are essential for civil-military coordination and marshalling civilian resources necessary for war. The production of roll-on and roll-off ships necessary for amphibious military operations also continues apace. China has also been working to rapidly set up a secure quantum communications channel. According to China's official *Guangming Daily* (February 24) as of the end of 2023, the length of the backbone network of optical fibre quantum secure communication built in China exceeded 10,000 kilometers, covering 17 provinces and connecting about 80 cities. Quantum communications are vital for ensuring speed and security of communications.

The People's Liberation Army (PLA)'s Southern and Eastern Theatre Commands also continue to regularly conduct air and sea military exercises. The Eastern Theatre Command Navy maintains eight daily combatants patrolling near Japan and Taiwan, or reportedly an estimated 14 percent of the Eastern Theatre Command Navy's warships. The East China Sea patrols are near China's claimed Air Defence Identification Zone (ADIZ). Chinese maritime research vessels have also visibly increased incursions into waters just 24 nautical miles off Taiwan's coast. For example, China's newest research ship the Zhu Hai Yun, which is loaded with cutting-edge technology and is a drone carrier with links to the People's Liberation Army (PLA), carried out nine missions in waters off Taiwan since September, in contrast to just two in each of the previous three years. This coincides with Beijing signalling its growing surveillance capabilities and collection of data crucial for naval warfare.

The recent appointment of Admiral Dong Jun as China's Defence Minister has effectively placed the PLA budget under the command of a PLA Navy officer. Dong Jun is a submariner. His appointment will mean increased emphasis on development of the PLA Navy and attention to military operations and planning for the reunification of Taiwan. The Taiwan election results have underscored that there is a clear sense of alienation between the people living on either side of the Taiwan Strait and Beijing would estimate that this would probably only become even more acute with the passage of time. At the same time, Xi Jinping's policy of pumping the Chinese people with nationalism since his ascendance to China's three top posts in 2012, means that they now consider the issue of Taiwan's reunification important to the unity, security and development of the country and the "great rejuvenation of the Chinese nation".

While Xi Jinping is certainly preparing for a possible military takeover of Taiwan, he will be deterred by the recent deployment of US Special Forces (Green Berets) on the Kinmen and Quemoy islands as it means any military operation against Taiwan will directly entail action against the US. There is additionally the real risk of Chinese action against Taiwan triggering a major global conflagration since it would adversely impact the supply of vitally needed semiconductors and AI chips and severely disrupt global trade. Xi Jinping would prefer a peaceful reunification so as to avoid direct retaliation from the US and West. Economic sanctions or direct military intervention by the US and West would completely derail the Chinese communist leadership's effort to improve the country's economy or rival the US, thereby endangering the Chinese Communist Party's legitimacy and position as China's sole ruling political party. The recent corruption scandal in the PLA involving senior Generals including his close associates and friends will also be a major inhibiting factor. One recent report suggested that senior PLA officers had advised against any military action against Taiwan as the PLA was not ready.

Taiwan's DDP leadership has in the meanwhile initiated steps to reduce dependence on the Chinese Mainland. Taiwan President Tsai Ing-wen's astute and strategic 'Southbound Policy' seeks to get Taiwanese businesses to move to other destinations. Though some have shifted operations to Vietnam and Malaysia, they have for various reasons been reluctant to move to India, which is today the world's largest untapped market. As part of the policy Taiwan is enlarging the areas of interaction with other countries. Lai Ching-te will continue this policy. Zhou Zhihuai, Deputy Director of the Academic Committee of the China Council for the Promotion of Peaceful National Reunification, which is affiliated to the Chinese Communist Party (CCP) Central Committee (CC)'s United Front Work Department, recently warned that Lai Ching-te "is the most dangerous leader to have led Taiwan since it first began to democratise in the late 1980s" He added that "The risk of his making reckless moves towards his dream of independence is real".

Xi Jinping has already activated the United Front Work Department (UFWD). There is apprehension among UFWD cadres that Lai Ching-te's DPP government is likely to take more steps in continuation of its policy of "de-sinicising" the island, promoting a distinct Taiwanese identity and subtly encouraging Taiwan (Republic of China) independence. This will heighten the sense of alienation between the people living on either side of the Taiwan Strait. The UFWD did mount propaganda and psywar operations in the months leading up to Taiwan's general elections, like personal attacks denigrating incumbent Taiwan President Tsai Ing-wen and the DPP candidate Lai Ching-te, but these failed to make much headway. Similarly, the effort to muster votes for opposition candidates by giving paid leave to Taiwanese workers in the Mainland to vote in the elections yielded no results. Aware of this, the UFWD can now be expected to make determined efforts to shore the KMT and Taiwan People's Party (TPP) against the DPP, subvert Taiwan's youth and intelligentsia, and use the example of Ukraine to highlight the dangers of confronting China.

Politburo Standing Committee member and Chairman of the Chinese People's Political Consultative Conference (CPPCC) Wang Huning, during a meeting on Taiwan affairs held in Beijing on February 22 and 23, emphasized "the need to advance national reunification efforts". He highlighted the "importance of implementing the Party's policies for resolving the Taiwan question and the decisions made by the CCP CC regarding Taiwan'. He called for strengthening China's strategic initiative for reunification, especially in the context of the 75th anniversary of the People's Republic of China and the goals set in the 14th Five-Year Plan. Wang Huning "also emphasized the need to combat 'Taiwan independence' forces and external interference to maintain peace in the region" and underscored the Party's leadership in Taiwan-related work. Wang Huning's remarks are a direct call for intensified United Front work inside and relating to Taiwan. They suggest more direct action against the DPP and its leaders.

Chinese President Xi Jinping is likely to pursue all three options of kinetic and covert action and political subversion. He will at the same time seek to further strengthen China's position in the South China Sea while watching the US Administration for signs of weakness or vacillation on the Taiwan issue. The latter dovetails neatly into Xi Jinping's larger ambition of rivalling and possibly surpassing the US as the preeminent world power.

This was first published by the Centre for China Analysis and Strategy (CCAS) and Vivekananda International Foundation (VIF) in March 1, 2024.

71. 'Rising Tension in Taiwan Strait is Cause for Concern'

Tension across the Taiwan Strait has risen in past weeks after the leader of the Democratic Progressive Party (DPP) Lai Ching-te took over as Taiwan's new President. Since then the Chinese authorities have mounted psychological and military pressure on Taiwan. Beijing has issued sternly worded warnings, accompanied by personal threats, to Lai Ching-te against making statements that Beijing perceives as provocative. Tensions were raised further when Chinese President Xi Jinping told the People's Liberation Army (PLA) to be ready to invade Taiwan by its hundredth founding anniversary in 2027. On May 7, 2024, the US Central Intelligence Agency Director Bill Burns repeated that "President Xi has instructed the PLA [People's Liberation Army], the Chinese military leadership to be ready by 2027 to invade Taiwan".

A few significant developments have contributed to the increase in tension. These include Chinese President Xi Jinping's three nation tour to Europe in early May, which came after an interval of five years, and Russian President Putin's summit with Xi Jinping in Beijing within a week thereafter. China and Russia, who claim a "no limits friendship", have endorsed each other's "core interests", "indivisible security" and territorial claims, and jointly articulated that the existing world order needs to be made more"fair" and "equitable". While Putin considers Ukraine as historically a part of Russia, the Chinese Communist Party (CCP) has made Taiwan's reunification with Mainland China an emotionally charged domestic issue and identified it as one of the country's three "core interests". Chinese President Xi Jinping has stoked this aspiration and made it an integral part of the "rejuvenation of the great Chinese nation". The goal is linked with Xi Jinping's personal ambition to go down in China's history as the leader who achieved the reunification.

The electoral victory of Taiwan's Democratic Progressive Party (DPP) for an unprecedented third time and the election of pro-independence DPP candidate Lai Ching-te as President was a setback for the Chinese Communist Party (CCP) and Xi Jinping. The DPP victory came despite Xi Jinping having strengthened the CCP Central Committee (CC)'s United Front Work Department (UFWD) in late 2016, by doubling its budget and personnel strength. He also brought retired veteran CCP cadre Song Tao out of retirement to head the crucial Taiwan Affairs Office of the State Council and the CCP CC's Taiwan Office.

Song Tao, currently Director of the Taiwan Affairs Office (TAO) of the State Council, (宋涛) worked in Fujian Province when Xi Jinping served as Governor there (1999-2002) and was even then considered a close confidant of Xi Jinping. Song Tao was also Xi Jinping's special envoy to North Korea in November 2017 and played similar roles on visits to Vietnam and Cuba. Song Tao is also close to Wang Huning, the fourth-ranking member of the Politburo Standing Committee of the CCP, Party ideologue and Deputy to Xi Jinping at the Central Leading Group for Taiwan Affairs. According to reports, of all the Directors of the Taiwan Affairs Office since the agency's inception, Song Tao is the one who has "the deepest knowledge of the DPP" and has had "many contacts and communications with" Chiu Tai-san the current Minister of the Mainland Affairs Council (MAC, 大陸委員會), Tao's counterpart in Taiwan. Of his three Deputy Directors: Pan Xianzhang, Qiu Kaiming and Wu Xi — Qiu Kaiming, holds a Ph.D. in International Politics from Fudan University in Shanghai, earned under the guidance of Wang Huning, Chairman of the National Committee of the Chinese People's Political Consultative Conference (CPPCC) and known as the "national mentor". Qiu Kaiming served as Director of the Cross-Strait Relations Research Centre at the Taiwan Affairs Office think-tank until 2019, when he assumed the role of Director of the Research Bureau at the Taiwan Affairs Office. With over 25 years of research experience on Taiwan-related issues, he now oversees cross-strait exchanges and formulates policies towards Taiwan.

The UFWD has been operating inside Taiwan and can now certainly be expected to intensify efforts. Already, interactions with the Kuomintang (KMT) have been stepped up with a KMT delegation visiting China almost every week. KMT leader and former Taiwan President Ma Ying-jeou has visited China at least twice and met Chinese President Xi Jinping. China's official Huaxia Ribao (Overseas Chinese Daily) publishes reports on Taiwan and the officials or politicians visiting China from Taiwan each day. Reports suggest that Taiwan's armed forces personnel are also being targeted and attempts made to win them over or get them to defect.

Ever since former US House Speaker Nancy Pelosi's visit to Taiwan in August 2022, China has maintained military and psychological pressure on Taiwan and kept alive the possibility of China using the military to effect the reunification. The PLA Eastern Theater Command has conducted numerous exercises in the Taiwan Strait and, departing from past practice, has now made crossing the median line almost routine. They have also, for the first time, begun carrying out exercises around Taiwan and on its eastern coast, prompting observers to assess that the Chinese Navy is rehearsing for a blockade. The number of warships and aircraft participating in these exercises has also increased. Most recently on July 10, Taiwan's defence ministry reported it had detected more than 66 aircraft and seven PLAN warships in the Taiwan Strait and that 56 of them had crossed the median line. Separately, PLA Ground Forces and Marines have carried out amphibious landing and para-drop exercises on the Chinese Mainland ostensibly in preparation for an invasion of Taiwan.

There are other indications of the Chinese Communist leadership working to a timetable for Taiwan's reunification, if necessary, by force. In fact, China's leadership has wanted to reunify Taiwan with the Mainland since 1947. The PLA has been preparing for this and with China having grown much more powerful the threat too has correspondingly grown. While Chinese Communist leaders have occasionally said that Taiwanese are their compatriots and they would not like to shed Chinese blood, their statements imply that the Taiwanese should agree to peacefully reunify with the Mainland.

In April 2024, for the first time the Work Report of the Government presented by Chinese Premier Li Qiang to the National People's Congress (NPC) plenum omitted the word "peaceful" while referring to the reunification of Taiwan. It was notable that the final version of his speech too did not include it, thereby confirming that the omission was deliberate. The frequency of assertions by senior Chinese leaders that China will not tolerate moves towards independence by Taiwan's leaders have also increased. At the 16th Straits Forum in Xiamen in June this year, Wang Huning, Politburo Standing Committee member and Chairman of the CPPCC, which is responsible for Taiwan's reunification with Mainland China, reiterated this. Separately confirming that the situation had changed, a senior CCP cadre recently revealed that the reunification process had entered the "fast track". Zhang Weiwei, a close associate and supporter of Chinese President Xi Jinping and former English Interpreter to Deng Xiaoping and late Chinese Premier Li Peng, is also a Professor of International Relations at Fudan University and Director of its China Institute. Zhang Weiwei is known to have briefed the Politburo. Speaking at a seminar in Malaysia on May 8, he said that reunification had entered the "fast track" and is targeted to be completed by 2027. Interestingly, Zhang Weiwei was in France around the time of Xi Jinping's visit and in lectures there underscored that the Taiwan issue was high on the CCP's agenda and that reunification would be effected soon. If Xi Jinping has returned from his European tour with the feeling that the US is distracted and Europe is preoccupied with the war in Ukraine, it would strengthen his view that they will possibly be reluctant to open a second front. In that case China has a window of opportunity to move against Taiwan with minimal possibility of intervention by the West.

The increased overt military pressure on Taiwan needs to be viewed in this backdrop. Reports have further revealed that China is rapidly expanding its nuclear arsenal and has been constructing hundreds of new silos in Xinjiang. A few years earlier, PLA officers had suggested that China is redeploying its nuclear warheads to reduce the time taken to marry warheads with the missiles. These measures build deterrence against any potential attack on China by the US and West. Reports yet to be confirmed claim that the fishing boat incident off Kinmen Island in March 2024 in which two fishermen were killed was actually an operation of the People's Liberation Army Navy (PLAN). If true, it would signal a significant escalation of pressure on Taiwan. Beijing also chose to interpret Lai Ching-te's inaugural speech as provocation and warned that such acts would not be tolerated. The following day the PLA conducted a majorday exercise around Taiwan when Taiwan's defence ministry claimed dozens of aircraft and vessels had crossed the median line. The spokesman of the PLA Eastern Theatre Command warned Taiwan that with each provocation China's armed forces would take one step further towards reunification. By saying so Beijing has effectively put Taiwan and its supporters on notice.

Whether China can successfully launch a military invasion of Taiwan is debatable. There is a reliable report that late last year a PLA General conveyed to Xi Jinping that the PLA is not ready for an invasion of Taiwan. Amphibious operations are difficult and crossing the Taiwan Strait will be a difficult operation as would be going over Taiwan's mountainous hinterland to get to its urban centres. A major uncertainty is whether the US will intervene and whether other countries in the region will react when their commercial shipping and lanes of communications are threatened. The Japanese Foreign Minister has already declared that "an attack on Taiwan means an attack on Japan"! If countries start preparing to support Taiwan, then Beijing will probably re-evaluate, or pause, its plans for Taiwan.

Nevertheless, Beijing retains the option of a sudden, swift operation to seize the three small islands of Penghu, Matsu and Kinmen sited only 129, 19 and 10 kms respectively off the coast of Mainland China. They are dependent on China for water and some daily essential supplies. Such a limited Chinese action will also end before the US or other nations can react and enable Xi Jinping to declare he has begun the process of reunification — becoming the first Chinese leader to achieve this! The US will then face the difficult choice of either responding militarily to ensure it remains the preeminent global power or imposing punitive economic sanctions on China. Enforcing the latter will be difficult as American business is already unhappy with the sanctions and restrictions on trade with China as the US Administration emphasises competition rather than confrontation. Europe, which is reluctant to dilute ties with China, will also drag its feet. Countries in the region like Japan, Vietnam and India can be expected to take serious note of China's actions and prepare options to counter its aggressive policy of forcibly grabbing territories it claims. It would, nevertheless, be imprudent to disregard the possibility of Xi Jinping embarking on such an adventure.

This was first published by the Centre for China Analysis and Strategy (CCAS) and Vivekananda International Foundation (VIF) in July 12, 2024.

Glossary

1. BLACK SWAN (Page 2)	refers to unexpected events that can have far reaching consequences for politics and markets.
2. GREY RHINO (Page 2)	foreseeable risk often overlooked Demographic crisis: China's rapidly aging population is eroding its growth momentum. Debt: China's debt, especially local government debt, is a growing threat. Bond defaults by state-owned firms have highlighted the country's debt problem. Decoupling: Decoupling is another threat to China's economy.
3. TIGERS (Page 6)	powerful leaders referred to as 'tigers' and lowly bureaucrats referred to as 'flies'.
4. CULTIVATE RED CADRES (Page 13)	Refers to Xi Jinping call for developing cadres with strong ideological training and loyal to the Party.
5. PRINCELINGS (Page 15)	Leaders whose parents belong to the first generation of CCP revolutionaries
6. RED DESCENDANTS (Page 15)	Descendants of the founders of the CCP.
7. GLOBAL DEVELOPMENT INITIATIVE (GDI) (Page 16)	Chinese President Xi Jinping proposed the Global Development Initiative (GDI) at the general debate of the 76th session of the United Nations (UN) General Assembly in 2021 calling for building a consensus on pursuing development, promoting shared growth and helping accelerate the implementation of the UN 2030 Agenda for Sustainable Development.

8. GLOBAL SECURITY INITIATIVE (Page 16)	China's Global Security Initiative (GSI) was first proposed by Chinese President Xi Jinping at the Boao Forum for Asia in April 2022. It was one of Three Major Initiatives (三大倡议) announced between 2021 and 2023 – the others being the Global Development Initiative (GDI) and the Global Civilization Initiative (GCI). The GSI also enveloped the aims of the Global Data Security Initiative (GDSI) that was announced in 2020. Together these initiatives form part of China's proposal for a reformed world order and have since been incorporated into its vision for a Community of Common Destiny for Mankind (人类命运共同体). This represents China's proposed alternative to the existing world order, which the Chinese Communist Party (CCP) claims has failed to solve global challenges and endangered world peace. China's global vision is deliberately defined along its critique of the United States' hegemonism and unilateralism.
9. COLOUR REVOLUTIONS (Page 17)	In the context of China, it means an attempt by Western countries to overthrow the socialist system, encouraging pro-democracy protests and posing a serious challenge to the supremacy of the Chinese Communist Party.
10. SELF-RESTORATION WITH THE BLADE INWARD AND BONE SCRAPING TO CURE THE POISON (Page 19)	China's security apparatus is called the 'knife handle' by the party cadres.
11. "610" OFFICE (Page 23)	The 610 Office is a central-authority level security agency associated with the Political and Legislative Affairs Committee of the Communist Party that tackles illegal cults. It gets its name from the date of its creation - June 10, 1999 - when it was set up to crack down on the Falun Gong sect.

12. TWO ESTABLISHMENTS 13. (Page 33)	Establishment of Comrade Xi Jinping's core position in the CCP CC and in the Party as a whole and the guiding role of Xi Jinping Thought on Socialism with Chinese Characteristics for a New Era
14. FOUR CONSCIOUSNESS (Page 33)	Coined by Xi Jinping, this refers to 'political consciousness", general awareness', leadership-core values'and alignment in ideology'.
15. LOW-LEVEL REDS AND HIGH-LEVEL BLACKS (Page 35)	Low-level red is to simplify and vulgarize the party's beliefs and political propositions. High-level black means conducting propaganda activities (high-level black) that are likely to mislead people and only produce negative effects
16. FENGQIAO MODEL (Page 41)	The Fengqiao model, so named after a town in Zhejiang Province, is an exemplar of Chinese community-level social governance
17. 1992 CONSENSUS (Page 51)	1992 Consensus is a political term which refers to a meeting held in 1992 between the semi-official representatives of the CCP led People's Republic of China in mainland China and Kuomintang led Republic of China in Taiwan. In this both recognized that there is only one China though both sides define China differently.
18. FOUR CONSCIOUSNESSES (Page 54)	It is a political concept of Xi Jinping. The concept includes "Confidence in Path, Confidence in Theories, Confidence in System, and Confidence in Culture." In 2021, the concept was expanded to include the idea of Historical Confidence.
19. XICHENG AUNT (Page 68)	Xicheng Aunts refer to a group of volunteers who roam Xicheng District in central Beijing acting as public security volunteers. Some 70 percent of them are females aged 58 to 65.
20. HAIDIAN NETIZENS" (Page 68)	They are volunteers who report clues to police and the top source of police's neighborhood intelligence.

21. FENGTAI PERSUATION TEAM (Page 68)	It is a powerful force that has been added to the Fengtai district government in the Chinese capital. The volunteers also act as the eyes and ears of police and report any suspicious activities.
22. TANGPING (Page 64)	a social phenomenon in China where young people, often frustrated by high pressure work culture and limited social mobility, choose to "lie flat" or passively resist to opt out of the competitive rat race.
23. LIN BIAO GROUP (Page 91)	Lin Biao was a Chinese politician and Marshal of the People's Republic of China who was pivotal in the Communist victory during the Chinese Civil War. Lin and his faction allegedly drew up a plan for a coup, or armed uprising, the *Wu qi yi* (571, a pun on 'armed uprising') plan. Before it could be implemented, Mao, Zhou Enlai and others found out. Fleeing the country with his family and staunch supporters, Lin's plane 'crashed' over the former Mongolian People's Republic in 1971.
24. GANG OF FOUR (Page 91)	the name given to a group of four Chinese Communist Party officials led by Jiang Qing, Mao Zedong's last wife.
25. THE TWO CENTENARY GOALS OF CHINA (Page 105)	The "centenaries" refer to the two 100-year anniversaries: The goals to be achieved by the first centenary was to achieve a moderately well-off society by 2021- the centenary of the founding of the Chinese Communist Party in 1921. The second centenary goal is to become a strong, democratic, civilized , harmonious, modern ,socialist country by 2049, the centenary of the founding of the People's Republic of China.

26. STATE EUNUCHIZATION (Page 133)	This term was mentioned in the 2015 essay by China's Rao Yi. It refers to a group of Xi Jinping's cronies promoted to positions, and other factions within the party purged or incorporated..
27. RO-RO SHIPS (Page 149)	Ro-Ro ships, or roll-on/roll-off ships, are cargo ships that transport wheeled cargo, such as cars, trucks, and buses, by allowing them to be driven on and off the ship
28. FOUR STRESSES AND FOUR LOVES (Page 178)	A new ideological campaign of the CCP aimed at diluting the negative impact of religion and strengthening education for the masses . This was particularly aimed at the TAR region. The four stresses include: Gratitude and loyalty for the CCP Unity of the motherland Appreciation and recognition for distinguished service Education and economic prosperity. The four loves include: Love for the "core interests" of the CCP Love for the motherland Love for one's hometown Love for one's livelihood
29. FOUR STANDARDS (Page 178)	The "four standards" policy requires Tibetan monks and nuns to demonstrate "political reliability," "moral integrity capable of impressing the public," and willingness to "play an active role at critical moments." In short, monks and nuns must support the Chinese government and prevent any resistance to the official policy on religion.
30. ETHNIC GROUPS IN TIBET (Page 185)	These mainly include Monpa, Lhoba, Lisu, Mongol, Deng etc.

31. COMPREHENSIVE TRANSPORT CORRIDORS (Page 203)	China's comprehensive transport corridors refer to a network of interconnected transportation routes, including highways, railways, waterways, and air routes, designed to facilitate efficient movement of goods and people across the country, with key corridors like the "Belt and Road Initiative" connecting major cities and regions, including the "Silk Road Economic Belt" and the "21st Century Maritime Silk Road
32. GAZELLE ENTERPRISES (Page 238)	In China, "gazelle enterprises" refer to small and medium-sized businesses that are experiencing rapid growth, typically defined by achieving at least 20 percent annual revenue growth over a sustained period and are often high-tech and considered important drivers of economic innovation in the country.
33. THE THUCYDIDES TRAP (Page 259)	It is a term popularized by American political scientist Graham T. Allison to describe an apparent tendency towards war when an emerging power threatens to displace an existing great power as a regional or international hegemon.

Index